Maximizing Social Science Research Through Publicly Accessible Data Sets

S. Marshall Perry
Saint Mary's College of California, USA

A volume in the Advances in Knowledge Acquisition, Transfer, and Management (AKATM) Book Series

IGI Global
DISSEMINATOR OF KNOWLEDGE

Published in the United States of America by
IGI Global
Information Science Reference (an imprint of IGI Global)
701 E. Chocolate Avenue
Hershey PA, USA 17033
Tel: 717-533-8845
Fax: 717-533-8661
E-mail: cust@igi-global.com
Web site: http://www.igi-global.com

Library of Congress Cataloging-in-Publication Data

Names: Perry, S. Marshall, 1973- editor.
Title: Maximizing social science research through publicly accessible data sets / S. Marshall Perry, editor.
Description: Hershey, PA : Information Science Reference, [2018]
Identifiers: LCCN 2017020272| ISBN 9781522536161 (hardcover) | ISBN 9781522536178 (ebook)
Subjects: LCSH: Social sciences--Research--Data processing. | Social sciences--Research--Statistical menthods.
Classification: LCC H61.3 .M39 2018 | DDC 300.72--dc23 LC record available at https://lccn.loc.gov/2017020272

This book is published in the IGI Global book series Advances in Knowledge Acquisition, Transfer, and Management (AKATM) (ISSN: 2326-7607; eISSN: 2326-7615)

British Cataloguing in Publication Data
A Cataloguing in Publication record for this book is available from the British Library.

All work contributed to this book is new, previously-unpublished material.
The views expressed in this book are those of the authors, but not necessarily of the publisher.

For electronic access to this publication, please contact: eresources@igi-global.com.

Advances in Knowledge Acquisition, Transfer, and Management (AKATM) Book Series

ISSN:2326-7607
EISSN:2326-7615

Editor-in-Chief: Murray E. Jennex, San Diego State University, USA

MISSION

Organizations and businesses continue to utilize knowledge management practices in order to streamline processes and procedures. The emergence of web technologies has provided new methods of information usage and knowledge sharing.

The **Advances in Knowledge Acquisition, Transfer, and Management (AKATM) Book Series** brings together research on emerging technologies and their effect on information systems as well as the knowledge society. **AKATM** will provide researchers, students, practitioners, and industry leaders with research highlights surrounding the knowledge management discipline, including technology support issues and knowledge representation.

COVERAGE

- Cognitive Theories
- Cultural Impacts
- Information and Communication Systems
- Knowledge acquisition and transfer processes
- Knowledge management strategy
- Knowledge sharing
- Organizational learning
- Organizational Memory
- Small and Medium Enterprises
- Virtual communities

IGI Global is currently accepting manuscripts for publication within this series. To submit a proposal for a volume in this series, please contact our Acquisition Editors at Acquisitions@igi-global.com or visit: http://www.igi-global.com/publish/.

The Advances in Knowledge Acquisition, Transfer, and Management (AKATM) Book Series (ISSN 2326-7607) is published by IGI Global, 701 E. Chocolate Avenue, Hershey, PA 17033-1240, USA, www.igi-global.com. This series is composed of titles available for purchase individually; each title is edited to be contextually exclusive from any other title within the series. For pricing and ordering information please visit http://www.igi-global.com/book-series/advances-knowledge-acquisition-transfer-management/37159. Postmaster: Send all address changes to above address.

Titles in this Series

For a list of additional titles in this series, please visit:
http://www.igi-global.com/book-series/advances-knowledge-acquisition-transfer-management/37159

Philosophical Perceptions on Logic and Order
Jeremy Horne (International Institute of Informatics and Systemic, USA)
Information Science Reference • ©2018 • 402pp • H/C (ISBN: 9781522524434) • US $225.00

Handbook of Research on Tacit Knowledge Management for Organizational Success
Dhouha Jaziri-Bouagina (University of Sousse, Tunisia) and George Leal Jamil (Informações em Rede Consultoria e Treinamento Ltda, Brazil)
Information Science Reference • ©2017 • 542pp • H/C (ISBN: 9781522523949) • US $275.00

Bio-Inspired Computing for Information Retrieval Applications
D.P. Acharjya (School of Computing Science and Engineering, VIT University, India) and Anirban Mitra (Vignan Institute of Technology and Management, India)
Information Science Reference • ©2017 • 388pp • H/C (ISBN: 9781522523758) • US $205.00

Managing Knowledge Resources and Records in Modern Organizations
Priti Jain (University of Botswana, Botswana) and Nathan Mnjama (University of Botswana, Botswana)
Business Science Reference • ©2017 • 280pp • H/C (ISBN: 9781522519652) • US $185.00

Analyzing the Role of Citizen Science in Modern Research
Luigi Ceccaroni (1000001 Labs, Spain) and Jaume Piera (ICM-CSIC, Spain)
Information Science Reference • ©2017 • 355pp • H/C (ISBN: 9781522509622) • US $185.00

Scholarly Communication and the Publish or Perish Pressures of Academia
Achala Munigal (Osmania University, India)
Information Science Reference • ©2017 • 375pp • H/C (ISBN: 9781522516972) • US $190.00

For an enitre list of titles in this series, please visit:
http://www.igi-global.com/book-series/advances-knowledge-acquisition-transfer-management/37159

IGI Global
DISSEMINATOR OF KNOWLEDGE

701 East Chocolate Avenue, Hershey, PA 17033, USA
Tel: 717-533-8845 x100 • Fax: 717-533-8661
E-Mail: cust@igi-global.com • www.igi-global.com

Table of Contents

Preface xiv

Section 1
Large Scale Data Set Collection and Institutional Use

Chapter 1
Sifting Through the Sets: The Significance and Availability of Open Data 1
Claudia McGivney, Stony Brook University, USA

Chapter 2
Using Public Data From Different Sources 23
Yair Cohen, Farmingdale State University of New York, USA

Chapter 3
Big Data Analytics in Higher Education 38
Tanveer H. Shah, University of Azad Jammu and Kashmir, Pakistan

Chapter 4
Retrieving HTML and XBRL Data With Microsoft Excel 2010 62
Jianing Fang, Marist College, USA

Section 2
Empirical Studies on Publicly Accessible Data Sets

Chapter 5
Principals and Student Achievement: A Comparative Study of Eight Countries 84
S. Marshall Perry, Saint Mary's College of California, USA
Karen M. Sealy, Independent Educational Consultant, USA
Héctor X. Ramírez-Pérez, Universidad Panamericana, Mexico
Thomas C. DeNicola, Independent Researcher, USA
Yair Cohen, Independent Researcher, USA

Chapter 6
Relationship Among Education, Income, and Life Satisfaction 118
Elsa-Sofia Morote, Farmingdale State University of New York, USA

Chapter 7
Pension Systems Dynamics: A Pooled Data Analysis 142
Salvador Rivas-Aceves, Universidad Panamericana, Mexico
Edmundo Marroquín-Tovar, Universidad Panamericana, Mexico
Héctor X. Ramírez-Pérez, Universidad Panamericana, Mexico

Chapter 8
Implementing Structural Equation Modeling on Public Data............................ 178
Yair Cohen, Farmingdale State University of New York, USA
Elsa-Sofia Morote, Farmingdale State University of New York, USA

Section 3
Empirical Studies Informed by Publicly Accessible Data Sets

Chapter 9
Elementary Teachers' Math Instructional Practices, Receptivity to Change, Instructional Leadership, and Academic Optimism... 197
Dennis D. Sullivan, Saint Joseph's College, USA

Chapter 10
What Are the Relationships Between Poverty, Attendance, Teacher Evaluations, and High School Graduation Rates? 229
Kenneth Forman, Stony Brook University, USA
Craig Markson, Stony Brook University, USA

Chapter 11
Effects of Annual Professional Performance Review on Teacher Efficacy, Instructional Practices, and Professional Development 247
Erica Murphy-Jessen, Huntington Union Free School District, USA

Chapter 12
Hiring Practices, Uses of Social Media, and Teacher Retention Differences 275
Bridgette Waite, Dowling College, USA
Elsa-Sofia Morote, Farmingdale State University of New York, USA

Compilation of References 293

About the Contributors 323

Index 326

Detailed Table of Contents

Preface xiv

Section 1
Large Scale Data Set Collection and Institutional Use

Chapter 1
Sifting Through the Sets: The Significance and Availability of Open Data 1
Claudia McGivney, Stony Brook University, USA

Data-driven decision making has become a driving factor across many industries and reliance on verifiable data is crucial in this environment. Equitable access to reliable data is a key component in establishing a just society. This chapter provides a brief overview and background to open data resources, including current initiatives and policies, along with an exploration of challenges to accessing this information. The researcher reviewed over 2,000 open data websites and repositories in order to provide a selection of these as exemplars. All resources have been annotated, with specific attention paid to repositories offering large datasets and government resources.

Chapter 2
Using Public Data From Different Sources 23
Yair Cohen, Farmingdale State University of New York, USA

The United States federal government agencies as well as states agencies are liberating their data through web portals. Web portals like data.gov, census.gov, healthdata.gov, ed.gov and many others on the state level provide great opportunity for researchers of all fields. This chapter shows the challenges and the opportunities that lie by merging data from different pubic sources. The researcher collected and merged data from the following datasets: NYSED school report card, NYSED Fiscal Profile Reporting System, Civil Rights Data Collection, and Census 2010 School District Demographics System. The challenges include data validation, data cleaning, flatting data for easy reporting, and merging datasets based on text fields.

Chapter 3
Big Data Analytics in Higher Education 38
Tanveer H. Shah, University of Azad Jammu and Kashmir, Pakistan

This chapter reviews the literature on the use of business analytics in higher education. Universities have large datasets available to predict future direction and generate actionable information. An important type of analytics used to improve management processes and to make informed decisions is big data business analytics. State university executive leaders may improve the effectiveness of their decisions by integrating business analytics in the decision-making models. However, there is a need to examine the use of big data business analytics in the decision-making process at the executive leadership level of the selected state universities. Especially in the context of how descriptive, predictive, prescriptive, decisive and basic analytics, and data collection influence the decision-making process at the executive leadership level of the state universities in terms of student retention and graduation rates.

Chapter 4
Retrieving HTML and XBRL Data With Microsoft Excel 2010.........................62
Jianing Fang, Marist College, USA

The Securities and Exchange Commission (SEC) has upgraded the Electronic Data Gathering, Analysis, and Retrieval (EDGAR) system, to the Interactive Data Electronic Applications (IDEA) platform, or the Next-Generation EDGAR (New EDGAR). The SEC issued its final mandate for XBRL adoption and the conversion target dates for all firms in January 2009. With this conversion, users can retrieve the financial statement information of listed companies at both the document level and data element level. This chapter reviews the fundamental concepts of XBRL and reports on the current compliance status of the SEC XBRL conversion mandate. The main task is to demonstrate how to retrieve data from the New EDGAR and how to process the data with Microsoft Excel 2010.

Section 2
Empirical Studies on Publicly Accessible Data Sets

Chapter 5
Principals and Student Achievement: A Comparative Study of Eight Countries...84
S. Marshall Perry, Saint Mary's College of California, USA
Karen M. Sealy, Independent Educational Consultant, USA
Héctor X. Ramírez-Pérez, Universidad Panamericana, Mexico
Thomas C. DeNicola, Independent Researcher, USA
Yair Cohen, Independent Researcher, USA

Connections between principal leadership activities, school context, and student achievement are examined within this paper. Data for this quantitative study are from the 2013 Teaching and Learning International Survey (TALIS) and the 2012 Programme for International Student Assessment (PISA). The eight countries of examination participated in both the TALIS and PISA and the researchers merged datasets, yielding a study sample of 1,301 schools. This paper supports a context-specific view of instructional leadership. When looking across countries, the researchers found different practices were more strongly associated with the academic achievement of students, and suggest that school leaders have a meaningful overall relationship with academic achievement, both directly and indirectly. This study therefore supports prior research about the direct and indirect effects of instructional leadership. Further study, which accounts for differences in family academic resources and school-level opportunities to learn, will better illuminate the connection between instructional leadership practices and academic achievement.

Chapter 6
Relationship Among Education, Income, and Life Satisfaction........................118
Elsa-Sofia Morote, Farmingdale State University of New York, USA

This study examines the relationships among Education, Income, and Life Satisfaction. The study also seeks to learn whether Unemployment can be a mediator of these relationships. For this study, database collected by the Quality of Government Institute was used. The database contains 194 countries' records on the topic and its variables collected in 2012. Correlation to test relationship, and partial correlation to test the relationship among the variables while controlling for unemployment was used. It was found that income strongly relates to life satisfaction, and years of schooling relates weakly to life satisfaction. Years of schooling, however, strongly relates to GDP per capita. Contrary to previous studies, it was found that unemployment was not a mediator of the relationship among Education, Income, and Life Satisfaction but shows slight indication that it can be a mediator between higher education and life satisfaction. It was advised that governments put more effort into education as well as future research on enhancing the quality and efficacy of education.

Chapter 7
Pension Systems Dynamics: A Pooled Data Analysis......................................142
Salvador Rivas-Aceves, Universidad Panamericana, Mexico
Edmundo Marroquín-Tovar, Universidad Panamericana, Mexico
Héctor X. Ramírez-Pérez, Universidad Panamericana, Mexico

The main focus of the chapter is to define directions and magnitudes of causality of the pension systems, labor force, and hours worked for selected OECD (Organization for Economic Co-operation and Development) countries through a pool data analysis.

The information is examined within basic, intermediate, and advanced statistical analyses by regional comparison of the OECD countries. Main results include: (a) a positive impact of Labor Force size on Pension Systems, (b) a negative effect of the Average Hours Worked on Pension Systems, (c) when introducing cross-section and time series heterogeneity, relations are sustained from both global and regional inquiry, (d) an insightful and meticulous investigation can be performed using public and open databases if depuration of the information is well conducted.

Chapter 8
Implementing Structural Equation Modeling on Public Data............................178
Yair Cohen, Farmingdale State University of New York, USA
Elsa-Sofia Morote, Farmingdale State University of New York, USA

The researchers used structural equation modeling (SEM) to create a model predicting fourth-grade student achievement in math by exploring the relationships among: student, household, school, and teacher factors. Public data from the New York State Education Department (NYSED) 2012–13 school report card data, NYSED fiscal reporting system, Census 2010 School District Demographics System, and 2011 Civil Right Data Collection were used from 1,263 schools in New York excluding New York City. Variables were chosen using this convenient sample and supported by our conceptual rationale. The model predicted fourth-grade math achievement with 67 percent of effect size. Household factors had strong predictive, while school attendance rate had medium predictive value for student achievement.

Section 3
Empirical Studies Informed by Publicly Accessible Data Sets

Chapter 9
Elementary Teachers' Math Instructional Practices, Receptivity to Change, Instructional Leadership, and Academic Optimism..197
Dennis D. Sullivan, Saint Joseph's College, USA

This study sought to identify the relationships among elementary teachers' instructional practices in mathematics pre- and post-Common Core Learning Standards (CCLS) implementation in relation to technological and pedagogical content knowledge (TPACK), formative assessment, reflective practice, receptivity to change, academic optimism, and instructional leadership across age, years of experience, grade level taught, and college math credits taken in high and low needs schools. Teacher responses from low and high need schools across age, years of teaching experience, grade level taught, and college math credits taken were examined with the dimensions of mathematics instructional practices to see if any relationships exist among the variables. The implementation of CCLS mathematics had an influence on elementary-school teachers' instructional practices and attitudes in both high and low needs schools. Teacher academic optimism was reported as overall higher in high needs districts, whereas teachers in low needs districts reported an increase in instructional motivation practices after the implementation of CCLS mathematics.

Chapter 10
What Are the Relationships Between Poverty, Attendance, Teacher Evaluations, and High School Graduation Rates? 229
Kenneth Forman, Stony Brook University, USA
Craig Markson, Stony Brook University, USA

The focus of this study was to examine the relationships among poverty, attendance rates, the New York State's Annual Professional Performance Review (APPR) teacher evaluation system, and student achievement. The setting of this study was high schools from New York State's Nassau and Suffolk counties, a suburban region of New York City. The results of this study showed that poverty had a strong negative correlation with graduation rates from the Regents Diploma, accounting for 31.02 percent of the variance. However, the negative impact that poverty had on the graduation rates from the Regents Diploma with Advanced Designation more than doubled. While high school student attendance rates had a weak, but statistically significant, positive correlation with Regents Diploma graduation rates, the positive correlation more than tripled with the Regents Diploma with Advanced Designation graduation rates. The New York State teacher evaluation system did not have the desired effect on student achievement.

Chapter 11
Effects of Annual Professional Performance Review on Teacher Efficacy, Instructional Practices, and Professional Development 247
Erica Murphy-Jessen, Huntington Union Free School District, USA

The purpose of this study was to examine the effects of new Annual Professional Performance Review (APPR) legislation on professional development, instructional practices, and teacher efficacy. Additionally, teacher perceptions of the impact of new APPR standards on the disability classification rate in their school districts were examined. A mixed-method survey was conducted comparing two Average Needs, public school districts, in New York. Although similar student demographics were reported, the disability classification rate in District 1 was above the state the average and District 2 below the state average. The results of this study revealed that the implementation of APPR legislation significantly affected teacher's perceptions of professional development, instructional practices, and teacher efficacy. Professional development proved to be of high importance for all teachers in both districts. However, there was little consensus about the effects of APPR on the disability classification rates.

Chapter 12
Hiring Practices, Uses of Social Media, and Teacher Retention Differences....275
Bridgette Waite, Dowling College, USA
Elsa-Sofia Morote, Farmingdale State University of New York, USA

This study assesses the differences between teacher retention rate and human resource (HR) managers' hiring practices, self-efficacy. Their use of social media websites (Facebook, LinkedIn, and Twitter) for hiring was evaluated. Turnover of teachers with fewer than 5 years of experience was gathered from New York State Education Department (NYSED) database. New York State schools were separated by high and low teacher retention rates. A Likert Scale Survey with one open ended question was sent to school districts HR managers. An independent sample t test was used to determine the differences between high and low teacher retention rates. A content analysis is presented using the responses to the open-ended question. Findings indicated that less than half of the HR managers used social media in the hiring process. No significant differences between teacher retention rates, HR managers' practices, and HR self-efficacy was found.

Compilation of References 293

About the Contributors 323

Index 326

Preface

OVERVIEW OF THIS BOOK

Maximizing Social Science Research Through Publicly Accessible Data Sets provides examples of quality research studies from the social sciences involving large datasets. Extensive methodological information, including download links and directions for data conversion, is provided.

The book presents research studies involving or informed by large datasets. Chapters were selected to obtain a wide range of methodologies and datasets. Research could be from the areas of education, political science, psychology, economics, sociology, business, or a number of other areas. Statistical approaches will range from descriptive and inferential statistics to more complex causal analysis including structural equation models. Because managing large datasets can be challenging, the book includes detailed information for researchers interested in conducting similar analyses, including information about data retrieval and importing and statistical methods used. While the majority of chapters will focus on quantitative analyses, the book concludes with examples of qualitative research that are grounded in complementing the limitations of quantitative findings.

Maximizing Social Science Research Through Publicly Accessible Data Sets is unique in that it emphasizes analytical methods with large scale datasets. It intends to present research that demonstrates novel approaches to managing big data for statistical analysis. While each empirical chapter includes a literature review, the expected impact of the book is its value in data management and research methods. The methodological emphasis is unique in research books, while the focus on publicly available datasets is particularly useful from an instructional standpoint. The structure and content of the book will allow readers to recreate presented research studies, or better yet, extend areas of research for the benefit of the social sciences.

Although it is not a traditional statistics textbook, it guides readers through a several publicly accessible data sets and provides multiple examples of applied statistical methods. This book could be therefore be useful for intermediate graduate and undergraduate courses in research methods. It should also interest researchers, evaluators, and policy analysts interested in exploring publicly available datasets. Because the research can involve theoretical frameworks from any of the social sciences, it is anticipated that researchers and students of education, political science, sociology, economics, business administration, and other areas could benefit by reading the book.

There are three sections in *Maximizing Social Science Research Through Publicly Accessible Data Sets.* Section one pertains to large-scale data set retrieval, maintenance, and institutional use. The first chapter, authored by information scientist Claudia McGivney, provides a curated list of websites with publicly accessible data sets. Chapter two, written by Yair Cohen, guides readers through the complexities of merging multiple datasets. The next two chapters explore the extent to which different institutions make use of "Big Data." Chapter three, written by Tanveer Shah, focuses on the data analytics used by institutions of higher education. The subsequent chapter by Jianing Fang explores how corporations file complex quantitative and qualitative financial information and guides users in obtaining these public data.

Section two consists of empirical studies on publicly accessible data sets. Each of the four chapters includes a literature review, theoretical framework, and research questions centered on constructs measured by various data sets. Chapter five, written by the book editor as well as Karen M. Sealy and three other co-authors, explores the relationship between school leadership and student achievement in eight countries using data from the 2013 Teaching and Learning International Survey (TALIS) and the 2012 Programme for International Student Assessment (PISA). In the next chapter, Elsa-Sofia Morote analyzed the Quality of Government Institute's standard dataset to explore the relationships among education, income, and life satisfaction. Salvador Rivas-Aceves, Edmundo Marroquín-Tovar, and Héctor X. Ramírez-Pérez wrote the seventh chapter. It employs a pool data analysis to examine dynamics in pension systems. Chapter eight makes use of New York State Education Department public data to create a structural equation model for fourth-grade student achievement in math using student, household, school, and teacher factors.

Section three consists of independent empirical studies that were informed by publicly accessible data sets. In each of the four chapters, public data from New York State were used to define a sample for a new study in which a new survey was created, distributed, and analyzed. Chapter 9 was written by Dennis D. Sullivan and examines elementary teachers' instructional practices in mathematics in relation to technological and pedagogical content knowledge, formative assessment, reflective practice, receptivity to change, academic optimism, and instructional leadership. The authors of chapters ten and eleven consider New York State's Annual Professional Performance Review (APPR) teacher evaluation system. In chapter ten, Kenneth Forman and Craig Markson examine the relationships among poverty, attendance rates, and high school graduation rates in this context. In chapter eleven, Erica

Murphy-Jessen examines the effect of Annual Professional Performance Review (APPR) legislation on professional development, instructional practices, differentiated professional development, teacher efficacy, and disability classification rate. An interesting aspect of this chapter and chapter twelve is that both quantitative and qualitative analytic methods are used. In chapter twelve, Bridgette Waite and a co-author assess differences between teacher retention level and human resource managers' hiring practices (recruiting, hiring and selection) and self-efficacy.

The Oxford English Dictionary (OED) recently defined big data as, "data of a very large size, typically to the extent that its manipulation and management present significant logistical challenges." While the term is relatively recent, large datasets, with over 100 variables and 100,000 cases, are not new. Examples include various datasets by the Organisation for Economic Co-Operation and Development, International Association for the Evaluation of Educational Achievement, World Bank, Quality of Government, UNESCO Institute for Statistics, and others. As public access to online big data expands and computer storage capacity and processing speed increase, the logistical challenges associated with data analysis remain. Together, the chapters of this book explore the retrieval, analysis, and use of publicly accessible large scale data sets. Before attending to these logistical challenges, this preface explores the conceptual and ethical considerations of using such quantitative data sets.

Quantitative data sets involve the extensive use of labels, and categorization, and ratings on variables of interest. Social psychologists have long acknowledged the inevitability of categorization in our lives (see Lippmann, 1922; Allport, 1954). Our world is a complex one. Through organizing information into categories, we are more able to navigate efficiently, because category membership allows perceivers to assume information in less time. Therefore, we classify things as plants, animals, minerals, friends, foes, tables, and chairs. Without categories, our world would seem overwhelming. As Gordon Allport (1954) has noted:

The human mind must think with the aid of categories. We cannot possibly avoid this process. Orderly living depends on it. Our experience in life tends to form itself into clusters (concepts, categories), and while we may call on the right cluster at the wrong time, or the wrong cluster at the right time, still the process in question dominates our entire mental life.

What problems can occur through the use of categories? Allport (1954) implies that at the simplest level, a person may use a category incorrectly or may assume too much from category membership. The use of racial categories offers a vivid example. Categorical beliefs about groups of people are stereotypes. There are different conceptions of what constitutes a stereotype. Ashmore and Del Boca's (1981) definition of prejudice as a set of beliefs about the attributes of a group of people illustrates the connection between stereotypes and the use of categories. A person may hold a set of beliefs or assumptions about a sycamore tree because it is a member of the plant and tree categories. Similarly, a person may hold a set of beliefs about a person because he is member of a specific group, for example, men of African descent.

Researchers from various disciplines have emphasized the need for caution in using and interpreting categories. Not all constructs lend themselves to categorization; error can occur when continuous variables are measured with only broad categories (Johnson and Creech, 1983). O'Brien (1981) has noted three types of errors in categorizing.

Transformation error results from distortions introduced when the distances between the measured categories are not linear transformations of the underlying variable's metric. Grouping error occurs when a limited number of categories are used to represent a large number of underlying values. Finally, misclassification error may occur when scores from the underlying variable are put in the wrong category. (cited in Johnson & Creech, 1983)

These errors will prove useful in considering potential adverse effects from categorizing students. In categorizing people generally, psychological essentialism can become a dangerous trap into which an otherwise open-minded person may fall. Essentialism views different categories as having unique essential elements. Combined with other possible false assumptions, such as mutual exclusivity and inalterability, essentialism breeds several false conclusions about inherent differences between groups of people (e.g., Rothbart & Taylor, 1992). If findings are viewed with a critical eye, the lack of logic may become apparent. Most would doubt that there are certain things that are shared by every single person belonging to a given country, ethnic group, or other defined category. Underlying this view is the belief that a person outside of a group cannot understand what it means to be a part of that group—the traditions, the beliefs, the joys, or the sufferings. The researcher, armed with an impressively large data set and equally impressive analytic methods, becomes an authority voice of how one group differs from another. Clearly, this belief divides us, and has the potential to undermine inter-group communication and deeper understanding that is not built around presumed category membership. Assumptions about category membership, and the inevitable rating that follows fits within social dominance theory, as theorized by Sidanius (1993). This theory asserts that societies are predisposed to organize into hierarchies based socially constructed groups and create processes that produce and maintain those hierarchies.

Perhaps the tendency to conduct errors in categorization and place too much blind faith in large data sets is best illustrated in United States educational policy in light of international assessment data, such as the Trends in International Mathematics and Science Study (TIMSS) or the Programme for International Student Assessment (PISA). In the past, assessment results for the United States have been used by policymakers to promote educational policy, based upon comparing aggregate achievement to other countries and comparing subgroup achievement differences within the country. For example, in 2009, then Secretary Arne Duncan proclaimed that the PISA results:

Show that American students are poorly prepared to compete in today's knowledge economy. ... Americans need to wake up to this educational reality—instead of napping at the wheel while emerging competitors prepare their students for economic leadership... As disturbing as these national trends are for America, enormous achievement gaps among black and Hispanic students portend even more trouble for the U.S. in the years ahead.

Unfortunately, public policy makers often make simplistic use of quantitative and qualitative data, starting with the example of the (1983) report, "Nation at Risk," and examining the accountability movement in the last three U.S. presidential terms. More recent academic examinations of the relationship between public policy and data, including Stone's *Policy Paradox* (2012) and the Economic Policy Institute's (2013) report, "What Do International Tests Really Show About U.S. Student Performance," suggest that this fascination with international comparative data continues.

In December of 2016, OECD released data from the 2015 PISA. Over a half million 15-year-old students from 72 countries/economies participated. They were assessed in science, mathematics, reading, collaborative problem solving and financial literacy. From this recent historical perspective, it is reasonable to expect that the 2015 PISA results will be used by policymakers to draw conclusions about the educational system in the United States. The recent obsession with data also suggests that some of these conclusions will be unwarranted.

Data could be used differently, however. In the example of the 2015 PISA, gaining a better understanding of the school leadership practices and their connection to teacher practice and student achievement is of international importance. Summarizing research from England, New Zealand, and the United States, Robinson (2010) noted:

There is no doubt that this body of evidence about the links between instructional leadership and student outcomes has been noticed by policymakers...While the attention being given by policymakers to this research is to be welcomed, a word of warning is needed. Evidence about effective leadership practices is not the same as evidence about the capabilities that leaders need to confidently engage in those practices. (p. 2)

As school leaders, principals are central to the success of external educational policies, in terms of both enacting the policies and translating policies into terms and conditions that have the most immediate presence in teachers' and learners' daily lives. While there is research literature that supports context-by-leadership interactions, several kinds of contexts that shape leadership most are likely to include national policy and economic environments as well as local school and professional communities. Although effective teaching and school leadership are common subjects of inquiry, researchers have not yet clarified the context-specific nature of teaching and instructional leadership practices that are available using large publicly accessible data sets such as those explored in the chapters that follow.

While publicly accessible data offers a great resource to researchers, the importance of careful interpretation of findings cannot be overstated. Hopefully, this book will encourage the thoughtful analysis that can leverage "Big Data" for greater understanding, rather than the simplistic use of data to support the hierarchies that separate us.

REFERENCES

Allport, G. W. (1954). The historical background of modern social psychology. In G. Lindley (Ed.), *Handbook of social psychology* (Vol. 1). Reading, MA: Addison-Wesley.

Ashmore, R. D., & Del Boca, F. K. (1981). Conceptual approaches to stereotypes and stereotyping. In D. L. Hamilton (Ed.), *Cognitive processes in stereotyping and intergroup behavior* (pp. 1–35). Hillsdale, NJ: Lawrence Erlbaum Associates.

Carnoy, M., & Rothstein, R. (2013). What Do International Tests Really Show About US Student Performance? Washington, DC: Economic Policy Institute. Retrieved from http://www.epi.org/publication/us-student-performance-testing/

Johnson, D. R., & Creech, J. C. (1983). Ordinal measures in multiple indicator models: A simulation study of categorization error. *American Sociological Review*, *48*(3), 398–407. doi:10.2307/2095231

Lippmann, W. (1922). *Public opinion*. New York: Harcourt Brace.

OBrien, R. M. (1983). Reducing grouping distortion in rank category variables. *American Journal of Political Science*, *25*(3), 605–616. doi:10.2307/2110821

Robinson, V. M. J. (2010). From Instructional Leadership to Leadership Capabilities: Empirical Findings and Methodological Challenges. *Leadership and Policy in Schools*, *9*(1), 1–26. doi:10.1080/15700760903026748

Rothbart, M., & Taylor, M. (1992). Category labels and social reality: Do we view social categories as natural kinds? In G. R. Semin & K. Fiedler (Eds.), *Language, interaction and social cognition* (pp. 11–36). London: Sage.

Sidanius, J. (1993). The psychology of group conflict and the dynamics of oppression: A social dominance perspective. In S. Iyengar (Ed.), *Explorations in political psychology* (pp. 183–219). Durham, NC: Duke University Press.

Stone, D. A. (2002). *Policy paradox: The art of political decision making*. New York: Norton.

United States. (1983). *A nation at risk: The imperative for educational reform*. Author.

Section 1

Large Scale Data Set Collection and Institutional Use

Chapter 1
Sifting Through the Sets:
The Significance and Availability of Open Data

Claudia McGivney
Stony Brook University, USA

ABSTRACT

Data-driven decision making has become a driving factor across many industries and reliance on verifiable data is crucial in this environment. Equitable access to reliable data is a key component in establishing a just society. This chapter provides a brief overview and background to open data resources, including current initiatives and policies, along with an exploration of challenges to accessing this information. The researcher reviewed over 2,000 open data websites and repositories in order to provide a selection of these as exemplars. All resources have been annotated, with specific attention paid to repositories offering large datasets and government resources.

INTRODUCTION

The growing volume of data being generated has significant implications for everyone, from students and academic researchers to citizens and world leaders. Curating, distributing, and analyzing this data is complex and unwieldy. At the same time, we are becoming more dependent on the communication and utilization of big data for both large-scale strategy and our day-to-day work. Increased demand for open data is similar in nature to the current movements for open access, open government, and open educational and open source resources and its impact is wide-ranging since the

DOI: 10.4018/978-1-5225-3616-1.ch001

access to this information has the potential for change across all sectors of daily life. Open data has been defined as research data that has been made available to copy, download, research, or re-use, without barriers - financial, legal, or technological - save the ability to access the internet (SPARC, 2016). With information increasing at unprecedented rates, the ability to access and make use of such information has raised many questions for librarians, scholars, and researchers.

BACKGROUND

The sheer amount of data being produced by open government initiatives such as Data.gov, Data.gov.uk, and Open.canada.ca have attempted to make data transparent, easily accessible and available, but this data must remain protected under the label of "open data." At the 2013 G8 summit, the US, UK, France, Canada, Germany, Russia, Italy, and Japan committed to the Open Data Charter (Sinai & Martin, 2013) and as of 2015 this mandates that data be: data should be: open by default, timely and comprehensive, accessible and usable, comparable and Interoperable, for improved governance and citizen engagement, and for inclusive development and innovation (Open Data Charter, 2015). In order to ensure that data remain available for everyone, resources must be allocated to support the data remaining accessible, and there must be a to assessing the use of this information, as well as a commitment by those providing the data to long-term support and continued growth.

The commitment to access, long-term availability, and growth has found support in the growing open access movement and legislation has begun to reflect this philosophy when it concerns research and information that have been government funded. The EU Horizon 2020 project has maintained the view that publicly funded information should be available for perpetual access by the public with no additional costs imposed in order to fully benefit citizens, researchers, and companies alike (Teixeira da Silva, J., & Dobránszki, J. (2015). The US has adopted similar policies, specifically The Office of Science and Technology Policy, as part of a larger plan for open government. These initiatives are key legislation in ensuring that publicly funded, open data remains available to the very people that supported the research for myriad uses for their direct benefit.

With many policies still relatively new and developing, the availability of data remains a key factor in determining strategic plans for open data since persistent access to digital information tends to decrease with age (Teixeira da Silva, J., & Dobránszki, J., 2015). Having caught the interest of businesses, government, and policy makers open data's spread has necessitated public sector organizations to actively develop policies concerning the availability of data (Runardotter, M. & Ståhlbröst, A., 2016). These initiatives and policies are significant to the open data movement since it can be challenging for the individual researcher to determine if data made available on various websites is truly open data, i.e. freely available for use and reuse without any restrictions or additional permissions necessary.

Open data has also garnered a great deal of attention from the scholarly community, specifically academic libraries, wherein the focus is on ensuring that researchers of all levels have access to verified and usable information that these individuals may analyze and reuse without any additional permissions needed. A clear example of support for open access to data within the research community is a policy adopted by the Public Library of Science's *Data Availability Statement*: "PLOS journals require authors to make all data underlying the findings described in their manuscript fully available without restriction, with rare exception" (Public Library of Science, 2014). PLOS specifically requests authors provide *Data Availability Statement* outlining compliance with the policy.

Additional challenges arise with the degree of access, organization, and consistency, of data being made available. It is not enough to provide access to data in large quantity, without information on how data is collected, organized and the intention for the data's use providing access to large amounts of data leaves the researcher sifting through massive amounts of information without context (Evans, A. M., & Campos, A., 2013). In order for this information to be relevant and engaging there must be methods in place for ensuring equitable levels of access and reliability.

Along with organizational challenges, there are privacy issues where initiatives like the open government movement are concerned. While the intent behind open government and open data support the larger intent of the right to information championed by the open access movement the rapid shift towards availability has increased the potential for privacy issues. The open government movement is part of a complex landscape in the blurring of public and private information that is accessible through newly emerging technologies (Scassa, T., 2014) and open data should not include any identifying information within the datasets. Statistical data remains highly useful, with myriad possibilities, but accessibility to public health information, while equally useful, presents new challenges. Legislation and policies surrounding data availability must maintain the ease of access while protecting private individuals' personally identifiable information (PII). In the United States, for example, safeguards are being established as some states (Arizona, Ohio, and Washington) have established Chief Privacy Officer positions and in February of 2016 the Federal Privacy Council was established by executive order.

Open data is driving change on a global scale for academia, business, government, healthcare and the general public as unprecedented access to this information expands potential innovative research and social change. Equitable access to these resources directly impacts to quality of individual lives and society as a whole. Access to wide-variety of open data resources such as, community health data, climate change and environmental data, housing and economic data, and many more sectors increase the ability for interdisciplinary research, as well as empowerment of the individual citizen for both personal and social gains. Increases in the production of, and access to, data also supports evidence-based decision and policymaking. Social benefits of open data are vast, and government accountability and transparency stand to be deeply impacted as legislation and policies are rapidly being produced to account for the revolutionary means in which data is being opened to the public.

MAIN FOCUS OF THE CHAPTER

Open data, like the movement for open access and the development of open educational resources, is recognized as highly valuable for the development of digital literacies and as an educational tool to support critical thinking, analytical skills and collaborative behaviors (Atenas, J., Havemann, L., & Priego, E., 2015). Different organizations and institutions have various methods, motivations and reasons for the publicization of data. A great deal of focus has been given to open data and open data policies as we move towards a more globalized research environment, but there are no standard policies beyond keeping the data "open" as defined by the movement towards open data (Zuiderwijk, A., & Janssen, M., 2014). Conversations surrounding access, curation, dissemination, ethics, privacy and social change are on the rise globally as the myriad benefits of this information have been recognized. Open data is an expansive resource with the potential uses and implications only just being realized.

Long-term access and preservation are additional challenges that will need to be addressed as open data resources expand as perennial access is imperative to the future of a data-driven society. Included in this chapter is a descriptive list of a sampling of open data available on the internet in order to ease into navigating some of these freely accessible data sets. The collected sample is by no means comprehensive, but rather seeks to act as a guide into readily accessible open data and act as initial point in familiarizing researchers with both large scale initiatives as well as specialized and local collections of open data. Additional sites with open data are listed in the Appendix.

ArcGIS Open Data (https://opendata.arcgis.com/)

Created by ESRI ArcGIS is a platform for organizations to share GIS data, with over 66,000 datasets from 4,000 publishers, and users are able to download datasets directly. Users can choose to create an ArcGIS Online Account to access additional features, such as creating a favorites list of saved datasets. Datasets are easily searched by topic and/or location, with results further filtered by category, source, or tag. The newest datasets may be browsed from the homepage and there are also sections for "noteworthy" datasets and featured organizations sharing data. Additional resources, such as ArcGIS Desktop and OpenStreetMap, allow for greater manipulation of data.

The Association of Religion Data Archives (ARDA) (http://www.thearda.com)

The goal of the Association of Religion Data Archives is to "democratize access to the best data on religion." Archiving data from over 900 surveys ARDA lets users browse alphabetically, by category, newest additions, or most popular files. There are also a number of tutorials aimed towards assistance in using the archive, general browsing, finding information on particular religious groups and international data. The "QuickStats" section is geared towards general users and provides easily readable survey responses on popular topics such as attitudes about moral issues, strength of religious affiliation and religious beliefs about the paranormal.

Big Cities Health Inventory Data (http://www.bigcitieshealth.org/city-data/)

Compiled by the Big Cities Health Coalition (BCHC), the Health Inventory Data Platform provides open data from 28 cities in the United States. Focused on public health, the platform curates data at the city level in order to provide current health information on the communities in urban areas. The majority of the data is reported from the cities directly and there are over 50 indicators that guide users in exploring data on public health. These indicators are grouped into 11 overarching categories: Behavioral Health /Substance Abuse; Cancer; Chronic Disease; Demographics; Environmental Health; Food Safety; HIV/AIDs; Infectious Disease; Injury and Violence; Life Expectancy and Death Rate (overall) and Maternal and Child Health. Data can be further sorted by city, ethnicity, or gender and visualizations can be viewed online, downloaded in various sizes or shared directly to social media.

Bureau of Economic Analysis (http://www.bea.gov/)

A key U.S. government agency, the Bureau of Economic Analysis provides economic statistical information including the gross domestic product and national income. Data is easily downloaded and browsable by keyword, but the layout of the page provides quick access to data through four basic categories: national, international, regional, industry, and there is a special category for interactive data. Each of the four main sections includes an explanation of the data provided, methodologies for collection, a release schedule, and staff contacts for the various topics included in each category. In addition, the interactive data category includes an app that allows for easy access to the data, sharing capabilities, and visualizations of the data.

Bureau of Labor Statistics (http://stats.bls.gov/)

The Bureau of Labor Statistics collects statistical data from Federal agencies, State and local governments, business, and labor representatives. The website is easily navigable and using the "Data Tools" tab will provide access to a number of data retrieval tools, and customized tables, as well as information about restricted data and discontinued database access. The Bureau of Labor Statistics Public Data Application Programming Interface (API) provides access to raw economic data including employment trends, such as: projections, unemployment, earnings, and workplace injuries. Making use of the Data Finder will take the user to the BLS Beta Labs and from there data sets can be customized by date range, manipulated on screen and instantly exported for use.

Census Bureau (http://www.census.gov/)

While the most well-known responsibility of the U.S. Census Bureau is the national census conducted every ten years, there are also more than 130 surveys conducted annually including the largest household survey (the American Community Survey) and business survey (Annual Retail Trade Survey). In addition access to the U.S. Economic Census (conducted every five-years) and the Current Population Survey (conducted monthly) is available. Also included in the available data is the State Data Center (SDC) Program which was created specifically to support access to data at the state and city level. The easiest method for accessing data is through the Surveys & Programs tab, which indexes all available surveys alphabetically. In addition to the surveys there are also a number of apps, data tools, infographics and visualizations to help users download, manipulate and reuse the data.

Chicago's Open Data Portal (https://data.cityofchicago.org/)

Launched in 2012 the City of Chicago's open data portal, like many government data repositories, was created with both novice citizens and researches in mind. With over 1,100 data sets, the portal is designed with the user in mind. Browsability and navigation are kept simple and links to other resources, such as apps, are visible from the main page. For those new to data tutorials are provided, including a YouTube tutorial channel (https://www.youtube.com/user/ChicagoITDept/playlists). The most popular datasets include salary and title of current City of Chicago employees, building permits, affordable housing developments, and crime statistics.Categories of datasets range from Administration & Finance and Education to Environment & Sustainable Development and Historic Preservation.

Dartmouth Atlas of Health Care (http://www.dartmouthatlas.org/)

The Dartmouth Atlas of Health Care is based at The Dartmouth Institute for Health Policy and Clinical Practice and designed to document "patterns of health care delivery and practice across the United States and evaluates the quality of health care Americans receive." Data is browsable by region, hospital, or topic and the topics provide overviews of what type of information would be contained in that category. Data downloads cover a broad range of healthcare information, including Medicare spending and variation in care, with data provided at the state, county, hospital service area (HSA) or hospital referral region (HRR) levels. Other sets, such as the *Variations in the Care of Surgical Conditions* are broken into categories such as: Obesity, Cerebral aneurysms, Diabetes and peripheral arterial disease, Spinal stenosis, End-stage renal disease, and Prostate cancer. Most of the data provided is indexed by year and available via direct download to an excel file.

Data.gov (https://www.data.gov/)

This repository of information from the United States Federal Government includes over 190,000 datasets from various government agencies. Launched in 2009, Data.gov aims to provide public and easily accessible information; available raw data include economic, environmental, and healthcare related information. Over 70 federal agencies are represented through these datasets and in addition there are hosted datasets from 40 US states, 46 US cities and counties, 52 international countries, and 164 international regions. Transportation to geospatial information is included and most recently data on marine transportation has been added and includes information on topics ranging from mammals to revenue. The website is meant to be a portal to the myriad agency, bureau, and department data sets that can be accessed, downloaded, used, and reused.

Economic Indicators (purl.access.gpo.gov/GPO/LPS1458)

Economic Indicators is compiled monthly by the Council of Economic Advisers for the Joint Economic Committee. Data is available online going back to 1995 and breaks out information on wide array of economic factors including: total output, income, and spending with data on gross domestic product, national income, and corporate profits. Other data sets cataloged are employment, production and business activity, which include housing, construction, and manufacturing data. All data provided is navigable by year and month and can be easily downloaded for re-use as XLS, PDF or text files.

ENVIRONMENTAL PROTECTION AGENCY'S ENVIRONMENTAL DATASET GATEWAY (HTTPS://EDG.EPA.GOV/)

The Environmental Protection Agency's (EPA) Environmental Dataset Gateway provides open data aimed at making environmental data sets discoverable for use, reuse, and sharing in a variety of formats. The search function of Environmental Dataset Gateway (EDG) allows users to search quickly by popular search terms, an interactive map and provides quick links to their most popular data sets. Data sets are most easily browsed through category, including topics such as air quality, climate change, environmental justice and sustainability. Metadata and descriptive information for the data sets include time period of the content, spatial domain, access, themes and an abstract. The EDG provides a review option for users to rate that data, as well as a "Relationships" option. Once a user has reviewed a particular dataset it is then possible to select "Relationships" which provides connections to other resources based on "Parent of," "Child to" and "Others from this publisher" as connected to the current dataset.

European Union Open Data Portal (https://data.europa.eu/euodp/en/data/)

The European Union Open Data Portal is meant to act as a centralized access point for data in the European Union. The portal also links to various member countries' government portals such as, Ireland (https://data.gov.ie/data), Italy (http://www.dati.gov.it/) and Malta (data.gov.mt). With over 10,000 data sets available for use, the easily navigable portal invites suggestions for data from any "EU institution, agency or other body that is not yet in our catalogue." Use, reuse and distribution of the data is encouraged and browsability is enhanced through datasets grouped by subject, most viewed, most recent, and a standard search bar. There is also an interactive word cloud of popular terms, highlighting statistics, geospatial data, gender equality, water, vector data and international trade as some of the most highly accessed.

Eurostat (http://ec.europa.eu/Eurostat)

As the statistical office of the European Union, Eurostat was designed to provide public access to statistics that will allow for research between countries and regions within the EU. Eurostat is committed to the belief that "democratic societies do not function properly without a solid basis of reliable and objective statistics." Statistical information available includes data on the topics of: agriculture and fisheries, economy and finance, environment and energy, industry, trade and services, and science, technology and digital society. Designed as a portal to European statistics the site is easily navigable by code, keyword, name, theme, and there is a bulk download option that is updated twice a day.

Federal Aviation Administration (FAA) (https://www.faa.gov/data_research/)

The Federal Aviation Administration maintains a Data & Research section on their website which acts as a portal to data and statistics that are publicly accessible. Research on the site includes information in the following categories: Accident & Incident Data, Aviation Data & Statistics, Aviation Forecasts, Commercial Space Data, Funding & Grant Data, Passengers & Cargo Research and Safety. The data presented is a bit more challenging to navigate than some of the regional and local government portals, but the site is updated weekly and data are readily downloadable for export into SPPS or other statistical programs.

Federal Reserve Economic Data (FRED) (https://fred.stlouisfed.org/)

The Federal Reserve Bank of St. Louis provides access to over 400,000 economic time series from both U.S. and international sources. Sources include a number of U.S. Federal Reserve Banks, international banks, and the National Bureau of Economic Research. Data can be browsed by Browse data through a number of ways including: Category, Series, Source or Release Calendar. Data is also tagged for easy browsing and keyword searching will also add tags to your search if one of your initial keywords is a tag used by FRED. Similar to many other open data resources FRED provide mobile apps to facilitate access to data and a helpful resource for working with data is the FRED Add-in for Excel.

FedStats (https://fedstats.sites.usa.gov/)

Around since 1997, this early repository of open data provides statistical information from over 100 agencies on more than 400 topics. FedStats can be used as a portal to a broad range of agencies with information on: agriculture, crime, education, energy use, health insurance, population trends and more. To find information on the site is fairly intuitive and statistical information can be searched by an A to Z topic list, agency name, keyword, subject, or phrase searching, and even press releases which are updated daily and fully browsable.

Gene Expression Omnibus (GEO) (https://www.ncbi.nlm.nih.gov/geo/)

The Gene Expression Omnibus (GEO) is part of the National Center for Biotechnology Information (NCBI) and hosts over 4,000 datasets. GEO classifies itself as "international public repository that archives and freely distributes microarray, next-generation sequencing, and other forms of high-throughput functional genomics data submitted by the research community." The database is generally constructed for use by researchers and professionals in the scientific community, but all data is open to the public and available for download. Files are available in variety of formats and generally they are compressed using gzip. Dataset records provide a summary, cluster analysis and sample count. A particularly helpful feature is the data analysis tool, which includes the ability to select the test to perform, the significance level, and sample groups from the data.

Global Biodiversity Information Facility (GBIF) (http://www.gbif.org)

The Global Biodiversity Information Facility (GBIF) is funded through global intergovernmental support and acts as a portal to over 30,000 datasets on biodiversity. GBIF believes that compiling data from member institutions "enables research not possible before, and informs better decisions to conserve and sustainably use the biological resources of the planet." The collected data is browsable by description, publisher, or title. Results can be further filtered by a number of options, including: type of dataset, keyword, country, publisher, or publishing country. Datasets are available through direct download with most including an interactive map that provides geographic information about the dataset.

Harvard Dataverse (https://dataverse.harvard.edu/)

The Harvard Dataverse compiles scientific data from all disciplines and currently holds over 70,000 datasets. There are over 30,000 datasets classified in the social sciences which makes the holdings one of the largest collections of this discipline's research data in the world. Along with the social sciences, other subjects include: Arts and Humanities, Earth and Environmental Sciences, Health and Life Sciences and Law. Data may be shared via social media and email, or downloaded in a variety of formats, and the Dataverse's TwoRavens tool to create statistical models on screen.

International Genome Sample Resource (IGSR) 1000 Genomes Project (http://www.internationalgenome.org)

The overarching mission of the portal is to make data from the 1000 Genomes Project available. From the portal, data is easily searchable, shared, and downloadable. Available data has been anonymized, but in the data disclaimer it is noted that "data made available by IGSR comes from many different owners and that consequently restrictions on different pieces of data within IGSR and rights claimed on pieces of data vary. These variations can occur both between and within subsets of data in IGSR. In addition, restrictions and claimed rights may vary over time" (http://www.internationalgenome.org/IGSR_disclaimer/, para. 2). The data portal provides a very user friendly interface for filtering and downloading data and allows users to search by sample, population or data collections.

ILOSTAT (http://www.ilo.org/)

The International Labour Organization (ILO) provides access to labor information Promoting tripartism between employers, workers, and member states. ILO's open data access is geared towards promoting dialogue and engaging all sides of labor standards, policies, and programs. Indicators are browsable by a number of subjects, including: labor productivity, social protection, and working time. Information for over 180 countries is accessible and the hyperlinked, summary tables provide at-a-glance access to general labor information about profiled countries. When accessing a set, such as, "Mean weekly hours actually worked per employed person by sex and occupation" users are able view all data and fully customize which data to include before downloading a CSV, Excel, or SDMX file.

Medicare Data (https://data.medicare.gov/)

Medicare's data portal is straightforward and, like many federal websites, designed to be user friendly. Many of the datasets are comparisons: hospital compare, dialysis facility compare, physician compare, etc. National survey results are included as well, for example, the Home Health Care - Patient survey (HHCAHPS) results are available for download under the Nursing Home Compare datasets. Datasets are easily viewed on screen, filtered, shared or exported and can be downloaded in a number of formats including CSV and Microsoft Access Database files. Users are also able to subscribe to RSS feeds so that they may track changes to a particular dataset.

NASA's Open Data Portal (https://open.nasa.gov/open-data/)

There are over 30,000 data sets available through NASA's open data portal and cover a broad range of categories, including: Aerospace, Applied Science, Apps, Earth Science, Management/Operations, Raw Data, Software, and Space Science. Data sets are browsable, but can be limited using types, categories and tabs. All data are available for download, as well as manipulation and visualization through the "View Data" tab. Further features for visualization are the "Calendar" option which allows researchers to see how data have changed over time and the "Data Lens" which lets researchers customize their view of the data through charts, graphs and maps. There is also an option to share data through an embed code using the "Social Data Player."

NOAA National Climatic Data Center (http://www.ncdc.noaa.gov/)

This data portal is the combined repository of NOAA's former three data centers—the National Climatic Data Center, the National Geophysical Data Center, and the National Oceanographic Data Center. The three data centers combined to form the National Centers for Environmental Information (NCEI). With this merge the NCEI is the world's largest repository for historic and current weather and climate data. The holdings are extensive and the categories of datasets range from radar and satellite data, to severe weather and paleoclimatology. NCEI also maintains Climate Data Online https://www.ncdc.noaa.gov/cdo-web/datatools, which contains an archive of global historical weather and climate data. The data include temperature, precipitation and degree measurements in monthly, seasonal, and yearly increments, as well as 30-year Climate Normals. Data are browsable, and samples can be downloaded, but certified hard copies do have a fee. The Climate Data Online Data Tools allow users to search across single or multiple datasets, access Climate Normals from 9,800 stations across the United States, as well as access hourly, daily, and monthly data from 2,400 locations. Tools for accessing storm events and severe weather data are also available.

The National Science Digital Library (https://nsdl.oercommons.org/)

The National Science Digital Library (NSDL) provides access to open educational resources in the sciences, technology, engineering, and mathematics (STEM) fields. These resources include over 2,200 datasets and subject areas include: Applied Science, Education, History, Life Science, Mathematics, & Physical Science. Since

NSDL has an educational focus, the datasets can be sorted by education level or standards. Datasets are compiled from other institutions, websites, or data portals so the providers are clearly listed with each dataset and they will often link out to the original source. Other resources are collections grouped by providers, for example" Teach the Earth" is a collection from Carleton College's Science Education Resource Center (SERC). The datasets provided collectively focus on geoscience education and have a range of application from middle school to graduate coursework with the majority focused on undergraduate education and teaching with data. Resource providers span from the American Association for Advancement of Science to PBS LearningMedia.

Network Repository (http://networkrepository.com)

Network Repository (NR) is an interactive data repository with visual analytics, graph mining, and graph visualization. Users can interact with a single dataset or cross-reference multiple datasets, which include: biological networks, brain networks, cheminformatics, machine learning and social science. All data sets are accessible, easily downloaded and shared. There is also an option for users to upload, share, and visualize their own data.

State of New York Open Data (https://data.ny.gov/)

Currently, 40 states within the United States provide data portals, easily found via lists at: https://www.data.gov/open-gov/. New York State's Open Data provides over 1,400 datasets, resources and tools related to health and government to recreation and transportation. The portal also publishes a quarterly report updating users on the latest additions to the datasets and highlighting specific resources and their potential uses. There is a wide range of public data available, including information on community health and of course standard budgetary and education information. There are even highlighted areas uniquely focused on transparency, crime on NY State college campuses and even farmer's markets throughout the state.

NYC Open Data (https://opendata.cityofnewyork.us/)

New York City's open data law (Local Law 11 of 2012) requires that all "public data be made freely available on a single web portal by December 31, 2018." The open data portal is designed with users in mind, and provides guidance and instructional materials for everyone from new users to "data veterans." As with many open data sets users can search by newest and most popular data, as well as make use of a traditional search bar. Results can be further sorted through categories, which include: Business, City, Government, Education, Environment, Health, Housing & Development, NYC BigApps, Public Safety, Recreation, Social Services, and Transportation. It is also possible to filter results by the originating agency and type of data. Once a user selects a particular dataset there are numerous options for downloading, sharing and interacting with visualization tools.

OpenDataPhilly (www.opendataphilly.org)

In 2012 the city of Philadelphia unveiled their Open Data Policy, one of the smaller, local data sets included in this chapter, OpenDataPhilly.org has been the main repository for accessing open data from schools, nonprofits and businesses for the city. Currently there are over three hundred data sets, easily navigable by topic and through a general keyword search feature. It has been established as the official open data repository for the Philadelphia region, including data sets from many organizations in the region. They can also be found on Twitter: @opendataphilly.

OpenEI Open Energy Information (http://en.openei.org)

Supported through the U.S. Department of Energy Open EI is run by the National Renewable Energy Laboratory to provide open access to energy information compiled by various resources. They liken themselves to a Wiki inviting users - everyone from individuals to research professionals to government agencies - to add, edit, share and use data. Committed to open data and crowdsourcing information the major contributors of data on OpenEI are the U.S. Dept. of Energy Open Data Catalog, International Utility Rate Database, and the U.S. Utility Rate Database. Results are further filtered by tags, catalogs, or sectors, such as: geothermal, solar, wind. It is also possible to explore datasets through an interactive map. The results list includes tags under each entry that quickly indicated the file formats available for download for each particular dataset.

Open Government Canada (http://open.canada.ca/en/open-data)

Canada's Open Government page provides a wide-ranging access to government information, and they have specific sections dedicated to explaining and working with data sets. Datasets are fully searchable - with a variety of limiters to drill down to specific sets quickly, and easily navigable since clear descriptions are provided for each data set. Topic range from economics, justice, and agriculture, to public services, immigration, and transportation. Through Canada's Federal Geospatial platform a great deal of data collected by a wide-range of sources such as scientists and surveyors. They acknowledge that the open maps section is a work in progress, but the website does provide access to geospatial data in a variety of formats. The open maps section includes a section on working with data and application programming interfaces, and like much of the website provides clear information about accessing and manipulating data, as well as contact information for additional help.

Organisation for Economic Co-Operation and Development (OECD) Data (https://data.oecd.org/)

The OECD includes international data provided by the governments of 35 member countries. Topics are wide ranging, including data on: agriculture, economics, education, energy, environment, health, technology, and society. Their collected indicators include information on everything from taxes and trade, to wireless mobile broadband subscriptions, and passenger car registrations. Their section for statistics news releases is very helpful in tracking frequency of reports and future release dates. Another useful feature provided by the OECD is the iLibrary which can be accessed from the publications tab. Data sets for statistical indicators are available to read online or download, as PDF or excel files, but a subscription is necessary to access full reports and data sets.

Registry of Research Depositories (http://www.re3data.org/)

Re3data defines itself as a "global registry of research data repositories" that "aims to promote a culture of sharing, increased access and better visibility of research data" (http://www.re3data.org/faq, para. 1) This unique resource is funded by the German Research Foundation (http://www.dfg.de/) and has collected over 1500 open data repositories, since launching in 2012, in an effort to contend with the challenges presented by trying to locate, sort, and access myriad data repositories across a wide expanse of disciplines. The key criteria of all data repositories included in the registry are that they: "be run by a legal entity, such as a sustainable institution (e.g. library, university), clarify access conditions to the data and repository as well as the terms of use, and have focus on research data." The repositories are easily searchable and each one is coded with icons to indicate the level of access, indicators of repository standards or policies and persistence of links. The breadth of subjects, countries, and content type is impressive and easily filtered. Browsing by subject can be done by text, but there is a graphic feature that allows for an interactive visual search of content, while browsing by country lets users engage with a map displaying the number of data repositories indexed in the portal. Entries provide the repository's URL, a description of the repository, subjects, keywords, and a mission statement when applicable.

Stanford Large Network Dataset Collection (https://snap.stanford.edu/data/)

Part of the Stanford Network Analysis Project (SNAP), the Stanford Large Network Dataset Collection is a collection of data focused on social and information networks. According to the website, the biggest project to date was the Microsoft Instant Messenger network from 2006 with 240 million nodes and 1.3 billion edges. Most datasets focus on a single social network tracked over time, such as Twitter or Livejournal. Most networks are grouped into categories such as Internet peer-to-peer networks, or online reviews, to make browsing datasets easier.

UK Data Service (https://www.ukdataservice.ac.uk/)

Funded by the Economic and Social Research Council (ESRC) UK Data Service contains the UK's largest collection of international social and economic data including census and population data. Data included on the site covers topics from employment and income to housing and quality of life and international macrodata on a variety of socio-economic topics is also available. UK Data Service collects data from a number of sources, much of which is provided by surveys funded through national and regional governments, as well as voluntary community sector organizations and universities. UK surveys are nationally-representative, including individual and household responses, and many have large sample sizes with data being updated regularly. Data can be browsed easily, but researchers must register in order to analyse and download data. Academic researchers may analyze sensitive or confidential data in a secure lab in a virtual research environment. Researchers are able to use, manage and deposit data, but some is restricted to UK users only and researchers should check both the access restrictions and collection development policies on the site.

UNData (http://data.un.org/)

The United Nations Statistics Division (UNSD) launched UNData in 2005 as part of an initiative for "Statistics as a Public Good." UNData is a fully searchable database that pulls information from international statistical databases provided by the UN System of agencies including ILO, World Bank and WHO. Searchable topics are wide-ranging and include data on Education, Employment, Energy, Environment, Health, Human Development, Industry, Information and Communication Technology, Refugees, Trade, and Tourism.

The World Bank DataBank (http://databank.worldbank.org/)

Consisting of five institutions - The International Bank for Reconstruction and Development, The International Development Association, The International Finance Corporation, The Multilateral Investment Guarantee Agency and The International Centre for Settlement of Investment Disputes - the World Bank gathers data on World Development Indicators. Development data includes of economic, social and environmental indicators, such as: education statistics, gender statistics, health, nutrition, and population statistics. Under the data tab, World Bank Open Data allows users to search by keyword, phrase, country, or indicator. Data can be easily exported, saved and shared and the site includes analysis, graphing, mapping, and visualization tools.

Zenodo: Open Data for Open Science (http://zenodo.org/)

Supported by The CERN & Society Foundation, Horizon 2020 and OpenAire Zenodo was designed to address long-term data management and access within the area scientific research.Zenodo includes a number of Open Science resources, and actively solicits the depositing of data, software, and materials is support of scholarly research. The majority of datasets archived at Zenodo are open access, over 4,000 of them in fact, but there is some data that is closed, restricted or embargoed. The initial limiter for search query results pertains to access level, and all information is clearly marked.

CONCLUSION

As society continues to adapt to changes in the digital age, governance, industry, medicine, and scholarly communication have all been deeply impacted by the need for open and reliable data. The access to large datasets through open data repositories is unprecedented and stands to improve research, government and civil life. As the open access movement gains ground the infrastructure to support access to open data is increasing, but there are still challenges facing these repositories. The most complex aspect of open data is perennial access to content. Repositories that are currently accessible require both support and maintenance to protect access for future generations. As the digital landscape shifts open data repositories are vital to support equity, transparency, and scholarship in an increasingly data-driven world.

REFERENCES

Atenas, J., Havemann, L., & Priego, E. (2015). Open Data as Open Educational Resources: Towards transversal skills and global citizenship. *Open Praxis*, *7*(4), 377–389. doi:10.5944/openpraxis.7.4.233

Evans, A. M., & Campos, A. (2013). Open government initiatives: Challenges of citizen participation. *Journal of Policy Analysis and Management*, *32*(1), 172–185. doi:10.1002/pam.21651

Karen, O. (2016). What is being done with open government data? An exploratory analysis of public uses of New York City open data. *Webology*, *13*(1), 1–12.

Krishnamurthy, R., & Awazu, Y. (2016). Liberating data for public value: The case of Data.gov. *International Journal of Information Management*, *36*(4), 668–672. doi:10.1016/j.ijinfomgt.2016.03.002

Open Data Charter. (2015). *Principles*. Retrieved from http://opendatacharter.net/principles/

Public Library of Science. (2014). *Data Availability*. Retrieved from http://journals.plos.org/plosone/s/data-availability

Runardotter, M. & Ståhlbröst, A., (2016). CLASH!: The open data policy meets an organizational context. *International Journal of Public Information Systems*, (1), 1.

Scassa, T. (2014). Privacy and open government. *Future Internet*, *6*(2), 397–413. doi:10.3390/fi6020397

Sinai, N., & Martin, M. (June 19, 2013). *Open Data Going Global*. Retrieved from https://www.whitehouse.gov/blog/2013/06/19/open-data-going-global

Teixeira da Silva, J., & Dobránszki, J. (2015). Potential Dangers with Open Access Data Files in the Expanding Open Data Movement. *Publishing Research Quarterly*, *31*(4), 298–305. doi:10.1007/s12109-015-9420-9

Zuiderwijk, A., & Janssen, M. (2014). Open data policies, their implementation and impact: A framework for comparison. *Government Information Quarterly*, *31*(1), 17–29. doi:10.1016/j.giq.2013.04.003

APPENDIX

Table 1.

Name	URL
Aachen Open Data	http://offenedaten.aachen.de/
Aberdeen City Council Open Data	http://www.aberdeencity.gov.uk/open_data/
Afganistan Open Data Project	http://afghanistandataproject.org
African Development Bank Group Open Data	http://dataportal.opendataforafrica.org/
Aid Data	http://aiddata.org
Alagoas em Dados e Informações	http://dados.al.gov.br/
Alameda County Data Sharing Initative	http://data.acgov.org/
Alaska Ocean Observing System	http://www.aoos.org/aoos-data-resources/
Alberta Open Data	https://open.alberta.ca/
Amsterdam Economic Board Open Data Exchange (ODE)	http://amsterdamopendata.nl
Aragon Open Data	http://opendata.aragon.es
Ashford Borough Council	http://www.ashford.gov.uk/transparency
Atlanta Open Data (Govathon)	http://govathon.com/data.html
Australian Antarctic Data Centre	https://data.aad.gov.au
Australian Data Archive	https://www.ada.edu.au
Australian Nation Data Service	http://ands.org.au
Austrian Government Open Data	http://data.gv.at
Balearic Islands Open Data	http://www.caib.es/caibdatafront/
Barcelona Open Data	http://opendata.bcn.cat/opendata/ca
Bari Open Data	http://opendata.comune.bari.it/
Bayern Open Data	https://opendata.bayern.de
Belarus Open Data	https://opendata.by/
Berlin Open Data	http://daten.berlin.de/
Bilbao Open Data	http://bilbao.net/opendata
Bochum Open Data	https://www.bochum.de/opendata
Boston's Open Data Hub	https://data.boston.gov/
Brazilian Open Data Portal	http://dados.gov.br/
British Columbia Open Data	http://www.data.gov.bc.ca/
Brussels-Capital Region Open Data Portal	http://opendatastore.brussels
Buenos Aires Data	http://data.buenosaires.gob.ar/

continued on following page

Table 1. Continued

Name	URL
California Open Data Portal	http://data.ca.gov/
Catalonia Open Data Catalog	http://dadesobertes.gencat.cat
City of Austin Open Data	http://data.austintexas.gov/
City of Berkeley Open Data	https://data.cityofberkeley.info/
City of Lucca Open Data	http://opendata.provincia.lucca.it/
City of Mannheim Open Data	https://opendata.mannheim.de
City of Turin Open Data	http://www.comune.torino.it/aperto
City ofAlburquerque Open Data	http://www.cabq.gov/abq-data/
Comune Di Firenze Open Data	http://opendata.comune.fi.it
Connecticut Open Data	https://data.ct.gov/
Copenhagen Data	http://data.kk.dk/
Data Gov HK	https://data.gov.hk/en
Data Tel-Aviv	https://www.tel-aviv.gov.il/Transparency/Pages/DataTelAviv.aspx
Data.gov.au	http://data.gov.au
Datos Argentina	http://www.datos.gob.ar/
Datos El Salvador	http://www.datoselsalvador.org/
Datos Peru	http://www.datosperu.org/
Fort Worth Open Data	http://data.fortworthtexas.gov
German Government Open Data	http://govdata.de/
Greece National Data Portal	http://data.gov.gr/
Indonesia Open Data Portal	http://data.go.id/
Ireland's Open Data Portal	https://data.gov.ie/data
Israel Open Data	http://data.gov.il/
Italy Open Data	http://dati.gov.it
Japan Open Data	http://www.data.go.jp/
Kenya Open Data	http://opendata.go.ke/
Latvia Open Data	http://opendata.lv/
London Datastore	http://data.london.gov.uk
Los Angeles Open Data	https://data.lacity.org/
Maine Open Data	http://www.maine.gov/data/
Melbourne Data	https://data.melbourne.vic.gov.au/
Montana Open Data	https://data.datamontana.us/
Moscow Open Data Portal	http://data.mos.ru

continued on following page

Table 1. Continued

Name	URL
Nebraska Open Data	http://www.nebraska.gov/data.html
New Zealand Open Data	http://data.govt.nz/
Niagara Open Data	http://niagararegion.ca/government/opendata
Ontario Open Data	http://www.ontario.ca/open-data
Open Data Aarhus	http://www.odaa.dk/
Open Data Alkmaar	http://www.alkmaar.nl/opendata
Open Data Banda Aceh	http://data.bandaacehkota.go.id/
Open Data Baton Rouge	http://data.brla.gov
Open Data Bologna	http://dati.comune.bologna.it/
Open Data Bulgaria	https://opendata.government.bg/
Open Data City of Antwerp	http://opendata.antwerpen.be/datasets
Open Data Euskadi	http://opendata.euskadi.net
Open Data Florence	http://dati.comune.firenze.it
Open Data For Africa	http://opendataforafrica.org/
Open Data For Kenya Development Bank Group Open Data	http://kenya.opendataforafrica.org/
Open Data Glasgow	https://data.glasgow.gov.uk/
Open Data Halifax	http://www.halifax.ca/opendata/
Open Data Hub Italy	http://www.sciamlab.com/opendatahub/
Open Data Netherlands	http://opendatanederland.org
Open Data of Nice Côte d'Azur	http://opendata.nicecotedazur.org
Open Data Portal City of Richmond	https://data.richmondgov.com/
Open Data Portal Munich	https://www.opengov-muenchen.de/
Open Data Portal of Badalona	http://opendata.badalona.cat/badalona/ca
Open Data Portal of Estonia	https://opendata.riik.ee/
Open Data Portal South Korea	http://data.go.kr
Open Data Regione Toscana	http://dati.toscana.it/
Open Data Seine Saint Denis	http://data.seine-saint-denis.fr/
Open Data Spain	http://datos.gob.es
Open Data Uganda	http://data.ug
Open Data Ville De Bordeaux	http://opendata.bordeaux.fr/
Open Government Data (OGD) Platform India	https://data.gov.in/
Open Nepal	http://data.opennepal.net/

continued on following page

Table 1. Continued

Name	URL
Open Public Data in Norway	http://data.norge.no/
Open Puerto Rico	http://abrepr.org/
Open Stockholm	http://open.stockholm.se/
openAFRICA	http://africaopendata.org/
OpenColorado	http://opencolorado.org/
OpenData Bolzano	http://dati.retecivica.bz.it/it/
OpenData City of Lecce	http://dati.comune.lecce.it
Opendata Corsica	http://opendata.corse.fr
Saudi National Portal	https://www.saudi.gov.sa/wps/portal/
Scottish Parliament's open data portal	https://data.parliament.scot/#/home
Seoul Open Data	http://data.seoul.go.kr
Serbia Open Data	http://rs.ckan.net/
Sierra Leone Data Portal	http://sierraleone.opendataforafrica.org/
State of Washington Open Data	http://data.wa.gov
Swiss Open Government Data	www.opendata.swiss
Taiwan Open Data Portal	http://data.gov.tw
Thailand Open Data Portal	http://data.go.th/
Vertex Alaska Satellite Facility Data Portal	http://vertex.daac.asf.alaska.edu
York Open Data	https://www.yorkopendata.org/
Zurich Open Data Catalog	https://data.stadt-zuerich.ch/

Chapter 2
Using Public Data From Different Sources

Yair Cohen
Farmingdale State University of New York, USA

ABSTRACT

The United States federal government agencies as well as states agencies are liberating their data through web portals. Web portals like data.gov, census.gov, healthdata.gov, ed.gov and many others on the state level provide great opportunity for researchers of all fields. This chapter shows the challenges and the opportunities that lie by merging data from different pubic sources. The researcher collected and merged data from the following datasets: NYSED school report card, NYSED Fiscal Profile Reporting System, Civil Rights Data Collection, and Census 2010 School District Demographics System. The challenges include data validation, data cleaning, flatting data for easy reporting, and merging datasets based on text fields.

INTRODUCTION

On January 21, 2009 on his first day in his office, President Obama signed two executive orders: The *Memorandum on Transparency and Open Government* and The *Memorandum on the Freedom of Information Act* (Cuillier & Piotrowski, 2009). These memorandums stated that the federal administration is committed to creating an unprecedented level of openness in Government, and that transparency will enhance the public trust. It encouraged government transparency as an important step toward government accountability and democracy. Directing the federal agencies to take affirmative steps to make information public and use modern technology to inform citizens about what is known and done by their Government. The executive orders

DOI: 10.4018/978-1-5225-3616-1.ch002

also called for the Chief Technology Officer (CTO) to present recommendations for Open Government Directive (Obama, 2009a). The recommendation of the federal CTO became the base for President Obama published Open Government Directive (OGD) presented in December 2009. The OGD was based on transparency, participation, and collaboration that were described as the cornerstone of an open government. The OGD has led to the development of data.gov website which provides direct access to enormous amounts of unrefined government data with the hope that researchers, private entities, and other government agencies will be able analyze and develop new uses for the data that will enhance government activities (Bertot & Jaeger, 2010). In 2016 data.gov was elected to be one of the *Best Free Business Websites*, the explanation stated that data.gov is the "home of the US government's open data," it is an online government data aggregator based on its OGD to embrace a new era of open and accountable government. In an age when data are seemingly abundant in our daily lives and with production expanding at an astonishing pace, Data.gov is in its eighth year of bringing data to the American public in an effort to foster government transparency, and is a recognized tool of the open data movement. The platform has spawned a host of data.gov sites in other countries (e.g., Canada, the UK, Australia, France, Singapore), with 106 countries now bringing the open data movement forward, according to a 2016 United Nations global survey. States also followed the OGD and developed websites on the state level. New York State launched in 2013 open.ny.gov a comprehensive state data website that provides user-friendly access to data from New York State agencies, localities, and the federal government. The state of California developed data.ca.gov in order "bring government closer to citizens and start a new shared conversation for growth and progress in our great state". The state of Texas developed data.tx.gov, each state has developed its own data sharing site following the footsteps of the federal initiative (Best of the best business websites, 2016). As of April 2017, data.gov hosts over 192,000 datasets across government offices. The data catalog includes data from the following departments: agriculture, climate, consumer, ecosystems, education, energy, finance, health, local government, manufacturing, maritime, ocean, public safety, and science & research.

However, not all government agencies connected to data.gov. For example, the US Census Bureau stored its massive data under census.gov, the site hold valuable information for social science researchers on topics like age, sex, migration, household, poverty, education, income, and more.

All the departments that connected to data.gov have created their own site in order to make it easy for the end users to find the dataset they are looking for. The US Department of Health and Human Services (HHS) issued their own website healthdata.gov that host data from the various department agencies (e.g. CCD, FDA, CMS, and others), the department also focused on making data easier for developers to use, while their goal is to "unleash the power of private-sector innovators and entrepreneurs to utilize HHS data to create applications, products, services and features that help improve health and health care" (healthdata.gov/content/about). The US Education departments created ed.gov/data where school district, schools, students, and other data can be retrieved easily. As mentioned above there is a link from data.gov to these datasets, however, accessing through the department/agency website is easier.

MAIN FOCUS OF THE CHAPTER

Finding the right dataset is one challenge the researcher face, as there are hundreds of thousands of government datasets in data.gov, census.gov and other government data sites. Another challenge is to handle the dataset as the data can origin from different sources and combined into complex data structures that increase the difficulty of data integration (Cai & Zhu, 2015). Another challenge involves merging multiple datasets from different sources. This chapter discusses these challenges and shows an example of how it can be done using MS-Excel and MS-Access.

Datasets Used in the Research

New York State Education Department (NYSED) School Report Card Database

New York State Education Department (NYSED) launched its data site data.nysed.gov with over 5.8 million page views, publicly reports education data for educators across the state. Users of the website can access statewide data reports and view reports for an individual school, district, BOCES, or county. The website has 2012-13 and 2013-14 educator data (APPR ratings and State-provided growth ratings), student data (public school enrollment data), school data (school report cards), 2012-13, 2013-14 and 2014-15 public school grades 3-8 assessment data, aggregate reports for the data work with SUNY and CUNY, as well as teacher and leader certification metrics (NYSED, 2016).

NYSED school report card database is published around May of each year for the previous school year (e.g. on May 2016 NYSED published 2014-15 school year report cards). It is a large MS Access database (~1.2GB in 2016), and consists of 37 tables. The data included data submitted by local school district officials and the results of the state assessments. The tables contained data about performance of designated subgroups (e.g. Gender, Ethnicity) are reported by total public school or charter school and can be aggregated by school district. The database is open to the public and can be downloaded at http://data.nysed.gov/downloads.php. The download is a zip file which includes two files: the first is a ReadMe PDF document that provides explanation on the different tables and their structure, the second file is the report card Access database. The zip file includes a ReadMe file that provides explanation on the different tables in the dataset; it also provides the changes from previous years. The data extracted from the report card database had two levels: 1. School level (e.g. teachers data and students' attendance data) 2. Grade level, for each school ELA and math achievement data is provided by grade (e.g. Fourth grade ELA achievement).

NYSED Fiscal Profile Reporting System (FPRS)

Around August of each year NYSED publish the school districts fiscal profile data of the precious year (e.g. in August 2015 the NYSED published the 2013-14 school district fiscal data). According the NYSED this data is used to:

- To provide data to State agencies, members of the Legislature and their staff, school districts, educational interest groups, the press and the public;
- To assist in the development of the Regents State Aid Proposal;
- To serve as a source of expenditure data for the School Report Card;
- To serve as the data source for the calculation of the cost of general education per pupil and special education per pupil;
- To assess the spending and revenue trends of districts; and,
- To suggest further analyses needed to better understand the spending and revenue trends of a particular district or group of districts.

This dataset comes in a form of Excel spreadsheet; it displays the district's reported expenditures and revenues by various categories per budget year for the 674 NY school districts. Each year had a separate Excel sheet starting from 1993-94. The list of Excel files and their description can be viewed and downloaded from NYSED Fiscal Analysis & Research Unit webpage (NYSED, n. d.).

Census 2010 School District Demographics System (SDDS)

Most districts in the Mid-Atlantic and New England states follow county, township, or city boundaries, while districts in the Midwest and Western states are generally independent of municipal boundaries and frequently intersect statistical areas like Census tracts and block groups.

The U.S. Census Bureau developed demographic, economic, geographic, and fiscal data for school districts, and many of these data collection activities are conducted in cooperation with the National Center for Education Statistics (NCES), part of the U.S. Department of Education's Institute of Education Sciences (IES). Most districts in the Mid-Atlantic and New England states follow county, township, or city boundaries, while districts in the Midwest and Western states are generally independent of municipal boundaries and frequently intersect statistical areas like Census tracts and block groups. School District Demographics System (SDDS) provides Census information for over 14,000 school districts across the US (census.gov). SDDS enables access to school district demographics and related geographic data that is not available in any other form. SDDS was developed to help community leadership, educators, researchers and analysts, and the public to access and use demographic data to understand current demographic characteristics and patterns of change better, as well as to plan for improved educational programs and opportunities (National Center of Educational Statistics, n.d.). This database is available online and includes hundreds of tables based on the Census report. The SDDS had many options to view data, for the purpose of this study the researchers used the following link was used Table P18 – Household Type and Table P28 Household Type by Household Size for the state of NY. The data is provided on a school district level for each of the 674 NY school districts and can be downloaded in Excel format.

Civil Right Data Collection (CRDC)

Since 1968, the U.S. Department of Education (ED) and the Office for Civil Rights (OCR) conducting a biennial (i.e., every other school year) survey named the Civil Rights Data Collection (CRDC). The CRDC collects data on leading civil rights indicators related to access and barriers to educational opportunity at the early childhood through grade 12 levels. The data is collected from all public local educational agencies (LEA) and schools, including long-term secure juvenile justice facilities, charter schools, alternative schools, and schools serving students with disabilities (CRDC, n. d.).

The CRDC has an important role in the overall enforcement and monitoring strategy used by OCR to ensure that public funded schools do not discriminate on the basis of race, color, national origin, sex, and disability (CRDC, n.d.).

In addition, the CRDC is a valuable resource for educational researchers who seek comprehensive state-wide data on student equity and opportunity. Starting 2009-10 CRDC started to collect and report data on teacher absents. Data is available online at http://ocrdata.ed.gov. In order to have the full database on a CD the researcher has to file a "request for flat-file format of civil rights data collection data". For our research the researchers used the 2011-12 CRDC CD-ROM. CRDC data is provided on a school level.

LIST OF VARIABLES USED IN THE RESEARCH

Student Grade Level Factors (Grade Level)

Students With Disabilities (SWD)

For the purposes of this study, students with disabilities (SWD) were defined as the percentage of students with physical and or mental impairments at a grade level. Data were retrieved from the 2012–13 New York State school report cards.

Limited English Proficiency (LEP)

For the purposes of this study, limited English proficiency (LEP) was defined as the percentage of students with limited English proficiency at a grade level. Data were retrieved from the 2012–13 New York State school report cards. In 2015 NYSED school report card data the term LEP was changed to English Language learners (ELL). In this chapter both LEP and ELL will be used.

Economically Disadvantaged

For the purposes of this study, economically disadvantaged was defined as the percentage of students who participated in, or whose family participated in economic assistance program (NYSED, 2014).

School Factors (School Level)

Attendance Rate

For the purposes of this study, attendance rate was defined as students' annual attendance rate in school as reported in the 2012–13 New York State school report card. It was calculated by dividing the school's total actual attendance by the total possible attendance for a school year (NYSED, 2015).

Suspension Rate

For the purposes of this study, the suspension rate was defined as the percent of students suspended from school as reported in the 2012–13 New York State school report card. It was determined by dividing the number of students who received out-of-school suspensions for one full day or longer anytime during the school year by the total student enrollment for that school year. A student was counted only once, regardless of whether the student was suspended one or more times during the school year (NYSED, 2015).

Per-Student Instructional Expenditures

For the purposes of this study, per-student instructional expenditures were the 2012–13 per-student expenditures reported for each school district by NYSED. Appendix A shows the description of the file provided by NYSED reporting the revenues and expenditures for each school district. Instructional expenditures included teacher salaries, curriculum development and support instructional salaries, BOCES instructional expenditures, other instructional salaries, and other instructional expenses – columns N, P, Q, T, and U in the file. Instructional expenditures were divided by the number of students in the district to establish the per-student instructional expenditure data.

School Size

For the purposes of this study, school size was defined as the student enrollment for each school reported on the 2012–13 school report cards.

Class Size

For the purposes of this study, class size was defined as the average student class size for each school as reported on the 2012–13 school report cards (NYSED, 2015).

Teacher Factors (School Level)

Percentage of Novice Teachers

For the purposes of this study, percentage of novice teachers was defined as the proportion of all teachers within the school who had fewer than three years of teaching experience as reported in 2012–13 New York State school report cards (NYSED, 2015).

Teachers With Master's Plus 30 Credits or Doctorate

For the purposes of this study, teachers with masters plus 30 credits or doctorate was defined as the percentage of all teachers within the school who had a master's degree plus 30 additional credits or a doctorate degree as reported on the 2012–13 New York State school report cards (NYSED, 2015).

Teachers Not Highly Qualified

For the purposes of this study, percent of teachers who are not highly qualified were those reported in the 2012–13 New York State school report card. To be highly qualified, a teacher must have at least a Bachelor's degree, be certified to teach in the subject area or otherwise in accordance with state standards, and show subject matter competency (NYSED, 2015).

Teacher Turnover Rate

For the purposes of this study, Teacher Turnover Rate for a specified school year is the number of teachers in that school year that were not teaching in the following school year, divided by the number of teachers in the specified school year, expressed as a percentage. Teachers who in year one were reported as providing instruction in one building, but in year two were reported under the district code or another building within the same district are included in the turnover rate (NYSED, 2015).

Teacher Absences

For the purposes of this study, teacher absences were the percentage of teachers in the school who were absent more than 10 days of the 2011–12 school year, excluded days missed for approved professional development.

Household Factors (District Level)

Household Structure

For the purposes of this study, household structure was defined by using the 2010 census categories of: (1) Family household included a. husband-wife family household, b. male family household and c. female family household, and (2) Nonfamily household included a. householder living alone and b. householder not living alone (U.S. Census Bureau, 2010). Same-sex families were counted in the Census report either in male family household or female family household based on their sex (U.S. Census Bureau, 2010).

Household Size

For the purposes of this study, household size was defined as the number of residents in a household. The 2010 Census data provided seven options for household size, from single resident householder to seven plus residents household.

Creating the Research Database

Eliminating Multiple years

The school report database was downloaded in MS-Access format. Many of the tables in the database contain more than one year, for example in 2015 database the table "BOCES and N/RC" contains data for three years (2013, 2014, 2015), and ELA and math achievement tables contain data for two years (2014, 2015). Any query that will merge, sum, or sort data has to cut the data for the specific year, otherwise the result table can have mixed year data.

Cleaning Tables

NYS will not publish data that can reveal the students; therefore, if there is a group of less than five students the state will not publish the data for that group. For example, in the third-grade ELA table, if the group "White" in a school has less than five students that group achievement data is not reported; however, the number of students of that group is reported. In addition, all gender ethnicity subgroups (e.g. "White female", "Black or African American male") the subgroup achievement data is not reported, however the number of students is reported. In all those cases where no achievement data was reported, the Access data field appears with "s". The issue with that is that it is better for the researcher to keep achievement as a numeric field so there is an option to run calculations, however, numeric field cannot contains the text ("s"). Therefore, there is a need to replace the "s" with blank in all occurrences. This will allow the achievement field to be numeric. The technique to do that is to open the achievement tables used in the research, highlight the relevant columns click CTRL+F, click Replace, Enter "s" in the "Find What" field, leave the "Replace Field" empty, on "Match" field select "Whole Field", Search "All", and check the "Match Case". Once doing that Access will clear the "s" from the table. Since the files are large there is a need to repeat this action five to six times until Access clears the entire table, Access 2010 which was used in this project can replace close to 95,000 occurrences per click.

Creating Queries

Another challenge working with Report card achievement tables is to transform the table look to single data line. For example, Figure 1 shows the "table look" for 2015 third grade ELA results at Powel Lane School. As seen in Figure 1 the first row in the table shows that 196 students took the third-grade ELA test in 2015 with a mean score of 288 at Powel Lane School. Out of them, 182 students were economically disadvantaged (ED) with a mean score of 286 and 14 were not economically disadvantaged (NED) with a mean score of 315, 135 students were not English language learners (NELL) with a mean score of 298 and 61 students were English language learners (ELL) with a mean score of 266, and 14 students were in the students with disabilities (SWD) group with a mean score of 258 and 182 students were in the general education (GE) group with a mean score of 291. For the purpose of this research the researcher wanted to flat the file so that grade data for each school will have a single line. Figure 2 shows an example of 2015 third grade ELA results at Powel Lane School flat data. As seen on Figure 2 ED_Num represents number of economically disadvantaged students and ED_Mean represents their score. NED_Num represents the number of not economically disadvantaged students and NED_M represents their score. NELL_Num represents the number of Non-English language learner students and NEEL_Mean represents their score. ELL_Num represents the number of English language learner students and ELL_Mean represents their score. SWD_Num represents the number of students with disabilities, and SWD_Mean represents their score. GE_Num represents the number of general education students and GE_Mean represents their score. All_Num represents the total number of students in the grade and All_Mean represents the grade mean. In order to do that, open a new Query choose the table (e.g. ELA3 Subgroup Results), select the following fields as ordered in the table Entity_CD, Entity_Name, and Year. Click on the ∑ symbol add to the ribbon as this query is a totals query, the "Group By" writing will appear near the variables at the Total line. Add criteria for the year (e.g. 2015). Now add a list of calculated fields, for example: ED_Num:Sum(IIf([SUBGROUP_NAME]="Economically Disadvantaged", [NUM_TESTED],0)). The researcher used the Sum function to sum number of students in each group and Max function for the Mean. In the Total line will appear "Expression" as seen in Figure 3. To verify the calculation, the researcher checked that the student groups added up to the total number of students:

ED_Num + NED_Num = NELL_Num+ELL_Num = SWD_Num + GE_Num = All_Num

The next step is to transfer the query results into a new table as in the researcher experience Access does not work properly when using a total query as the new query source. In order to do that go to design view, click on "Make a Table" on the ribbon, a pop-up window asks for the name of the new table, fill it and click on the Run button. A new table will be created in your table list containing the data from the Query (see Figure 4).

Figure 1.

ENTITY_CD	ENTITY_NAME	YEAR	SUBGROUP_NAME	NUM_TESTED	MEAN_SCORE
280401030005	POWELLS LANE SCHOOL	2015	All Students	196	288
280401030005	POWELLS LANE SCHOOL	2015	American Indian or Alaska Native	1	
280401030005	POWELLS LANE SCHOOL	2015	American Indian or Alaska Native Female	1	
280401030005	POWELLS LANE SCHOOL	2015	Asian or Native Hawaiian/Other Pacific Islander	4	
280401030005	POWELLS LANE SCHOOL	2015	Asian or Native Hawaiian/Other Pacific Islander Female	3	
280401030005	POWELLS LANE SCHOOL	2015	Asian or Native Hawaiian/Other Pacific Islander Male	1	
280401030005	POWELLS LANE SCHOOL	2015	Black or African American	51	293
280401030005	POWELLS LANE SCHOOL	2015	Black or African American Female	28	
280401030005	POWELLS LANE SCHOOL	2015	Black or African American Male	23	
280401030005	POWELLS LANE SCHOOL	2015	Economically Disadvantaged	182	286
280401030005	POWELLS LANE SCHOOL	2015	Non-English Language Learners	135	298
280401030005	POWELLS LANE SCHOOL	2015	Female	86	290
280401030005	POWELLS LANE SCHOOL	2015	General Education	182	291
280401030005	POWELLS LANE SCHOOL	2015	Hispanic or Latino	136	285
280401030005	POWELLS LANE SCHOOL	2015	Hispanic or Latino Female	52	
280401030005	POWELLS LANE SCHOOL	2015	Hispanic or Latino Male	84	
280401030005	POWELLS LANE SCHOOL	2015	English Language Learners	61	266
280401030005	POWELLS LANE SCHOOL	2015	Male	110	287
280401030005	POWELLS LANE SCHOOL	2015	Not Economically Disadvantaged	14	315
280401030005	POWELLS LANE SCHOOL	2015	Not Migrant	196	288
280401030005	POWELLS LANE SCHOOL	2015	Small Group Total	9	313
280401030005	POWELLS LANE SCHOOL	2015	Students with Disabilities	14	258
280401030005	POWELLS LANE SCHOOL	2015	White	4	
280401030005	POWELLS LANE SCHOOL	2015	White Female	2	
280401030005	POWELLS LANE SCHOOL	2015	White Male	2	

Figure 2.

SCHOOL_NAME	ED_Num	ED_Mean	NED_Num	NED_Mean	NELL_Nun	NELL_Mean	ELL_Num	ELL_Mean	SWD_Num	SWD_Mean	GE_Num	GE_Mean	All_Num	AllMean
POWELLS LANE SCHOOL	182	286	14	315	135	298	61	266	14	258	182	291	196	288

Figure 3.

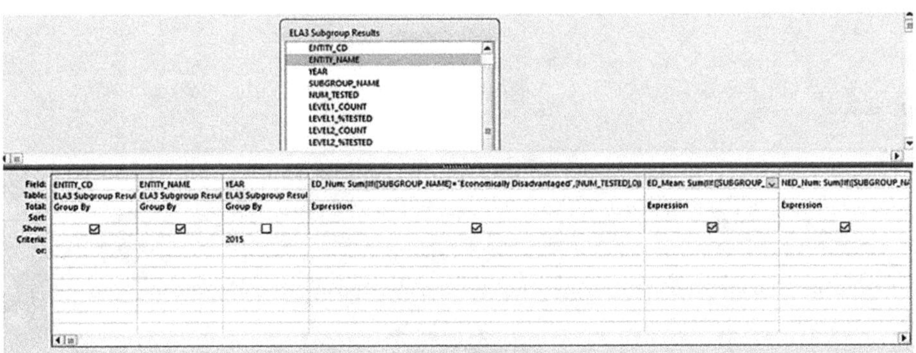

Figure 4.

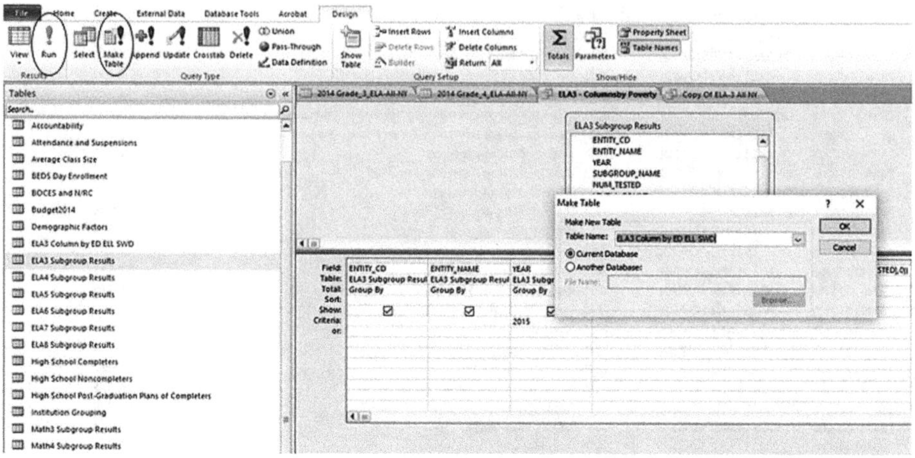

Merging Tables With Different Hierarchy

The research database contains data from three hierarchies Grade, School and District (see Figure 5). Trying to merge district level table with school level table in Access will result in a new school level table where the district data is spread over all the schools that are in the same district. And when merging it with grade level data, the school and district data will spread over all the grades in that school. In order to simplify, our study used only one grade level data (fourth grade) per school so that the research dataset was per school with fourth grade data.

Figure 5.

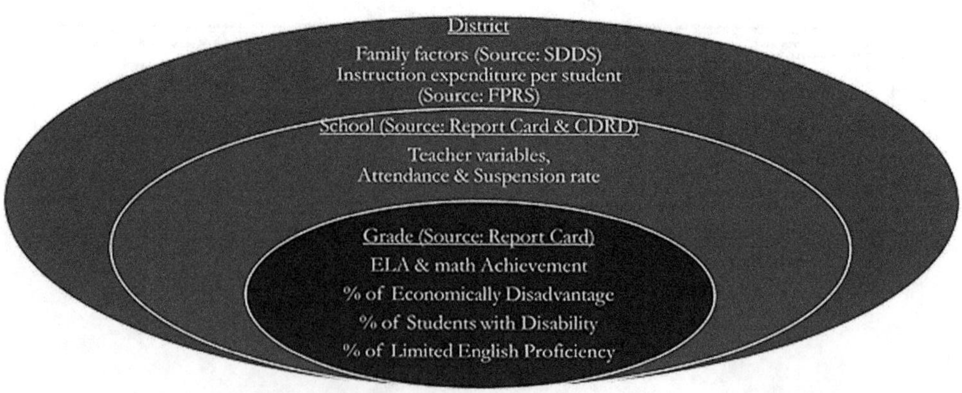

Merging Fields

Merging different tables within the same database is relatively easy as the key fields are the same for all tables. For example, in the report card database each school has an ID field called Entity_CD and the tables can be easily merged by using that field. However, the only common field for merging report card tables with SDDS tables is district name, and the only common field for merging report card tables with CRDC tables in school name. Merging tables by textual fields is not trivial as in many cases the text is not exactly the same. For example, Haverstraw-Stony Point Central School District is called on SDDS "Haverstraw-Stony Point Central School District" while in the report card tables it appears as "Haverstraw-Stony Point CSD (North Rockland)". On those cases the researcher has to manually change the name on one of the tables in order for the merge to be completed. In order to find all the cases where the district and school name spelled differently the researcher opened the "Join properties" and used the option "Include all records from 'ELA Column by ED ELL SWD' and only those from 'Household type' when the join fields are equal. In our research the researcher decided to use NYSED terminology for district and school names.

Figure 6 shows the different tables that were used to collect the data for the research. As mentioned before Entity_CD was the most used join field for NYSED data. District name was the join field with Household type table. School name was the join field with Teacher absences table. And District ID was the join field with District expenditure 2013 table.

Figure 6.

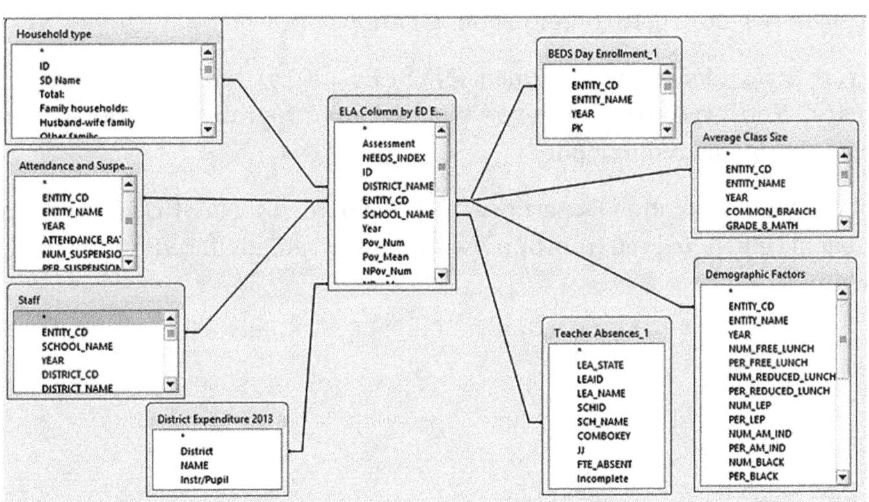

CONCLUSION

There is an enormous amount of available data waiting to be analyzed. Federal data at Data.gov and other federal agencies, state data portals, and state agencies data portals change the researcher focus from "how to" to "where to" as data may already been collected. In this new world, the researcher has to master data management, data cleaning techniques, and data query tools in order to analyze the data properly.

REFERENCES

Bertot, J. C., Jaeger, P. T., & Grimes, J. M. (2010). Using ICTs to create a culture of transparency: E-government and social media as openness and anti-corruption tools for society. *Government Information Quarterly*, *27*(3), 264–271. doi:10.1016/j.giq.2010.03.001

Best of the best business websites. (2016). *Reference & User Services Quarterly*, *56*(2), 130-134. Retrieved from http://jerome.stjohns.edu:81/login?url=http://search.proquest.com.jerome.stjohns.edu:81/docview/1860278455?accountid=14068

Cai, L., & Zhu, Y. (2015). The Challenges of Data Quality and Data Quality Assessment in the Big Data Era. *Data Science Journal*, *14*(0), 2. doi:10.5334/dsj-2015-002

Civil Rights Data Collection (CRDC). (n. d.). About the Civil Rights Data Collection. Retrieved from http://ocrdata.ed.gov/downloads/AboutTheCRDC.pdf

Cuillier, D., & Piotrowski, S. J. (2009). Internet information-seeking and its relation to support for access to government records. *Government Information Quarterly*, *26*(3), 441–449. doi:10.1016/j.giq.2009.03.001

New York State Education Department (NYSED). (2016). Race to the top executive summary. Retrieved from https://www2.ed.gov/programs/racetothetop/state-reported-sharing/nyexsumm.pdf

New York State Education Department (NYSED). (n. d.). NYSED Fiscal Analysis & Research Unit. Retrieved from http://www.oms.nysed.gov/faru/Profiles/profiles_cover.html

Obama, B. (2009a). Transparency and open government. Memorandum for the Heads of Executive Departments and Agencies, Retrieved data from http://www.whitehouse.gov/sites/default/files/microsites/ostp/ostp_public_access_memo_2013.pdf

Obama, B. (2009b). Memorandum for the Heads of Executive Departments and Agencies: Freedom of Information Act (Presidential memorandum). Retrieved from http://www.whitehouse.gov/the_press_office/Transparen

Chapter 3
Big Data Analytics in Higher Education

Tanveer H. Shah
University of Azad Jammu and Kashmir, Pakistan

ABSTRACT

This chapter reviews the literature on the use of business analytics in higher education. Universities have large datasets available to predict future direction and generate actionable information. An important type of analytics used to improve management processes and to make informed decisions is big data business analytics. State university executive leaders may improve the effectiveness of their decisions by integrating business analytics in the decision-making models. However, there is a need to examine the use of big data business analytics in the decision-making process at the executive leadership level of the selected state universities. Especially in the context of how descriptive, predictive, prescriptive, decisive and basic analytics, and data collection influence the decision-making process at the executive leadership level of the state universities in terms of student retention and graduation rates.

INTRODUCTION

The range of challenges that state universities face today is vast and continuously expanding. These challenges are political, economic, societal, and cultural. Higher educational leaders are struggling to meet these challenges and compete in a highly competitive environment. Universities have taken several initiatives to meet these challenges. One of these initiatives is the use of analytics to make informed decisions at the executive leadership level. Universities have large datasets available to predict future direction and generate actionable information. The integration of big data

DOI: 10.4018/978-1-5225-3616-1.ch003

business analytics in decision-making processes at the executive leadership level of state universities may result in their increased effectiveness. Delen and Demirkan (2013) stated that big data analytics offer a great potential to provide much needed information for effective decision-making. In order to use big datasets and analytics effectively, it is important to understand what is big data and what is analytical process.

BACKGROUND

The term big data referred to large datasets first coined in the 1990s. The definition of these large datasets had been changing over time. In the 1980s, this term referred to a size of data that was so large that magnetic tapes were required to store it. In the 1990s, big data referred to any size of data that was beyond the limitations of Microsoft Excel and desktop PC. Currently, big data refers to any data that is too large to place and analyze in a desktop relational database and such data require specialized software and computing techniques (Jacobs, 2009).

Diebold et al. (2012) claimed that big data emerged from statistics, econometrics, and computer science disciplines. Big data utilized knowledge, skills, and techniques of these disciplines in a coordinated manner. John Mashey at a lunch table in Silicon Graphics Inc. coined the term big data and elaborated on its use. Diebold et al. (2012) further claimed that Mashey, Weiss and Indurkhya, Diebold, and Laney were among the earlier contributors to the term big data. Diebold concluded that big data had emerged as a discipline of its own.

Buhl (2013) indicated that there was a lot more to come in the field of big data such as sensor-generated data. The term big data did not only refer to traditional data but it also included the analysis of huge amounts of data. Analysis provided new opportunities to improve the management and decision-making processes. Big data provided more options for decision-making, but it also added complexity to this process. Therefore, besides knowing big data itself, knowing how to use big data was equally important (Buhl, 2013).

Buhl, Röglinger, Moser, and Heidemann (2013) claimed that big data was multidiscipline and evolved from the combination of emerging technologies of data storage and data processing. The characteristics of big data include volume, velocity, variety, and veracity of data. Veracity meant maintaining the quality of data.

According to Davenport, Barth, and Bean (2013), in big data, data flows were more important than data stocks. In a big data environment, quick analysis, decisions, and actions were required. It was important to keep pace with the emerging trends in data flows that kept changing continuously. Observing trends was useless unless leaders took specific actions identified by recognizable trends (Davenport et al., 2013).

Davenport further explained that big data environment needed data scientists instead of data analysts. These professionals possessed multidisciplinary skills of information technology, analytics, social network sociology, statistics, communication, and programming skills (Davenport et al., 2013).

In the journal *Strategic Direction*, the publishing director Tony Roche (2013) pointed out important differences between big data and traditional data. It was not only size but also the form of data that mattered. Big data was not just storage of historical data like traditional data rather it was constant, current, live, dynamic data that flew through an organization. It forced the organization to change information management systems in order to take advantage of these qualities of big data. Big data was not meant to be buried within the computers. Rather, it had to go to decision-makers who could use it to act quickly. The process of using big data would make the core functions of organizations appear completely different (Direction, 2013).

Schermann, Hemsen, Buchmüller, Bitter, Krcmar, and Markl (2014) elaborated the big data definition further. According to their study, big data referred to technologies used to provide right information to the right persons in the right volume and the right quality at the right time.

Daniel and Butson (2014) while describing features of big data added that beside volume, velocity, veracity, and variety, big data entailed features like verification and value. These six Vs represent fundamental characteristics of big data:

- Volume refers to challenging size of data.
- Velocity means ever rising speed of flow of data in an institution.
- Veracity explains quality of data.
- Variety means that big data includes numerous types of format including both structured and unstructured.
- Verification is authenticity and security of data.
- Value depicts whether data generates useful insights and benefits for management processes (Daniel & Butson, 2014).

Daniel et al. pointed out two additional important features of big data:

- Validity refers to accuracy of data.
- Volatility refers to how data changes constantly.

Therefore, these eight 'Vs' representing key characteristics of big data elaborate the importance and complexity of big data and how organizations used it for value creation. Following Figure is adapted from (Daniel & Butson, 2014) by adding two more Vs and renaming it as Eight Vs of Big Data. Figure 1 elaborates eight characteristics of big data.

Figure 1.
This figure was adapted from (Daniel & Butson, 2014) and work by Buhl, Röglinger, Moser, and Heidemann (2013). Two Vs were added and renamed as 'Eight Vs of big data'

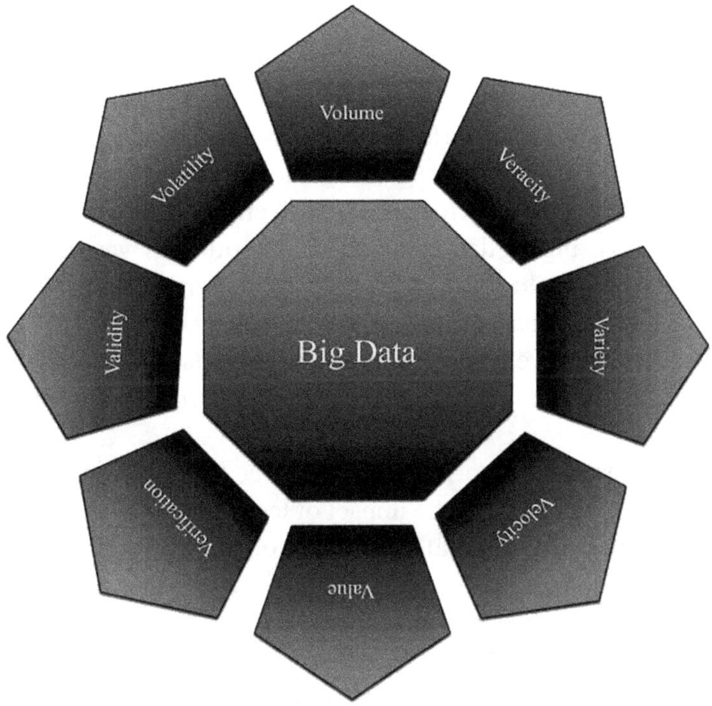

Manyika et al. (2011) noted that big data offered great potential to leadership in organizations to generate value by improving their management of human and material resources. In addition, data management increased efficiency, accountability, and transparency, and added opportunities for creativity and innovation. Many sectors including education could benefit from the use of big data. The use of big data could bring efficiency and transparency to different departments of academic institutions. According to Manyika, in the public sector institutions, employees consumed 20% of their time searching for information from non-digital sources and travelling and walking from point to point in order to obtain information.

Manyika et al. (2011) studied how individuals shared large amounts of data on social websites and expressed their opinions, needs, and preferences that could inform decision-making and make management more scientific. Leaders in data driven organizations could make hypotheses before reaching their decisions. They could test those hypotheses with this large amount of data by designing experiments, using control groups, and analyzing quantitative results. Academic research had proven advantages for informed decision-making (Manyika et al., 2011).

Robust analytics would help leadership improve their decision-making process in the educational sector. This could minimize risks and help administrators and policy makers discover critical hidden aspects needed to create value (Manyika et al., 2011).

Manyika observed that there was a productivity difference among the units with the same organization at different locations in spite of using same work processes. Sharing the same information at different locations and among similar organizations could minimize this variability in performances without any other incentive. Employees could match their performances with employees of other units.

A major hurdle in using big data in educational institutions was systemic-barriers, which once removed, would result in greater productivity. One potential area was measuring teacher performance in the form of student achievement (Manyika et al., 2011). Leaders who were able to interpret large datasets could find ways to remove barriers between divisions and improve in productivity, innovation, and competitiveness.

Organizations were under enormous pressure, because of the continued recession of 2010 and higher education felt the impact of technology (Picciano, 2012). After all, higher educational institutions also depended on political and economic systems within the country. Leadership in universities needed to cope with the problems of retention and graduation rates that demanded higher educational institutions find creative solutions to these problems.

Informed decision-making helped university management to generate innovative solutions to student retention problems. Picciano (2012) concluded that informed decision-making entered into a new era when big data offered new opportunities to expand options that helped develop strategies to resolve problems in low retention and graduation rates (Picciano, 2012).

Organizations in this era of information have tremendous access to data, but it is very challenging to convert this data into knowledge that ultimately will inform decisions to generate positive results. It is important to develop capacity and capabilities to analyze and use data to make informed decisions. An important aspect is to develop skills to gather and clean relevant data (Thomas, Jeanne, David, & Alvin, 2001).

The first step towards informed decision-making is to develop analytical ability in an organization. Factors like transactional data environment and supportive top management play a critical role in creating analytical capacity, an ability to convert data into meaningful insights. These analytical capacities through technology help the institutions in converting analysis into informed decisions (Thomas et al., 2001).

Drigas and Leliopoulos (2014) noted that big data could help in shaping educational systems and make them more dynamic, optimized, and modernized to benefit each student. Big data helped to make good educational decisions and could provide educational leaders and teachers with new tools to use in their decision-making.

Drigas et al. further said that there was a need to create an environment where educational leaders, teachers, and students could use these tools for desired results.

Luan (2002) noted that as a result of increasing competition and economic constraints, leaders at higher educational institutions have to proactively look for probable students. Leaders in higher education institutions need to design academic programs that address needs and demands of students instead of forcing the students into programs that did not consider what students wanted. Luan (2002) recommended that data mining techniques to determine students' needs be used in exploratory and predictive data analysis methods. Data mining processes could predict student desires for education by identifying patterns and underlying meanings in the large datasets available in institutions and online. These data mining techniques could forecast probable student entrants, likely graduates, and assist in decision-making by analyzing student data stored within an institution and online.

Similarly, leaders in higher educational institutions could also utilize big data to meet their challenges and to create evidence based decisions. Most of these institutions already had large datasets that they could use to predict future challenges. These challenges existed at different levels including institutional, teacher, and student levels (Daniel & Butson, 2014). For instance, mining unstructured and informal information produced by students on social media with motion sensors and location-based data could provide beneficial facts and patterns not uncovered before. This information could relate to retention of students and be useful as an input for policy-making.

Phillips-Wren and Hoskisson (2015) concluded that there was increasing evidence for organizations to gain strategic competitive advantage by using big data analytically. However, due to lack of human capital, leadership with strategic vision, and big data platforms, mid and small sized organizations were facing challenges in benefiting big data potentials.

According to Zhang (2015), big data silently entered into universities and gradually took roots. Characteristics of big data like volume, velocity, variety, veracity, and value revealed the impact of big data on different aspects of management of modern universities including management, classrooms, and teaching models. These influences have revolutionized internal management systems of universities (Zhang, 2015).

Daniel (2015) proclaimed that the environment in which universities functioned usually posed mounting pressure and high competition for students. Using big data could enable universities to cope with these challenges and respond to a need to increase students in certain academic areas, equip students with skills required at real work, and guarantee they meet both national and international standards. Daniel further claimed that big data offered tremendous opportunities to use data analysis for informed decision-making by efficiently aggregating and correlating large datasets to generate repetitive patterns of behavior and provide meaningful insights. However, he noted that there was limited research conducted on big data in higher education.

Daniel (2015) stated that there were three stages of implementing big data in any organization including data collection, analysis, and visualization and application. Data collection was about recognizing data that could generate valuable information. Data analysis generated actionable information after analyzing complex and diverse data by linking, correlating, and connecting different datasets. Visualization and application was about presenting information to relevant receivers in interpretable form so that they abled to integrate into existing processes of decision-making.

Thomas et al. (2001) noted that although organization leaders had incredible access to data, it was hard to generate useful information to inform decisions and achieve valuable outcomes. In many cases, personnel became confused because of the availability of abundant data. Currently, organizations needed to develop the capacity to combine, analyze, and use data to inform decisions and enable personnel to take quick actions and create true value.

Thomas et al. (2001) presented a model for converting transactional data into valuable information and outcomes. This model had three basic elements including context, transformation, and outcomes. Context included aspects related to strategies, organizational culture, organization, skills, technologies, and data. Transformation was where data were analyzed and used for the decision-making. Outcomes included the changes adopted from decision-making. These outcomes could alter behaviors, programs, and finances (Thomas et al., 2001).

According to Thomas et al. (2001) most personnel within an organization focused on technology and data and ignored other critical factors of organizational structure, culture, level of skills and experience. Contextual elements were important to design successful strategies for a particular environment. Experts who analyzed data needed to know the business processes, statistics, and communication skills so that they could present information in a useful way for decision-makers.

Thomas et al. (2001) claimed that in order to create a data driven culture, management needed to learn faster and be smarter with the use of information. The proper use of data required continuous improvement. The success of this analytic capability depended on a data driven culture across an organization that promoted the importance of data analysis and informed decision-making. Leadership in organizations needed to differentiate between automated transaction systems and analytics that required high involvement of personnel and their human insights.

Keeping in view strategies, skills and experience, structure, culture, and technological level of an organization, data transformed into knowledge influenced policies through interrelated phases of analysis and decision-making (Thomas et al., 2001).

Thomas et al. (2001) concluded that automated basic business procedures generated transactional data and there was a need to convert this data into valuable knowledge. Some decision-making processes required less human intervention but complex and unstructured processes required skilled humans using analytics.

Harris, Craig, and Light (2011) claimed that making full use of analytics required the integration of analysis and data processes throughout an organization. Furthermore, those who advocated for analytics had to be people with the right analytical skills, and capable to change a culture, process, and behavior at an organizational level. Finding right opportunities to implement analytics was important in order to get maximum output.

Kiron et al. (2011) found that organizations gained substantial competitive advantage by integrating analytics into strategies and processes. Organizations achieved sophistication in analytics by acquiring mastery in analytical skills and tools, robust information management practices, creating a data driven environment, and by improving those who lagged behind. Organizations without reasonable analytics strategies remained uncompetitive and their future was at risk. A continuous emerging and widening gap of competitive advantage was found between organizations that used analytics and those that did not (Kiron et al., 2011).

According to LaValle, Lesser, Shockley, Hopkins, and Kruschwitz (2011), organizations that used field related information, insights, and analytics in their decisions and strategies in day-to-day functioning performed better than those who did not. There was a strong correlation between use of analytics-driven leadership and performance. The use of analytics provided an organization with efficiency, progression, and competitive advantage. LaValle et al. recommended to start with the biggest and most significant challenge. The use of diagrams and available data could elaborate processes and applications and demonstrate where and how analytics would be most effective. For example, in the case of universities, retention of students was a major challenge and analytics could visualize and group issues related to retention.

Kiron and Shockley (2011) claimed that organizations that developed integrated data-driven environment across the organization gained the maximum potential from analytics. A data-driven culture required a strategic use of analytics, leadership supportive for analytics, availability of information, and insights for those who needed guidance in future decisions.

Beside creating a data-oriented culture, transformed organizations managed information and analytics in an excellent way (Kiron & Shockley, 2011). The mastery of analytics required talent, tools, and technology. Good information management provided the right information at right time to the right people. Robust data governance and data management practices delivered strong information management (Kiron & Shockley, 2011).

Barneveld, Arnold, and Campbell (2012) stated that data driven decision-making, another term for informed decision-making, was a process to provide critical data and support in decision-making for managerial and financial processes.

According to Picciano (2012), because of the recent 2008 recession, higher education like all other sectors found itself under tremendous pressure. Universities needed to find the means and ways to retain students, and have them complete their degrees. Many universities already used big data analytics in order to inform their decision-making, and to identify and evaluate strategies that could improve student retention (Picciano, 2012).

Rajesh (2013) elaborated that big data analytics were valuable for all organizations that wanted to make sense out of huge databases available on internet and on their networks. These organizations used analytics to improve their decision-making to compete with their competitors.

Kiron, Ferguson, and Prentice (2013) claimed that big data analytics would influence all decisions in coming years, and serve as an important driving force. They further elaborated that leaders could benefit from analytics by considering data as a core asset, by challenging the status quo, and by opening their minds to new thinking. They called it rethinking or reimagining.

Macfadyen, Dawson, Pardo, and Gasevic (2014) noted that education, as compared to all other sectors was much slower in utilizing the potential of big data analytics. This situation persisted in educational institutions all over the world, because of a lack of capacity to collect, manage, and analyze big data, effectively. Macfadyen et al. (2014) explained further that big data analytics provided educators with a useful alternative to get rid of time-consuming longitudinal and personalized assessment along with their ever-increasing workload.

Baer and Duin (2014) claimed that universities needed to rethink, readjust, and reinvent their institutional policies and practices to focus on student success. They insisted that a complete paradigm shift would result in a new model and culture to exploit the power of big data analytics.

Daniel (2015) observed that although the use of data in higher educational institutions grew in recent years, most of data were still stored across desktop computers in different departments making the integration and retrieval of data difficult for analysis. One important factor in using big data analytics in higher education institutions was how data sharing was implemented. Security of sensitive information was another key consideration. Daniel insisted that there was a need to define processes to store, retrieve, and secure information, and to authorize employees to access data.

MAIN FOCUS OF THE CHAPTER

There are many types of big data analytics that can be used in higher education for addressing different challenges. One of these analytics are business analytics that can provide solutions for informed decision-making to the leaders at higher educational institutions.

Business Analytics

In business, value creation was a major driving force behind the development of business analytics. This development occurred in all related fields including organizational processes and advanced technologies. One single focus of all this development was satisfaction and fulfillment of customer needs. Customer needs were driving force in making these technologies more accessible, reliable, and user-friendly. Gradually, data gathering, storing, and analyzing technologies became an integral part of almost every organizational process with a promise to generate actionable information that would produce business value (Kohavi, Rothleder, & Simoudis, 2002).

Eckerson (2006) claimed that organizational leaders would get an advantage from using information in their decision-making processes. He used examples of scorecards and dashboards that provided relevant information to make effective decisions and achieve strategic goals. These systems were capable of generating visual data to view an overall picture and analysis of operational data for actionable information. These instruments also enabled managers to monitor the performances of employees and keep track of the execution of their strategic objectives.

Research in business analytics continuously progressed over decades, and resulted in development of powerful analytical and performance management tools. In order to inform decisions, complex systems like expert systems, decision support systems, and data mining systems were devised to unearth complicated patterns and relationships in order to generate actionable information (Baars & Kemper, 2008).

According to Chaudhuri, Dayal, and Narasayya (2011), gradually, the business intelligence field progressed both in research and practice. One reason for this development was the availability of data and easy access to larger datasets. More diversity in the data, and the availability of text data resulted in systems to analyze data more intelligently. Beside availability of data, unprecedented advancement in computer technologies, and reduction in their prices also helped create technologies like cloud computing. These technologies were the backbone of business intelligence and business analytics. Chaudhuri et al. (2011) further hinted that the use of continuously advancing smartphone technologies would create further opportunities for business intelligence and business analytics in different fields and professions.

Watson (2011) argued that in spite of great potential, success of business analytics depended on how leaders made essential organizational and technological changes, and how much value they created from the use of these technologies.

Viaene and Van den Bunder (2011) reported that business analytics accompanied uncertainty and changes in requirements that required special skills for managers to lead in this field. New managers should expect changes in their starting plan at any phase in the progression of the project. These business analytics leaders were capable of involving all the concerned parties in the description and justification for new expectations. They strongly believed in experimentation based on iterative trial and error process and meaningful insights. This intelligent experimentation started with clear objectives, followed by a four-step cycle comprised design, build, run, and analyze (Viaene & Van den Bunder, 2011).

Klatt et al. (2011) noted that less bureaucratic organizations performed better in business analytics. There was a need for a clear and target-oriented strategic communication system, assignments, and actions. Success of business analytics depended on the planning style of analytical leadership. Successful organizations in implementing business analytics distributed across-the-board rational data analysis (Klatt et al., 2011).

Hsinchun, Chiang, and Storey (2012) observed that business analytics became an emerging trend in academia and business in the last two decades. Educational institutions need a new vision for information systems to use emerging analytical skills meet the needs of their traditional students.

According to Shanks and Bekmamedova (2012), organizations required a state of art technological and data setup for success in business analytics. Business analytics should be imbedded into different organizational process and required real-time relevant data feeds. Moreover, business analytics needed to advance continuously to give competitive advantage to institutions.

Delen and Demirkan (2013) claimed that business analytics became famous faster than any other management practice because of their potential to provide relevant information for effective decision-making. Delen et al. described that business analytics consisted of three types of analytics including descriptive, predictive, and prescriptive. Descriptive analytics or business reporting used data to pinpoint problems and business opportunities. Predictive analytics used mathematical modeling techniques on data to generate patterns to predict relationships between input and output. Predictive analytics accurately forecasted future events and reasoning behind them. Prescriptive analytics used different mathematical algorithms to provide different courses of actions or decision alternatives (Delen & Demirkan, 2013).

Kumar (2014) claimed that there was a fourth type of business analytics that was called decisive analytics. Decisive analytics used modeling techniques and visual analytics to support decisions and reasoning. According to Kumar, business analytics consisted of four types of analytics: descriptive, predictive, prescriptive, and decisive.

Descriptive Analytics

Descriptive analytics provided answers to questions like what happened and what is happening. These analytics were called business reporting (Delen & Demirkan, 2013). According to Delen et al. to identify well-defined business opportunities and problems, descriptive analytics generated different types of reports including periodic, on-demand, and interactive reports. Business reporting, data warehousing, dashboards, and scorecards were used to identify business opportunities and deficiencies (Delen & Demirkan, 2013).

Baer and Duin (2014) noted that higher education institutions rarely used information from data buried in their networks. Fewer people used this information for basic reporting and even less people used the data in their decision-making processes. Using these analytics enabled personnel in educational institutions to use past data of student enrollment records, types of admissions, and courses with high dropouts and failures to know where the problems rose and what was happening (Baer & Duin, 2014).

Kumar (2014) stated that descriptive analytics provided management with information from historical data to make their decisions more informed. Descriptive analytics used data from separate sources to integrate and generate accurate information of occurrence of past events.

Dashboards were enablers of descriptive analytics and used to present information to management in visual form including icons, graphs, text, and charts. This consolidated information presented a clear overview on a screen for monitoring and building further details (Santiago Rivera & Shanks, 2015).

Wilder and Ozgur (2015) suggested that skills and knowledge required for descriptive analytics were the abilities to describe and communicate past events in an effective manner within a variety of formats. Personnel using these analytics employed several techniques including descriptive statistics, frequency distributions, discrete distributions, continuous distributions, sampling distributions, and statistical inference (Wilder & Ozgur, 2015).

In the context of higher education, Daniel (2015) stated that descriptive analytics described and analyzed historical data of students, teachers, policies, administration, and academic activities including research and teaching. This analysis generated patterns to identify present trends on student enrollment, graduation and retention rates. Descriptive analytics enabled higher education institutions to look into frequency of student logins into certain pages, page views, course completion rates, activities of successful students compared to those of less successful students, and what material they searched for (Daniel, 2015).

Predictive Analytics

According to Agosta (2004), efforts in data mining technologies gave birth to predictive analytics. These analytics discovered patterns in data to make a hypothesis about future events. It was important to acknowledge that data itself was not information because it did not have qualities like organization, consistency, and conceptual constructs. Predictive analytics informed data with meaning.

Hair (2007) reported that predictive analytics used correlations of data and explanatory variables to predict chances of occurrence and relationships. Predictive analytics and data mining shared an interactive process. Data mining identified prospective correlations and patterns in past data including but not limited to text, numbers, visual data, and web clicks. Predictive analytics utilized confirmed relationships to identify future patterns, behaviors, events, and tendencies. Data mining examined large datasets in two phases. The first phase identified high value hidden relationships in valuable datasets that could potentially create knowledge to improve decision-making. This phase used automated machine learning processes to identify patterns of information. The second phase verified and identified correlations to confirm or reject by hypotheses (Hair, 2007).

Predictive analytics used these confirmed correlations for wide-ranging data analysis. These analytics used predictive, descriptive, and decision models with different statistical methods. Predictive models predicted the occurrence of a behavior in the future based upon the analysis of historical data. Abrupt patterns identified a risk or opportunity. Descriptive models grouped customers and events by describing correlations in data. Often descriptive models categorized individuals based on their choices, behaviors, and age levels. Decision models explained different aspects critical for a decision including explaining data, correlations, decision itself, and effect of the decision after implementation (Hair, 2007).

Jalonen and Lönnqvist (2009) claimed that observation, analysis, and optimization were basic factors of the predictive analysis process. Observation provided answers to questions such as, what happened, how much, how often, and where. Analysis was about why something happened and what would happen next. Whereas, optimization was about what was best to happen and what actions needed to be taken next. Jalonen and Lönnqvist (2009) claimed that predictive process could reveal the processes behind even unsystematic incidents.

Harris et al. (2011) identified that in order to improve retention of employees in an organization, knowing their preferences was crucial. Data could determine what employees like most. An analytical model based on data related to their preferences would predict actions to improve retention of employees. However, to tap maximum potential across the board, integration of data analysis and of analytical processes was mandatory.

Delen and Demirkan (2013) described that predictive analytics discovered patterns like tendencies, relations, and similarities by using data. These patterns represented integral relations between data inputs and outputs. Predictive analytics responded to queries like what and why something would happen. Techniques like data mining, text mining, web mining, and media mining helped in finding answers to these queries.

According to Waller and Fawcett (2013), predictive analytics was a subgroup of data science that used both qualitative and quantitative methods for forecasting. Besides predicting the future, these analytics were used to explore questions like what would happen in the past under a number of different conditions. Predictive analytics were very fast and a cost-effective way of drawing conclusions using processes of deductive mathematics. This was done through estimating relations between different variables.

Holsapple, Lee-Post, and Pakath (2014) noted that predictive analytics engaged sources to predict what would happen. The global consulting company Capgemini presented the threefold taxonomy of analytics in 2010. This taxonomy was comprised of descriptive, predictive, and prescriptive dimensions. Holsapple et al. (2014) also hinted about the fourth dimension of evaluation that would be discussed under decisive analytics.

Baer and Duin (2014) noted that predictive analytics could provide a plan to achieve optimum student learning while considering both individual and collective needs of students. Predictive analytics could play a vital role in students' readiness, advisement, continuous training of teachers, learning needs of students, and scheduling courses for students' success. As Baer and Duin (2014) observed, predictive analytics would enable educational intuitions management to track the progress of students. It was important to know where students were, where they were supposed to be, and how they would reach their goal.

Gandomi and Haider (2015) stated that predictive analytics employed several techniques to forecast results using past and present data. Almost all disciplines could utilize predictive analytics to predict outcomes of actions. Predictive analytics identified patterns and relations in data. A basic technique used in predictive analytical process was moving averages on historical data and their extension to the future to predict outcome variables. Another technique was linear regression in which interdependent relations between explanatory and outcome variables were identified and used to make predictions. This forecasting differed from traditional data analysis whose sample size was much less than the population. In predictive analysis sample size reffered to a majority if not the whole population (Gandomi & Haider, 2015).

Wilder and Ozgur (2015) emphasized the skills and knowledge for predictive analysis and how to exploit the outcomes of this analysis. They noted how to comprehend a problem, conduct analysis, and communicate the outcomes in simple language. Analytical techniques employed in predictive analysis included ANOVA, regression, correlation, time series, and nonparametric approaches (Wilder & Ozgur, 2015).

Daniel (2015) insisted that predictive analytics provided organizations with valuable insights derived from data analysis that would lead further actions. These analytics would forecast events by identifying trends and patterns in data, and acknowledging relations between different variables. This analysis would identify any opportunity or threat in the future. In contrast to descriptive analytics, predictive analytics would uncover unseen relations such as completion rates and demographic changes. They could also forecast behaviors of students earlier in their academic programs that would result in their failure or exit from programs. This would help educators make informed decisions for future courses of actions (Daniel, 2015).

Prescriptive Analytics

Evans (2012) described that optimization techniques were used in prescriptive analytics to select best available option to act upon in order to achieve certain goals such as maximizing retention rate of students in a university or minimizing dropouts in an academic program. Several processes of organizational management could benefit from prescriptive analytics including but not limited to operations, finance, and marketing. Mathematical and statistical techniques used in predicative analytics together with optimization techniques could result in informed decisions that accounted for the uncertainty of data (Evans, 2012).

Delen and Demirkan (2013) stated that prescriptive analytics obtained a set of valuable alternatives for taking actions or decisions to improve organizational performance. Algorithms used in prescriptive analysis could employ data in reliable processes. Simulation, optimization, multi-criteria decision modeling techniques, and expert systems could enable these analytics to produce best decisions and actions under certain situations and constraints. Prescriptive analytics provided answers to questions what and why one would do an action. Best possible decisions, actions, and transactions were outcomes of prescriptive analysis (Delen & Demirkan, 2013).

Power (2014) viewed prescriptive analytics as a planned quantitative analysis of real-time data capable of triggering events. Information generated through prescriptive analysis suggested desirable actions.

According to Kumar (2014), prescriptive analytics used results of both descriptive and predictive analytics to produce a set of actions. Organizational leaders used prescriptive analytics to get a reliable course of action to solve problems.

Wilder and Ozgur (2015) suggested that the successful use of prescriptive analytics required skills and knowledge of calculus, simulation, and optimization. Experts in these analytics needed skills to recognize patterns within a problem and interpret them using good communication skills. Prescriptive analytics helped analysts recommend what should happen.

Daniel (2015) stated that universities used prescriptive analytics to select alternatives. These alternatives were created through authentic and reliable predictions of events. Prescriptive analytics used analytical outputs of descriptive and predictive analytics to seek and establish a new course of action to achieve desired goals in a given situation within constraints. These analytics helped decision-makers in higher education to seek opportunities and identify threats in their future actions as well as act in time to take advantage of this foresight.

Decisive Analytics

Thomas and Cook (2005) stated that visual models were a multidiscipline analytical reasoning having interacting visual interfaces. Techniques used in visual models were analytical reasoning, data representation, and visual representation.

Analytical reasoning techniques empowered users to gain deep insights that directly facilitated evaluation, planning, and decision-making processes. The basic philosophy behind the use of visual models was to assist human judgment with limited time of analysis. These visual models enabled a quick analysis of past and present situations, trends and events that created current situations, and future probable courses of actions and their alarming signs. These techniques helped users to monitor occurrence of any alarming signs or any unexpected situations, helping analysts to determine a need to take an action, and supporting decision-makers in critical situations (Thomas & Cook, 2005).

Thomas and Cook (2005) stated that data representations and transformation techniques shaped conflicting and dynamic data in forms that supported visualization and analysis. These representations were in structured forms that existed already or derived from original data in order to fit in computer-based transformations. Production, presentation, and dissemination techniques used to communicate the results of an analysis in an appropriate perspective to a range of audiences (Thomas & Cook, 2005).

Visual representations and interaction techniques while taking advantage of the human eye's wide-ranging bandwidth path into the mind allowed users to see, explore, and comprehend large volumes of information immediately. Visual representations interpreted data in an observable form that underlined important features, including commonalities and abnormalities. These visual representations made it easy for users to identify significant characteristics of their data swiftly. Enhancing the cognitive reasoning process with perceptual reasoning through visual representations allowed the analytical reasoning process to act faster and be more attentive (Thomas & Cook, 2005).

According to Chang et al. (2007) visual analytical models could confront problems that were stubborn because of their size and complexity. These complex problems needed a combined human and machine analysis for their solution. Kielman et al. (2009) reported that visual analytical models employed advanced techniques for analytical reasoning, communication, data transformations, and representations. These techniques used computation, visualization, analytic reporting, and technology transition. Visual models derived from collaborative work of several scientific and technical communities in computer science, information visualization, cognitive and perceptual sciences, interactive design, graphic design, and social sciences. Visual models employed tools like geographic maps, info graphics, heat maps, spark lines, and fever charts (Kielman et al., 2009).

Holsapple et al. (2014) considered that there were two major taxonomies of business analytics including a threefold and alternative fourfold model. In 2010, a global consultation company Capgemini presented threefold taxonomy comprising descriptive, predictive and prescriptive dimensions. Steps involved in the fourfold taxonomy of business analytics included how to sense a situation, make predictions, make evaluations, and take decisive action (SPED). SPED taxonomy enabled management to do evidence based problem solving through sensing, predicting, and evaluating. Problem solving was a broader term not necessarily always decisional. Making sense was more related to understanding the problems rather than making decisions (Holsapple et al., 2014).

Hargreaves and Ding (2014) recommended construction of a decision agent within the business analytics framework. This agent's work would be based on recorded effects of recommended decisions that were accepted by a user and performed recommended actions. Recording this impact would be the only update that required human involvement. An evaluation agent would evaluate future decisions by comparing current choices and conditions with recorded impacts of past decisions. The evaluative agent acted only when an effect of a decision was recorded.

According to Kumar (2014) fourth a type of business analytics was decisive analytics. Managers used decisive analytics to create visual models to support their decisions and reasoning. Visual analytics supported human decisions with virtual representations of expressed reasoning.

CONCLUSION

Higher educational leaders are struggling to meet these challenges and compete in a highly competitive environment. Retention of students is one of the important challenges that state universities face today. Retaining students is crucial for universities not only for their financial resources but also for their reputation. One of the initiatives to address this issue is to make informed decisions is the use of big data analytics. Universities have large datasets available to predict future direction and generate actionable information. An important type of analytics used to improve management processes and to make informed decisions is big data business analytics. State university executive leaders may improve the effectiveness of their decisions by integrating business analytics in the decision-making models.

However, there is a need to examine the use of big data business analytics in the decision-making process at the executive leadership level of the selected state universities. Especially in the context of how descriptive, predictive, prescriptive, decisive and basic analytics, and data collection influence the decision-making process at the executive leadership level of the state universities in terms of student retention and graduation rates.

REFERENCES

Agosta, L. (2004). Data Mining is Dead-Long Live Predictive Analytics! *Information & Management*, *14*(1), 37.

Alavi, M., Yoo, Y., & Vogel, D. R. (1997). Using information technology to add value to management education. *Academy of Management Journal*, *40*(6), 1310–1333. doi:10.2307/257035

Astin, A. W. (1997). How good is your institutions retention rate? *Research in Higher Education*, *38*(6), 647–658. doi:10.1023/A:1024903702810

Avolio, B. J., Jung, D. I., Murry, W., & Sivasbramaniam, N. (1996). Building highly developed teams: Focusing on shared leadership process, efficacy, trust, and performance.

Baars, H., & Kemper, H.-G. (2008). Management Support with Structured and Unstructured Data—An Integrated Business Intelligence Framework. *Information Systems Management*, *25*(2), 132–148. doi:10.1080/10580530801941058

Baer, L., & Duin, A. H. (2014). Retain Your Students! The Analytics, Policies and Politics of Reinvention Strategies. *Planning for Higher Education*, *42*(3), 30.

Basham, L. M. (2010). Transformational and transactional leaders in higher education. *International Review of Business Research Papers*, *6*(6), 141–152.

Bryman, A. (2007). Effective leadership in higher education: A literature review. *Studies in Higher Education*, *32*(6), 693–710. doi:10.1080/03075070701685114

Buhl, H. U. (2013). Interview with Martin Petry on Big Data. *Business & Information Systems Engineering*, *5*(2), 101–102. doi:10.1007/s12599-013-0253-9

Buhl, H. U., Röglinger, M., Moser, F., & Heidemann, J. (2013). Big Data. *Wirtschaftsinformatik*, *55*(2), 63–68. doi:10.1007/s11576-013-0350-x

Burns, J. M. (2003). *Transforming leadership: A new pursuit of happiness* (Vol. 213). Grove Press.

Chang, R., Ghoniem, M., Kosara, R., Ribarsky, W., Yang, J., Suma, E., . . . Sudjianto, A. (2007). Wirevis: Visualization of categorical, time-varying data from financial transactions. *Paper presented at the IEEE Symposium on Visual Analytics Science and Technology VAST '07.*

Chang, R. M., Kauffman, R. J., & Kwon, Y. (2014). Understanding the paradigm shift to computational social science in the presence of big data. *Decision Support Systems*, *63*, 67–80. doi:10.1016/j.dss.2013.08.008

Chaudhuri, S., Dayal, U., & Narasayya, V. (2011). An overview of business intelligence technology. *Communications of the ACM*, *54*(8), 88–98. doi:10.1145/1978542.1978562

Daniel, B. (2015). Big Data and analytics in higher education: Opportunities and challenges. *British Journal of Educational Technology*. doi:10.1111/bjet.12230

Daniel, B., & Butson, R. (2014). Foundations of Big Data and Analytics in Higher Education. Retrieved from http://engineering.nyu.edu/files/ICAS2014-Proceedings-Publication.pdf

Daniel, B. K., & Butson, R. (2013). Technology enhanced analytics (TEA) in higher education. *Paper presented at the Proceedings of the International Conference on Educational Technologies.*

Davenport, T. H., Barth, P., & Bean, R. (2013). How 'big data' is different. *MIT Sloan Management Review, 54*(1).

Delen, D., & Demirkan, H. (2013). Data, information and analytics as services. *Decision Support Systems*, *55*(1), 359–363. doi:10.1016/j.dss.2012.05.044

Dhar, V., & Sundararajan, A. (2007). Information Technologies in Business: A Blueprint for Education and Research.

Diebold, F. X., Cheng, X., Diebold, S., Foster, D., Halperin, M., Lohr, S., & Pospiech, M. (2012). *A Personal Perspective on the Origin (s) and Development of "Big Data"*.

Direction, S. (2013). So, are the geeks inheriting the earth?: Big Data, big decisions and best practice for information management. *Strategic Direction, 29*(9).

Drigas, A. S., & Leliopoulos, P. (2014). The Use of Big Data in Education. *International Journal of Computer Science Issues*, *11*(5), 58.

Dupin-Bryant, P. A., & Olsen, D. H. (2014). Business Intelligence, Analytics And Data Visualization: A Heat Map Project Tutorial. *International Journal of Management & Information Systems*, *18*(3), 185–200.

Dziuban, C., Moskal, P., Cavanagh, T., & Watts, A. (2012). Analytics that Inform the University: Using Data You Already Have. *Journal of Asynchronous Learning Networks*, *16*(3), 21–38.

Eckerson, W. W. (2006). Deploying dashboards and scorecards. The Data Warehouse Institute, 1-24.

Evans, J. R. (2012). Business analytics: the next frontier for decision sciences.

Franks, E. E. (2014). *State of the art analytics and managers in the defense industry*. CAPELLA UNIVERSITY.

Fullan, M. (2011). *Change leader: Learning to do what matters most*. John Wiley & Sons.

Fullan, M., & Scott, G. (2009). *Turnaround leadership for higher education*. John Wiley & Sons.

Gandomi, A., & Haider, M. (2015). Beyond the hype: Big data concepts, methods, and analytics. *International Journal of Information Management*, *35*(2), 137–144. doi:10.1016/j.ijinfomgt.2014.10.007

Hair, J. F. Jr. (2007). Knowledge creation in marketing: The role of predictive analytics. *European Business Review*, *19*(4), 303–315. doi:10.1108/09555340710760134

Hargreaves, C. A., & Ding, L. (2014). Business Analytics as a Framework for an Evolving Multi-Agent System. *Journal on Computing*, *2*(3).

Harris, J. G., Craig, E., & Light, D. A. (2011). Talent and analytics: New approaches, higher ROI. *The Journal of Business Strategy*, *32*(6), 4–13. doi:10.1108/02756661111180087

Harrison, L. M. (2011). Transformational leadership, integrity, and power. *New Directions for Student Services*, *2011*(135), 45–52. doi:10.1002/ss.403

Holsapple, C., Lee-Post, A., & Pakath, R. (2014). A unified foundation for business analytics. *Decision Support Systems*, *64*, 130–141. doi:10.1016/j.dss.2014.05.013

Hopkins, M. S. (2011). Big Data, analytics and the path from insights to value. *MIT Sloan Management Review, 52*(2), 21-22. Retrieved from http://0-search.ebscohost.com.library.dowling.edu/login.aspx?direct=true&db=buh&AN=57750727&site=ehost-live

Hsinchun, C., Chiang, R. H. L., & Storey, V. C. (2012). Business intelligence and analytics: from big data to big impact. *Management Information Systems Quarterly*, *36*(4), 1165–1188. Retrieved from http://0-search.ebscohost.com.library.dowling.edu/login.aspx?direct=true&db=lxh&AN=83466038&site=ehost-live

Jacobs, A. (2009). The pathologies of big data. *Communications of the ACM*, *52*(8), 36–44. doi:10.1145/1536616.1536632

Jagadish, H. V., Gehrke, J., Labrinidis, A., Papakonstantinou, Y., Patel, J. M., Ramakrishnan, R., & Shahabi, C. (2014). Big Data and Its Technical Challenges. *Communications of the ACM*, *57*(7), 86–94. doi:10.1145/2611567

Jalonen, H., & Lönnqvist, A. (2009). Predictive business – fresh initiative or old wine in a new bottle. *Management Decision*, *47*(10), 1595–1609. doi:10.1108/00251740911004709

Kielman, J., Thomas, J., & May, R. (2009). Foundations and Frontiers in Visual Analytics. *Information Visualization*, *8*(4), 239–246. doi:10.1057/ivs.2009.25

Kiron, D., Ferguson, R. B., & Prentice, P. K. (2013). From value to vision: Reimagining the possible with data analytics. *MIT Sloan Management Review*, *54*(3), 1.

Kiron, D., & Shockley, R. (2011). Creating business value with analytics. *MIT Sloan Management Review*, *53*(1), 57.

Kiron, D., Shockley, R., Kruschwitz, N., Finch, G., & Haydock, M. (2011). Analytics: The widening divide. *MIT Sloan Management Review*, *53*(3), 1–22.

Klatt, T., Schlaefke, M., & Moeller, K. (2011). Integrating business analytics into strategic planning for better performance. *The Journal of Business Strategy*, *32*(6), 30–39. doi:10.1108/02756661111180113

Knapp, M. S., Swinnerton, J. A., Copland, M. A., & Monpas-Huber, J. (2006). *Data-Informed Leadership in Education*. Center for the Study of Teaching and Policy.

Kohavi, R., Rothleder, N. J., & Simoudis, E. (2002). Emerging trends in business analytics. *Communications of the ACM*, *45*(8), 45–48. Retrieved from http://0-search.ebscohost.com.library.dowling.edu/login.aspx?direct=true&db=buh&AN=11863428&site=ehost-live doi:10.1145/545151.545177

Kumar, B. S. (2014). Business Analytics: A way forward to Decision Making.

Lau, L. K. (2003). Institutional factors affecting student retention. *Education-Indianapolis Then Chula Vista*, *124*(1), 126–136.

LaValle, S., Lesser, E., Shockley, R., Hopkins, M. S., & Kruschwitz, N. (2011). Big Data, Analytics and the Path from Insights to Value. *MIT Sloan Management Review*, *52*(2), 21-32.

Luan, J. (2002). Data mining and its applications in higher education. *New Directions for Institutional Research*, *2002*(113), 17–36. doi:10.1002/ir.35

Macfadyen, L. P., Dawson, S., Pardo, A., & Gasevic, D. (2014). Embracing big data in complex educational systems: The learning analytics imperative and the policy challenge. *Research & Practice in Assessment*, *9*(2), 17–28.

Manyika, J., Chui, M., Brown, B., Bughin, J., Dobbs, R., Roxburgh, C., & Byers, A. H. (2011). Big data: The next frontier for innovation, competition, and productivity.

March, J. G., & Simon, H. A. (1958). Organizations.

Marsh, J. A., & Farrell, C. C. (2015). How leaders can support teachers with data-driven decision making A framework for understanding capacity building. *Educational Management Administration & Leadership*, *43*(2), 269–289. doi:10.1177/1741143214537229

Murtaugh, P. A., Burns, L. D., & Schuster, J. (1999). Predicting the retention of university students. *Research in Higher Education*, *40*(3), 355–371. doi:10.1023/A:1018755201899

Nandeshwar, A., Menzies, T., & Nelson, A. (2011). Learning patterns of university student retention. *Expert Systems with Applications*, *38*(12), 14984–14996. doi:10.1016/j.eswa.2011.05.048

OReilly, K., & Paper, D. (2012). Want Value from Big Data? Close the Gap between the C-Suite and the Server Room. *Journal of Information Technology Case and Application Research*, *14*(4), 3–10. doi:10.1080/15228053.2012.10845709

Phillips-Wren, G., & Hoskisson, A. (2015). An analytical journey towards big data. *Journal of Decision Systems*, *24*(1), 87–102. doi:10.1080/12460125.2015.994333

Picciano, A. G. (2012). The Evolution of Big Data and Learning Analytics in American Higher Education. *Journal of Asynchronous Learning Networks*, *16*(3), 9–20.

Power, D. J. (2014). Using Big Data for analytics and decision support. *Journal of Decision Systems*, *23*(2), 222–228. doi:10.1080/12460125.2014.888848

Rajesh, K. (2013). Big Data Analytics: Applications and Benefits. *IUP Journal of Information Technology*, *9*(4), 41.

Ravishanker, G. (2011). Doing academic analytics right: Intelligent answers to simple questions. *Research Bulletin (Sun Chiwawitthaya Thang Thale Phuket)*, 2.

Rogers, D. L. (2000). A paradigm shift: Technology integration for higher education in the new millennium. *AACE Journal*, *1*(13), 19–33.

Santiago Rivera, D., & Shanks, G. (2015). A Dashboard to Support Management of Business Analytics Capabilities. *Journal of Decision Systems*, *24*(1), 73–86. doi:10.1080/12460125.2015.994335

Senge, P. M. (2014). *The dance of change: The challenges to sustaining momentum in a learning organization*. Crown Business.

Shanks, G., & Bekmamedova, N. (2012). Achieving benefits with business analytics systems: An evolutionary process perspective. *Journal of Decision Systems*, *21*(3), 231–244. doi:10.1080/12460125.2012.729182

Thomas, D., Jeanne, G., David, W., & Alvin, L. (2001). Data to Knowledge to Results, Building an Analytic Capability. *California Management Review*, *43*(2).

Thomas, J. J., & Cook, K. A. (2005). Illuminating the Path: The R&D Agenda for Visual Analytics National Visualization and Analytics Center.

Tinto, V. (2006). Research and practice of student retention: What next? *Journal of College Student Retention*, *8*(1), 1–19. doi:10.2190/4YNU-4TMB-22DJ-AN4W

Tinto, V. (2007). *Taking student retention seriously*. Syracuse University.

Tucker, B. A., & Russell, R. F. (2004). The influence of the transformational leader. *Journal of Leadership & Organizational Studies*, *10*(4), 103–111. doi:10.1177/107179190401000408

van Barneveld, A., Arnold, K. E., & Campbell, J. P. (2012). Analytics in higher education: Establishing a common language. *EDUCAUSE learning initiative*, *1*, 1-11.

Viaene, S., & Van den Bunder, A. (2011). The secrets to managing business analytics projects. *MIT Sloan Management Review*, *53*(1), 65–69.

Waller, M. A., & Fawcett, S. E. (2013). Data science, predictive analytics, and big data: A revolution that will transform supply chain design and management. *Journal of Business Logistics*, *34*(2), 77–84. doi:10.1111/jbl.12010

Watson, H. (2011). Business analytics insight: Hype or here to stay? *Business Intelligence Journal*, *16*(1), 4–8.

Whitchurch, C. (2004). Administrative managers–A critical link. *Higher Education Quarterly*, *58*(4), 280–298. doi:10.1111/j.1468-2273.2004.00274.x

Wilder, C. R., & Ozgur, C. O. (2015). Business Analytics Curriculum for Undergraduate Majors. *INFORMS Transactions on Education*, *15*(2), 180–187. doi:10.1287/ited.2014.0134

Zhang, K. (2015). Four Changes of Modern Universities from the Perspective of "4V" of Big Data. *Canadian Social Science*, *11*(3).

Chapter 4
Retrieving HTML and XBRL Data With Microsoft Excel 2010

Jianing Fang
Marist College, USA

ABSTRACT

The Securities and Exchange Commission (SEC) has upgraded the Electronic Data Gathering, Analysis, and Retrieval (EDGAR) system, to the Interactive Data Electronic Applications (IDEA) platform, or the Next-Generation EDGAR (New EDGAR). The SEC issued its final mandate for XBRL adoption and the conversion target dates for all firms in January 2009. With this conversion, users can retrieve the financial statement information of listed companies at both the document level and data element level. This chapter reviews the fundamental concepts of XBRL and reports on the current compliance status of the SEC XBRL conversion mandate. The main task is to demonstrate how to retrieve data from the New EDGAR and how to process the data with Microsoft Excel 2010.

INTRODUCTION

Since the Securities and Exchange Commission's (SEC) eXtensible Business Reporting Language (XBRL) conversion mandate was issued in 2009, most of the registrants have successfully followed suit. Many have converted their annual financial reports (10K), quarterly financial reports (10Q), and other required financial reports from the Hyper Text Markup Language (HTML) format under the old Electronic Data Gathering, Analysis, and Retrieval (EDGAR) system, which

DOI: 10.4018/978-1-5225-3616-1.ch004

reported only at the document level, to the XBRL format under Interactive Data Electronic Applications (IDEA) – otherwise known as the Next-Generation EDGAR (New EDGAR) – which reports at both document level and data element level (Du, Vasarhelyi & Zheng, 2013). This provided a more efficient and cheaper source of data for financial analysts, investors, students, and other users needing information on the annual or quarterly financial reports of all publicly traded companies (Jones & Willis, 2003). XBRL has since been "ranked as one of [the] top ten technologies for accounting and auditing professionals" (Liu, 2013, p. 60).

This new data element level data depository is a very valuable addition to the existing and ever enlarging stores of qualitative and quantitative data online and available for researcher use publicly. While these public resources can be invaluable to the skilled researchers in many specific fields, there are inherent technical challenges and differences between data reuse and traditional researcher-collected qualitative and quantitative data. Especially in the XBRL domain—due to the lacking efforts and limited opportunities for education and training, many users do not have the necessary knowledge or skills to make full use of this new source of financial data (Harris & Morsfield, 2012; Fang, 2013). In this chapter, the author will review the SEC's XBRL conversion mandate and the compliance status. Additionally, this chapter will walk through the entire process of retrieving financial data on the New EDGAR system with a simple and practical example and step-by-step instructions with plenty of screenshots for Windows operating systems. The detailed instructions will not only show how to search for companies and their data on IDEA, but it will also demonstrate how to correctly set up Excel worksheets to import and process the HTML and XBRL data.

BACKGROUND

One of the most significant legacies of the G. W. Bush Administration for US corporations occurred on January 30, 2009: the SEC issued the final mandate for XBRL adoption with firm conversion target dates (SEC, 2009). The mandate required the largest domestic and foreign public companies using U.S. Generally Accepted Accounting Principles (GAAP) to file their financial statements in XBRL format by June 15, 2009. Medium-sized filers had to switch to XBRL by June 15, 2010, and the rest of the filers, either using U.S. GAAP or International Financial Reporting Standards (IFRS), needed to convert by June 15, 2011 (Aguilar, 2009; Fang, 2011; Harris & Morsfield, 2012).

The new rules aimed to render financial information into easier formats for investors to analyze and to assist in automating regulatory filings and business information processing. The New EDGAR system provides information at both the document level, such as the entire set of financial statements for a given firm, and at the data element level, such as a firm's Inventory or Net Income. Data tagged at data element level in XBRL format can function across multiple platforms or application programs. Thus, XBRL has the potential to increase the speed, accuracy, and usability of financial disclosure, eventually reducing costs for financial reporting and business transaction processing (Fang, 2009; Bizarro & Garcia, 2010; Harris & Morsfield, 2012).

When a company files its XBRL-formatted financial statements or its related registration statements with the SEC, the commission also requires a filer to post its financial statements in interactive data format on its corporate website for at least twelve fiscal months. The new rules will not eliminate or change existing filing requirements for financial statements, accompanying reports, schedules, and footnotes to be filed in the traditional HTML format. The SEC believes that some investors and analysts may still wish to use the HTML format to obtain copies of entire registration statements or financial reports, either in addition to or in lieu of interactive data.

XBRL can also improve security market efficiency. The Semi-Strong form of the Efficient Market Hypothesis (EMH) is about how financial data and other related information can affect an individual security or the market as a whole (Fama, 1970). As discussed above, XBRL and IDEA can dramatically improve both the speed and accuracy of financial reporting, and as the sophistication of these XBRL and IDEA technologies improves, market efficiency will improve. Thus, IDEA affords significant advantages over EDGAR in terms of speed and accuracy not only for financial reporting but also for utilizing reported financial information for investment purposes.

Before the SEC's mandate for XBRL conversion, a user could download financial statements directly from the SEC's old EDGAR system. However, with financial information reported only at the document level, the user had to meticulously sift through pages of statements and footnotes in order to manually extract the relevant data needed. He or she then must manually re-enter this information into a spreadsheet or into an investment analysis system or similar specialized software. Manual data entry is both time-consuming and error-prone (Taylor & Dzuranin, 2010).

To improve efficiency and accuracy, many users had often turned to the costly commercial data providers, such as Compustat or Mergent, to obtain the necessary data. With IDEA, users can retrieve this data directly from the SEC's website without any middleman; as a result, there is the potential for investors, accountants, and financial professionals not only to save huge amounts of time and costs, but also obtain the needed data with higher accuracy and speed. While this is beneficial to all users, this change is particularly important to institutions with limited resources, such as small businesses, students, and small CPA practices. Using Microsoft Excel, a widely available tool, anyone can procure detailed information directly from the New EDGAR system with great ease and efficiency.

THE CURRENT COMPLIANCE STATUS

How has the United States fared in its efforts to convert financial statements to XBRL? The author has prepared Table 1 using registrant filing data published on RR Donnelley's website[1] to display the number of companies who registered with the New EDGAR system and the total number of filings at various dates:

The SEC estimated that there are about 500 large accelerated issuers, 1,000 accelerated issuers, and 8,700 other issuers, making a total of 10,200 registrants. According to the Table 1, only 8,066 companies successfully converted to the required XBRL filing format by the final conversion deadline of December 30, 2011. That can hardly be called a roaring success for the SEC's XBRL conversion

Table 1. SEC registrant filing data (cumulative)

Date	Note	Companies	Filings
August 29, 2011		5,970	13,935
October 15, 2011		7,281	15,642
October 30, 2011		7,383	16,379
November 30, 2011		7,875	22,238
December 30, 2011	Deadline for all issuers	8,066	23,184
January 26, 2012		8,175	23,708
February 16, 2012		8,227	25,138
March 06, 2012		8,271	27,181
June 15, 2012		8,710	35,796
October 19, 2012		8,974	44,612
February 11, 2013		9,142	53,296
August 15, 2013		9,582	71,716
September 12, 2013		9,631	72,875
November 19, 2013		9,777	79,243
December 20, 2013		9,837	80,252
January 22, 2014		9,872	81.032
February 28, 2014		9,912	84,079
March 18, 2014		9,931	85,699

mandate. In fact, about 21% of the registrants had failed to convert to XBRL by the final deadline (Harris & Morsfield, 2012; Fang, 2013).

One of the primary reasons for this subpar performance is that most companies and colleges are still reluctant to allocate financial and human resources for their XBRL projects and training programs. Despite many leading researchers' early identification of the serious shortage of qualified professionals who are equipped with sufficient XRBL skills in the CPA field (Sheridan & Drew, 2012), and despite urgent calls for increased efforts for integrating XBRL into accounting curricula (Debreceny & Farewell, 2010; Fang, 2011, 2013), most colleges and universities have yet to offer full courses dedicated to teaching XBRL (Harris & Morsfield, 2012; Cable & Healy, 2013). In addition to the lack of XBRL specialists, many companies have neither invested enough resources to acquire the necessary computer programs nor trained their XBRL specialists through other means (e.g. training modules provided by their software vendors). Most of all, the author believes that the main reason is that the SEC does not have a strong and functional mechanism to enforce its mandates regarding the XBRL conversion deadlines.

Any registrant who fails to either file the company's financial reports in XBRL format with the SEC by the applicable due dates or to post the related interactive data on the company website on time is prohibited from using the short form registration statements on Form S-3, F-3, or S-8. This penalty brings considerable burdens on non-compliant companies in terms of additional cost, time, and labor because the companies are forced to prepare the required long forms for the registration statements, instead of the short forms, to file with the SEC. Also, under the exemption clause set forth in Section 4(1) of the Securities Act [15 U.S.C. 77d (1)], Rule 144 creates a safe harbor for the resale of securities. In order to enjoy the benefit of this exemption, the issuer of the securities must be deemed to have adequate current public information available as specified by Rule 143(C)(1) [17 CFR 230.144(C)(1)]. Thus, when an issuer fails to file the company's financial reports in XBRL format with the SEC by the applicable due date, or fails to post the related interactive date on the company Web site on time, the Final Rule specifies that during the disqualification period, the filer will be deemed not to have available adequate current public information to take the Rule 144 resale safe harbor exemption. Nevertheless, the author believes that this "slap on the wrist" type of penalty is too light to be effective. For details of the consequences of and solutions to noncompliance with the SEC's XBRL conversion mandate, see "The Progress of XBRL Conversion: Reviewing the Rules, Consequences, and Potential Remedies" (Fang, 2013).

The result is that as the eighth anniversary of the SEC's XBRL conversion mandate approaches in late January 2017, reports indicate that only a small fraction of the promised benefits of the costly XBRL filings have been realized by investors and financial analysts. The main disappointments among the many problems are the lack of user training, poor data quality, and unavailability of data retrieval and processing software (Hoffelder, 2012; Harris & Morsfield, 2012; Provost, 2013), again, confirming our discussion above.

The detrimental consequence is that while U.S. companies are dragging their feet, the rest of the world has been passing us by very rapidly. If a reader simply spends 10 minutes visiting XBRL International's website (http://www.xbrl.org), he or she will find that many other countries have moved beyond XBRL for financial reporting (XBRL FR) to XBRL Global Ledger (XBRL GL), which is being used for business process reengineering. This means international competitors have gained tremendous competitive advantages over US companies, not only in terms of their efficiency of financial reporting, but in business transaction processing.

Educators in accounting and other related fields can play an important part in helping along the adoption and implementation of XBRL reporting (Corkern & Morgan, 2012). In the following section, building on the foundation established by Tribunella and Tribunella (2010), the author will walk you through the whole process of retrieving financial data on the New EDGAR system with a practical example and play-by-play explanations of the process with screenshots. The demonstration will not only show you how to search for companies and their data on the New EDGAR system, but it will also demonstrate how to correctly set up your Excel worksheets to import and process the HTML and XBRL data on Microsoft Excel 2010 using the Windows operating system.

A HTML AND XBRL DATA RETRIEVING EXAMPLE

The following example demonstrates how to retrieve relevant data from financial statements on the New EDGAR system to complete a three-year Net Profit Ratio trend analysis with step-by-step instructions and plenty of helpful screenshots:

Step 1: Preparing the Excel workbook.

To begin, you should create an "XBRL" subdirectory in your "Document" folder on your laptop or PC. Naturally, you will save all of the files used in this example in that subdirectory. This will help you find any file very quickly.

The first action to take after opening a new Excel workbook is to check whether the "Developer" tab is displayed in the Ribbon. If not, click the "File" tab and then click on "Options" in the pane on the left-hand side (see Figure 1) to open the "Excel Options" window.

Choose "Customize Ribbon" in the left pane. In the right-hand column beneath "Customize the Ribbon", check the selection box next to "Developer" (see Figure

Figure 1. Dropdown manual of the "File Tab"

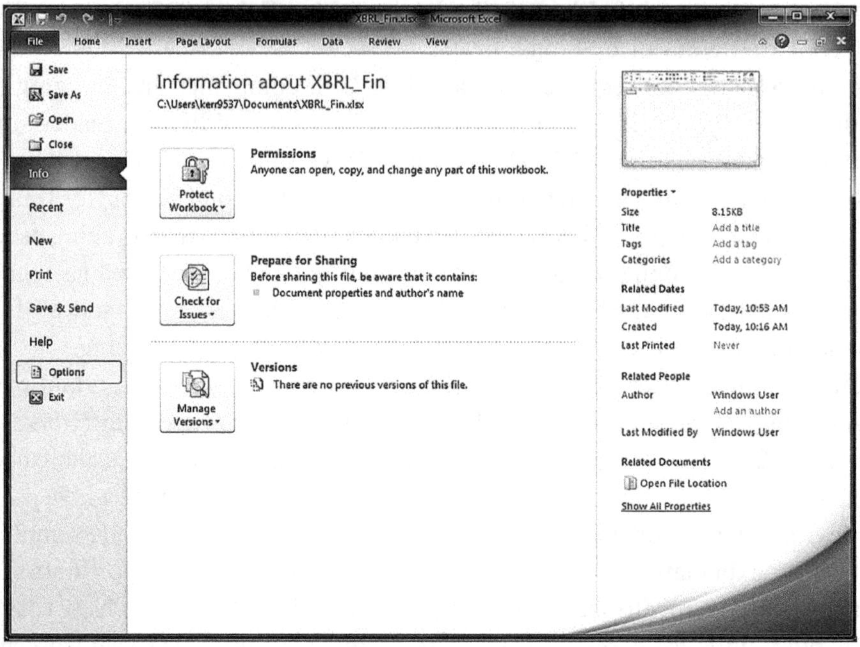

2). Click the "OK" button at the bottom of the "Excel Options" window to confirm your selections and return to your Excel worksheet.

Step 2: Retrieving XBRL file on IDEA to PC.

The next step is to download the necessary data from the New EDGAR system. Go to the SEC's EDGAR website by searching "SEC EDGAR" in an Internet search engine and clicking on the SEC's EDGAR link. From the "SEC Structured Data" homepage, you can search for any of the companies registered with the SEC by clicking on the "Filings" tab in the upper right-hand corner, and then click on "Company Filings Search" (see Figure 3). You may also go to this site directly by entering its web address – https://www.sec.gov/edgar/searchedgar/companysearch.html – into your Internet browser's URL bar.

The SEC provides a few different ways to search company filings. Since Apple Inc. is one of the most watched companies these days, its filings will be used in this example. You can use the name search method by typing "Apple Inc." into the "Company Name" field on the left search pane, and then click on the "Find Companies" button. This will open an "EDGAR Search Results" window (see Figure 4) displaying a list of company names that begin with "Apple."

Figure 2. The "Excel Options" window

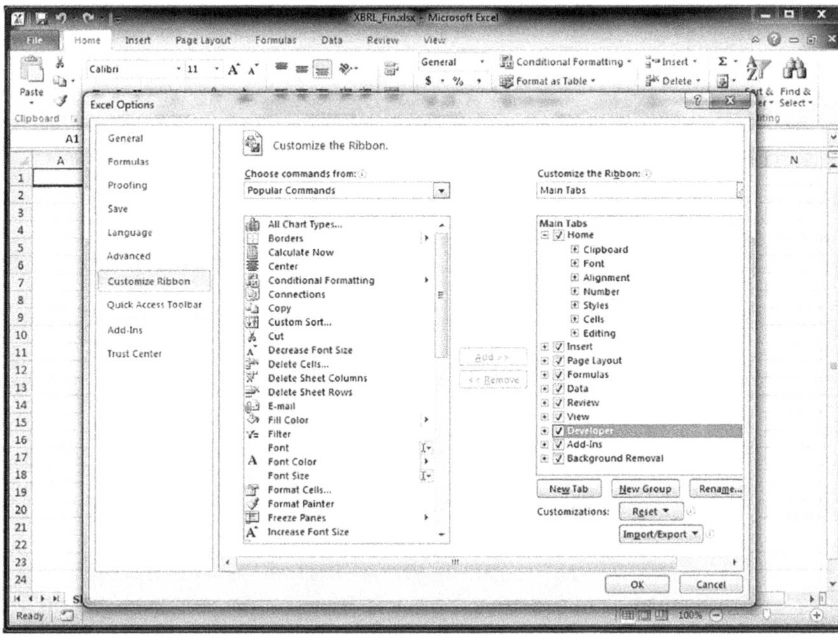

Figure 3. The "SEC Structured Data" homepage

Figure 4. The "EDGAR Search Results" window

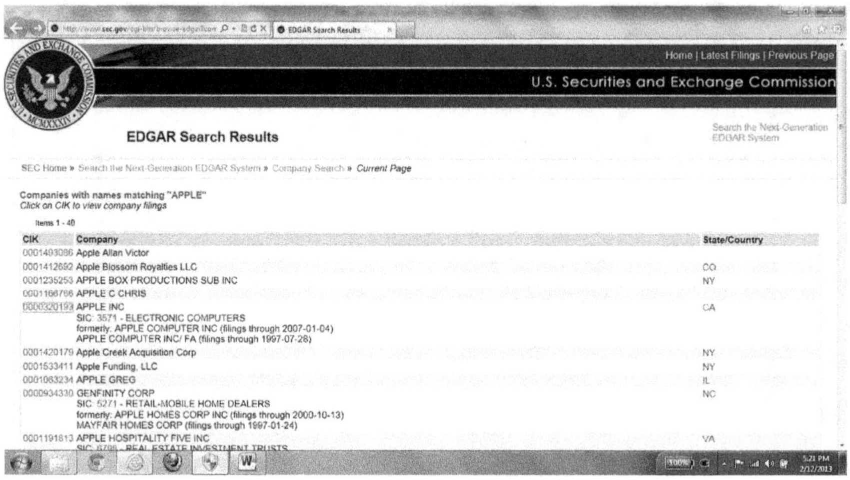

Move down the "Company" column you will find "Apple Inc." Click on the assigned CIK code to the left of the company name, and it will open a list of all of the documents that the company has filed with the SEC in chronological order. 40 documents can be displayed at a time along with all of the pertinent registrant information. That is the default setting; however, you can change it to your own preferences (e.g. 20 or 100). A blue "Interactive Data" tag next to the "Documents" link in the "Format" column identifies all of the filings in XBRL format (see Figure 5). The fillings without a blue "Interactive Data" tag are in other data formats such as ".txt," ".jpg," or ".htm." Retrieving HTML data will be covered later in this chapter.

When you scroll down the list, you will find the 2012 10-K report filed on 2012-10-31 with the SEC. Click on the blue "Interactive Data" tag next to the "Documents" link, and that will open up the "View Filing Data" window (see Figure 6). Click on the "Financial Statements" tag on the left pane and select "Consolidated Statements of Operations" from the dropdown menu.

This will provide Apple Inc.'s Consolidated Statements of Operations from September 29, 2010 to September 29, 2012 (see Figure 7). You can click the printer icon (or the "Print Document" tab) to print a hard copy of the statements as a reference. This will be helpful in ensuring the accuracy of the XBRL data you will download later, and it will help you find the correct XBRL data label when you begin your analysis.

Figure 5. The "Filing List" window

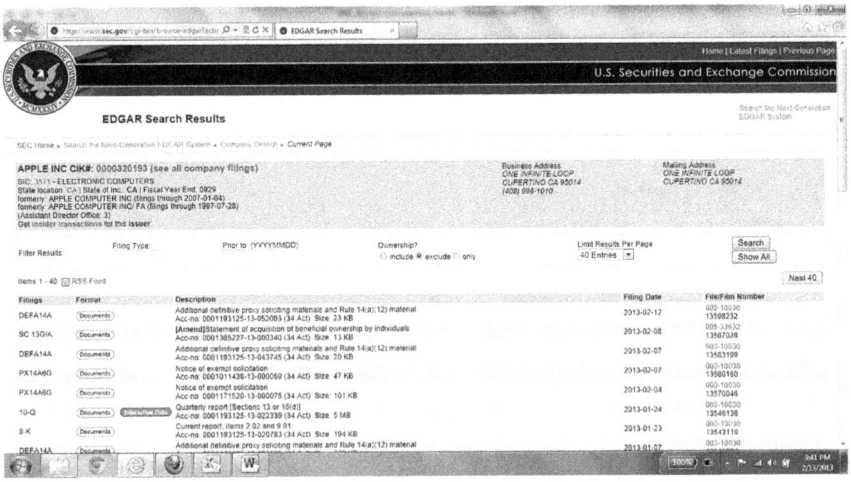

Figure 6. The "Document List" window

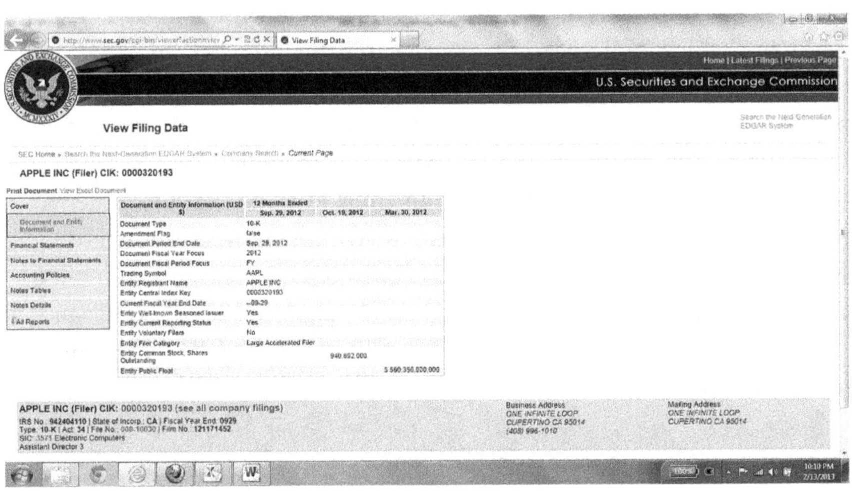

You can also save the information on your PC by first opening a new Microsoft Word document and then capturing a screenshot of your internet browser by holding down the "Ctrl" ("Fn" on some keyboards) key and then pressing the "PrtSc" key on your keyboard. Then, switch back to the Word document, right-click, and select "Paste", or press "Ctrl" and "v" on your keyboard. This will input the screenshot to the Word document, which you can save for future use. Another option is to save the reports as a Portable Document Format (PDF). Most Internet browsers have the

Figure 7. The "View Filing Data" window

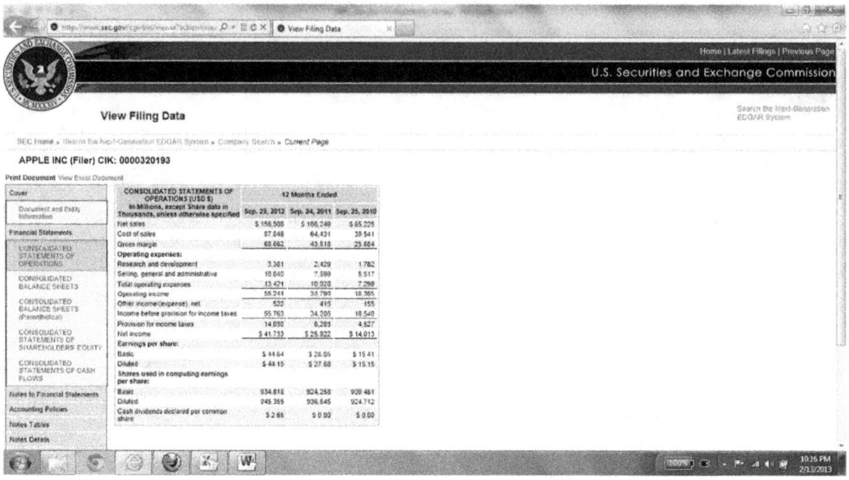

ability to either save or "print" a web page as a PDF. The advantage with this option is that instead of simply saving an image of the report, you can save a searchable text document, which will speed up your search for relevant information later in your analysis.

Next, you must download the financial statement data in XBRL format. Return to your Internet browser and navigate back to the document list window (see Figure 5). Scroll down to the same 10-K report, but this time, click on the "Documents" button and the "Filing Detail" window (see Figure 8) will open. Scroll down to locate the file with the description "XBRL INSTANCE DOCUMENT" marked "Seq. 7" for this document. Right-click the file link named "aapl-20120929.xml" and choose "Save Target As …". You should save this file in the "XBRL" subdirectory that you created earlier.

Step 3: Mapping XML on the Excel workbook.

The next step is to import the XBRL data you need for your analysis into an Excel worksheet. Click on the Excel tab on the taskbar at the bottom of your window. Open the instance document by clicking on the "File" tab, and then click "Open". You will need to navigate to your "XBRL" subdirectory to select the "aapl-20120929.xml" file. After you press the "Open" button, Excel can recognize that the file is in XML format, and it will provide an "Open XML" dialog box (see Figure 9). Select the "Use the XML Source task pane" option and press the OK button.

Figure 8. The "Filing Detail" window

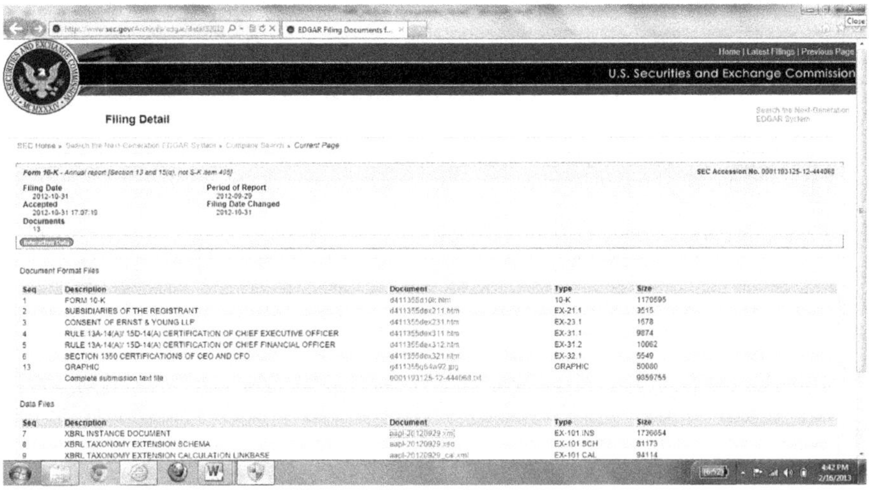

Figure 9. The "Open XML" dialog box

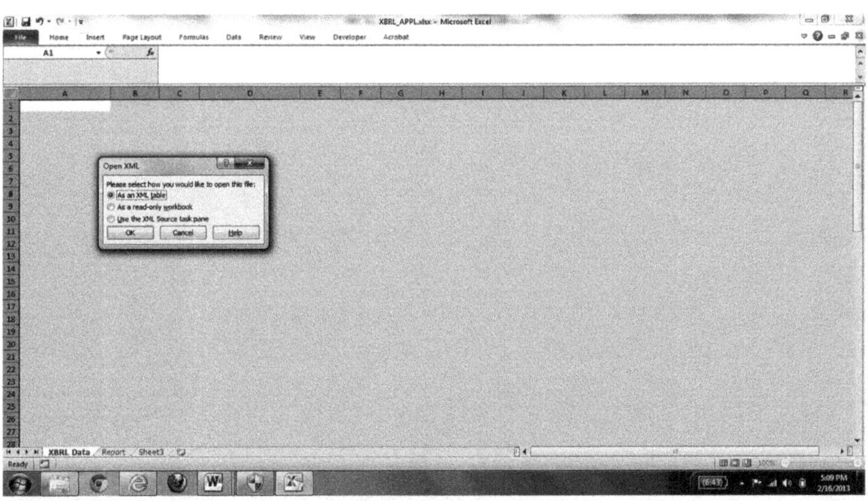

A warning box (see Figure 10) will pop up to tell you "…Excel will create a schema based on the XML source data". That is exactly what you want, so press the OK button to proceed.

An "XML Source" pane (see Figure 11) will open on the right side of your Excel worksheet. In order to map the data quickly and accurately, it is recommended that you display the associated value of each XML data element. Click the "Options" button at the bottom of the "XML Source" pane and select all of the options. To

Figure 10. The "XML Schema Notification" dialog box

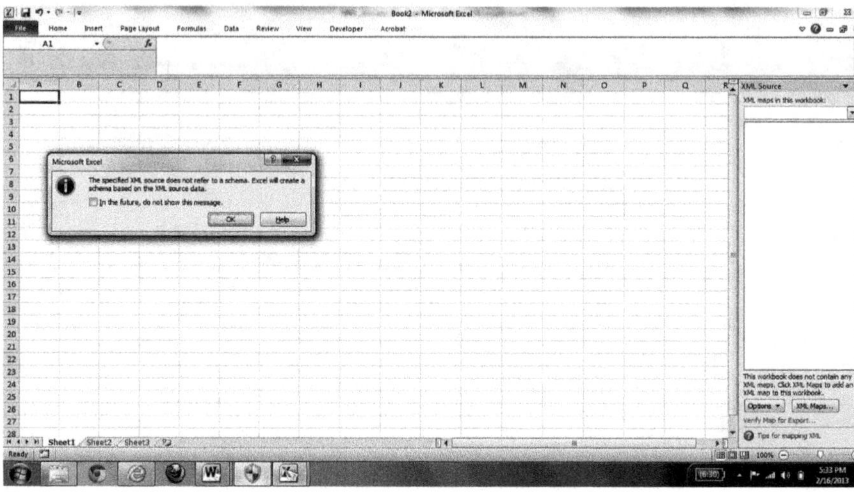

Figure 11. The "XML Source" pane

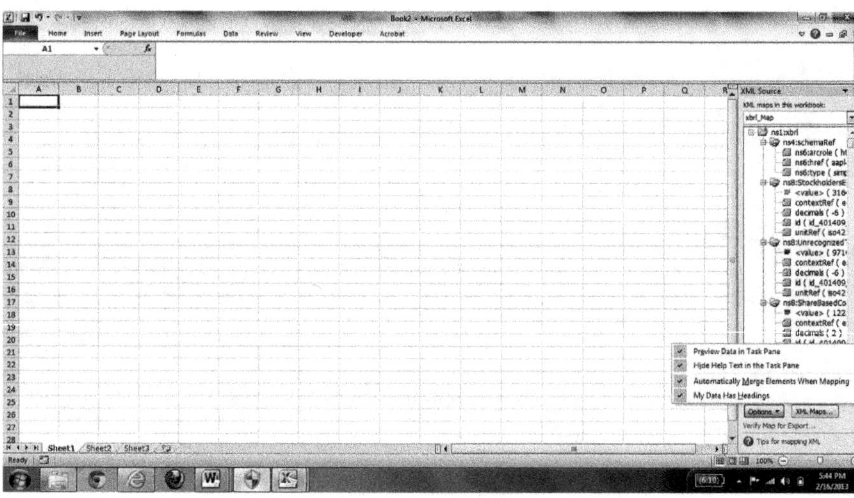

see the full content of each tag, you can make the "XML Source" pane wider by dragging its left border towards the center of the screen.

Now, you need to map the XBRL data elements equivalent to "Net Income" onto your Excel worksheet. This is necessary because XBRL is still in its infancy and all of the XBRL taxonomies, which are XBRL financial statement filing standards for various accounting standards and/or industries (e.g. IFRS vs. US GAAP, general industry vs. insurance industry), provide many different labels to tag the same or similar data elements (Capozzoli & Farewell, 2010; Harris & Morsfield, 2012). This presents a formidable challenge for the users—especially an XBRL novice. Looking for the correct tag from a list with thousands upon thousands of data elements for any new instance document is like searching for a tiny needle in a huge haystack because the label a given company uses to tag a particular data element is not standardized; therefore, it is often unknown to external users. For this reason, the author had recommended earlier either printing out a hard copy of the Consolidated Statements of Operations or saving a PDF or screenshot of the financial statement and displaying the data value in the "XML Source" pane on the right-hand side of your screen.

Step 4: Importing XBRL data to Excel.

When you scroll down the instance document on the "XML Source" pane, about three-quarters of the way down the list, you will find a data element named "ns8:NetIncomeLoss" with a <value> of "14013000000" (for fiscal year ending on Sep. 25, 2010). Refer to your printed hard copy or screenshot of the Consolidated Statements of Operations for Apple Inc. You can verify that the two amounts match each other, and you will also learn that the company uses the label of "ns8:NetIncomeLoss" to tag its "Net Income."

Now, click on <value> (next to its associated amount of 14013000000), and drag it to cell A1 on your Excel worksheet or any other field in which you would like to map the XBRL data element labeled "ns8:NetIncomeLoss". Click on the "Developer" tab in the Excel Ribbon on top of the window and choose "Import". Excel will display an "Import XML" window. Again, you need to navigate to your "XBRL" subdirectory to select the same "aapl-20120929.xml" file. After you press the "Import" button at the bottom of the window, Excel will import and place Apple Inc.'s "Net Income" for all of the reporting periods – in this example, for 2010, 2011 and 2012 – below the XBRL data element of "ns8:NetIncomeLoss". You should label the data with the corresponding year by referring to your printed hard copy or screenshot of the Consolidated Statements of Earnings, as shown in Figure 12.

Following the same procedures, you can map Apple Inc.'s XBRL data element equivalent to "Net Sales" onto your Excel spreadsheet. Scroll down the XML Source pane, about halfway down the list, to find the "Net Sales" or the XBRL equivalent data element of "ns8:SalesRevenueNet" to map it to cell D1 on your Excel worksheet. Following the procedures described above, repeat the same process for the "Net Sales" data for the last three years. At the bottom of the window, right-click on the Excel worksheet tab labeled "Sheet 1" and rename it as "XBRL Data" and rename "Sheet 2" as "Report" (see Figure 13). Save the Excel workbook in your "XBRL"

Figure 12. Mapping and importing XBRL data

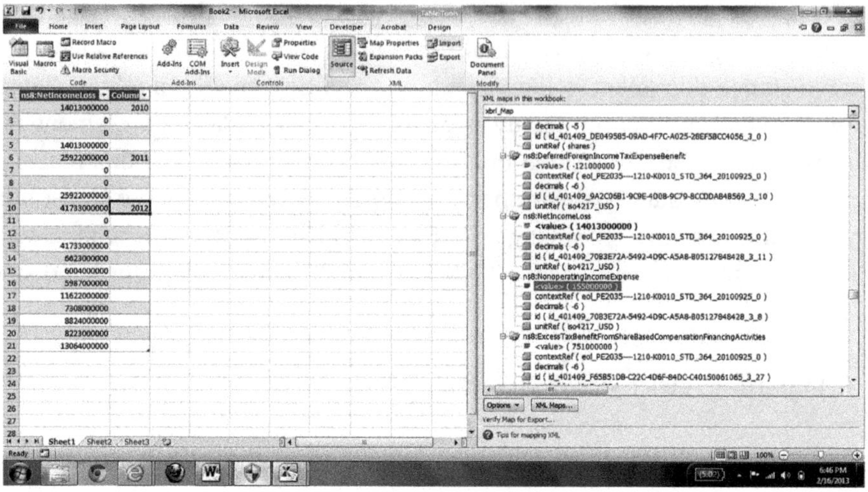

Figure 13. Renaming worksheets

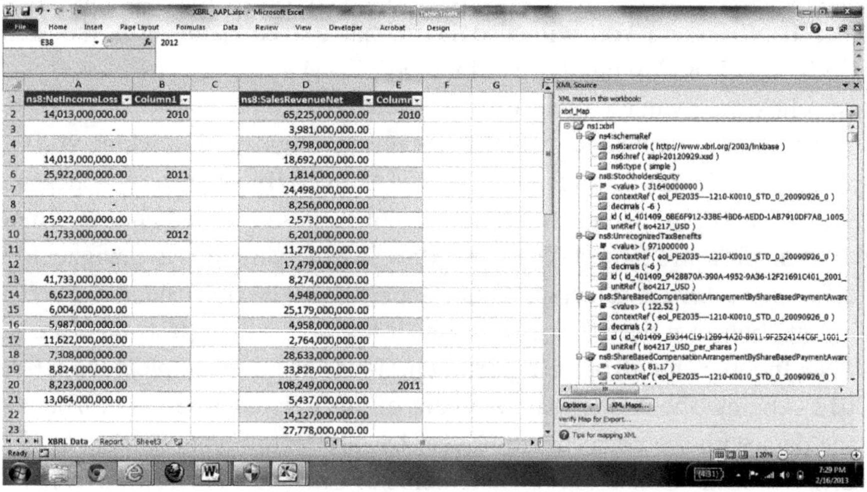

subdirectory as "AAPL_XBRL". Later, the "XBRL Data" Excel worksheet will serve as a template for importing all of the necessary XBRL data and the "Report" Excel worksheet that will be used for the trend analyses and reports.

Step 5: Processing XBRL data on Excel.

On the "Report" Excel worksheet, you can set up a section to calculate the three-year Net Profit Ratio trend analysis for Apple Inc. The next step is to link all of the necessary data from your "XBRL Data" Excel worksheet to your "Report" Excel worksheet. For example, the formula pane of the "Report" Excel worksheet displays the content of cell D6 (see Figure 14). The technical meaning of "='XBRL Data'!A2" is that the value of cell D6 on the "Report" Excel worksheet is equal to the value of cell A2 on the "XBRL Data" Excel worksheet within the same Excel workbook. You should also set up all of the formulas needed for the Net Profit Ratio trend analysis. For example, the formula in cell F9 is "=F6/F7", and in cell F11, the formula is "=(F9-E9)". You only need to enter each of these formulas once and then copy and paste them to the other years to save time. Click the "Save File" icon to save your Excel workbook.

Following the same procedure, you can download Apple Inc.'s financial statement data for 2009 (which includes data for 2008 and 2007) and for as many years as you need after 2009 to complete your analysis. If you need to expend your Excel worksheet to include more years for a longer trend analysis, it will be simple because you have set up the XBRL mapping and the "Report" Excel worksheet already. You will only need a minute or two to retrieve all of the necessary data without any "input errors", which is a significant gain in both efficiency and accuracy.

To complete the demonstration, the author wishes to indicate that, except for the companies that took part in the SEC's voluntary XBRL filing program, most filers

Figure 14. The Report worksheet

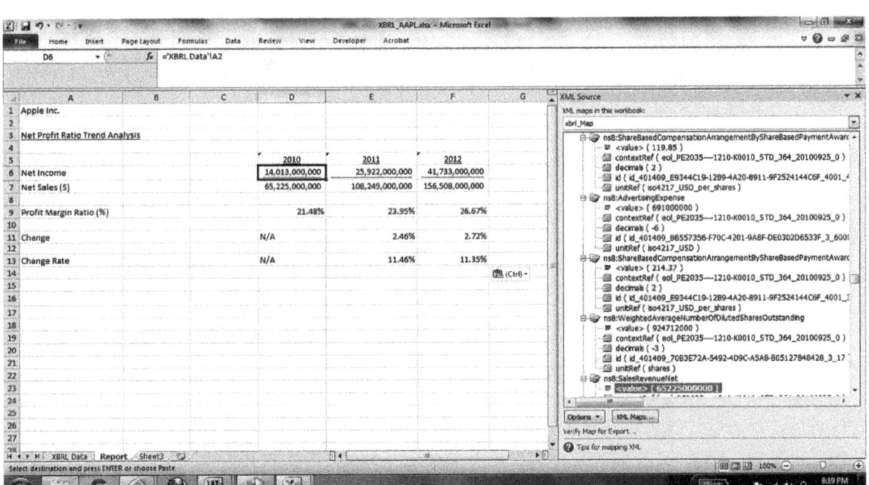

have started to file their financial reports in the XBRL format after the SEC's XBRL conversion mandate in 2009. Nevertheless, the New EDGAR system is "backward-compatible," so you can continue to download their HTML financial statements at the document level from the SEC by following similar procedures when searching for your target company (Apple Inc. for our example). After you navigate to the "Filings List" window (see Figure 5), click on the "Next 40" button at the bottom-right of the window until you find Apple Inc.'s 10-K report for 2008. Click on the "Documents" button, and a "Filing Detail" window (see Figure 15) will open up.

This time, you will need to click on the "d10k.htm" link (marked "Seq. 1") under "Document". The EDGAR system will provide you with the full 10-K report in HTML. You will have to sift through the report to manually find the data needed for your analysis, and then you will have to manually enter the amounts in the "Report" Excel worksheet. This manual entry is much slower than XBRL data import, and more importantly, it is much more susceptible to "input errors" (Fang, 2009; Du, Vasarhelyi & Zheng, 2013). However, if you search for information online or in your saved PDF, you can improve your search accuracy and efficiency because these formats maintain the integrity of the reports at the document level. By using the search function – "Ctrl" and "f" is the shortcut for most programs – you can instantly locate every occurrence of a given word or phrase in your document. This method is still subject to human error though; you need to be very careful of misspellings.

Figure 15. The "Filing Detail" window (HTML)

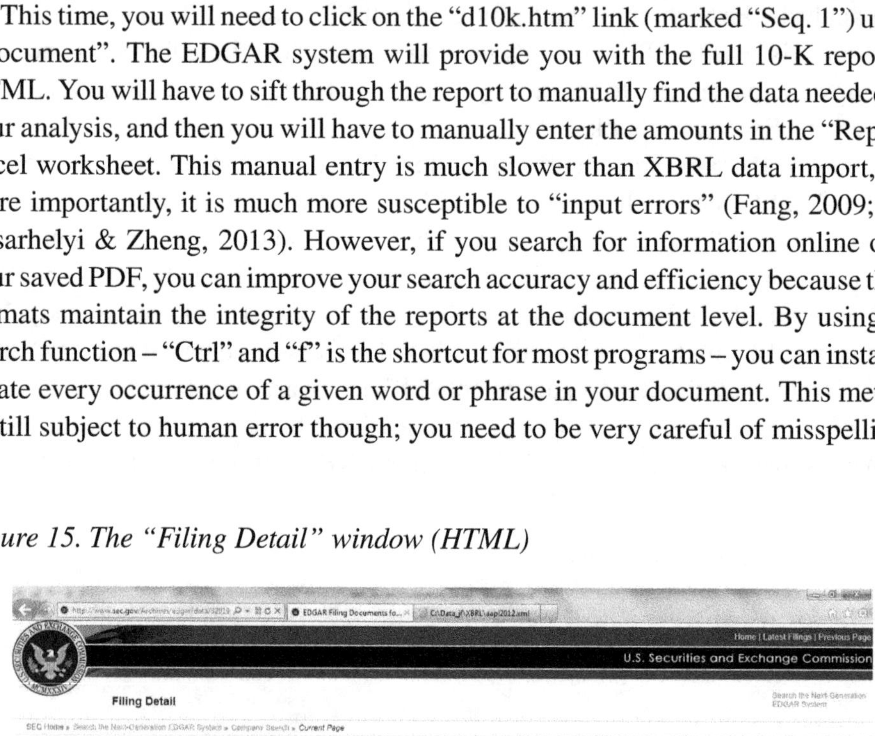

FUTURE RESEARCH DIRECTIONS

More and more companies throughout the world are adopting XBRL for financial reporting, and more and more sophisticated and user-friendly IDEAs are developed, driven by stronger market demands and the need for financial information efficiency with regards to both distribution speed and content accuracy (XBRL US, 2016). Consequently, as demonstrated in the background section above, capital market efficiency will improve as well, both domestically and internationally. Going forward, in addition to conducting similar follow-up studies to monitor the effects of XBRL for financial reporting on EMH for international markets, it will be important to promote the global adoption of XBRL for financial reporting and to search for more and better ways to develop more powerful IDEAs by successfully integrating XBRL with other information technologies, such as cloud computing, artificial intelligence, ASP, big data, and data analytics. The combined and coordinated efforts of information systems, finance, and accounting researchers and professionals will help achieve these goals faster.

CONCLUSION

Over the past five years, the SEC has made considerable progress in building a functional IDEA system. It has successfully implemented the Next-Generation EDGAR system, which provides its users with many convenient search options such as multiple links and RSS (really simple syndication) feeds. This new system is "backward-compatible" and seamlessly combines the old document level EDGAR system with the new data element level IDEA system. Thus, a user can retrieve a company's financial data in the XBRL format at data element level as well as in the electronic document level in the HTML format.

In this chapter, the author has explained all of the necessary XBRL related concepts, demonstrated how to directly retrieve XBRL data from financial reports filed with the SEC, and illustrated how to import the necessary data into Excel 2010 using the Windows operating system. To be better prepared to handle this challenge of increased XBRL financial data reporting in the near future, business schools and institutions with modest resources should train their faculty, students and/or staff with the necessary XBRL theories and skills. By now, most of the big software houses have developed their own proprietary XBRL modules to work with their Enterprise Resource Planning systems for filing financial reports with the SEC and for retrieving IDEA data for financial analyses. However, Microsoft Excel remains the most cost-effective and accessible XML-capable software for most users of limited resources.

REFERENCES

Aguilar, M. K. (2009, February). SEC Mandates XBRL; Filings to Start by July 2009. *Compliance Week*, *6*(61), 14–15.

Bizarro, P., & Garcia, A. (2010). XBRL—Beyond the basics. *The CPA Journal*, *80*(5), 62.

Cable, R., & Healy, P. (2013, May). XBRL in the accounting curriculum. *Paper presented at the American Accounting Association Mid-Atlantic Region Annual Meeting*, Parsippany, NJ.

Capozzoli, E., & Farewell, S. (2010). SEC XBRL filing requirements: An instructional case on tagging financial statement disclosures. *Issues in Accounting Education*, *25*(3), 489–511. doi:10.2308/iace.2010.25.3.489

Corkern, S. M., & Morgan, M. I. (2012). Introduce XBRL to business students. *American Journal of Business Education*, *5*(3), 319–323.

Debreceny, R., & Farewell, S. (2010). XBRL in the Accounting Curriculum. *Issues in Accounting Education*, *25*(3), 379–403. doi:10.2308/iace.2010.25.3.379

Du, H., Vasarhelyi, M. A., & Zheng, X. (2013). XBRL mandate: Thousands of filing Errors and so what? *Journal of Information Systems*, *27*(1), 61–78. doi:10.2308/isys-50399

Fama, E. F. (1970). Efficient capital markets: A review of theory and empirical work. *The Journal of Finance*, *25*(2), 383–417. doi:10.2307/2325486

Fang, J. (2009). How CPAs can master XBRL. *The CPA Journal*, *79*(5), 70.

Fang, J. (2011). Why is the U.S. XBRL conversion process so slow? *The CPA Journal*, *81*(1), 1.

Fang, J. (2013). The progress of XBRL conversion: Reviewing the rules, consequences, and potential remedies. *The CPA Journal*, *83*(2), 68.

Harris, T., & Morsfield, S. (2012). An evaluation of the current state and future of XBRL and interactive data for investors and analysts (White Paper No. 3). *Columbia University, Center for Excellence in Accounting and Security Analysis*.

Hoffelder, K. (2012). *Finance Execs Find XBRL Useless*. Retrieved December 20, 2013 from http://ww2.cfo.com/gaap-ifrs/2012/11/finance-execs-find-xbrl-useless/

Jones, A., & Willis, M. (2003). The challenge of XBRL: Business reporting for the investor. *Balance Sheet*, *11*(3), 29–37. doi:10.1108/09657960310491172

Liu, C. (2013). XBRL: A new global paradigm for financial reporting. *Journal of Global Information Management, 21*(3), 60–80. doi:10.4018/jgim.2013070104

Provost, T. (2013). *No-so-happy anniversary, XBRL.* Retrieved December 20, 2013 from http://ww2.cfo.com/gaap-ifrs/2013/01/not-so-happy-anniversary-xbrl

SEC. (2009). *Interactive Data to Improve Financial Reporting*. Retrieved December 12, 2013 from http://www.sec.gov/rules/final/2009/33-9002.pdf

Sheridan, B., & Drew, J. (2012, June). The future is now: XBRL emerges as career niche. *Journal of Accountancy.* Retrieved May 23, 2016 from http://www.journalofaccountancy.com/issues/2012/jun/20124962.html

Taylor, E. Z., & Dzuranin, A. C. (2010). Interactive financial reporting: An introduction to eXtensible Business Reporting Language (XBRL). *Issues in Accounting Education, 25*(1), 71–83. doi:10.2308/iace.2010.25.1.71

Tribunella, T., & Tribunella, H. (2010). Using XBRL to analyze financial statements. *The CPA Journal, 80*(3), 69.

XBRL US. (2016). *Who else uses XBRL?* Retrieved May 25, 2016 from https://www.xbrl.org/the-standard/why/who-else-uses-xbrl

KEY TERMS AND DEFINITIONS

EDGAR: The Electronic Data Gathering, Analysis, and Retrieval system, or EDGAR, is the data depository established by the Securities and Exchange Commission (SEC) in order to store its registrants' electronic filings of all the required financial reports in HTML format at the document level. It has been upgraded to Interactive Data Electronic Applications (IDEA) since 2011.

HTML: Hypertext Markup Language is a computer language devised to allow webpage and website creation. It provides detailed formatting tags for static textual contents such as font, color, image, and table.

IDEA: Interactive Data Electronic Applications (IDEA), or the Next-Generation EDGAR system, is the new data depository established by the Securities and Exchange Commission (SEC) to store its registrants' electronic filings of all the required financial reports in XBRL format at the data element level. It has replaced the old Electronic Data Gathering, Analysis, and Retrieval (EDGAR) system since 2011.

Registrant: A registrant is an interchangeable name of filer or issuer who is required to file his or her company's financial reports with the SEC.

SEC's XBRL Mandate: In April 2009, the Securities and Exchange Commission (SEC) issued a mandate to require all registrants to convert their financial reports from the Hyper Text Markup Language (HTML) format under the old Electronic Data Gathering, Analysis, and Retrieval (EDGAR) system at the document level to the eXtensible Business Reporting Language (XBRL) format under IDEA, or the Next-Generation EDGAR, at both the document level and the data element level.

XBRL: eXtensible Business Reporting Language is a subset of XML. It is specifically designed for business reporting and exchanging business information.

XML: Extensible Markup Language, or XML, is a global and freely available standard. It follows a set of rules and specifications to code documents into a format that is readable by both humans and computers.

ENDNOTE

1 RR Donnelley provided a "XBRL Filing Dashboard" on its homepage to report daily SEC XBRL compliance statuses. The company took the dashboard off of its website around the end of March 2014, when most registrants had fully complied with the SEC's XBRL Mandate.

Section 2

Empirical Studies on Publicly Accessible Data Sets

Chapter 5
Principals and Student Achievement:
A Comparative Study of Eight Countries

S. Marshall Perry
Saint Mary's College of California, USA

Karen M. Sealy
Independent Educational Consultant, USA

Héctor X. Ramírez-Pérez
Universidad Panamericana, Mexico

Thomas C. DeNicola
Independent Researcher, USA

Yair Cohen
Independent Researcher, USA

ABSTRACT

Connections between principal leadership activities, school context, and student achievement are examined within this paper. Data for this quantitative study are from the 2013 Teaching and Learning International Survey (TALIS) and the 2012 Programme for International Student Assessment (PISA). The eight countries of examination participated in both the TALIS and PISA and the researchers merged datasets, yielding a study sample of 1,301 schools. This paper supports a

DOI: 10.4018/978-1-5225-3616-1.ch005

context-specific view of instructional leadership. When looking across countries, the researchers found different practices were more strongly associated with the academic achievement of students, and suggest that school leaders have a meaningful overall relationship with academic achievement, both directly and indirectly. This study therefore supports prior research about the direct and indirect effects of instructional leadership. Further study, which accounts for differences in family academic resources and school-level opportunities to learn, will better illuminate the connection between instructional leadership practices and academic achievement.

INTRODUCTION

Gaining a better understanding of the specific school leadership practices that best predict student achievement is of international importance, even though the existence of a connection is widely presumed. As Robinson (2010) noted:

There is no doubt that this body of evidence about the links between instructional leadership and student outcomes has been noticed by policymakers. For example, it has informed the development of educational leadership standards in the United States (Council of Chief State School Officers, 2008), the work of the National College of School Leadership in England (Leithwood, Day, Harris, & Hopkins, 2006), and the development of a leadership framework for New Zealand principals (New Zealand Ministry of Education, 2008).

As school leaders, principals are often considered central to student success, in terms of enacting organizational practices and translating external policies into terms and conditions that have strong presence in daily interactions between teachers and learners. How specifically might school leadership practices be connected to teachers and students? A (2012) meta-analysis of research studies on principal effectiveness entitled *Ripple Effect: A Syntheses of Research on Principal Influence to Inform Performance Evaluation Design* was conducted by the American Institute for Research. The framework that emerged from the meta-analysis of more than 20 studies provided a framework for understanding principal effectiveness that included direct and indirect effects of principal practices on student achievement.

The foundation of the ripple effect theory is principal practice. This is informed by principal knowledge and dispositions and can take different forms including traditional manager, supervisor of standards, adaptive leader, instructional leader, and leader of leaders. This behavior has direct effects upon teacher quality, instructional quality, and student achievement, and can be mediated by school conditions and community contexts. There can also be indirect effects of principal practice, which can include providing feedback to teachers to signal preferred methods of instruction, allocating resources in concert with priorities, or having a role in teacher evaluation based upon student learning.

While ripple effect theory includes school conditions and community contexts that can mediate principal practice quality, it does not identify relevant principal constructs such as the principal's life experiences. Nor does ripple effect theory identify the barriers to principal efficacy in supporting high student achievement.

Although effective school leadership is a common subject of inquiry, researchers have not uncovered the context-specific leadership practices that become available using the most recent international datasets from the Organisation for Economic Co-operation and Development (OECD). The objectives of the chapter are to address this concern through the following research questions:

- What are the relationships among principal leadership practices activities, school culture and climate, perceived hindrances, professional background, and student achievement in the countries of Australia, Finland, Latvia, Mexico, Portugal, Romania, Singapore, and Spain?
- How does the nature of these relationships differ by country?

To answer these questions, the researchers merged variables from two datasets, the 2013 Teaching and Learning International Survey (TALIS) principal questionnaire and the 2012 Programme for International Student Assessment (PISA) student assessment. Individual student level PISA data on achievement in mathematics, reading, and science were first merged to create school mean scores. These data were then matched with TALIS principal data for the subset of schools that participated in both the PISA and TALIS administrations. The resultant dataset included 1,301 schools from the countries of Australia, Finland, Latvia, Mexico, Portugal, Romania, Singapore, and Spain. These countries were the only ones that allowed for matching at the school level. All eight countries were included for study to maximize sample size and geographical diversity.

BACKGROUND

Leadership Practices

Leadership styles that principals employ are reflective of their training and experience. Deming (1986) described the necessity of building trusting relationships, celebrating differences, and have a focus on continuous improvement throughout the organization. He asserted the attention on individuals as people, not as statistical factors within an organization. Senge (1990) took the organizational perspective that each part of the organization could be leveraged to make improvements through a comprehensive understanding of systems thinking. The system of any organization is an interconnection of the deep personal knowledge and beliefs of the people involved, as well as group learning and shared vision. Fullan (2001) bridged the emphasis from organizational behavior in a business frame to educational leadership. Developing teacher leaders, team learning, professional communities, and sharing leadership were central concepts in developing more effective learning organizations.

Kouzes and Posner (2002) echoed the concentration on human capital with a description of five leadership practices emphasizing modeling to teach others, sharing leadership, encouraging passion within people, moving together towards goals, and challenging the status quo. DuFour, DuFour, and Eaker (2008) built upon the human capital focus within the educational leadership frame by developing a deeper understanding of professional learning communities. The priorities of the learning communities included working together toward a common vision through collaborative work, data-informed decision making, and ongoing efforts of improvement. Manley and Hawkins (2010) expanded upon contemporary educational leadership literature by describing the bridge from theory to practice. The core function of a leader within a learning organization is to design, teach, and steward. From an honest understanding of current reality through creating a shared vision, the leader's role is to design a system that moves toward the collective goals of the stakeholders involved, teach others how to move toward that vision, and support them along the way.

Studies published within the past decade have added to the growing body of literature that has been written in support of the direct and indirect effects of instructional leadership on student achievement (Waters, Marzano, & McNulty, 2004; Provost, Boscardin, & Wells, 2010; Soehner & Ryan, 2011; Taylor & LaCava, 2011; and Clifford, Behrstock-Sherratt, & Fetters, 2012).

Provost et al. (2010) discussed the themes discovered when studying the perceptions of principal leadership behaviors from the viewpoints of educational administrators. The two main themes that emerged through the analysis of responses connected with more effective principals were instructional leadership and site-based management. Through the lens of site-based management, the factors that were emphasized included shared governance and accountability, as well as an implementation of goals that focused on student learning. Soehner & Ryan (2011) discussed the indirect effect of principal leadership on student achievement. Through the review of recent literature, the authors' discussed the links of teachers as leaders and their direct impact on student achievement, and then continued to discuss how the principal leadership directly influences the framework of teacher leadership within the building.

In contrast, Taylor & LaCava (2011) framed their study around the actions that would lead most directly to urgent and significant changes resulting in student achievement. The following actions were identified by Taylor and LaCava (2011):

Focusing the school's culture on all students achieving a high level, making decisions for student learning, data-based decision making, and personally investigating the change. Monitoring of instruction and assessments within the school year leading to the annual accountability assessment represents personally investing in the change. Furthermore, principals specifically identified curricular and instructional foci of intervention and research-based instruction particularly for student subgroups. (p. 239)

Clifford et al. (2012) considered the existing research on the direct and indirect impact of principal leadership on student achievement. The policy perspectives that emerged from their review of research were: "1. A practice perspective from which principal effectiveness is defined by the quality of the principal's leadership or administrative practices (and) 2. An impact perspective from which principal effectiveness is defined by the principal's impact on his or her school" (Clifford et al., 2012, p 4).

To further describe the impact of the principal on teacher quality, instructional quality, and student achievement, a framework was described as *the ripple effect* which "reflects the broad impact and context-dependent nature of principals' practice," (Clifford et al., 2012, p. 7). "Although more research on principal effectiveness is needed, available research provides a framework for understanding principal effectiveness that includes principals' practice, direct effects on schools and teachers, and indirect effects on instruction and learning," (Clifford et al., 2012, p. 13).

Data-informed decision-making is a process in which the gap between the current reality and goals are considered, analyzed, and acted upon (Ovando & Cavazos, 2004; Ayala et. al, 2008; Bakula, 2010; and Lange, Range, & Welsh, 2012). One step in employing data-informed focus on improvement is to have a clear understanding of how the program measures against the established goals that are aligned vision and mission. Ovando and Cavazos (2004) applied a multiple case study approach to examine how principals use instructional leadership to improve academic success. The three dimensions of instructional leadership that were highlighted within the study included the development of student-centered academic performance goals and implementation, as well as school culture and instructional management. By sharing the responsibilities of developing formal goals with the faculty and staff, an interdisciplinary accountability system can be established and the gap between goals and achievement can be traversed.

School Culture and Climate

Deal and Peterson (1999) described a school's culture as consisting of unwritten rules and traditions, norms, and expectations that are through all aspects of the organization. Culture is found in the actions, discussions, and interactions between people. It is also evident in how teachers discuss their students and their work amongst colleagues. Various research studies from the late 1970s and early 1980s, suggested that organizational culture was consistently identified when describing effective schools as being purposeful and conducive to learning (Levine & Lezotte, 1990). Clear, student-centered missions that illuminated high expectations for the organization were the embedded within cultures, becoming a dominant theme within the literature.

More recently, the focus of organizational culture shifted to implementing change in schools. In 1998, Fullan delineated the improvement of teaching and learning through the lens of strong organizational culture. Studies suggested that the static organizational culture lead to a stall in results and a lack of lasting improvements. The counter balance of research suggested that improvement efforts in organizational cultures resulted in a reinforcement of strong educational missions and ultimately positive and enduring change (Rossman, Corbett, & Firestone, 1988).

A shift in focus from teaching to learning was espoused by Dufour and Mattos (2013) as a key lever in improving student outcomes through establishing positive school cultures. According to DuFour and Mattos (2013), "The most powerful strategy for improving both teaching and learning, however, is not by micromanaging instruction but by creating the collaborative culture and collective responsibility of a professional learning community" (p. 37).

Research published by the Center on Organization and Restructuring of Schools (Newmann & Wehlage, 1995); the National Commission on Teaching and America's Future (Carroll, Fulton, & Doerr, 2010); the Annenberg Institute for School Reform (2005); the Wallace Foundation (Louis, Leithwood, Wahlstrom, & Anderson, 2010); and the American Educational Research Association (Holland, 2005) provide a foundation of literature in support of the impact of culture on teaching and learning. As a review of the research on organizational culture concluded, "The collective results of these studies offer an unequivocal answer to the question about whether the literature supports the assumption that student learning increases when teachers participate in professional learning communities. The answer is a resounding and encouraging yes" (Vescio, Ross, & Adams, 2008, p. 87).

School climate influences perceptions of stress, teaching efficacy, and job satisfaction (Collie et al. 2012), as well as organizational commitment (Collie, Shapka, & Perry, 2011). The theoretical framework on which Leech and Fulton's (2008) study was built included the earlier findings of Block and Rafaeli (1993). Reform in education requires a cultural change. "Block (1993) proposed that organizations must embrace democratic participative structures to effect cultural change. These structures demand a new vision of leadership, in which the decisional ownership and accountability is distributed among all members of the organization" (Leech & Fulton, 2008, p. 632). Considering the impact of shared decision making on employees, they referenced a study from the mid-1980s. "In an examination of employees participating in quality circles, Rafaeli (1985) reported that employees involved in participatory management have a sense of influence and greater interaction with other employees" (Leech & Fulton, 2008, p. 632).

Perceived Hindrances

School poverty, location, size, and lack of resources, including parental involvement, can contribute to negative perceptions and higher degrees of social and behavioral problems in both students and teachers at a school, including absenteeism and decreased morale (Garmezy, 1991; Welsh, 2000; Wilson, 2004; Gottfredson et al., 2005; Louis et al, 2010; and Urick et al., 2015). While these issues might be characteristics of struggling schools, school leadership has been shown to mediate the effects of student background and broader social issues (McEvoy & Welker, 2000).

The problems associated with teacher absenteeism are a focus of increasing concern among educators. In a financial cost study conducted by Hill (1982), the researcher estimated the costs associated with paying absent teachers and their substitutes at 2 billon dollars per year. Norton (1994) reported that 71% of school personnel directors reported teacher absenteeism as one of the leading problems that they face. Norton went on to espouse that the difficulty of finding qualified substitute personnel is also a growing problem for many school districts.

Research literature supports a connection between teacher absenteeism, student achievement, and school climate. In a study conducted by Summers and Raivetz (1982), the researchers explored the relationship between fourth-grade reading results and teacher absenteeism. The findings suggest that teacher absenteeism adversely affected student achievement related to reading assessment results. Negative effects of teacher absenteeism and student achievement were also delineated in a study reported by O'Brien et al., (1985). Imants and Van Zoelen (1995) explored the relationship between school climate on teacher absenteeism. The findings of the study suggest that collegial relationships and the leadership style of the principal were associated with the rate of teacher absences. Dworkin et al. (1990) ascertained that teachers who perceived that they had supportive principals were less likely to be absent than teachers that perceived that their principal was unsupportive.

Literature supports a connection between parental involvement and students' success in school (Pattnaik & Sriram, 2010). When schools engage families in discourse related to their children's education, parents are more connected to the school and student achievement increases (Epstein et al., 2009). According to Epstein et al. (1997) parental involvement includes the following five dimensions: parenting, assisting with homework, communicating with the school, volunteering at the school, and participating in school decision-making.

Principals play a key role in creating and sustaining successful parent-school partnerships. According to Gordon and Seashore-Louis (2009), principals must be willing and able to delegate decision-making power to stakeholders while concurrently guiding the process. Topics related to budgeting, student safety, curriculum, and policy lend themselves well to community and parental input. This process of shared decision-making and collaboration among stakeholders creates a sense of ownership and responsibility for the success of students. The organization of a system that fosters parental involvement requires a multi-dimensional approached, strong leadership, a focus on student learning, equity, and partnerships at the school and classroom levels (Epstein & Rodriguez-Jansorn, 2004).

Principal Professional Background

Principals are the instructional leaders and building managers of their schools. The direct and indirect influence of principals on the students in which they serve has been described in multiple studies (e.g., Leithwood et al., 2006; Clifford et al., 2012). Qualities and capacities that are evident in effective leaders include goal setting, improving instructional practices, and measuring changes in student learning (Prytula, Noonan, & Hellsten, 2013). Additional leadership attributes include shared purpose, prioritizing teaching and learning, and allocating time and resources for meaningful professional development for their faculty and staff (Leithwood, Strauss, & Anderson, 2007).

Principals are required to play multiple roles in their positions as school building leaders. Pierson (2014) summarized the roles into "human capital manager; school operations manager; instructional leader; visionary; and community and family outreach coordinator" (p. 8). Previous leadership experiences may increase the likelihood of teachers moving into building leader positions. As found through an exploratory study, Muth, Borwne-Ferrgno, Bellamy, Fulmer, and Silver (2013) identified patterns in which participants had "1) expressed commitment to becoming formal leaders, (2) had already held responsible leadership roles in their schools working with adults, or (3) had earned an advanced degree before entering a preparation program were more likely to take administrative posts" (p. 122).

Through a meta-analysis of 70 published studies, Waters et al. (2004) found that leadership does matter. The findings indicate that when leadership improves, student achievement does, as well. The 21 key areas of responsibility of educational leaders included: culture; order; discipline; resources; curriculum, instruction, and assessment; knowledge of curriculum, instruction, and assessment; focus; visibility; contingent rewards; communication; outreach; input; affirmation; relationship; change agent role; optimizer role; ideals and beliefs; monitoring and evaluation; flexibility; situational awareness; and intellectual stimulation.

The professional background of principals may account for their readiness and efficacy in pursuing leadership roles. According to Pierson (2014),

Prior education and professional experience may influence the likelihood that a principal undertakes certain actions as well as the effectiveness of those actions; a principal with a background as an assistant principal, for example, may have a better understanding of how to manage people and other resources at a school and may be a more effective manager than a principal without that experience. Certain educational and professional experiences might better prepare principals to fill the key roles described above and may increase their effectiveness (p. 24).

MAIN FOCUS OF THE CHAPTER

Issues, Controversies, Problems

This paper employed quantitative analysis to address the objectives of the study. Researchers used Statistical Package for the Social Sciences, version 21 to merge datasets and conduct statistical analyses. Variables of study are summarized below.

2013 TALIS Principal Questionnaire:

- Country Identification number
- School Identification number
- Personal (Background) Information: Age (2), Education (3), Experience (4), Status (5), Training (6), Professional Development (7)
- School (Background) Information: Student Characteristics (15)
- School Leadership: Task Responsibility (18), Percentage of Time (19), Leadership Activities (21) [P3], Participation and Collaboration (22)
- School Climate: School Culture (30), School Capacity (31), Student and Teacher Behavior (32)

2012 PISA:

- Country Identification Number
- School Identification Number
- Student Predicted Composite Scores in Science
- Student Predicted Composite Scores in Reading
- Student Predicted Composite Scores in Mathematics

To access the data, researchers navigated the site https://data.oecd.org. This site, developed by the Organisation for Economic Co-operation and Development, houses databases, along with research, articles, and a wide variety of topics and resources to engage with. The topics embedded within the data and larger site include agriculture, development, economy, education, energy, environment, finance, government, health, innovation and technology, jobs, and society. The site also offers a user guide to assist with navigation and use.

Once the data were obtained, researchers first created a new database of school means for the PISA student predicted composite scores in science, reading, and mathematics. Because the data had been transformed from a student level of analysis to a school one, the resultant file was then merged with the TALIS file, and matched based upon country identification number and school identification number. Once the merged dataset was created, there were only 1,301 schools across eight countries from the original PISA dataset. To analyze the relationship between individual items (with ordinal ranking) and mean student achievement in the eight countries, researchers split the file by country identification number and calculated Spearman's rank correlation coefficients using SPSS software.

Australia

Leadership Practices

Percentage of time spent on other tasks in school had a moderate correlation with math ($rho_m = .220$) in which the variables shared 4.8% of the variance. Principals who spent more time on other tasks tended to work in schools with higher average achievement in mathematics.

School Culture and Climate

Providing parents or guardians with information had a moderate correlation with math, reading, and science achievement ($rho_m = .220$, $rho_r = .222$, $rho_s = .233$) in which the variables shared 4.8%, 4.9%, and 5.4% of the variance respectively. Opportunities for parents to actively participate in decisions had a moderate inverse correlation with math ($rho_m = -.201$) in which the variables shared 4.0% of the variance. While providing parents and guardians was directly associated with higher mean achievement, opportunities for parents to actively participate in decisions was associated with lower achievement in mathematics.

Perceived Hindrances

Principal perceptions that inadequate school budget and resources limit their effectiveness had a moderate inverse correlation with math, reading, and science achievement (rho_m= -.276, rho_r = -.208, rho_s = -.236), in which the variables shared 7.6%, 4.3%, and 5.6% of the variance respectively. Teachers' absences had a strong inverse correlation with math, reading, and science achievement (rho_m= -.486, rho_r = -.477, rho_s = -.442) in which the variables shared 23.6%, 22.8%, and 19.5% of the variance respectively. Lack of parent or guardian involvement and support also had a strong inverse correlation with math, reading, and science achievement (rho_m= -.452, rho_r = -.432, rho_s = -.430) in which the variables shared 20.4%, 18.7%, and 18.5% of the variance respectively. In addition, lack of opportunities for teachers' professional development had a moderate inverse correlation with math achievement (rho_m = -.211) in which the variables shared 4.5% of the variance. These four areas that principals perceived as hindrances (inadequate school budgets, teacher absences, lack of parent or guardian involvement and support, and lack of opportunities for teacher professional development) were all associated with lower mean achievement.

Principal Professional Background

There was a moderate correlation between year(s) working in other school management roles had with math, reading, and science achievement (rho_m= .257, rho_r = .240, rho_s = .224), in which the variables shared 6.6%, 5.8%, and 5.0% of the variance respectively. Principals with more years working in other school management roles was associated with higher achieving schools as indicated by mean achievement in mathematics, reading, and science.

Finland

School Culture and Climate

Supporting co-operation among teachers had a weak inverse correlation with math achievement (rho_m = -.193), in which the variables shared 3.7% of the variance. In addition, collaborating with principals from other schools had also a weak inverse correlation with math achievement (rho_m = -.164), in which the variables shared 2.7% of the variance. While the relationships were weak, these relationships illustrate

Table 1. Significant correlations with PISA achievement in Australia

		Mathematics	Reading	Science
Leadership Practices				
Percentage of time spent on other tasks in school	rho	.220*	.146	.137
	r^2	.048	.020	.017
	N	100	100	100
School Culture and Climate				
Providing parents or guardians with information	rho	.220*	.222*	.233*
	r^2	.048	.049	.054
	N	101	101	101
Opportunities for parents to actively participate in decisions	rho	-.201*	-.181	-.192
	r^2	.040	.032	.036
	N	100	100	100
Perceived Hindrances				
Inadequate school budget and resources	rho	-.276**	-.208*	-.236*
	r^2	.076	.043	.056
	N	101	101	101
Teachers' absences	rho	-.486**	-.477**	-.442**
	r^2	.236	.228	.195
	N	101	101	101
Lack of parent or guardian involvement and support	rho	-.452**	-.432**	-.430**
	r^2	.204	.187	.185
	N	101	101	101
Lack of opportunities for teachers' professional development	rho	-.211*	-.152	-.138
	r^2	.045	.023	.017
	N	101	101	101
Principal Professional Background				
Year(s) working in other school management roles	rho	.257**	.240*	.224*
	r^2	.066	.058	.050
	N	104	104	104

** Correlation is significant at the 0.01 level (2-tailed).
* Correlation is significant at the 0.05 level (2-tailed).

that principals who support cooperation among teachers or collaborate with other principals tend to work in schools with lower achievement in mathematics.

Perceived Hindrances

Inadequate school budget and resources had a weak to moderate inverse correlation with math and reading achievement (rho_m = -.164, rho_r = -.219), in which the variables shared 2.7% and 4.8% of the variance respectively. In addition, lack of parent or guardian involvement and support had a weak inverse correlation with reading achievement (rho_r = -.163), in which the variables shared 2.7% of the variance. In schools where principals perceived that inadequate school budgets and resources or lack of parent or guardian involvement were hindrances, students tended to score lower in mathematics and reading.

Table 2. Significant correlations with PISA achievement in Finland

		Mathematics	Reading	Science
Climate of Collaborative Culture and Communication				
Supporting co-operation among teachers	rho	-.193*	-.114	-.086
	r^2	.037	.012	.006
	N	147	147	147
Collaborating with principals from other schools	rho	-.146	-.163*	-.067
	r^2	.027	.003	.002
	N	147	147	147
Perceived Hindrances				
Inadequate school budget and resources	rho	-.164*	-.219**	-.137
	r^2	.027	.048	.017
	N	147	147	147
Lack of parent or guardian involvement and support	rho			
	r^2	.020	.027	.004
	N	147	147	147

** Correlation is significant at the 0.01 level (2-tailed).
* Correlation is significant at the 0.05 level (2-tailed).

Latvia

Leadership Practices

Percentage of time spent on student interactions had a moderate inverse correlation with math, reading, and science achievement (rho_m = -.266, rho_r = -.232, rho_s = -.234) in which the variables shared 7.1%, 5.4%, and 5.5% of the variance respectively. In addition, Percentage of time spent on other tasks in school had a moderate correlation with math (rho_m = .212) in which the variables shared 4.5% of the variance. Degree of distributed leadership in the school had a moderate inverse correlation with math achievement (rho_m= -.2.10), in which the variables shared 4.4% of the variance. Only one item within this variable was associated with higher mean achievement in mathematics: the percentage of time principals spend on other tasks. Other items, including time spent on student interactions and the degree of distributed leadership, were associated with lower achieving schools.

School Culture and Climate

Opportunities for staff to actively participate in decisions had a moderate inverse correlation with math (rho_m = -.209) in which the variables shared 4.4% of the variance. Opportunities for parents to actively participate in decisions had a moderate inverse correlation with math (rho_m = -.204) in which the variables shared 4.2% of the variance. In addition, there is a collaborative culture had also a moderate inverse correlation with math achievement (rho_m = -.225) in which the variables shared 5.1% of the variance. These three items in School culture and climate were all associated with lower student achievement in mathematics.

Perceived Hindrances

Teachers' absences had a moderate correlation with math, reading, and science achievement (rho_m= .204, rho_r = .204, rho_s = .206), in which the variables shared 4.2%, 4.2%, and 4.2% of the variance respectively. This finding was surprising and unique to Latvia. Principals who perceived that teacher absences were hindrances tended to work in schools with higher academic achievement on average.

Principal Professional Background

There was a moderate inverse correlation between year(s) working as a teacher in total had with science achievement (rho_s = -.203), in which the variables shared 4.1% of the variance respectively. This finding was also unexpected. Principals with

Table 3. Significant correlations with PISA achievement in Latvia

		Mathematics	Reading	Science
Leadership Practices				
Degree of Distributed Leadership in the School	rho	-.210*	-.152	-.178
	r^2	.044	.023	.029
	N	103	103	103
Percentage of time spent on student interactions	rho	-.266**	-.232*	-.234*
	r^2	.071	.054	.055
	N	103	103	103
Percentage of time spent on other tasks in school	rho	.212*	.182	.160
	r^2	.045	.032	.026
	N	103	103	103
School Culture and Climate				
Opportunities for staff to actively participate in decisions	rho	-.209*	-.148	-.190
	r^2	.044	.020	.032
	N	103	103	103
Opportunities for parents to actively participate in decisions	rho	-.204*	-.129	-.148
	r^2	.042	.014	.020
	N	103	103	103
There is a collaborative culture	rho	-.225*	-.188	-.129
	r^2	.051	.032	.014
	N	103	103	103
Perceived Hindrances				
Teachers' absences	rho	.204*	.204*	.206*
	r^2	.042	.042	.042
	N	102	102	102
Principal Professional Background				
Year(s) working as a teacher in total	rho	-.166	-.076	-.203*
	r^2	.026	.005	.041
	N	102	102	102

** Correlation is significant at the 0.01 level (2-tailed).

* Correlation is significant at the 0.05 level (2-tailed).

more years working as a teacher tended to work in schools with lower achievement in science.

Mexico

Leadership Practices

Degree of distributed leadership in the school had a moderate inverse correlation with reading, and science achievement (rho_r = -.207, rho_s = -.195), in which the variables shared 4.3%, and 3.8% of the variance respectively. Principals who believed they distributed leadership tended to work in schools with lower achievement in reading and science.

School Culture and Climate

Percentage of time spent on interactions with community, business and industry had a moderate inverse correlation with reading (rho_r = -.209) in which the variables shared 4.4% of the variance. Opportunities for staff to actively participate in decisions had a moderate inverse correlation with math, reading, and science achievement (rho_m= -.261, rho_r = -.280, rho_s = -.309) in which the variables shared 6.8%, 7.8%, and 9.5% of the variance respectively. Opportunities for parents to actively participate in decisions had a moderate inverse correlation with reading and science (rho_r = -.206, rho_s = -.177), in which the variables shared 4.2% and 3.1% of the variance. Principals who promote a higher degree of collaboration and communication in these items tend to lead schools that have lower achievement.

Perceived Hindrances

Inadequate school budget and resources had a moderate inverse correlation with math, reading, and science achievement (rho_m= -.236, rho_r = -.189, rho_s = -.223) in which the variables shared 5.6%, 3.6%, and 5.0% of the variance respectively. Teachers' career-based wage system also had a moderate correlation with reading achievement (rho_r = .201), in which the variables shared 4.0% of the variance. Principals that perceived that inadequate budgets were hindrances tended to work in schools with lower achievement, while principals who were more concerned with teachers' career-based wages tended to work in schools with higher achievement in reading.

Table 4. Significant correlations with PISA achievement in Mexico

		Mathematics	Reading	Science
Leadership Practices				
Degree of Distributed Leadership in the School	rho	-.151	-.207*	-.195*
	r^2	.023	.043	.038
	N	137	137	137
School Culture and Climate				
Percentage of time spent on interactions with community, business and industry	rho	-.165	-.209*	-.142
	r^2	.026	.044	.020
	N	133	133	133
Opportunities for staff to actively participate in decisions	rho	-.261**	-.280**	-.309**
	r^2	.068	.078	.095
	N	137	137	137
Opportunities for parents to actively participate in decisions	rho	-.134	-.206*	-.177*
	r^2	.017	.042	.031
	N	137	137	137
Perceived Hindrances				
Inadequate school budget and resources	rho	-.236**	-.189*	-.223**
	r^2	.056	.036	.050
	N	138	138	138
Teachers' career-based wage system	rho	.120	.201*	.146
	r^2	.014	.040	.020
	N	137	137	137

** Correlation is significant at the 0.01 level (2-tailed).
* Correlation is significant at the 0.05 level (2-tailed).

Portugal

Leadership Practices

Checking for mistakes in school procedures had a weak correlation with math achievement (rho_m = .176), in which the variables shared 3.1% of the variance. Checking for mistakes in school procedures was associated with slightly higher mean achievement in mathematics.

School Culture and Climate

Percentage of time spent on interactions with community, business and industry had a weak inverse correlation with reading achievement (rho_r = -.182) in which the variables shared 3.3% of the variance. In addition, collaborating with principals from other schools had a weak inverse correlation with reading achievement (rho_r = -.176) in which the variables shared 3.1% of the variance. Spending more time on interactions with the community or collaborating with principals from other schools was associated with slightly lower achievement in reading.

Perceived Hindrances

Inadequate school budget and resources had a weak inverse correlation with math achievement (rho_m= -.184), in which the variables shared 3.4% of the variance. Teachers' absences had a moderate inverse correlation with math, reading, and science achievement (rho_m= -.222, rho_r = -.177, rho_s = -.203) in which the variables shared 4.9%, 3.1%, and 4.1% of the variance respectively. Lack of parent or guardian involvement and support also had a moderate inverse correlation with math, reading, and science achievement (rho_m= -.285, rho_r = -.286, rho_s = -.306) in which the variables shared 8.1%, 8.2%, and 9.4% of the variance respectively. In addition, lack of shared leadership with other school staff members had a weak correlation with reading achievement (rho_r = .178) in which the variables shared 3.2% of the variance. While principal concerns about a lack of shared leadership was associated with slightly higher achievement in reading, the other perceived hindrances (inadequate school resources, teacher absences, and lack of parent or guardian support) were all associated with lower achievement.

Romania

School Culture and Climate

Collaborating with principals from other schools had a weak to moderate inverse correlation with math, reading, and science achievement (rho_m = -.176, rho_r = -.267, rho_s = -.243) in which the variables shared 3.1%, 7.1%, and 5.9% of the variance respectively. Principals who collaborated with principals from other schools tended to work in schools with lower academic achievement.

Table 5. Significant correlations with PISA achievement in Portugal

		Mathematics	Reading	Science
Leadership Practices				
Checking for mistakes in school procedures	rho	.176*	.121	.164
	r^2	.031	.014	.026
	N	137	137	137
School Culture and Climate				
Percentage of time spent on interactions with community, business and industry	rho	-.130	-.182*	-.126
	r^2	.017	.033	.014
	N	135	135	135
Collaborating with principals from other schools	rho	-.111	-.176*	-.106
	r^2	.012	.031	.010
	N	137	137	137
Perceived Hindrances				
Teachers' absences	rho	-.222**	-.177*	-.203*
	r^2	.049	.031	.041
	N	136	136	136
Lack of parent or guardian involvement and support	rho	-.285**	-.286**	-.306**
	r^2	.081	.082	.094
	N	136	136	136
Lack of shared leadership with other school staff members	rho	.142	.178*	.146
	r^2	.020	.032	.020
	N	136	136	136

** Correlation is significant at the 0.01 level (2-tailed).
* Correlation is significant at the 0.05 level (2-tailed).

Perceived Hindrances

Lack of parent or guardian involvement and support had a moderate to strong inverse correlation with math, reading, and science achievement (rho_m= -.366, rho_r = -.287, rho_s = -.244) in which the variables shared 13.4%, 8.2%, and 6.0% of the variance respectively. Schools with lower mean achievement tended to have principals who were concerned about the lack of parent or guardian involvement and support.

Table 6. Significant correlations with PISA achievement in Romania

		Mathematics	Reading	Science
School Culture and Climate				
Collaborating with principals from other schools	rho	-.176*	-.267**	-.243**
	r^2	.031	.071	.059
	N	140	140	140
Perceived Hindrances				
Lack of parent or guardian involvement and support	rho	-.366**	-.287**	-.244**
	r^2	.134	.082	.060
	N	140	140	140

* Correlation is significant at the 0.05 level (2-tailed).
** Correlation is significant at the 0.01 level (2-tailed).

Singapore

Leadership Practices

Resolving problems with the lessons timetable had a weak correlation with science achievement ($rho_s = .173$) in which the variables shared 3.0% of the variance. This was the one leadership practices item associated with higher academic achievement.

School Culture and Climate

Percentage of time spent on interactions with community, business and industry had a weak correlation with science achievement ($rho_s = .162$) in which the variables shared 2.6% of the variance. There is a collaborative culture had a moderate correlation with math, reading, and science achievement ($rho_m = .264$, $rho_r = .260$, $rho_s = .249$), in which the variables shared 7.0%, 6.8%, and 6.2% of the variance respectively. A school climate of mutual respect had a moderate relationship with math, reading, and science achievement ($rho_m = .233$, $rho_r = .201$, $rho_s = .212$), in which the variables shared 5.4%, 4.0%, and 4.5% of the variance respectively. Principals who spent more time on interactions with the community, had more of a collaborative culture, and supported a climate of mutual respect tended to work in schools with higher academic achievement.

Perceived Hindrances

Teachers' absences had a moderate inverse correlation with math, reading, and science achievement (rho_m= -.269, rho_r = -.272, rho_s = -.272) in which the variables shared 7.2%, 7.4%, and 7.4% of the variance respectively. Lack of parent or guardian involvement and support had a strong inverse correlation with math, reading, and science achievement (rho_m= -.446, rho_r = -.435, rho_s = -.437) in which the variables shared 19.9%, 18.9%, and 19.1% of the variance respectively. In addition, lack of shared leadership with other school staff members had a moderate inverse correlation with math, reading, and science achievement (rho_m= -.226, rho_r = -.212, rho_s = -.217) in which the variables shared 5.1%, 4.5%, and 4.7% of the variance respectively. Schools with lower achievement tended to have principals who perceived the following barriers to their efficacy: teacher absences, lack of parent or guardian involvement, and lack of shared leadership.

Principal Personal Background

There was a weak significant inverse correlation between year(s) working in other school management roles and science achievement (rho_s = -.193), in which the variables shared 3.7% of the variance. There was also a weak inverse correlation between year(s) working as a teacher in total and math and science achievement (rho_m = -.166, rho_s = -.164), in which the variables shared 2.8 and 2.7% of the variance respectively. In addition, time in a professional network, mentoring or research activity had a weak to moderate relationship with math, reading, and science achievement (rho_m= .228, rho_r = .247, rho_s = .184), in which the variables shared 5.2%, 6.1%, and 3.4% of the variance respectively. While the relationships were weak, principals with more years working in other school management roles or working as a teacher tended to work in schools with lower mean achievement in mathematics or science. Principals with more time in a professional network, mentoring or research activity tended to work in schools with higher mean achievement.

Spain

Leadership Practices

Percentage of time spent on administrative and leadership tasks had a weak correlation with science achievement (rho_s = .113), in which the variables shared 1.3% of the

Table 7. Significant correlations with PISA achievement in Singapore

		Mathematics	Reading	Science
Leadership Practices				
Resolving problems with the lessons timetable	rho	-.148	-.150	-.173*
	r^2	.020	.020	.030
	N	148	148	148
School Culture and Climate				
Percentage of time spent on interactions with community, business and industry	rho	.156	.135	.162*
	r^2	.023	.017	.026
	N	149	149	149
A school climate of mutual respect	rho	.233**	.201*	.212**
	r^2	.054	.040	.045
	N	148	148	148
There is a collaborative culture	rho	.264**	.260**	.249**
	r^2	.070	.068	.062
	N	149	149	149
Perceived Hindrances				
Teachers' absences	rho	-.269**	-.272**	-.272**
	r^2	.072	.074	.074
	N	149	149	149
Lack of parent or guardian involvement and support	rho	-.446**	-.435**	-.437**
	r^2	.199	.189	.191
	N	149	149	149
Lack of shared leadership with other school staff members	rho	-.226**	-.212**	-.217**
	r^2	.051	.045	.047
	N	149	149	149
Principal Professional Background				
Year(s) working in other school management roles	rho	-.151	-.154	-.193*
	r^2	.023	.023	.037
	N	149	149	149
Year(s) working as a teacher in total	rho	-.166*	-.137	-.164*
	r^2	.028	.017	.027
	N	149	149	149
Time in a professional network, mentoring or research activity	rho	.228**	.247**	.184*
	r^2	.052	.061	.034
	N	135	135	135

** Correlation is significant at the 0.01 level (2-tailed).

* Correlation is significant at the 0.05 level (2-tailed).

variance. In addition, percentage of time spent on student interactions had a weak inverse correlation with math, reading, and science achievement (rho_m= -.175, rho_r = -.174, rho_s = -.199) in which the variables shared 3.1%, 3.0%, and 4.0% of the variance respectively. In addition, important decisions being made by the principal had a weak inverse correlation with science achievement (rho_s = -.126) in which the variables shared 1.6% of the variance. Degree of distributed leadership in the school had a weak to moderate inverse correlation with math, reading, and science achievement (rho_m= -.226, rho_r = -.245, rho_s = -.168) in which the variables shared 5.1%, 6.0%, and 2.8% of the variance respectively. Instructional leadership had a weak correlation with math, reading, and science achievement (rho_m= .116, rho_r = .139, rho_s = .126) in which the variables shared 1.3%, 1.9%, and 1.6% of the variance respectively. Among the leadership practices items, only the percentage of time spent on administrative and leadership tasks and instructional leadership were associated with higher mean student achievement.

School Culture and Climate

Collaborating with teachers to solve discipline problems had a weak inverse correlation with math, reading, and science achievement (rho_m = -.190, rho_r = -.158, rho_s = -.177) in which the variables shared 3.6%, 2.5%, and 3.1% of the variance respectively. Teachers having responsibility for improving teaching skills had a weak correlation with reading achievement (rho_r = .135), in which the variables shared 1.8% of the variance. In addition, teachers having responsibility for learning outcomes had a weak correlation with science achievement (rho_s = .118), in which the variables shared 1.4% of the variance. Opportunities for staff to actively participate in decisions had a weak inverse correlation with math, reading, and science achievement (rho_m = -.195, rho_r = -.193, rho_s = -.119), in which the variables shared 3.8%, 3.7%, and 1.4% of the variance respectively. Opportunities for parents to actively participate in decisions had a weak to moderate inverse correlation with math, reading, and science achievement (rho_m = -.229, rho_r = -.262, rho_s = -.177), in which the variables shared 5.2%, 6.9%, and 3.1% of the variance respectively. Opportunities for students to participate had a weak to moderate inverse correlation with math, reading, and science achievement (rho_m = -.204, rho_r = -.223, rho_s = -.143), in which the variables shared 4.2%, 5.0%, and 2.0% of the variance respectively. A school climate of mutual respect had a weak relationship with math, reading, and science achievement (rho_m= .156, rho_r = .186, rho_s = .143) in which the variables shared 2.4%, 3.5%, and 2.0% of the variance respectively. While having a school climate of mutual respect was associated with higher achievement, the other significant correlations in school culture and climate were all inversely associated.

Perceived Hindrances

Teachers' absences had a weak inverse correlation with math, reading, and science achievement (rho_m= -.123, rho_r = -.125, rho_s = -.129), in which the variables shared 1.5%, 1.6%, and 1.7% of the variance respectively. In addition, lack of parent or guardian involvement and support had a moderate to strong inverse correlation with math, reading, and science achievement (rho_m= -.316, rho_r = -.296, rho_s = -.300) in which the variables shared 10.0%, 8.8%, and 9.0% of the variance respectively. Principals who were concerned with teacher absences or a lack of parent or guardian involvement and support tended to work in schools with lower achievement.

Principal Professional Background

There was a weak correlation between year(s) working in other school management roles had with math, reading, and science achievement (rho_m= .134, rho_r = .135, rho_s = .133) in which the variables shared 1.8%, 1.8%, and 1.8% of the variance respectively. While the relationship was weak, more years working in other school management roles was associated with higher achievement in mathematics, reading, and science.

SOLUTIONS AND RECOMMENDATIONS

Leadership Practices

The variable leadership practices captured principals' perceptions of their use of time, leadership styles, and tasks within the scope of their direct responsibilities. The direct and indirect influences of principals on achievement were explored and the findings were aligned with the study of Clifford et al. (2012).

While findings suggested that Finland had no significant relationships between leadership practices and academic achievement, the remaining seven countries had weak to moderate relationships. In Australia and Latvia, a moderate relationship was identified math achievement when describing the percent of time spent on other tasks. This finding suggests that in schools where principals reportedly spend time on other tasks, there was a positive and significant relationship with math achievement.

The principals' report of the degree of distributed leadership within their schools had an inverse relationship with achievement in Latvia, Mexico, and Spain. This finding indicates that schools with distributed leadership tend to experience lower levels of achievement in mathematics (Latvia and Spain), reading (Mexico and Spain), and science (Mexico and Spain). This suggests that in schools where principals

Table 8. Significant correlations with PISA achievement in Spain

		Mathematics	Reading	Science
Leadership Practices				
Degree of Distributed Leadership in the School	rho	-.226**	-.245**	-.168**
	r^2	.051	.060	.028
	N	307	307	307
Instructional Leadership	rho	.116*	.139*	.126*
	r^2	.013	.019	.016
	N	307	307	307
Percentage of time spent on administrative and leadership tasks	rho	.074	.082	.113*
	r^2	.005	.006	.013
	N	306	306	306
Percentage of time spent on student interactions	rho	-.175**	-.174**	-.199**
	r^2	.031	.030	.040
	N	306	306	306
Important decisions being made by the principal	rho	-.041	-.042	-.126*
	r^2	.002	.002	.016
	N	307	307	307
Collaborating with teachers to solve discipline problems	rho	-.190**	-.158**	-.177**
	r^2	.036	.025	.031
	N	307	307	307
School Culture and Climate				
Teachers having responsibility for improving teaching skills	rho	.110	.135*	.106
	r^2	.012	.018	.010
	N	307	307	307
Teachers having responsibility for learning outcomes	rho	.103	.105	.118*
	r^2	.010	.010	.014
	N	307	307	307
Opportunities for staff to actively participate in decisions	rho	-.195**	-.193**	-.119*
	r^2	.038	.037	.014
	N	307	307	307
Opportunities for parents to actively participate in decisions	rho	-.229**	-.262**	-.177**
	r^2	.052	.069	.031
	N	307	307	307

continued on following page

Table 8. Continued

		Mathematics	Reading	Science
Opportunities for students to participate	rho	-.204**	-.223**	-.143*
	r^2	.042	.050	.020
	N	307	307	307
A school climate of mutual respect	rho	.156**	.186**	.143*
	r^2	.024	.035	.020
	N	307	307	307
Perceived Hindrances				
Teachers' absences	rho	-.123*	-.125*	-.129*
	r^2	.015	.016	.017
	N	307	307	307
Lack of parent or guardian involvement and support	rho	-.316**	-.296**	-.300**
	r^2	.100	.088	.090
	N	307	307	307
Principal Professional Background				
Year(s) working in other school management roles	rho	.134*	.135*	.133*
	r^2	.018	.018	.018
	N	307	307	307

** Correlation is significant at the 0.01 level (2-tailed).
* Correlation is significant at the 0.05 level (2-tailed).

described a degree of distributed leadership, the academic outcomes were lower. Further exploration should be conducted to understand the connection between distributed leadership opportunities and academic achievement. The findings are further informed by the study of Leech and Fulton (2008) as they noted that sharing decision-making may improve accountability of organizational members.

The remaining relationships between leadership practices, and academic achievement remained varied by country. The limited shared relationships across countries that developed between the principal practices and learning outcomes indicate that those relationships are context bound. Countries have unique customs and norms influencing their educational system and their school leadership. This variation may explain the differences found across the study.

School Culture and Climate

The focus on a school culture and climate considered an environment of mutual respect, working together with parents, students, and teacher input, and providing opportunities for inclusion in decision making.

In schools where principals reported an opportunity for parents and guardians to participate in decision-making, there was a moderate inverse relationship with math achievement in Australia and Latvia, a weak to moderate inverse relationship with math, reading, and science achievement in Spain, a moderate inverse relationship found in reading and science in Mexico. These inverse relationships suggest that in schools where principals' report shared decision making with parents, academic achievement tends to be lower. This is counterintuitive to the research that suggests parental involvement improves learning outcomes for students. Further research into the types of decisions families are invited to participate in may serve to clarify this finding.

Schools that provided opportunities for staff to actively participate in decision-making experienced inverse relationships with math (Latvia, Mexico, and Spain) and reading and science (Mexico and Spain).

Weak inverse relationships were identified between collaboration with principals in other school and math achievement (Finland), reading (Portugal), and weak to moderate inverse relationships with math, reading, and science (Romania). The findings suggest that schools with principals who collaborate with peers from other schools also experienced lower academic achievement.

In Mexico and Portugal, there were moderate inverse relationships between reading and the percentage of time principals reportedly spend on interactions with community, business and industry. In contrast, a weak positive relationship was found in Singapore with science. This discrepancy further illustrates the unique needs and perspectives across countries.

In a time where collaboration is an increasing focus of educational policy and practice, the inverse relationships found within this variable were unexpected. Further investigation into the types of collaborative and decision-making opportunities should be explored. Additionally, ensuring effective collaboration is explicitly taught and practiced is essential for successful outcomes. Professional development for all stakeholders is required in considering how to effectively communicate and work together for the improvement of teaching and learning. Drago-Severson (2012) connected the principals' influence on climates to supporting teacher development.

Although there were inverse relationships found among the collaborative efforts in this study, literature strongly indicates the need for professional learning communities (Dufour & Mattos, 2013; Vescio, Ross, & Adams, 2008).

Perceived Hindrances

Principals identified their perceptions of barriers to accomplishing their goals as the leader of their school. Common themes of inadequate school budget and resources, limited family involvement and support, and teacher absenteeism were identified by a majority of the countries in this report.

Moderate inverse relationships were found between inadequate school budget and resources and math, reading, and science in Australia and Mexico. Weak inverse relationships were found with math in Finland and Portugal. A weak inverse relationship with reading was also identified in Finland. These inverse relationships suggest that in schools where there is a perceived deficit of financial resources, there is also lower academic achievement.

A lack of family involvement had a strong inverse relationship with math, reading, and science in Australia and Singapore, and a moderate to strong inverse relationship with the same academic indicators in Romania and Spain. In Portugal, the inverse relationship with math, reading, and science was moderate. A weak inverse relationship was found with reading in Finland. These findings allude to the importance of family involvement and engagement in the academic outcomes across multiple countries.

Teacher absenteeism had a strong inverse relationship with math, reading, and science in Australia. A moderate inverse relationship was found with math, reading, and science in Portugal and Singapore, while a weak inverse relationship was found with the same academic indicators in Spain. The findings were aligned with O'Brien et al. (1985), as they also reported an inverse relationship between teacher absenteeism and achievement. A discrepancy was found in the moderate relationship that teacher absenteeism had with math, reading, and science in Latvia. This contradiction indicated that in schools where teachers were not present, the academic outcomes improved.

Principal Professional Background

The background experiences of principals influence their leadership styles and efficacy. Consideration for the time in teaching, years working as a leader prior to becoming a principal, and time spent in a professional network or mentoring relationship was analyzed.

In Australia, there was a weak relationship between years working in other school management positions and math, reading, and science achievement. Additionally weak relationships with science were found in Singapore and Spain. In Spain, there were also weak relationships between years working in other school management positions and math and reading. These findings suggest that there are experiences that may influence school building leaders about positive academic outcomes prior to becoming a principal. The findings were aligned with the work of Pierson (2014) as the study described beneficial outcomes between experience and principal effectiveness.

Inverse relationships were found with science (moderate in Latvia / weak in Singapore) and years working as a teacher in total. This finding is interesting in that the time in teaching appears to have diminishing returns on student outcomes when moving out of the classroom into the leadership role. Further studies may reveal ways in which the gap between teaching and leading can be reduced.

CONCLUSION

This paper supports a context-specific view of instructional leadership. When looking across countries, the researchers found that different practices, school climates, and principal background characteristics were more strongly associated with the academic achievement of students, and suggest that school leaders do have a meaningful overall relationship with academic achievement in both direct and indirect ways. Finland and Romania were notably different from the other six countries that had several weak to moderate associations with academic achievement. This study therefore supports prior research about the direct and indirect effects of instructional leadership in connection to building management and instructional practices and school culture and climate. It is important, however, to recognize that this paper explored relationships, and not causality. Further study, which accounts for differences in family academic resources and school-level opportunities to learn, will better illuminate the connection between instructional leadership practices and academic achievement. Future research could also explore the relative predictive ability of principal leadership practices activities, school culture and climate, principal perceived hindrances, and principal professional background on student achievement, in conjunction with information on student and teacher characteristics.

REFERENCES

Ayala, C. C., Shavelson, R. J., Ruiz-Primo, M., Brandon, P. R., Yin, Y., Furtak, E., & Tomita, M. K. et al. (2008). From formal embedded assessments to reflective lessons: The development of formative assessment studies. *Applied Measurement in Education*, *21*(4), 315–334. doi:10.1080/08957340802347787

Bakula, N. (2010). The Benefits of Formative Assessments for Teaching and Learning. *Science Scope*, *34*(1), 37–43.

Carroll, T., Fulton, K., & Doerr, H. (2010). *Team up for 21st century teaching and learning: What research and practice reveal about professional learning*. Washington, DC: National Commission on Teaching and America's Future.

Clifford, M., Behrstock-Sherratt, E., & Fetters, J. (2012). *The ripple effect: A synthesis of research on principal influence to inform performance evaluation design.* American Institutes for Research. A quality School Leadership. *Issue Brief.*

Collie, R. J., Shapka, J. D., & Perry, N. E. (2011). Predicting teacher commitment: The impact of school climate and social-emotional learning. *Psychology in the Schools*, *48*(10), 1034–1048. doi:10.1002/pits.20611

Collie, R. J., Shapka, J. D., & Perry, N. E. (2012). School climate and social-emotional learning: Predicting teacher stress, job satisfaction, and teaching efficacy. *Journal of Educational Psychology*, *104*(4), 1189–1204. doi:10.1037/a0029356

DataO. E. C. D. © OECD, https://data.oecd.org

Deal, T., & Peterson, K. D. (1999). *Shaping school culture: The heart of leadership*. San Francisco, CA: Jossey-Bass.

Deming, W. E. (1986). *Out of the crisis*. Cambridge, MA: Massachusetts Institute of Technology, Center for Advanced Engineering Study.

Drago-Severson, E. (2012). New opportunities for principal leadership: Shaping school climate for enhanced teacher development. *Teachers College Record*, *114*, 1–44. PMID:24013958

DuFour, R., DuFour, R., & Eaker, R. (2008). *Revising professional learning communities at work: New insights for improving schools*. Bloomington, IN: Solution Tree Press.

DuFour, R., & Mattos, M. (2013). How do principals really improve schools? *Educational Leadership*, *70*(7), 34–40.

Dworkin, A. G., Haney, C. A., Dworkin, R. J., & Telschov, R. L. (1990). Stress and illness behavior among urban public school teachers. *Educational Administration Quarterly*, *26*(1), 60–72. doi:10.1177/0013161X90026001004

Epstein, J., & Rodriguez-Jansorn, N. (2004). School, family, and community partnerships link the plan. *Education Digest*, *69*(6), 19–24.

Epstein, J. L., Coates, L., Salinas, K. C., Sanders, M. G., & Simon, B. S. (1997). *School, family and community partnerships*. San Francisco: Corwin Press.

Epstein, J. L., Sanders, M. G., Sheldon, S., Simon, B. S., & Salinas, K. C. (2009). *School, family, and community partnerships: Your handbook for action*. Thousand Oaks, CA: Corwin Press.

Fullan, M. (1998). Leadership for the 21st century: Breaking the bonds of dependency. *Educational Leadership*, *55*, 6–11.

Fullan, M. (2001). *Leading in a Culture of Change*. San Francisco: Jossey-Bass.

Garmezy, N. (1991). Resiliency and vulnerability to adverse development outcomes associated with poverty. *The American Behavioral Scientist*, *34*(4), 416–430. doi:10.1177/0002764291034004003

Gordon, M., & Seashore-Louis, K. (2009). Linking parent and community involvement with student achievement: Comparing principal and teacher perceptions of stakeholder influence. *American Journal of Education*, *116*(1), 1–31. doi:10.1086/605098

Gottfredson, G., Gottfredson, D., Payne, A., & Gottfredson, N. (2005). School climate predictors of school disorder: Results from a national study of delinquency prevention. *Journal of Research in Crime and Delinquency*, *42*(4), 412–444. doi:10.1177/0022427804271931

Hill, S. T. (1982). You can't afford, for teachers to be out, so take these steps now to stop absenteeism. *ERIC Document Reproduction Service ED*, *214*, 233.

Holland, H. (2005). Teaching teachers: Professional development to improve student achievement. Research Points: Essential Information for Educational Policy, 3(1), 1–4. Washington, DC: American Educational Research Association.

Imants, J., & Van Zoelen, A. (1995). Teachers' sickness absence in primary schools, school climate and teachers' sense of efficacy. *School Organization*, *15*(1), 77–86.

Kouzes, J. M., & Posner, B. J. (2002). *Leadership challenge* (3rd ed.). San Francisco: Jossey-Bass.

Lange, C., Range, B., & Welsh, K. (2012). Conditions for Effective Data Use to Improve Schools: Recommendations for School Leaders. *International Journal Of Educational Leadership Preparation*, *7*(3), 1–11.

Leech, D., & Fulton, C. (2008). Faculty perceptions of shared decision making and the principal's leadership behaviors in secondary schools in a large urban district. *Education*, *128*(4), 630–644.

Leithwood, K., Aitken, R., & Jantzi, D. (2006). *Making schools smarter: Leading with evidence*. Corwin Press.

Leithwood, K., Strauss, T., & Anderson, S. E. (2007). District Contributions to School Leaders' Sense of Efficacy: A Qualitative Analysis. *Journal of School Leadership*, *17*(6), 735–770.

Levine, D. K., & Lezotte, L. W. (1990). Unusually Effective Schools: A Review and Analysis of Research and Practice. Madison, Wise: Nat. Centre for Effective Schools Research and Development.

Louis, K., Leithwood, K., Wahlstrom, K., & Anderson, S. (2010). *Learning from leadership: Investigating the links to improved student learning*. New York: Wallace Foundation.

Manley, R., & Hawkins, R. J. (2010). *Designing school systems for all students: A toolbox to fix America's schools*. New York: Rowman & Littlefield.

Muth, R., Browne-Ferrigno, T., Bellamy, T., Fulmer, C., & Silver, M. (2013). Using Teacher Instructional Leadership as a Predictor of Principal Leadership. *Journal of School Leadership*, *23*(1).

Newmann, F., & Wehlage, G. (1995). *Successful school restructuring: A report to the public and educators by the Center on Organization and Restructuring of Schools*. Madison: University of Wisconsin.

Norton, M. S. (1994). *The personnel administrator in Arizona: A research study*. Tempe, AZ: Arizona State University.

O'Brien, L. M., Meszaros, B., & Pulliam, W. (1985). Effects of teacher use of objectives on student achievement in social studies. In A. Summers (Ed.), *Productivity Assessment in Education*. San Francisco, CA: Jossey-Bass, Inc. doi:10.1080/00933104.1985.10505506

Ovando, M. N., & Cavazos, M. (2004). Principals' Instructional Leadership in Successful Hispanic Majority High Schools. *Scholar-Practitioner Quarterly*, *2*(3), 7–24.

Pattnaik, J., & Sriram, R. (2010). Father/male involvement in the care and education of children. *Childhood Education*, *86*(6), 354–359. doi:10.1080/00094056.2010.10523169

Pierson, A. (2014). *What makes a successful principal?: Incorporating school principal background in state and district policy* [Doctoral dissertation].

Provost, J., Boscardin, M., & Wells, C. (2010). Perceptions of principal leadership behaviors in Massachusetts in the era of education reform. *Journal of School Leadership*, *20*(5), 532–560.

Prytula, M., Noonan, B., & Hellsten, L. (2013). Toward Instructional Leadership: Principals' Perceptions of Large-Scale Assessment in Schools. *Canadian Journal of Educational Administration and Policy*.

Robinson, V. J. (2010). From instructional leadership to leadership capabilities: Empirical findings and methodological challenges. *Leadership and Policy in Schools*, *9*(1), 1–26. doi:10.1080/15700760903026748

Rossman, G. B., Corbett, H. D., & Firestone, W. A. (1998). Change and effectiveness in schools: A cultural perspective. *Curriculum Inquiry*, *21*(1), 127–131.

Senge, P. (1990). *The fifth discipline: the art and practice of a learning organization*. New York: Currency Doubleday.

Soehner, D., & Ryan, T. (2011). The Interdependence of Principal School Leadership and Student Achievement. *Scholar-Practitioner Quarterly*, *5*(3), 274–288.

Summers, A., & Raivetz, M. (1982). What helps fourth grade students to read? In A. Summers (Ed.), *Productivity Assessment in Education*. San Francisco, CA: Jossey-Bass, Inc.

Taylor, R. T., & La Cava, G. S. (2011). Urban Principals' Second Order Change Leadership. *Planning and Changing*, *42*(3-4), 224–240.

Tschannen-Moran, M., Hoy, A. W., & Hoy, W. K. (1998). Teacher efficacy: Its meaning and measure. *Review of Educational Research*, *68*(2), 202–248. doi:10.3102/00346543068002202

Urick, A., Wilson, A., Paes de Carvalho, C., Oliveira, A. C., Perry, S. M., & Campelo Koslinski, M. (2015). Does school leadership influence opportunity to learn for 15 year olds in US and Brazil? *Paper presented at American Education Research Association annual meeting*, Chicago, IL.

Vescio, V., Ross, D., & Adams, A. (2008). A review of the research on the impact of professional learning communities on teaching practice and student learning. *Teaching and Teacher Education*, *24*(1), 80–91. doi:10.1016/j.tate.2007.01.004

Waters, J. T., Marzano, R. J., & McNulty, B. (2004). Leadership that sparks learning. *Educational Leadership*, *61*(7), 48.

Welsh, W. (2000). The effects of school climate on school disorder. *The Annals of the American Academy of Political and Social Science*, *567*(1), 88–107. doi:10.1177/000271620056700107

Wilson, D. (2004). The interface of school climate and school connectedness and relationships with aggression and victimization. *The Journal of School Health*, *74*(7), 293–299. doi:10.1111/j.1746-1561.2004.tb08286.x PMID:15493706

Chapter 6
Relationship Among Education, Income, and Life Satisfaction

Elsa-Sofia Morote
Farmingdale State University of New York, USA

ABSTRACT

This study examines the relationships among Education, Income, and Life Satisfaction. The study also seeks to learn whether Unemployment can be a mediator of these relationships. For this study, database collected by the Quality of Government Institute was used. The database contains 194 countries' records on the topic and its variables collected in 2012. Correlation to test relationship, and partial correlation to test the relationship among the variables while controlling for unemployment was used. It was found that income strongly relates to life satisfaction, and years of schooling relates weakly to life satisfaction. Years of schooling, however, strongly relates to GDP per capita. Contrary to previous studies, it was found that unemployment was not a mediator of the relationship among Education, Income, and Life Satisfaction but shows slight indication that it can be a mediator between higher education and life satisfaction. It was advised that governments put more effort into education as well as future research on enhancing the quality and efficacy of education.

INTRODUCTION

An important duty of nearly every Western government is improving-the wellbeing of its people, and education is considered a key element in increasing the efficacy of the production system to produce the wealth that supports the common weal. It is clear

DOI: 10.4018/978-1-5225-3616-1.ch006

that in order to achieve economic development, it is necessary to have highly skilled people; many researchers (Duvall, 2001, Miller, 2013) and international organizations (King & World Bank, 2011) (21st Century Partnership, 2008) affirm that "education is crucial for economic and social progress in less developed countries" (Rondinelli & Montgomery, 1995). Also, most agree that the linkage between higher education and economic development is a two-way process. However, few researchers include employment and happiness in the equation.

Although some may disagree that the assurance of happiness for its citizens is a governmental responsibility, several governments in the world consider doing so their responsibility. For example, in 1933, Herbert Hoover, President of the United States, highlighted the importance of assuring happiness of the citizenry (Mitchell & USA, 1933) by connecting happiness with the economic situation of the country. Bhutan's Fourth Dragon King Jigme Singye Wangchuck took that responsibility seriously creating the famous *Gross National Happiness* (GNH) as a measurement of the success of the Bhutanese economy in serving the wellbeing of Bhutan's people and Buddhist culture, replacing the GDP (Gross Domestic Product) as the sole standard for judging Bhutan's economy. This was codified in Bhutan's legal code that included the maxim stating that, "...if the Government cannot create happiness (*dekid*) for its people, there is no purpose for the Government to exist"– Legal Code of Bhutan 1972 (O.E.C.D., Ura, Alkire, & Zangmo, 2011)

Throughout the past, the happiness and wellbeing of the individual has captured the attention of several researchers (Malik, & Singh, 2012; Nicolae, 2012). In the United States, one of the lead researchers is Diener of the University of Illinois offers the following comprehensive definition: "a person is said to have high [well-being or happiness] if she or he experiences Life Satisfaction and frequent joy, and only infrequently experiences unpleasant emotions such as sadness or anger. Contrariwise, a person is said to have low [well-being or happiness] if she or he is dissatisfied" (In Bok, 2010, p. 9). Diener prefers to measure Life Satisfaction, and his five survey questions show high reliability and have been tested several times (Diener, Emmons, Larsen, & Griffin, 1985; Pavot, Diener, Colvin, & Sandvik, 1991).

Happiness and economic development has been object of a research in several countries. For example, Knight and Gunatilaka (2012) found that in China current income has a positive and significant effect on happiness. On the contrary, the economist Easterlin (2013) concluded that average levels of happiness in the United States have risen very little if at all over the past 50 years despite substantial growth in *per capita* incomes, although Easterlin admitted that "rich people, as a whole, are happier than poor people." In addition, after analyzing 17 developed countries, nine developing countries, 11 transition countries, Easterlin concluded that in the short term, happiness and economic growth are positively related.

Governments are aware of the need to reduce unemployment, as well as the need for economic progress. However, most governments and international agencies do not directly correlate the relationship of these two key variables of economic development to tertiary education. Today, the debate about the connections between higher education and the labor market is again on the table. In 1994, The World Bank considered that the tension between higher education and unemployment is one of the crises of higher education related to mismatch of supply and demand of graduates and lack of contact with the market. In the emerging economies, labor has adjusted, wage levels and employment patterns have shifted, and in many countries pay differentials have begun creating incentives for workers to acquire new skills. In 2014, 20 years after the World Bank report, the *World Economic Forum Global Agenda Council on Employment in Matching Skills and Labour Market Needs Building Social Partnerships for Better Skills and Better Jobs* put this in its agenda (World Economic Forum Global Agenda Council on Employment, 2014).

The central premise of this study is that increasing the educational attainment of the population can help to improve economic development through strengthening GDP *per capita*; however, this impact will depend on other variables, such as employment. All of this will ultimately affect Life Satisfaction. This premise is based on the theory that education is an investment in human capital that increases an individual's skills and competencies. To an extent this investment is rewarded in the labor market through higher earnings. It is also the premise that economic wellbeing will affect the individual's Life Satisfaction.

In the first years following World War II, economic development was viewed primarily as a problem of capital accumulation and growth of output. Thus, the emphasis in development planning rested on maximizing the rate of growth in the capital stock, and little explicit consideration was given to implications of growth of employment (Gregory, 1986). Today, unemployment and underemployment affect a substantial proportion of the labor forces in emerging countries, and the development strategists can no longer afford to ignore the implications for alternative paths of employment.

Education is a key element in human resource development that has to be further explored, especially in the area of tertiary education, because of its importance in the new global economy. In 2008, The U.S. Bureau of Labor Statistics identified 271 jobs with high-growth potential over the next 10 years; 71 are likely to increase by 20 percent or more during this period. All of these jobs require at least some college education; most require one or more college degrees (US Bureau of Labor Statistics, 2008).

Some researchers mention the importance of having human resources with highly developed skills, but they do not go any farther. Other researchers (e.g. Daisi, 2011; De Meulmester & Rochet, 1995; Hanushek, & Woessmann, 2007; Jorgenson & Fraumeni, 1998; Psaharoupolous, 1988 and Ritzen, 1977) have analyzed the importance of education in economic growth, but none of them have reviewed the importance of other variables, such as unemployment and Life Satisfaction. In 2001, Morote analyzed the causal relationship between higher education, education, employment and economic development in Peru and Mexico, using an Akaike model of causal analysis with time series analysis, Morote found a Trivariate causality in Peru that showed the importance of employment as a key concept to reestablish the connection between higher education and economic growth. Now the question is how all of this related to Life Satisfaction.

Consequently, this study seeks that to evaluate the relationship between education, income and Life Satisfaction. How these variables affect each other will become an important subject of discussion in the coming years. Even though prior studies have been undertaken in this regard, they have rarely included an analysis of all three variables together, and few studies include Life Satisfaction. For instance, many quantitative studies have taken a narrow approach focusing on the link between economic growth and education, while ignoring various other aspects of development, such as employment rates.

To investigate this premise as an empirical study, the Quality of Government Institute (QoG) Standard dataset, 2012 (http://qog.pol.gu.se/data) was used. The data include more than 100 variables from194 countries. This study has selected five variables:

- Two that measure education (Percentage of Tertiary Complete, Years of Schooling
- Two that measure the income (GDP per capita, and unemployment)
- One that measures Life Satisfaction. Individuals rated the question "How satisfied are you with your life?"

Empirical analysis using correlation and partial correlation will be used to answer two main questions:

1. Is there a relationship among Tertiary Enrollment, Years Of Schooling, Unemployment, *Per Capita* GDP Rates and Life Satisfaction?
2. What is the correlation among Tertiary Enrollment, Years of Schooling, *Per Capita* GDP Rates, and Life Satisfaction, controlling the Unemployment?

BACKGROUND

Education, Income, and Happiness

Human Capital theorists (e.g. Becker, 1967, 1993; Shultz, 1988, 1994, 1997; Denison, 1971; Fitz-Enz, 2009) have investigated the relationship between education and economic growth. They assert that, by increasing human capital, education improves a country's productivity. It was not until late in the twentieth century that researchers undertook formal and scientific analysis of this relationship between economic growth and human capital development.

These theoretical explanations have been accompanied by empirical explanations. They were part of an extensive study in the early 1960s, beginning with the research of Denison and Schultz. In 1962, in an analysis of the factors of economic growth in the U.S. between 1910 and 1960, Denison (1971) followed traditional methods using only the classic variables of the function of production: labor and capital. After applying econometric methods, he found a "residual" that could be explained by both factors of production: labor and capital. However, this residual could also be explained by the increase of quality in human resources based on an increase in education. Denison (1971) concluded that between 1930 and 1960, 23% of the growth rate of the *per capita* product in the United States could be explained by the expansion of education.

Later, Schultz confirmed the conclusions of Denison. In 1963, Schultz compared the return rates of one dollar invested in education versus one dollar invested in physical capital. He concluded that the return rate of the money invested in education was equal to or higher than that invested in physical capital. Therefore, Schultz proposed that education should not be considered as a consumption activity, but as an investment.

These two studies began the Human Capital Revolution, which was based on the methodology used by Schultz and Denison. Becker (1967) was another classic investigator who presented a seminal work of the Human Capital Theory of education demand. Becker had estimated that the rate of return to investment in college education was high, theorizing that it was higher, in fact, than the rate of return on alternative investments. Various empirical research studies have been produced. These studies in general do not refute the fundamental conclusions of Denison and Schultz, but they have refined them.

Several studies have investigated the relationship between economic growth and education, such as Psaharoupolous, 1988; Pencavel, 1993; De Meulmester and Rochet, 1995; Jorgenson and Fraumeni, 1998, Miller, 2013. Their starting point was always the root of the economic growth itself. The pioneer theorists hypothesized that economic development depended on the increase of capital and the labor factor in the productive processes. A fundamental reason for economic growth was found to be the increase of productivity in these factors of production. Whereas researchers such as Pencavel (1993) affirmed that correlations exist across countries between economic growth rates and schooling enrollment rates including enrollment in higher education, another group of researchers such as De Meulmester and Rochet 1995; Morote, 2001, using more sophisticated econometric techniques, found that this relationship is not always a direct one.

Beginning in the 1960s and 1970s, economists in development agencies began to view education as an investment in economic development. National plans began to emphasize the importance of education in creating the skills necessary for economic enhancement. This line of thinking, relating to education and the economy, continued into the 1980s and 1990s, as international development institutions such as the World Bank began to focus their attention on education as a means to promote economic development (Jones, Ogawa, & Williamson, 1993). For instance, a 1995 publication by the Inter-American Development Bank (IDB) that examined various factors in the development of Brazil supports the contention that the lack of a strong educational system had hindered economic development and political stability (Birdsall & Sabot, 1996).

Researchers from the 2000s and 2010s continuing to assert previous years' findings (Krueger and Lindahl 2001; Sianesi and Van Reenen, 2003, and Sala-I Martin et al., 2004) concluded that education has a positive effect on economic performance. Some researchers began adding *quality of education* to the equation.

Development research has also firmly demonstrated the value of higher levels of education for socioeconomic development, poverty reduction, and higher incomes. The increased competition and globalization of economic activity, the acceleration in technological and scientific knowledge, and the information revolution continue to raise the value of education and training in preparing individuals for future employment. In addition, these help in upgrading skills for greater workplace mobility, in underpinning wealth creation, and in economic development through human capital formation.

Several researchers have focused on the relationship between education and happiness. There is a greater association between education and happiness for individuals with lower incomes compared to individuals of higher incomes (Diener et al., 1998). Hosen, Solovey-Hosen, and Stern (2003) stated that formal education contributes to the development of human capital and enhances subjective well-being. Quamruzzaman (2013) tested the hypothesis that education impacts happiness using data from the 1998 wave of the General Social Survey (GSS). A total of 2,832 respondents above 18 years of age were interviewed in person using a standard questionnaire resulting in the finding that the odds of enjoying happiness are about 1.66 times higher for those with a high school diploma and about 1.94 times higher for those with a college or beyond education compared to those with less than a high school diploma.

Happiness, Education, Income, and Unemployment

After the crisis in 2008, unemployment was a variable that was considered by several researchers in the United States. In 2008, Mahadea and Rawat found that there is a significant relationship between income and happiness. Previously, Morote (2001) researched the impact of higher education to economic development, using unemployment as a mediator. The study was based on time series analysis in two countries, Mexico and Peru. Morote found that unemployment was mediator of the causal relationship between higher education and economic growth. A causal relationship from the system higher education and employment to economic growth was found in both countries. In addition, in the case of causality between employment and higher education, a bi-directional causality was found in Mexico, and a unidirectional causality from employment to higher education was found in Peru.

Globalization has been blamed because employment has suffered multiple transformations due to technological changes, internationalization of companies, and changes in productive processes, which replace workers with low skills with others who possess the knowledge required for the new trends. The effectiveness of higher education has also been questioned although a natural unemployment rate will continue to be inversely related to educational attainment, and unless recent gains are unexpectedly reversed, it will remain low (DePrince & Morris, 2008)

The question of the connections between higher education and the labor market has been a topic for investigation and discussion for the last three decades. The key issues are debated whenever challenges for innovation in higher education are at stake (Teichler, 1999; DePrince & Morris, 2008). For example, in its 1994 report entitled "Higher Education: Lessons of Experience," the World Bank cited the tensions between higher education and employment as one of the key elements of the higher education crisis related to mismatch of supply and demand of graduates and lack of contact with the market (The World Bank, 1994). In the same way, The Organisation for Economic Cooperation and Development (OECD) addressed the transition from higher education to employment in one of its largest projects in the early 1990s. Between 1990 and 2003, the percentage of workers having either college or university education increased from 5.7 percent to 17.5 percent.

In this context, higher education is being challenged to reconsider its fundamental objectives—for example, should a balance be struck between supply and demand of graduates, between responding to the demands directly expressed by the employment system and influencing the labor market, and between its relationship with business and industry, and government? Most definitively, there will need to be an adjustment made between higher education policies and the employment sector. Not only is higher education being challenged, but government's policies toward unemployment are also being questioned.

In the Twentieth century, high educational gains were made in terms of enrollment throughout most of the world, but the rate of employment did not have a corresponding rise, in part because of structural developments and government policies toward the economy. Structural unemployment arises from a fundamental mismatch between supply and demand, including skill or locational mismatches in the labor market. This situation puts higher education and governmental policy makers under stress.

Furthermore, Howe (1993) stated that the labor market's response to the rising education level of an expanding labor force was a relative weakening of the labor market position for high school graduates, compared with those who had higher levels of education. Also, Howe noted that in the case of a cyclical economy (as is common in emerging economies), unemployment rises and falls for all educational groups during the course of a business cycle, and the degree of cyclical movement is generally smaller for the more highly educated groups.

There is no question that higher education affects unemployment, or that a higher level of education reduces the probability of being unemployed. It has become an increasingly important criterion for job market success over time. It is likely that the competitive advantage held by college graduates will continue into the future. On the other hand, government policies toward the economy affect the business cycle and in the same way, affect unemployment.

The connections between higher education and the labor market are among the most frequently discussed issues of higher education, but systematic knowledge of these connections is relatively poor. Most of these theories are not founded on systematic empirical evidence (Teichler, 1999). This does not mean that there is a lack of any information available. Overviews provide evidence that a substantial number of studies have been undertaken (Psacharopoulus, 1987; Carnoy, 1994; Sanyal, 1987; Miller, 2013).

There are two important points of view on higher education, unemployment, and economic growth, which are divided as follows: *Human Capital Theory*: Education provides people with skills to develop and manage the economy, and therefore, investment in education is investment in human capital. The positive correlation between education and wages has stimulated many attempts to establish a causal connection at the micro-economic level. Human Capital Theory, which dominates some literature, considers education as an investment, making individuals more productive. Like growth accounting models, the micro studies of the effects of education and training on productivity have limited value as policy makers must respond to a changing environment. Human Capital Theory claims that people are rewarded with good jobs to the degree that they possess human capital—i.e., knowledge and skill achieved through formal training (e.g. Shultz, 1988, 1994, 1997; Denison, 1971; see also Becker, 1967, 1993, Psaharoupolus, 1988, 21st Century Partnership, 2008).

This theory was extended by additional researches (e.g. Fields, 1980; Leipziger and Lewis, 1989, Ferre-i-Carbonell, 2005). They considered that education not only provided skills for performing occasional tasks, but also promoted social values by encouraging upward mobility in society and by acting as a screening device to select the most able people for the best jobs. Education not only impacts economic growth, but also it impacts income distribution and levels of poverty. For instance, finding suitable employment can contribute to the level of income distribution. The relationship between education, income distribution and poverty can be explained because with education, people are more productive. Without distortions in the labor market, this is normally seen as an increase in salaries. This effect is important for individuals attempting to escape poverty. Education is one of the main vehicles for social mobility because it allows workers access to higher salary jobs, changing their economic level and diminishing social inequalities.

Human Capital Theory accepts the idea of education's contribution to the social and economic development of people. Extensions of the theory raise doubts about the role of education in the social and economic development of people.

Regarding higher education and employment, empirical research is required. There have been some studies focusing on how employment and higher education enrollment match supply and demand (e.g., Abowd & Card, 1987; King & World Bank, 2011). However, most of them are related to social mobility and distribution of income (Leipziger & Lewis, 1989; Tilak, 1987). Other studies relate employment to economic cycles and the probabilities of employment (e.g., Howe, 1993). Since both theories (Human Capital and Labor Market Segmentation) predict that people with more education will have higher earnings and that people with little education will be economically deprived, what difference does it make which is correct? In actuality, it makes a significant difference. For example, if everyone's educational attainment is raised by one year, will everyone have a better job and higher pay? While Human Capital theorists will answer affirmatively because they consider that income reflects productivity, which reflects cognitive skills, which reflect education, the Labor Market Segmentation theorists will answer negatively because they affirm that no one's position in the labor queue will change. There will be no effect. Furthermore, if compensatory education or skill training is given to those with low income, will their incomes rise? Will overall poverty fall? Both theories will answer positively. Human Capital theorists will affirm that the low incomes will rise. No one else's incomes will fall, and poverty will decline. Labor Market

Segmentation theorists will also predict that income of the poor will rise. They will move ahead of other people in the labor queue, and those who are displaced will move toward the back, although the job distribution will not be affected, and neither will income distribution. Poverty will not decline, although it will be redistributed.

Based on the research studies reviewed, it can be inferred that education has an impact on the socio-economic structure of any country, but it is important to take into account that the economic levels reached because of education depend upon the kind and quality of education, the economic model followed by a nation (e.g., open economy, closed economy) and the economic level of a country (e.g., underdeveloped, developed). Ritzen (1977) concluded that investment in education without investment in physical capital had no impact on income distribution. Therefore, a skilled labor force requires a high amount of capital if the goal of the economic policy is to reduce the income distribution inequalities. Also, it can be implied that it is necessary to use new and advanced techniques to evaluate the impact of higher education on economic growth.

To date economic research has primarily focused on subjective well-being as an outcome variable (see Frey & Stutzer, 2001, for an overview) whose effect of unemployment has received particular attention, due to its important social implications, with a broad consensus asserting that unemployment leads to a decline in happiness (e.g., Winkelmann, 2016; Hosen, Solovey-Hosen, & Stern, 2003; Ohtake, 2012). Quamruzzaman (2013) found that the odds ratio of the currently unemployed is .28, which means that unemployed people have 72% less chance of being happy than currently employed people.

Recent studies show that higher national income goes hand-in-hand with a reduced spread in happiness, but they did not find evidence that economic growth has been accompanied by higher mean levels of subjective well-being (Clark, Fleche, & Senik, 2014). More research is needed.

MAIN FOCUS OF THE CHAPTER

Data Sources

To investigate this premise by making an empirical study, the Quality of Government Institute (QoG) Standard dataset, 2012 (http://qog.pol.gu.se/data) was used (University of Gothenburg, Sweden, 2016).

(The data include more than 100 variables from194 countries. This study has selected five variables—two that measure education, two that measure the economics of the country and one that measures Life Satisfaction. These include: (a) How satisfied are you with your life? (b) Real GDP per capita (Constant Prices: Chain series), (c) Percentage of the population that has tertiary education completed, (d) Years of Schooling, and (e) Unemployment (%)

Table 1 presents information of selected countries.

Methodology

The following research questions guide this study

1. Is there a relationship among tertiary enrollment, years of schooling, unemployment, *per capita* GDP rates, and Life Satisfaction?
2. What is the correlation between tertiary enrollment, years of schooling, *per capita* GDP rates and Life Satisfaction, controlling the unemployment?

To describe the strength of the relationship, the study followed the general guidelines provided by Cohen (1988): Strength of Association $0.1 < | r | < .3$ small correlation; $0.3 < | r | < .5$ medium/moderate correlation, and $| r | > .5$ large/strong correlation

The researcher has reviewed the assumptions that apply to those techniques. All variables showed normal distribution except GDP *per capita* (skewness = 2.0, kurtosis 4.6, 185 countries) and unemployment (skewness = 2.2, kurtosis 7.1, 155 countries).

Testing for normality and finding significant outliers: Three countries were deleted from the data. One was Djibouti, which showed a 60% unemployment rate; the other two—Qatar and Luxemburg—showed extremely high GDP *per capita*.

After removing these three countries, unemployment (skewness = 1.5, kurtosis 1,8, 152 countries) and GDP *per capita* (skewness = 1.5, kurtosis 1.4, 182 countries) showed normal distribution.

Table 2 shows the descriptive statistics of the variables consider in this study. The descriptive statistics show that some data were missing. For example, of the 191 countries left after removing the outliers, only 152 were able to collect % of unemployment. The mean value of Life Satisfaction was 6.5 (with a standard deviation of 1.1), Unemployment was 10.08 (with a standard deviation of 7.67), and finally, the Years of Schooling was seven years (with a standard deviation of 2.98 years), with a 6.5 percent on Tertiary complete (with a standard deviation of 1.12).

Table 1. Selected countries

Country	Life Satisfaction	GDP per Capita	% of Tertiary Education	Years of Schooling	Unemployment Rate
Argentina	7.3	8,157.34	6.42	8.56	17.9
Australia	7.3	34,769.59	21.35	11.86	6.4
Belgium	7.43	31,879.62	16.86	10.04	7.5
Brazil	7.64	6,999.47	5.79	5.57	9.1
Canada	7.85	34,364.23	18.46	11.06	7.7
Chile	7.12	9,788.57	8.37	8.75	8.9
Colombia	8.31	5,953.29	6.2	6.5	14.5
Cyprus	7.35	17,703.94	17.15	9.68	3.4
Denmark	8.24	33,280.58	10.55	9.99	4.6
Egypt	5.36	3,933.74	1.84	4.66	10.2
El Salvador	7.5	5,607.84	5.41	5.73	6.2
Finland	7.87	29,298.99	5.16	8.21	9
France	7.01	29,767.70	7.22	9.3	8.7
Germany	7.55	31,127.87	9.03	10.49	8.6
Guatemala	7.95	5,506.54	2.06	3.79	3.1
India	5.14	1,981.19	1.95	3.58	4.4
Israel	7.03	21,814.52	24.09	11.6	10.3
Italy	6.89	29,388.08	5.83	8.58	9.2
Jordan	5.6	3,886.38	4.04	7.34	16.2
Malaysia	6.84	9,667.74	2.37	8.16	3.5
Mexico	8.14	10,380.95	8.31	7.43	2.9
Morocco	6.06	2,738.58	3.01	3.37	11.6
Netherlands	7.85	34,772.74	12.43	10.81	2.6
Norway	7.96	45,798.07	10.58	11.52	3.9
Peru	6.44	5,159.27	16.61	7.73	7.7
Poland	7.02	11,892.04	8.45	9.51	19.9
Portugal	7.04	19,511.10	3.59	6.78	5
Russia	4.65	9,815.02	18.74	11.35	7.9
Tanzania	3.87	778.46	0.43	4.57	5.1
Thailand	7.21	6,157.38	4.84	5.37	1.8
U.K.	7.41	31,378.20	9.54	8.58	5.1
USA	7.66	39,148.70	29.39	13	5.8
Venezuela	7.52	7,596.66	3.92	5.58	16.2
Zimbabwe	3.94	308.35	0.57	5.89	4.2

Table 2. Descriptive statistics

	Unemployment (%)	Real GDP per Capita	How Satisfied Are You with Your Life	Percentage of Tertiary Complete	Years of Schooling
N	152	182	93	141	141
M	10.08	9776.26	6.50	6.23	7.01
SD	7.67	11209.56	1.12	6.10	2.98
Skewness	1.48	1.52	-0.34	1.35	-0.17
SE Skewness	0.20	0.18	0.25	0.20	0.20
Kurtosis	1.88	1.47	-0.81	1.59	-0.98
SE Kurtosis	0.39	0.36	0.50	0.41	0.41

FINDINGS

Research Question 1

Is there a relationship among tertiary enrollment, years of schooling, unemployment, *per capita* GDP rates and Life Satisfaction? Correlations were used to test this relationship.

Table 3 shows the relationships among tertiary enrollment, years of schooling, unemployment, per capita GDP rates and Life Satisfaction. A Pearson's product-moment correlation was run to assess the relationship between Life Satisfaction, GDP *per capita*, Years of Schooling, Percentage of Tertiary Education and Unemployment.

Table 3 shows that there was a strong positive correlation between Life Satisfaction and GDP per capita, r (91) = .65, p < .0005. Life Satisfaction and GDP per capita share a variance of 42%. This is represented in Figure 1.

Table 3 shows that there was a small positive correlation between Life Satisfaction and Years of Schooling, $r\,(83) = .27, p < .000$, with Years of School explaining 8% of the variation in the Life Satisfaction score. In addition, there was a strong positive correlation between GDP per capita and Percentage of Tertiary Complete, $r\,(140) = .54, p < .000$, with percentage of tertiary complete explaining 29% of the variation in GDP *per capita*. The same case applies to Years of Schooling, explaining 39 percent of the GDP *per capita*.

Table 3. Correlation among GDP per capita, tertiary complete, years of schooling and unemployment

		Life Satisfaction	Real GDP per Capita	Percentage of Tertiary Complete	Years of Schooling
Real GDP per capita	r	0.65			
	r^2	0.42			
	P	0.00			
	N	91			
Percentage of Tertiary Complete	r	0.20	0.54		
	r^2	0.04	0.29		
	P	0.06	0.00		
	N	83	140		
Years of Schooling	r	0.27	0.62	0.75	
	r^2	0.08	0.39	0.56	
	P	0.00	0.00	0.00	
	N	83	140	141	
Unemployment (%)	r	-0.34	-0.26	-0.09	0.02
	r^2	0.12	0.07	0.01	0.00
	P	0.00	0.00	0.28	0.75
	N	88	149	127	127

A Pearson's product-moment correlation was run to assess the relationship between unemployment and Life Satisfaction, GDP *per capita*, Years of Schooling, and Percentage of Tertiary Education. There was a small to moderate negative correlation between unemployment and GDP per capita $r(149) = -.26, p < .0005$, and Life Satisfaction, $r(88) = -.34, p < .0005$, with unemployment explaining 12% of the variation in Life Satisfaction (inverse relationship), and 7% of the variation in GDP *per capita* (inverse relationship).

Research Question 2

What is the correlation between tertiary enrollment, years of schooling, *per capita* GDP rates and Life Satisfaction, controlling the unemployment? Partial correlation was used to answer this question.

Table 4 presents the results of the partial correlation controlling for unemployment. A partial correlation was run to determine the relationship between an individual's Life Satisfaction, Years of Schooling, Percentage of Tertiary Education and GDP

Figure 1. Strong correlation between life satisfaction and GDP per capita (N = 91)

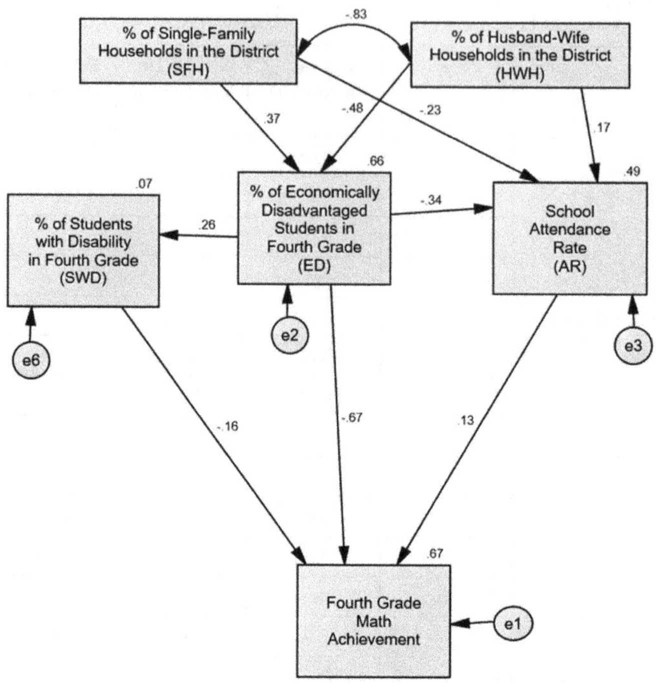

per capita controlling for unemployment. There was a strong, positive partial correlation between Life Satisfaction (6.5 ± 1.12) and GDP per capita (9,776 ± 11,209) controlling for unemployment (10.08 ± 7.67 years), which was statistically significant, r (79) = 0.598, p = .00. zero-order correlations showed that there was a statistically significant, strong correlation between Life Satisfaction and GDP per capita r (80) = .64, p < .000, indicating that unemployment had very little influence in controlling for the relationship between Life Satisfaction and GDP *per capita*. The same situation with the rest of the variables. Unemployment is not a controlling variable. However, there is a slight change from p = .065 to p = .111 in the case of the relationship between Percentage Tertiary Education and Life Satisfaction, unemployment may have some control. The researcher recommends continuing to observe this relationship with different years.

CONCLUSION

The central premise of this study was that increasing the educational attainment of the population can help to increase the economic wellbeing; however, this relationship

Table 4. Relationship between life satisfaction and education and GDP per capita, while controlling for unemployment

Control Variables		Life Satisfaction	GDP per Capita	Percentage of Tertiary Complete	Years of Schooling
Real GDP per capita	r	0.639			
	p	0			
	df	80			
Percentage of Tertiary Complete	r	0.204	0.5		
	p	0.065	0		
	df	80	80		
Years of Schooling	r	0.274	0.635	0.732	
	p	0.013	0	0	
	df	80	80	80	
Unemployment (%)	r	-0.304	-0.342	-0.117	0.021
	p	0.006	0.002	0.295	0.854
	df	80	80	80	80
Unemployment Real GDP per capita	r	0.598			
	p	0			
	df	79			
Percentage of Tertiary Complete	r	0.178	0.493		
	p	0.111	0		
	df	79	79		
Years of Schooling	r	0.295	0.683	0.739	
	p	0.008	0	0	
	df	79	79	79	

is not always direct, and there are some key variables, such as employment, and Life Satisfaction that can affect this relationship.

To pioneering human capital theorists, a fundamental reason for economic growth was to be found in the increase of productivity of the factors of production. Education will increase the quality of human resources, and human resources is one of the factors of production, and as a consequence, education will contribute to economic growth. In this study, growth rate was not used; rather, the actual GDP *per capita* was used. This study supports the hypothesis that education contributes to the GDP *per capita*, and remains on the same track of studies with Pencavel (1993), De Meulmester and Rochet (1995), and Quamruzzaman (2013). The findings indicate that education in general, and specifically percentage of tertiary education influences the GDP per capita (sharing a variance of 29%). Number of years of schooling accounted for 39% of the variances of GDP per capita. In the same way, years of schooling shared a variance of Life Satisfaction up to 8%. Thus, education contributes to Life Satisfaction, as previously pointed by Easterlin (2013).

After the 2008 U.S. economic crisis, unemployment rates became part of the discussion, so new findings were presented about this relationship, showing that unemployment inversely correlates with GDP *per capita* and Life Satisfaction. This study extends this theory specifically to higher education which provides high skill and quality in labor. Nevertheless, investment would not contribute to improvements in economic growth if policy makers did not also relate education to labor. In other words, higher education must provide the education related to and needed by the labor market, especially in the case of tertiary education

The connections between higher education and the labor market are among the most frequently discussed issues of higher education. Teichler (1999) showed his preoccupation with the need for systematic knowledge and empirical evidence. While testing trivariate causalities, Morote (2001) found a causal relationship between higher education enrollments and employment rates. This study adds empirical evidence to the testing of this relationship. However, in this study unemployment and education did not have a direct relationship.

The results of this study confirm that the employment rate is a key factor in that it affects Life Satisfaction and GDP per capita. In this study, unemployment was not found related to education—a finding that contradicts previous studies. However, in the case of tertiary education, some tendencies suggested that this relationship may exist. Once unemployment was included, this relationship became non-significant. Variables such as quality of education should be included in future studies.

The results of this study coincided with the findings of Howe (1993) and Daisi (2011) who stated that higher levels of education increase the labor market's response to the rising education level of an expanding labor force. Life Satisfaction shows a strong relationship with the GDP per capita. This is a similar finding to that of Clark, Fleche, and Senik in 2014. Based on previous Human Capital studies combined with this research, it can be inferred that higher education impacts the economy of a country; however, it is highly important to take into account that the economic levels reached because of education will depend on the economic model followed by nation, and specifically, whether the nation's economy is an open economy or a closed economy. Findings match certain empirical patterns identified the income-happiness literature. Future work should include time series analysis on this relationship.

REFERENCES

Abdalla, S., Thompson, S., & Marks, N. (2008). Estimating Worldwide Satisfaction. *Ecological Economics*, *47*(1), 35–42. retrieved from http://www.uvm.edu/pdodds/files/papers/others/everything/abdallah2007a.pdf doi:10.1016/j.ecolecon.2007.11.009

Abowd, J., & Card, D. (1989). On the Covariance Structure of Earnings and Hours Changes. Econometrica, 57(2), 411-445.

Becker, G. (1967). *Human capital and the personal distribution of income; an analytical approach*. Ann Arbor: Institute of Public Administration.

Becker, W., & Lewis, D. (1993). *Higher education and economic growth*. London: Kluwer Academic Publishers. doi:10.1007/978-94-015-8167-7

Birdsall, N., & Sabot, R. (Eds.). (1996). *Opportunity foregone: Education in Brazil. Washington, D.C.: Inter-American Development Bank*. Baltimore, Md.: John Hopkins University Press.

Blaug, M. (1985). Where are we now in the economics of education? *Economics of Education Review*, *4*(1), 17–28. doi:10.1016/0272-7757(85)90034-2

Bok, D. (2010). *The Politics of Happiness: What Government Can Learn from the New Research on Well-Being*. USA: Princeton University Press. doi:10.1515/9781400832194

Carnoy, M. (1994). *Economics of education: research and studies*. Oxford: Pergamon.

Daisi, O. (2011, January 13). The Impact of Human Resource Development on Economic Growth in Nigeria: An Empirical Investigation (1902-2008). doi:10.2139/ssrn.1739492

De Meulmester, J. C., & Rochet, D. (1995). A causality analysis of the link between higher education and economic development. *Economics of Education Review*, *144*(4), 351-361.

Denison, E. F. (1971). Education and the economics of human capital. In R. A. Wykstra (Ed.), Education and Economic Growth. New York Free Press.

DePrince, A., & Morris, P. (2008, April). The Effects of Education on the Natural Rate of Unemployment. *Business Economics (Cleveland, Ohio)*, *43*, 45. doi:10.2145/20080205

Diener, E., Emmons, R. A., Larsen, R. J., & Griffin, S. (1985). The Satisfaction with Life Scale. *Journal of Personality Assessment, 49*(1), 71–75. doi:10.1207/s15327752jpa4901_13 PMID:16367493

Duvall, R. (2001, January) Economic Education: Building on Strength, the Key to the Future

Easterlin, R. (2013, January). Happiness and Economic Growth: The Evidence (IZA Discussion Paper No. 7187). University of Southern California.

Easton, P., & Klees, S. (1990). Education and the economy: Considering alternative perspectives. *Prospects, 20*(4), 413–428. Retrieved from http://poseidon01.ssrn.com/delivery.php?ID=150124106095081120016088118092103022031075036012049018106011111015069015046088024084031004029052040127086090090120127123027104126121123102101107082095029121076068104092017115067&EXT=pdf doi:10.1007/BF02195115

Fitz-Enz, J. (n. d.). The ROI of Human Capital: Measuring the Economic Value of Employee Performance

Frey, B., & Stutzer, A. (2001). *Happiness and Economics: How the Economy and Institutions Affect Human Well-Being*. Princeton University Press.

Gregory, P. (1986). *The myth of market failure, employment and the labor market in Mexico*. Baltimore, London: The Johns Hopkins University Press, Published for the World Bank.

Hanushek, E., & Woessmann, L. (2007, February 1). The Role of Education Quality for Economic Growth (Working Paper No. 4122). World Bank Policy Research. Retrieved from http://ssrn.com/abstract=960379

Hosen, R., Solovey-Hosen, D., & Stern, L. (2003, Spring). Education and Capital Development: Capital as Durable Personal, Social, Economic and Political Influences on the Happiness of Individuals. *Education, 123*(3).

Howe, W. J. (1993). The effects of higher education on unemployment rates. In W. E. Becker & D. R. Lewis (Eds.), *Higher education and economic growth* (pp. 129–145). Netherlands: Kluwer Academic Publishers Group. doi:10.1007/978-94-015-8167-7_6

ILO. (2016). Statistics. Retrieved from http://www.ilo.org/stat/lang--en/index.htm

Jones, G., Ogawa, N., & Williamson, J. (1993). *Human resources in development along the Asia-Pacific Rim*. New York, Singapore: Oxford University Press.

Jorgenson, H. (1984). The contribution of education to U.S. economic growth. In E. Dean (Ed.), *Education and economic productivity* (pp. 95–163). Cambridge, Massachusetts: Ballinger Publishing Company.

Jorgenson, H., & Fraumeni, M. (1998). *Investment in education and U.S. economic growth.* Netherlands: Kluwer Academic Publishers.

King, E., & World Bank. (2011). Education is fundamental to develop and growth. Retrieved from http://blogs.worldbank.org/education/education-is-fundamental-to-development-and-growth

Knight, J., & Gunatilaka, R. (2012). Subjective Well-being and Social Evaluation in a Poor Country (CSAE Working Paper WPS/2014-09). Centre for the Study of African Economies, University of Oxford.

Krueger, A., & Lindahl, M. (2001). Education for Growth: Why and for Whom? *Journal of Economic Literature*, *39*(4), 1101–1136. doi:10.1257/jel.39.4.1101

Learn.org. (2016). tertiary education. Retrieved from learn.org

Malik, A., & Singh, D. (2012). Happiness: A Central Objective of Positive Psychology. *Indian Journal of Positive Psychology, 3*(1).

Miller, D. (2013, July-September). Universities and Colleges as Economic Drivers: Measuring Higher Education's Role in Economic Development. *Planning for Higher Education, 41*(4).

Mitchell, W. C., & United States, President's Research Committee on Social Trends. (1933). Recent Social Trends in the United States: Report of the President's Research Committee on Social Trends (Vol. 1). New York: McGraw-Hill. Retrieved from Questia

Morote, E.-S. (2001). Relationship Among Higher Education, Economic Growth and Employment in Latin American Leading Emerging Markets (Dissertation). University of Pittsburgh.

Nicolae, E. (2012). Happiness, Economics and Politics. towards a Multi-Disciplinary Approach. *The Journal of Philosophical Economics, 5*(2).

O'Neill, B. (2014, January). What's the Economy for, Anyway? Why It's Time to Stop Chasing Growth and Start Pursuing Happiness. *Journal of Financial Counseling and Planning.*

OECD DOCUMENTS. (1996). *Employment and growth in the knowledge–based economy*. Paris: OECD.

Ohtake, F. (2012). Unemployment and Happiness. Japan Labor Review, vol. 9, no. 2, Spring 2012

Partnership for 21 Century Skills (2008). 21st Century Skills Education and Competitiveness. http://www.p21.org/storage/documents/21st_century_skills_education_and_competitiveness_guide.pdf 2008

Pavot, W. G., Diener, E., Colvin, C. R., & Sandvik, E. (1991). Further validation of the Satisfaction with Life Scale: Evidence for the cross-method convergence of well-being measures. *Journal of Personality Assessment, 57*(1), 149–161. doi:10.1207/s15327752jpa5701_17 PMID:1920028

Pencavel, J. (1993). Higher education, economic growth, and earnings. In W. E. Becker & D. R. Lewis (Eds.), *Higher education and economic growth* (pp. 51–87). Netherlands: Kluwer Academic Publishers Group. doi:10.1007/978-94-015-8167-7_3

Psacharopolous, G. (1988, Fall). Returns to Education: A further international update and implications. *Journal of Human Resources, 20*(4), 893-921.

Psacharopoulos, G. (Ed.). (1987). *Economics of education: Research and studies*. New York: Pergamon Press.

Psacharopoulos, G., & Woodhall, M. (1985). *Education for development: An analysis of investment choices*. USA: World Bank, Oxford University Press.

Quamruzzaman, A. (2013, February). The Pursuit Of Happiness: An Analysis Of Aggregate Difference In The Distribution of Happiness In The United States. *Mcgill Sociological Review, 3*.

Ritzen, J. (1977). Education, economic growth, and income distribution. New York: North-Holland Pub. Co.

Rondinelli, D., & Montgomery, J. (1995). *Great policies: Strategic innovations in Asia and The Pacific Basin. Rotterdam, Netherlands: Erasmus Universiteit Rotterdam, Institute for Economic Research*. Published Westport, Conn: Praeger Publishing.

Saha, L., & Faberlind, I. (1994). Education and development. In H. Torsten, & T. Neville (Eds.), The international encyclopedia of education. USA: Pergamon.

Sala-i-Martin, X., Doppelhofer, G., & Miller, R. (2004). Determinants of Long Term Growth: ABayesian Averaging of Classical Estimates (BACE) Approach. *The American Economic Review, 94*(4), 813–835. doi:10.1257/0002828042002570

Sanyal, B. C. (1987). *Higher education and employment*. Great Britain: The Falmer Press, UNESCO.

Schultz, T. (1988). *Education, investment and returns. In handbook of development economics*. The Netherlands: North Holland.

Shin, D., & Johnson, D. (1978). Happiness as the Overall Assesment of the Quality of Life. *Source Social Indicators Research*, *5*(1-4), 475–492. doi:10.1007/BF00352944

Shultz, P. (1994). Human capital investment in women and men. Occasional Papers (N. 44). San Francisco, California: International Center for Economic Growth.

Shultz, P. (1997). *Latin American education: Comparative perspectives* (C. A. Torres & A. Puiggrós, Eds.). Boulder, Colo.: Westview Press.

Sianesi, B., & Van Reenen, J. (2003). The returns to education: Macroeconomics. *Journal of Economic Surveys*, *17*(2), 157–200. doi:10.1111/1467-6419.00192

21. st Century Partnership. (2008). 21st Century Skills Education and Competitiveness. USA: http://www.p21.org/storage/documents/21st_century_skills_education_and_competitiveness_guide.pdf

Teichler, U. (1999). Higher education policy and the world of work: Changing conditions and challenges. *Higher Education Policy*, *12*(4), 285–312. doi:10.1016/S0952-8733(99)00019-7

The QoG Institute. (2016). The QoG Standard Data Set. Code Book. Retrieved from http://www.qogdata.pol.gu.se/data/qog_std_jan16.pdf (10/4/2016)

The QoG Institute. (2016). The QoG Standard Data Set. http://qog.pol.gu.se/data/datadownloads/qogstandarddata

University of Gothenburg. Sweden. (2016, 1 1). Quality of Government Institute. Retrieved from http://qog.pol.gu.se/data

Ura, D. K., Alkire, S., & Zangmo, T. (2011). The Gross National Happiness Index of Bhutan: Method and Illustrative Results. Retrieved from OECD presentations: http://www.oecd.org/site/ssfc2011/48920513.pdf

US Bureau of Labor Statistics. (2008, 1 1). US Bureau of Labor Statistics. Retrieved 10 1, 2016 from US Bureau of Labor Statistics: http://www.bls.gov/

World Economic Forum Global Agenda Council on Employment. (2014, 1 22-25). Matching Skills and Labour Market Needs Building Social Partnerships for Better Skills and Better Jobs. Retrieved from http://www3.weforum.org/docs/GAC/2014/WEF_GAC_Employment_MatchingSkillsLabourMarket_Report_2014.pdf

KEY TERMS AND DEFINITIONS

GDP per Capita: According to the World Bank GDP per capita is equal to the GDP "The gross domestic product of a country is the total value added by all the residents in the country in the last period plus any product taxes and minus any subsidies that are not included in the total value of the products". (https://www.reference.com/world-view/gdp-per-capita) In this document the Real GDP per capita is estimated of real GDP per Capita in constant US dollars at base year 2000 (The QoG Institute, 2016).

Gross Domestic Product (GDP): The total market value of all final goods and services produced in a country in a given year; equals total consumer, investment and government spending, plus the value of exports minus the value of imports.

Life Satisfaction: Global assessment of a person's quality of life according to his or her chosen criteria (Shin & Johnson, 1978). Life Satisfaction. In the QoG, it consists of approximately 300 variables from 75 different data sources. Life Satisfaction, taken from the World Value Survey (WVS), has involved four waves of surveys across 81 countries and entities, carried out between 1990 and 2005. All of those surveys have included the following question: "All things considered, how satisfied are you with your life as a whole these days?" Respondents answered on a 1–10 scale (The QoG Institute, 2016).

Tertiary Education: Tertiary education, more commonly referred to as postsecondary education, refers to academic pursuit undertaken after high school. Undergraduate programs include any postsecondary education that takes up to four years to complete, including certificates, diplomas, and associate and bachelor's degrees. Graduate programs typically require prior completion of an undergraduate degree and include diploma, certificate, master's and doctoral degree programs. Tertiary education programs can be found at vocational schools, community colleges, technical schools, professional schools, colleges, and universities (Learn.org, 2016). Data were taking from the Educational Attainment Dataset- the Barro-Lee Data, explained in the previous section (years of schooling).

Unemployment: The general definition that International Labor Office (ILO) (ILO, 2016) used for unemployment: "(a) workers available for employment whose contract of employment had been terminated or temporally suspended and who were without jobs and seeking work for pay or profit. (b) Persons who are available for work, and were seeking work for pay or profit and were never previously employed. (c) Persons without a job and currently available for work who had made an arrangement to start a new job at a date subsequent to the specified period. (d)

Persons on temporary or indefinite lay-off without pay." (https://stats.oecd.org/glossary/)) In this study the QoG data was original collected from World Economic Outlook Database The World Economic Outlook (WEO) database contains selected macroeconomic data series from the statistical appendix of the World Economic Outlook report. Use this database to find data on national accounts, inflation, and unemployment rates (The QoG Institute, 2016).

Years of Schooling: The QoG collected this data from the Educational Attainment Dataset- the Barro-Lee Data. It provides educational attainment data for 146 countries in 5-year intervals from 1950 to 2010. It also provides information about the distribution of educational attainment of the adult population over age 15 and over age 25 by sex at seven levels of schooling- no formal education, incomplete primary, complete primary, lower secondary, upper secondary, incomplete tertiary, and complete tertiary. Average years of schooling at all levels - primary, secondary, and tertiary - are also measured for each country and for regions in the world. Aside from updating and expanding our previous estimates (1993, 1996, and 2001), QoG improve the accuracy of estimation in the current version by using more information and better methodology (The QoG Institute, 2016).

Chapter 7
Pension Systems Dynamics:
A Pooled Data Analysis

Salvador Rivas-Aceves
Universidad Panamericana, Mexico

Edmundo Marroquín-Tovar
Universidad Panamericana, Mexico

Héctor X. Ramírez-Pérez
Universidad Panamericana, Mexico

ABSTRACT

The main focus of the chapter is to define directions and magnitudes of causality of the pension systems, labor force, and hours worked for selected OECD (Organization for Economic Co-operation and Development) countries through a pool data analysis. The information is examined within basic, intermediate, and advanced statistical analyses by regional comparison of the OECD countries. Main results include: (a) a positive impact of Labor Force size on Pension Systems, (b) a negative effect of the Average Hours Worked on Pension Systems, (c) when introducing cross-section and time series heterogeneity, relations are sustained from both global and regional inquiry, (d) an insightful and meticulous investigation can be performed using public and open databases if depuration of the information is well conducted.

INTRODUCTION

The use of a database to conduct research is a helpful way to gain an understanding of the behavior of a phenomenon by identifying its causes and consequences. Podestà (2002) stated that pooled data analysis, also called pooled time series cross-section

DOI: 10.4018/978-1-5225-3616-1.ch007

analysis, is the combination of time series and cross-section data analysis. In order to conduct such an analysis, one must first perform a statistical analysis, which can be executed at three different levels: basic, medium and advanced analysis.

The purpose of this chapter is to gain a phenomenological understanding of pension systems by conducting a statistical analysis. Data on demography and hours worked were retrieved to identify their relationships to pension systems. The authors compared and analyzed trends, differences, and similarities.

The first step was to identify the relationship of each country's pension system to its demography. Then the authors described the relationship of hours worked to pension systems. Finally, a joint estimation measured the simultaneous effects of demography and hours worked on pension systems. This research includes OECD member countries divided by regions. The main objective of this study is to present a methodology for performing research through OEDC open access data sets and OEDC publications. The topics selected serve as an example of the quality research available through open access libraries and data sets.

BACKGROUND

The scope of the literature review was set to open access publications from OECD, according to the objective of this study. After reviewing the main sources and publication dates of the publications retrieved, the authors realized that chapters, graphs, and tables can be found in books written and published by OECD, so they are included in the publications retrieved by the search engine. The main source was *Pensions at a Glance*, published every two years; the latest version was published in 2015. The authors decided to narrow the search to editions in English with a publication date on or after 2012, considering that *Pensions at a Glance* (2015) included the findings from previous OECD's publications and compiled updated data related to pensions of the OECD countries and several non-OECD countries.

The main concern of this research was that "pension systems are facing crucial and far-reaching challenges" (OECD, 2014B, p. 9) due to demography and life expectancy, so "reforms in the pension system are needed to extend coverage" (De la Maisonneuve, 2015, p. 3). The OECD stated, "pensions are under pressure from the retiring of the baby boom generations, [as well as] the improvements in mortality and life expectancy" (OECD, 2014B, p. 9).

OECD (2015A) established that "first-tier old-age pensions are defined as the first layer of protection of the elderly" and may have three components: (a) a basic pension, (b) a minimum pension, and (c) social assistance. Pension systems around the globe have been changing from a common fund for elderly people using a basic pension scheme to a pension based on individual's contributions using a defined contribution scheme, according to OECD: "Most OECD countries have already moved or are moving towards a more diversified pension system, where PAYG [pay as you go] pensions need to be complemented with funded pension arrangements and other savings in order to ensure retirement income adequacy" (OECD, 2012, p. 101).

However, those efforts are not enough due to changes in many factors, including demography, life expectancy, hours worked, wages, and technology. Fall and Bloch (2014) found that pension schemes have been reformed in most OECD countries over the last twenty years to cope with the demographic trend towards ageing populations; yet, more efforts are needed to ensure the long run financial sustainability of pension schemes while preserving pension adequacy, and a sound, prudential regulatory framework for private and defined-contribution schemes is needed to protect individuals' pensions.

The change in the labor market is caused by several factors, including "the introduction of labor mobility in an overlapping-generations model with PAYG pensions [that] implies that labor flows are not only driven by differences in wages, but also by differences in the generosity of the welfare state" (Fedotenkov & Meijdam, 2013, p. 178), and "the amount of labor absorbed by the 'new economy' will probably continue to decrease… New forms of employment are spreading: part-time jobs, outsourcing, fixed-length contracts replace full-time employment and the traditional employer-employee link" (Augusztinovics, 2002, p. 22). Augusztinovics stated that:

Sooner or later, however, it will have to become evident that employment-based pension insurance is no longer compatible with the new scope and structure of the labor market, and that large fractions of the present working-age generation will be left without sufficient income in old age—not because of demographic but because of economic trends. It would be more reasonable to start planning ahead as soon as possible, rather than pass on the problem to future generations. A task, then, for pension system design, maybe comparable only to what the founding fathers of pension systems accomplished in their time. This is the real challenge of the twenty-first century. (p. 31)

Ageing Population

The Pension system is one of the most important economic indicators analyzed by many countries because of its long-term implications regarding age of the population and the funds needed to provide adequate living conditions for older people. According to OECD's *Pensions at a Glance* (2015), in the last decade many OECD and G20 countries (the most economically developed countries) implemented reforms in their pension systems to adapt their economic systems to a new reality of an increasing ageing society. The most visible change in several countries was moving up the official pension age parameter from 65 to 67 years old because the employment rates of workers aged 55 to 64 years went from 52 to 57 percent of the population of the OECD countries.

The outcomes of the pension systems among countries present substantial variations. For example, the future gross replacement rates for workers with average work earnings of the 34 countries in the OECD averages 53 percent for men and 52 percent for women. However, Mexico and United Kingdom offer the lowest future replacement rates of 25 to 30 percent, while The Netherlands offers replacement rates of slightly more than 90 percent.

French (2005) stated, "pension benefits typically depend on years of service at the firm, the highest annual earnings at the firm (usually the average of the five highest earnings years), and a formula that depends on age and years of service at the firm. The part of the pension formula that depends on age and years of service generates the incentive to leave the firm by the normal retirement age… therefore, delaying exit from the firm after the normal retirement age results in a reduction in the present value of pension benefits" (p. 400).

According to Militaru (2011) "the acceleration of the aging process is a major phenomenon worldwide; Europe and Japan face this situation in particular" (p. 175). With the combination of two factors, the baby boomers retiring and the labor market shrinking in terms of the number of employees, the deficit of the Pension Fund will increase and thus the target budget subsidy will have to be increased (Obidziński, 2010).

Poverty among those of 65 and older is different in the OECD countries. On average, 12.6 percent of older people are poor; however, in countries such as Korea (50 percent), Australia (36 percent), and Mexico (31 percent), older people tend to be poorer. In contrast, countries such as The Netherlands and Czech Republic have the lowest poverty rates of two and three percent, respectively (OECD, 2015A).

According to the OECD report, public pensions expending are the largest single item of social expenditure; it reaches 18 percent of total government expending on average when in 2011 it represented 7.9 percent of the Gross Domestic Product (GDP) of the OECD countries. Similarly to previous measures, there are cross-national differences with countries with low levels of expenditure as a percentage of GDP such as Mexico, Iceland, and Korea with 1.8, 2.1, and 2.2 percent respectively of public pensions expenditure as a percentage of the GDP, compared to countries such as Italy, Greece, or France, in which public pension expenditures represent 15.8, 14.5, and 13.8 percent respectively of the GDP.

Life Expectancy

Having an older society represents new financial challenges that countries had not faced before. On the one hand, it is expected that by year 2050, 27 percent of the population in the OECD countries will be 65 or more years old in comparison to 16 percent of the people in 2015. On the other hand, employment rates falls with age even before the official retirement age; in 2014, 67 percent of people with 55 to 59 years had jobs, but the percentage decreased to 44 and 20 percent for those aged 60-64 and 65-69, respectively in OECD and G20 countries.

Even though some reforms assure better financial outcomes to handle an ageing society, countries are facing another challenging reality as the fertility rate is below the replacement level of about 2.1 children needed to keep the total population constant. Only two countries, Israel and Mexico, are above that replacement level. In 2013, the average replacement level of the OECD countries was 1.67, and it is expected to grow to 1.85 in 2060, when replacement level would still be below the required rate. In the future, we will have not only an older population, but also a lower rate of people employed and fewer births; fewer people capable of working for an increasing population in retirement age.

Pensions were designed and calculated with a life expectancy age around 65 years but life expectancy has been increasing rapidly. In the period of 2010 to 2015, on average for OECD countries, women lived almost 21 years longer after age 65—a number that would increase to almost 26 years more longevity by 2060-65. Men lived 17.4 years after retirement in the period of 2010-15, and they will live almost 22 years after retirement by 2060-65. Therefore, the dependency ratio will go from 28 percent of people 65 and older in 2016 to 55 percent of people of 65 or older in 2075. More than half of the population will be retired in 60 years and with an increased life expectancy.

Extending the retirement age is a way to postpone the pension plan, but this measure may have other impacts on the level of wages and put pressure to provide enough jobs for new young entrants. Nevertheless, it is a viable option due to the extended life expectancy and the quality of life or health that senior workers will have. OECD (2014C) stated that life expectancy at retirement keeps increasing, and governments may want to keep either the average period spent in retirement stable in absolute terms or decide to keep the ratio between the time spent in work and the time spent in retirement constant and to index the pension age to life expectancy (OECD, 2014C).

The recommendation from OECD (2014C) was "encouraging retention in work of older people and of improving the opportunities for recruiting senior workers" (p. 103). Fall and Bloch (2014) agreed with the retirement age extension, stating that "in most countries, the retirement age has been increased and early retirement schemes phased out to improve the financial sustainability of pension schemes" (p. 7).

OECD (2014A) stated that the remarkable decline in mortality, as evidenced by the increase in life expectancy, is one of the greatest achievements of the last century. Lives continue to get longer, and this trend is predicted to continue. In 2010-15, life expectancy at birth averaged 70.7 years for men and 76.6 years for women. (p. 42)

However, OECD also remarked that, "while living longer and healthier lives is fundamentally good news, population ageing challenges the financial sustainability, solvency and adequacy of pension systems" (p. 9), and Knell (2012) added that, "increasing life expectancy is of particular interest, since it represents an ongoing process with considerable and far-reaching budgetary consequences" (p. 1).

Fall and Bloch (2014) found that many countries have introduced adjustment mechanisms to take into account changes in life expectancy. The adjustment can link the pension level, the retirement age or the contribution period to life expectancy. In national defined-contributions schemes (Sweden, Chile, Estonia, Mexico and Italy) and some defined-contributions plans, accumulated contributions and investment returns are converted into a pension or annuity in retirement, with the conversion factor depending on life expectancy. Denmark, Greece and Italy have introduced reforms to index the retirement age to life expectancy. In France, the automatic adjustment mechanism targets the contribution period, which is adjusted according to life expectancy gains in order to maintain a constant ratio between the duration of activity (2/3) and the expected duration in retirement (1/3). (p. 16) Fall and Block (2014) also found that:

Life expectancy gains are combined with a decrease in fertility rates in almost all OECD countries. These two phenomena are jointly lowering the old-age support ratio (the working age population (20-64) over the retirement age (65+) population). It is projected that between 2010 and 2050, the average OECD old-age support ratio will be halved from 4.4 to 2.1. Japan is expected to have the lowest support ratio (1.3) in 2050, while Mexico is projected to show the most rapid decline (going from 9.1 to 2.8). (p. 10)

Additionally, Augusztinovics (2002) pointed out, "Pension systems are exposed to the system-dependency ratio (number of pensioners over the number of contributors) rather than to the demographic old-age dependency ratio and the two ratios may significantly diverge because of trends on the labor market." (p. 22)

Pension Policy Challenges

Regarding the Latin-American region, OECD stated that "the biggest pension policy challenge faced by most countries in Latin America and the Caribbean (LAC) today is low coverage of formal pension systems, both in terms of the proportion of workers participating in pension schemes and the proportion of the elderly receiving some kind of pension income"(OECD, 2014A, p. 9) and "active coverage (i.e. contribution payments of workers to mandatory pension schemes) is low in LAC countries; on average in the region, only 45 in 100 workers are contributing to or affiliated with a pension scheme." (OECD, 2014A, p. 9)

An issue for this region is the proportion of formal employment versus self-employed workers that increase pressure on pension funds; OECD affirmed, "A key determinant of pension coverage in LAC is the type of employment. On average, 64 out of 100 salaried workers contribute to a pension scheme in LAC compared to only 17 out of 100 self-employed workers" (OECD, 2014A, p. 9). For example, "Colombia is one of the most unequal countries in Latin America. The high level of informality in the labor market and many characteristics of the pension system leave many elderly in poverty. Only formal-sector employees earning more than the relatively high minimum wage are covered." (De la Maisonneuve, 2015, p. 3)

The low pensions of elderly people in Latin America create an obligation for family members to support them or they have to keep working. OECD found that "a large share of older people in LAC will have to rely on other sources of income than contributory pensions, such as work income, assets such as housing, transfers, social pensions and informal family support" (OECD, 2014A, p. 10). To solve this issue, different countries have been taking different approaches; OECD stated "the countries in Latin America and the Caribbean are attempting to address the coverage issue in different ways but the most evident trend and the policy that appears to be having the most impact is the extension of social pensions." (OECD, 2014A, p. 32)

Regarding replacement rates for the Latin-American region "the total fertility rate is above the replacement level – the number of children needed to keep the total population constant – in 20 out of 26 LAC countries for 2005-10" (OECD, 2014A, p 40) and "The gross replacement rate shows the level of pensions in retirement relative to earnings when working. For workers with average earnings, the gross replacement rate averages 62% in the 26 LAC countries.

More funds have to be raised by the pension systems; OECD recommended, "increasing the mandatory contribution rate, but gradually" (OECD, 2016C, p. 4). The recommendation applies also to other regions different to LAC, as well; Fall and Bloch (2014) affirmed, "there is a need to ensure the financial sustainability of pension systems. In most BRIC countries (Brazil, Russia, India, and China), even though pension system coverage is far from universal, pension spending is already weighing on public finances" (Fall & Bloch, 2014, p. 6). Other actions are to "consider introducing mandatory contributions for self-employed workers to increase coverage and lengthen contributions periods" (OECD, 2016C, p. 16) and "increasing coverage of voluntary private pensions in countries where they represent an important complement to (relatively low) public pensions." (Fall & Bloch, 2014, p. 7)

The Swedish pension system, for example, has "a large National Defined Contribution (NDC) tier with automatic balancing mechanism, a defined contribution tier with centralized administration of accounts and a state-sponsored default fund" (Kent & Willén, 2014, p. 2). For the case of Israel, Giorno and Adda (2016) stated that the country is financially well prepared to withstand this development, thanks to the reforms implemented since the mid-1990s and it considers its performance in terms of avoiding poverty among the elderly, and more generally assesses its fairness and effectiveness in ensuring that everybody receives a sufficient pension; but it is already beginning to face the consequences of population ageing." (Giorno & Adda, 2016, p. 3)

Regarding demography, OECD (2012) stated, "to adapt pension systems to demographic trends, many countries are reducing pay-as-you-go (PAYG) public pension levels and lifting retirement ages" (OECD, 2012, p. 99). Fall and Bloch (2014) mentioned that demographic developments are unfavorable to the financing of pension systems in most OECD countries, because of rising life expectancy and declining fertility rates. The resulting decline in the old age support ratio is particularly challenging for PAYG pension schemes as pension spending is financed by contributions of current workers. In Germany, the revaluation of retirement points (which determine the pension level) takes into account the evolution of the demographic dependency ratio. (Fall & Bloch, 2014) Fall and Bloch (2014) proposed the following strategy:

The sustainability of pension systems can be ensured by a combination of different policy measures. Many countries are phasing in increases in the retirement age to restore the financial health of pension schemes. Adjusting key parameters automatically to cope with changes in structural variables can increase the financial robustness of pension systems. Many countries have introduced adjustment mechanisms to take into account changes in life expectancy. The adjustment can link the pension level, retirement age or contribution period to life expectancy. Increasing the contribution rate would improve financial sustainability, but could have a negative impact on labor markets. (p. 7)

MAIN FOCUS OF THE CHAPTER

Issues, Controversies, Problems

Decrease of Employment Rates

A big concern besides an ageing population, as presented in the background section, is the decrease of employment rates of the population. From 1960 to 2012 the employment rates of men decreased approximately by 10 percent, as showed in Figure 1. This situation might be explained because of the increase in number of older people in age of retirement that influenced the total population, however that assumption might not be accurate when analyzing the increase in employment rates among women. In the same period, female work force went from 40 percent to almost 60 percent, even though women tend to live longer than men do. If the reason is the share of people in retirement, then the trend in women's workforce would also be decreasing and there is no such thing. There is the need of more research to find out the reasons men are working less, but the reality is that more women are finding more working opportunities and they are becoming more protagonists in the workforce shape.

If labor force does influence pension systems, the decrease in the number of men involved in the workforce might represent a main problem in the near future, especially when over one quarter of the population will be in age of retirement by 2050. In this chapter, the aim is to work with long-size databases to find out if there are any connections between this demographic phenomenon and economic outcomes. In addition, to find out how useful databases are in research to discover new explanations of a phenomenon, in this case, if the pension system has a relationship with the size of labor force.

If women were substituting men in working positions, there would be no concern because while men decreased approximately 10 percent, women increased by 18 percent in the same period, which would result in an increasing labor force, no matter the gender. However, there is another risk associated to the only increase of women in the workforce effect: women tend to have more part-time jobs than men do. As presented in Figure 2 in the OECD countries over 20 percent of women have part-time jobs vs. less than 10 percent of men having part-time jobs.

There are countries such as Hungary where less than 10 percent of men and women have a part-time job; on contrary, there are countries such as the Netherlands that over 50 percent of working women have a part-time job. In general, working women tend to have more part-time jobs than men do. The OECD study defines part-time job as a job of less than 30 hours. For the analysis presented in this chapter, it would be valuable to define if average of hours worked had an impact on the pension

Figure 1. Employment rates among men and women
Source: Data extracted from OECD Employment and Labor Market Statistics, www.oecd-ilibrary.org/employment/data/oecd-employmentand-labour-market-statistics_lfs-data-en.

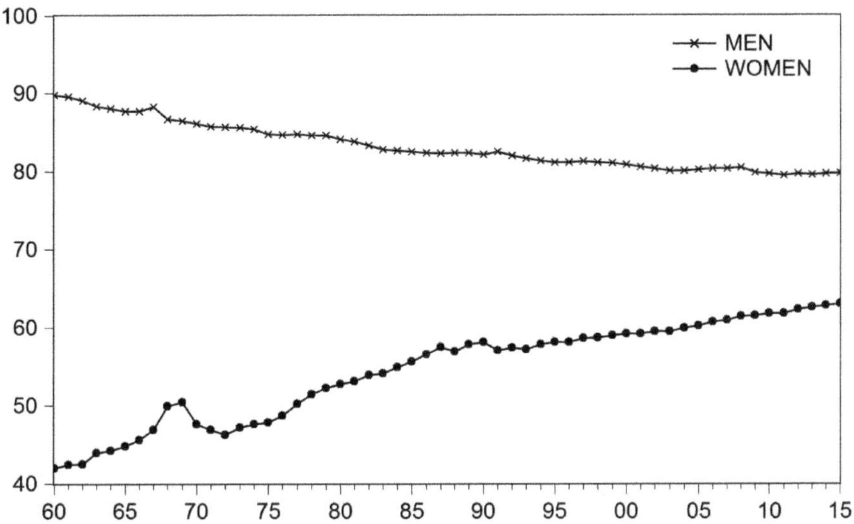

systems. If increasing the average hours worked have a positively impact in pension systems, there might be the conclusion that having more part-time jobs might affect pension systems negatively because there might be more people working, but with fewer hours and therefore without a positive contribution. However, if average hours worked does not have a positive impact on pension systems, then there would be no worries if a new job is either part- or full-time.

Furthermore, there is another concern when the increase of labor force is represented only by women. The maternal employment rates of women differ when having children. According to Figure 3, in the OECD countries the maternal employment rate represents only above 50 percent when the youngest children ages 0 to 2 years old. When the youngest child is at the age between 6 and 14, the maternal employment rate represents almost 80 percent of the women´s employment rate.

Therefore, the concern is having an older society and fewer hands to produce enough funds for all because the group of people with the higher increase are women, and part of this group tend to exit job when having kids. At this point, there are no elements to assure that having more people working or working more hours have an impact on pension systems.

OECD (2014D) defines hours worked as the total number of hours actually worked per year divided by the average number of people in employment per year.

Figure 2. Incidence of part-time employment by gender, 2013
Source: OECD Family Database, www.oecd.org/els/family/database.htm and OECD Employment and Labor Market Statistics, www.oecdilibrary.org/employment/data/oecd-employment-and-labour-market-statistics_lfs-data-en.

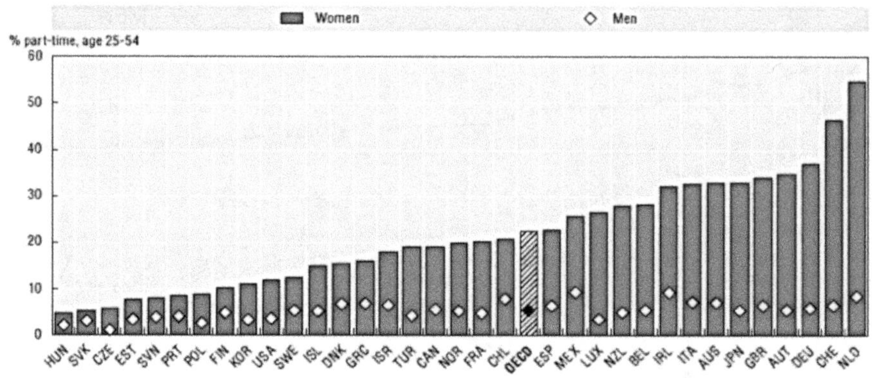

Actual hours worked include regular work hours of full-time, part-time and part-year workers, paid and unpaid overtime, hours worked in additional jobs, and exclude time not worked because of public holidays, annual paid leave, own illness, injury and temporary disability, maternity leave, parental leave, schooling or training, slack work for technical or economic reasons, strike or labor dispute, bad weather, compensation leave and other reasons. The data cover employees and self-employed workers.

According to OECD (2016D), hours worked have fallen in all OECD countries over the period of 2000 to 2012. In 2014, the average hours worked for OECD's countries was 1,770 hours. Germany had the lowest average with 1,371 hours. Germany, Netherlands, Norway, Denmark and France had an average below 1,500 hours. Mexico had the highest average with 2,228 hours. Mexico, Costa Rica, Korea and Greece had an average above 2,000 hours. OECD (2014D) states that lower hours worked are one of the forms in which the benefits of productivity growth have been shared by people.

For this chapter, the authors focused their attention on three variables: average work hours and labor force as independent variables and pension systems as the dependent variable. In the following section, an analysis is presented as an example of the use of databases as a source to expand knowledge through research. The information is a comparison between two important economic groups of countries such as NAFTA (North American Free Trade Agreement) and the European Union (EU).

Figure 3. Maternal employment rate by the age of the youngest child
Source: OECD Family Database, www.oecd.org/els/family/database.htm.

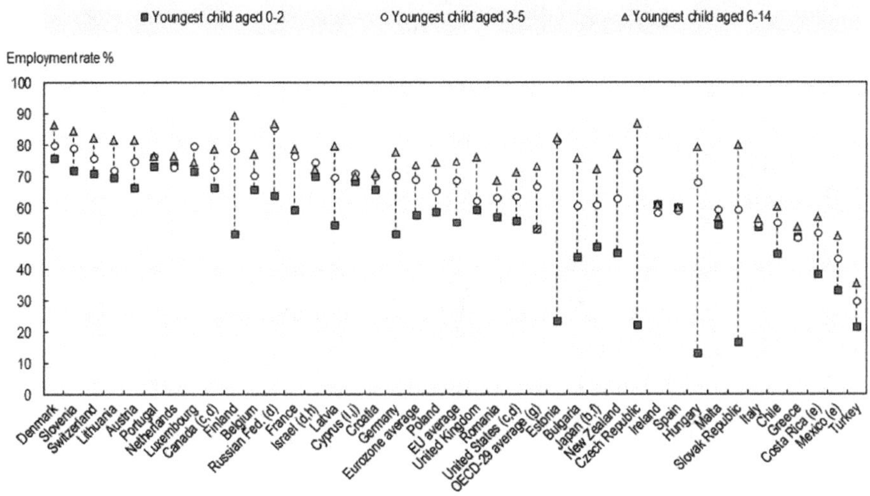

Country's Pension Systems, Labor Force and Hours Worked: A Pool Data Analysis

Analyzing the Pension System (PS) is the main objective in this research. Then considering the Average of Hours Worked (AHW) by workers and the size of Labor Force (LF) as the main determinants of a Pension System, a statistical study in all three levels will be carried out: basic, medium, and advanced level statistical analysis. Open database covers from several disaggregated variables of all three most of them available for most countries, so variables' measures are categorized in:

- Pension System
  - Pension plans
    - Occupational pension plans
    - Personal pension plans
    - Total
  - Benefit type
    - Hybrid benefit
    - Traditional benefit
    - Contribution protected
    - Unprotected contribution
    - Total

    - Plan type
        - Employee contributions
        - Employer contributions
        - Investment
- Average Annual Hours Worked per Worker
    - Dependent employment
    - Total employment
- Labor Force
    - Civilian employment
        - Civilian employment females: agriculture, industry, and services
        - Civilian employment males: agriculture, industry, and services
    - Civilian labor force
        - Civilian labor force females
        - Civilian labor force males
    - Population
        - Population females: between 15-64 years old, over 65, and under 15
        - Population males: between 15-64 years old, over 65, and under 15
        - Population over 65
        - Population under 15
        - Total employment
        - Total labor force
        - Unemployment
        - Persons
        - Index
        - Percentage

Under this categorizing, there are 47,935 observations available for study. Hence, information provided by the database was simplified as follow:

- Pension System
    - Total pension plans
    - Total Benefit plan
    - Investment
- Average Annual Hours Worked per Worker
    - Total employment
- Labor Force
    - Total labor force
    - Persons

Therefore, sample size decreased to 149 across 11 countries during 14 years from 2001 to 2014.

Basic Level Statistical Analysis

At this level, one can identify short run changes as well as long run tendencies; also, it is possible to get main statistical indicators for each variable to get an idea or intuition of how understand the variables' dynamics. For instance, see Figure 4 where it can be perceived a growing trend in pension systems of the USA (United States of America) and Canada, which are very similar, and how the 2008 international financial crisis affected both in a negative way; Mexican pension system remained constant. It is relevant to highlight that the United States Pension System is at least 10 times bigger than the Canadian one and even more considering the Mexican one.

As seen on Figure 5, the Average of Hours Worked in the NAFTA zone shows a decreasing comportment for Mexico and Canada. Even when Mexican average is greater than the rest of them, it seems to be converging towards the American one. When analyzing the Labor Force size in the zone, as shows Figure 6, labor force in United States and Mexico is growing while in Canada remains constant; the size of the labor force in USA is 4 times bigger than Mexican one.

Regarding the EU and Norway, most pension systems were constantly growing form 2001 to 2013 but by the end of 2014, all pension systems started to decrease, particularly Finland's Pension System showed a great decrease at 2011. In Figure 7 it can be noticed that Britain Pension System is 10 times bigger than German one, which the latter being the most vigorous system respect the rest with except of Great

Figure 4. Pension systems for NAFTA zone in millions of dollars
Source: Own elaboration with OECD database. Right side scaling belongs only to US PS.

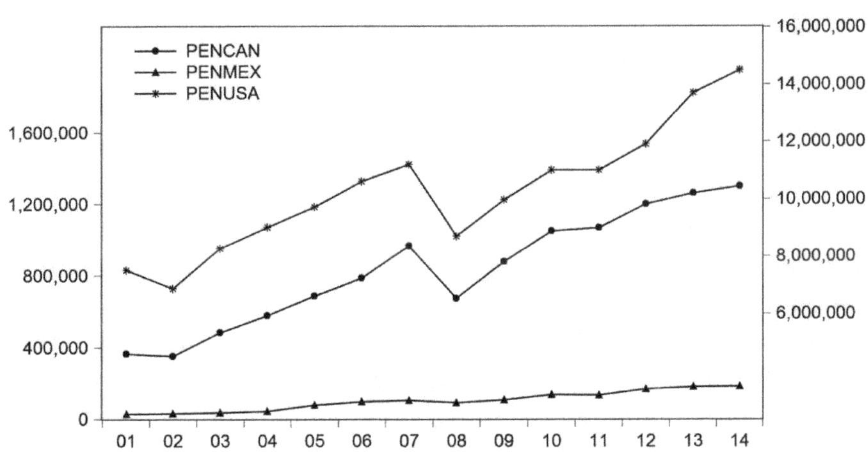

Figure 5. Average of hours worked for NAFTA zone
Source: Own elaboration with OECD database. Right side scaling belongs only to Mexican AHW

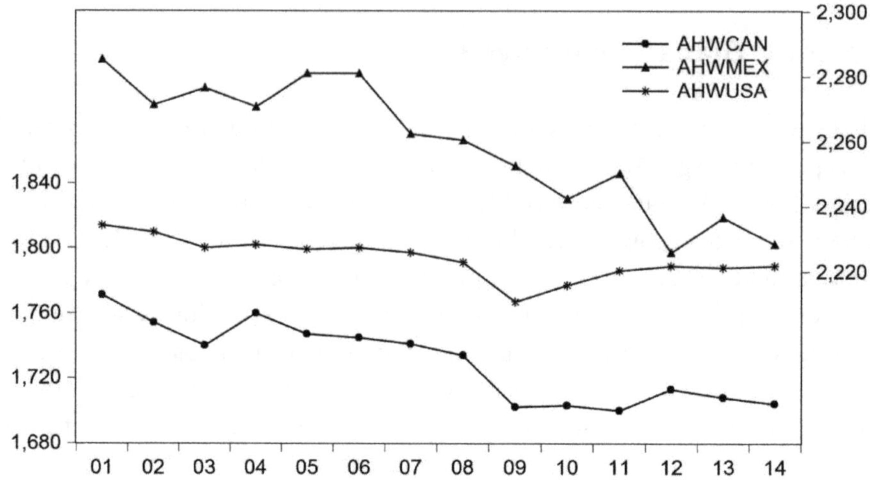

Figure 6. Labor force size for NAFTA zone measured in persons
Source: Own elaboration with OECD database. Right side scaling belongs only to US LF.

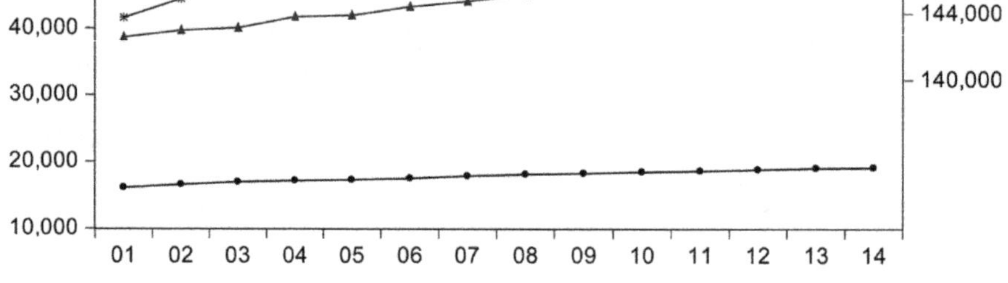

Britain (GB) system. If Figure 8 is analyzed, it can be acknowledged that AHW in the EU is been slightly decreasing during the analyzed period while in Norway it has been constant, thus being consistent with the behavior seen in the NAFTA zone. Additionally France, Norway and Germany are the counties with less average of hours worked while Poland has the highest average.

Figure 7. Pensions systems for EU and Norway in millions of dollars
Source: Own elaboration with OECD database. Right side scaling belongs only to GB PS.

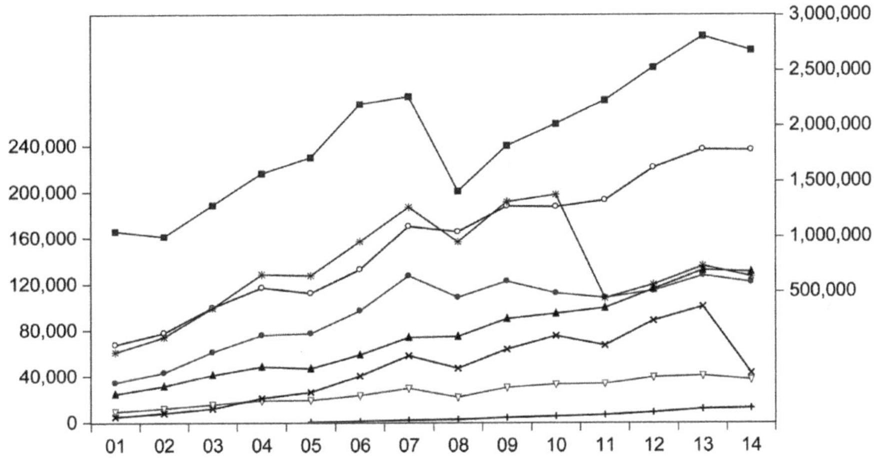

Figure 8. Average of hours worked in EU and Norway
Source: Own elaboration with OECD database.

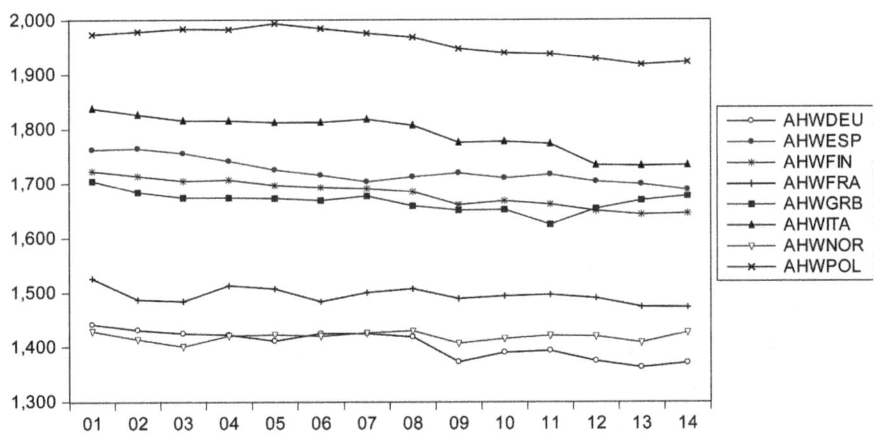

At the same time, the labor force in considered European countries is been mostly constant with the Finland's and the Norway's labor forces being the smallest ones and the German's one the biggest, as shown in Figure 9.

Considering all analyzed countries as a cluster, Table 1 shows the main statistical indicators obtained; there are 149 observations in total within 11 nations.

Particularly, the NAFTA zone provides 42 observations that is 28% of the total and together stands 3 times bigger the mean value of PS respect the global view; regarding the AHW of the NAFTA zone is above the world wide mean value due

Figure 9. Labor force size in EU and Norway measured in persons
Source: Own elaboration with OECD database.

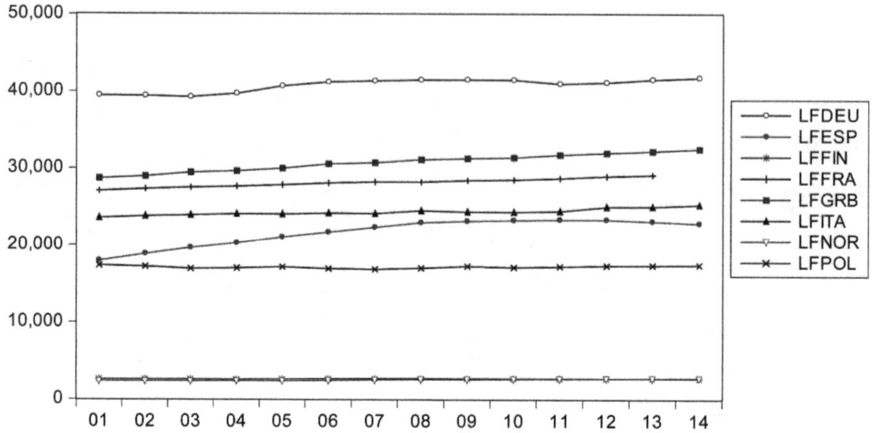

Table 1. Main statistical indictors of all considered countries (2001 – 2014)

	M	**Max**	**Min**	*SD*	**Skewness**	**Kurtosis**	*N*	**Cross Sections**
PEN	1283117.00	14460340.00	388.12	3037092.00	2.84	9.96	149	11
AHW	1727.79	2285.23	1362.50	236.39	0.66	3.23	149	11
LF	35,008.97	155921.80	2342.00	39824.37	2.25	7.07	149	11

Source: Own elaboration with OECD database.

mainly to Mexico since is the country with the higher average of all sample; Labor Force mean value is also above of global mean behavior, see table 2.

Contrary to NAFTA zone, the EU indicators display that the mean value of PS is 10 times smaller than the NAFTA zone and 4 times smaller than the global performance as was saw previously. AHW is closer to the global value as well as the Labor Force value for EU. Within these countries, there is a sample of 107 observations that is 72% of the range. See Table 3.

From the complete analysis performed so far, it can be summarized that there is a growing trend in the Pension Systems in the considered countries, a similar tendency was found when LF is studied, however AHW has revealed a decreasing behavior during the time period contemplated. When looking countries individually, the Unites States and Great Britain Pension Systems are the biggest in relation to global systems, and Mexico stands as the country with the more hours worked, while Germany with the less within the range. Finally, Labor Force in the EU is mostly constant as in NAFTA zone raises.

Table 2. Main statistical indictors of NAFTA zone (2001 – 2014)

	M	Max	Min	*SD*	Skewness	Kurtosis	*N*	Cross Sections
PEN	3739611.00	14460340.00	27187.64	4856886.00	0.90	2.11	42	3
AHW	1927.50	2285.23	1700.00	239.35	0.66	1.52	42	3
LF	71479.97	155921.80	16094.10	58368.58	0.59	1.51	42	3

Source: Own elaboration with OECD database.

Table 3. Main statistical indictors of EU and Norway (2001 – 2014)

	M	Max	Min	*SD*	Skewness	Kurtosis	*N*	Cross Sections
PEN	318885.80	2810564.00	388.12	651942.90	2.56	8.27	107	8
AHW	1649.40	1994.00	1362.50	183.99	0.10	2.02	107	8
LF	20693.25	41779.00	2342.00	12756.20	-0.15	1.98	107	8

Source: Own elaboration with OECD database.

Medium Level Statistical Analysis

From the previous section, it can be inferred that a possible relationship between the PS, AHW and LF exists. The hypothesis behind that relationship proposed in this section defines a Pension System being affected by the Average Hours Worked and by the Labor Force size. If this relationship is true, and by considering the long run tendencies disclosed in the previous section, it is expected to find a positive relationship between PS and LF, but a negative impact of AHW on PS value. This expected relationship turned out to be proved by a Covariance and Correlation analysis performed in Table 4.

Within the time period, covariance and, therefore, correlation across NAFTA countries between Pension Systems and Labor Force size is positive and high as well; covariance and correlation between Pension System and the Average Hours Worked is negative. The same results were found when EU and Norway observations were analyzed, because of the huge size of the correspondently table results are not presented.

Advanced Level Statistical Analysis

Since a relationship has been proven, as well as the direction of it between the variables considered, now through an advanced analysis it can be determined the magnitude of each relationship. Therefore, an econometric analysis was conducted.

The correspondently methodology dictates that first a hypothesis needs to be established (already done in the previous section), and second, a regression model has to be characterized; by operating the relationship found, the regression equation proposed is:

$$PS_{it} = \alpha + \beta_1 AHW_{it} + \beta_2 LF_{it} + u_{it} \tag{1}$$

where β_1 and β_2 parameters of the regression model will measure the magnitude of the relationship established, α is the autonomous behavior of a Pension System, u_{it} considers the perturbation among other not included phenomenon in the model and where the sub index of cross sections

$$i = \{CAN, MEX, USA, GRB, ITA, ESP, POL, \ldots, NOR\}$$

as well that the sub index of time series $t = \{2011, 2002, \ldots, 2014\}$.

Pool Least Squared Method performed the model by desegregating data in three different groups, as the same as the previously statistical analysis, which are for the global range, for NAFTA zone and for EU and Norway region. Global stats for the regression are shown in Table 5 where suffix (?) represents each country considered in the estimation.

At the global glance PS depends in a positive way on LF as found before and each time Labor Force increases in one person Pension System will increase in \$71.43 million dollars. On the other hand, the negative impact of AHW on PS is corroborated since for every additional hour worked per year a Pension System will decrease in an average of \$717.28 million dollars. This estimation gives the magnitude of the relationship already established and explains the 85% of the Pensions System dynamics. If heterogeneity between autonomous behaviors of PS is allowed across countries, then AHW variable explains even less (in fact this variable becomes not statistically significant) the dynamics of PS while LF variable explains more, an increase in one person in LF will produce an increase in \$208.58 million dollars in the PS, see Table 6.

Across time, heterogeneity also shows a negative impact of AHW on PS while LF has a positive effect. There is not a single observation across time of AHW with a positive impact all the contrary of LF in the Pooled Estimation, as notice in Table 7.

The same results are found if the NAFTA zone estimation is carried out. As it can be seen, AHW still affects in a negative way on PS since for each additional hour worked the PS value will decrease in \$1,073 million dollars. In fact, this negative impact is greater than the one in a global estimation; at the same time, an increase

Table 4. Covariance and correlation matrix within NAFTA zone (2001 – 2014)

Correlation	PENCAN	PENMEX	PENUSA	LFCAN	LFMEX	LFUSA	AHWCAN	AHWMEX	AHWUSA
PENCAN	9.58E+10								
	1								
PENMEX	1.59E+10	2.74E+09							
	0.98	1							
PENUSA	6.25E+11	1.04E+11	4.44E+12						
	0.96	0.94	1						
LFCAN	2.69E+08	45828242	1.69E+09	831058.9					
	0.95	0.96	0.88	1					
LFMEX	1.35E+09	2.32E+08	8.52E+09	4023919	20663772				
	0.96	0.98	0.89	0.97	1				
LFUSA	1.13E+09	1.93E+08	7.00E+09	3520222	16336752	16052369			
	0.91	0.92	0.83	0.96	0.9	1			
AHWCAN	-6155114	-1045349	-35878335	-19486.36	-94323.48	-80066.04	554.98		
	-0.84	-0.85	-0.72	-0.91	-0.88	-0.85	1		
AHWMEX	-5221244	-901184.8	-31847663	-15862.11	-82329.47	-62368.48	384.43	370.45	
	-0.88	-0.89	-0.79	-0.9	-0.94	-0.81	0.85	1	
AHWUSA	-2488863	-413229.4	-13313443	-8430.78	-37131.05	-37997.38	250.21	153.22	142.82
	-0.67	-0.66	-0.53	-0.77	-0.68	-0.79	0.89	0.67	1

Source: Own elaboration with OECD database.

Table 5. Estimation for a global pension system

Dependent Variable: PEN?				
Method: Pooled Least Squares				
Sample: 2001 2014				
Included Observations: 14				
Cross-Sections Included: 11				
Total Pool (Unbalanced) Observations: 149				
Variable	**Coefficient**	***SE***	**t-Statistic**	***p***
AHW?	-717.28	73.96	-9.70	0.000
LF?	71.44	2.44	29.32	0.000
r^2	0.854649	Mean dependent var	1283117	
Adjusted r^2	0.853661	S.D. dependent var	3037092	
S.E. of regression	1161819			

Source: Own elaboration with OECD database.

of one person in LF will produce a rise of $79.73 million dollars. Thus, explains the 90% of PS dynamics for the zone as Table 8 shows.

If heterogeneity is allowed in both autonomous behaviors across countries and across time, then the same results regarding AHW and LF from a global point of view are found in the NAFTA zone analysis, that is, negative impacts from AHW and positive ones from LF when coefficients were significant. See Tables 9 and 10.

To conclude with the analysis, the regression model was also performed for the EU and Norway region, and as it can be expected, results are the same. First if the estimation as a group within these 8 countries is carried out (see Table 11), then results show AHW negatively affecting PS even when there is none significance relationship; on the contrary LF affects positively since for each person that increases then PS enhance in $15.85 million dollars.

Across countries and time heterogeneity, in the EU and Norway results turned to be ambiguous because the direction of the relationships were corroborated, but magnitudes are not statistically significant, therefore even when for some countries LF has positives impacts on PS, as a group it cannot be inferred the same results. See Tables 12 and 13.

This section has provided a detailed point of view of how PS is affected by AHW and LF in different regions. In the NAFTA region, LF affects PS in a positive way meanwhile AHW impacts in a negative way PS. If the analysis is conducted within European countries, then LF affects positively PS and AHW has a negative impact on PS with some little statistical significance.

Table 6. Estimation for a global pension system with fixed effects

Dependent Variable: PEN?				
Method: Pooled Least Squares				
Sample: 2001 2014				
Included Observations: 14				
Cross-Sections Included: 11				
Total Pool (Unbalanced) Observations: 149				
Variable	**Coefficient**	***SE***	**t-Statistic**	***p***
C	-12175231.00	4724067.00	-2.58	0.01
AHW?	3562.90	2432.89	1.46	0.15
LF?	208.59	26.78	7.79	0.00
Fixed Effects (Cross)				
CAN--C	3121145.00			
DEU--C	-1179345.00			
ESP--C	1604704.00			
FIN--C	5765681.00			
FRA--C	922275.00			
GRB--C	1724655.00			
ITA--C	796713.00			
MEX--C	-5214410.00			
NOR--C	6623192.00			
POL--C	1658841.00			
USA--C	-15494068.00			
r^2	0.966635	Mean dependent var	1283117	
Adjusted r^2	0.963691	S.D. dependent var	3037092	
S.E. of regression	578712.3			
F-statistic	328.3476	Prob. (F-statistic)	0	

Source: Own elaboration with OECD database.

SOLUTIONS AND RECOMMENDATIONS

Throughout this study, it was proved that long-size databases are useful to understand phenomena and that it is possible to simplify the analysis that would produce specific outcomes. In addition, the researchers showed three types of statistical methodologies (basic, medium, and advanced level) to explore the situation of pension systems among several countries in the World.

Table 7. Estimation for a global pension system across time period

Dependent Variable: PEN?				
Method: Pooled Least Squares				
Sample: 2001 2014				
Included Observations: 14				
Cross-Sections Included: 11				
Total Pool (Unbalanced) Observations: 149				
Variable	**Coefficient**	***SE***	**t-Statistic**	***p***
AHW?--2001	-520.44	266.42	-1.95	0.05
AHW?--2002	-474.24	268.60	-1.77	0.08
AHW?--2003	-564.09	269.44	-2.09	0.04
AHW?--2004	-600.61	270.01	-2.22	0.03
AHW?--2005	-686.12	264.54	-2.59	0.01
AHW?--2006	-725.43	265.48	-2.73	0.01
AHW?--2007	-751.47	265.75	-2.83	0.01
AHW?--2008	-612.49	266.89	-2.29	0.02
AHW?--2009	-692.74	270.29	-2.56	0.01
AHW?--2010	-778.54	272.26	-2.86	0.01
AHW?--2011	-784.53	273.38	-2.87	0.00
AHW?--2012	-836.22	275.64	-3.03	0.00
AHW?--2013	-982.40	276.58	-3.55	0.00
AHW?--2014	-993.19	282.29	-3.52	0.00
LF?--2001	55.16	9.35	5.90	0.00
LF?--2002	49.95	9.30	5.37	0.00
LF?--2003	59.51	9.19	6.47	0.00
LF?--2004	64.12	9.14	7.02	0.00
LF?--2005	68.36	9.02	7.58	0.00
LF?--2006	73.29	8.90	8.24	0.00
LF?--2007	76.31	8.80	8.67	0.00
LF?--2008	59.08	8.74	6.76	0.00
LF?--2009	67.57	8.75	7.73	0.00
LF?--2010	74.60	8.77	8.50	0.00
LF?--2011	74.96	8.81	8.50	0.00
LF?--2012	79.98	8.75	9.14	0.00
LF?--2013	91.88	8.73	10.52	0.00
LF?--2014	96.44	8.70	11.08	0.00

r^2	0.885806	Mean dependent var	1283117
Adjusted r^2	0.860325	S.D. dependent var	3037092
S.E. of regression	1135055		

Source: Own elaboration with OECD database.

Table 8. Estimation for NAFTA zone of pension system

Dependent Variable: PEN?				
Method: Pooled Least Squares				
Sample: 2001 2014				
Included Observations: 14				
Cross-Sections Included: 3				
Total Pool (Balanced) Observations: 42				
Variable	**Coefficient**	***SE***	**t-Statistic**	***p***
AHW?	-1073.92	181.01	-5.93	0.00
LF?	79.74	3.83	20.83	0.00

r^2	0.907965	Mean dependent var	3739611
Adjusted r^2	0.905664	S.D. dependent var	4856886
S.E. of regression	1491751		

Source: Own elaboration with OECD database.

Table 9. Estimation for NAFTA zone of pension system with heterogeneity across countries

Dependent Variable: PEN?				
Method: Pooled Least Squares				
Sample: 2001 2014				
Included Observations: 14				
Cross-Sections Included: 3				
Total Pool (Balanced) Observations: 42				
Variable	**Coefficient**	***SE***	**t-Statistic**	***p***
CAN--AHWCAN	-2273.17	1909.32	-1.19	0.24
USA--AHWUSA	-24488.90	3660.77	-6.69	0.00
MEX--AHWMEX	-166.79	862.03	-0.19	0.85
CAN--LFCAN	267.06	184.91	1.44	0.16
USA--LFUSA	358.22	43.37	8.26	0.00
MEX--LFMEX	10.55	42.80	0.25	0.81

r^2	0.976982	Mean dependent var	3739611
Adjusted r^2	0.973786	S.D. dependent var	4856886
S.E. of regression	786372.1		

Source: Own elaboration with OECD database.

Table 10. Estimation for NAFTA zone of pension system with heterogeneity across time

Dependent Variable: PEN?				
Method: Pooled Least Squares				
Sample: 2001 2014				
Included Observations: 14				
Cross-Sections Included: 3				
Total Pool (Balanced) Observations: 42				
Variable	**Coefficient**	***SE***	**t-Statistic**	***P***
AHW?--2001	-750.84	778.92	-0.96	0.35
AHW?--2002	-702.02	790.03	-0.89	0.39
AHW?--2003	-836.31	791.31	-1.06	0.31
AHW?--2004	-917.93	794.62	-1.16	0.27
AHW?--2005	-959.50	793.10	-1.21	0.25
AHW?--2006	-1046.69	796.30	-1.31	0.21
AHW?--2007	-1081.66	803.57	-1.35	0.20
AHW?--2008	-879.87	808.52	-1.09	0.29
AHW?--2009	-1002.22	817.65	-1.23	0.24
AHW?--2010	-1177.45	837.91	-1.41	0.18
AHW?--2011	-1186.73	840.34	-1.41	0.18
AHW?--2012	-1292.75	850.60	-1.52	0.15
AHW?--2013	-1547.48	850.85	-1.82	0.09
AHW?--2014	-1642.16	853.38	-1.92	0.07
LF?--2001	61.13	17.76	3.44	0.00
LF?--2002	55.54	17.74	3.13	0.01
LF?--2003	66.01	17.52	3.77	0.00
LF?--2004	71.41	17.48	4.09	0.00
LF?--2005	75.77	17.23	4.40	0.00
LF?--2006	81.37	17.03	4.78	0.00
LF?--2007	84.57	16.91	5.00	0.00
LF?--2008	65.70	16.82	3.91	0.00
LF?--2009	75.12	16.84	4.46	0.00
LF?--2010	83.77	17.16	4.88	0.00
LF?--2011	83.96	17.27	4.86	0.00
LF?--2012	89.87	17.23	5.22	0.00
LF?--2013	103.88	17.20	6.04	0.00
LF?--2014	109.27	17.16	6.37	0.00

r^2	0.953557	Mean dependent var	3739611
Adjusted r^2	0.863988	S.D. dependent var	4856886
S.E. of regression	1791208		

Source: Own elaboration with OECD database.

Table 11. Estimation for EU and Norway of pension system

Dependent Variable: PEN?				
Method: Pooled Least Squares				
Sample: 2001 2014				
Included Observations: 14				
Cross-Sections Included: 8				
Total Pool (Unbalanced) Observations: 107				
Variable	**Coefficient**	***SE***	**t-Statistic**	***p***
AHW?	-2.85	66.41	-0.04	0.97
LF?	15.86	4.54	3.49	0.00
r^2	0.103327	Mean dependent var	318885.8	
Adjusted r^2	0.094787	S.D. dependent var	651942.9	
S.E. of regression	620275.8			

Source: Own elaboration with OECD database.

For example, throughout the use of basic level statistics it is possible to conclude that even though in the NAFTA area the three countries tended to decrease the number of AHW in the 14 year-period under study (Figure 5), in the same period their pension systems increased (Figure 4), but not at the same pace. The gap between the USA and Canada versus Mexico is considerably high, even though Mexicans tend to work many more hours than Americans or Canadians. In this case, Mexico should create a methodology to measure the effectiveness of the workforce in some industries, compared to best practices of other countries where people tend to work fewer hours and contribute more to the pension systems. If those indicators show a positive trend, the methodology could be expanded to other industries.

Another recommendation when dealing with long-size databases is to narrow down the number of observations in order to detect specific relationships between key variables. This would allow interpreting fundamental directions and magnitudes of any kind of relationship throughout a statistical analysis. For the present study, when considering only three variables from a long-size database with 47,935 observations, it was possible to reduce it to 149 observations with information from 11 countries and from a period of 14 years. At the beginning of a study of this kind, it is relevant to define a possible relationship between variables that can be proved or rejected by the use of advanced statistical methods.

Table 12. Estimation for EU and Norway of pension system with heterogeneity across countries

Dependent Variable: PEN?				
Method: Pooled Least Squares				
Sample: 2001 2014				
Included Observations: 14				
Cross-Sections Included: 8				
Total Pool (Unbalanced) Observations: 107				
Variable	**Coefficient**	***SE***	**t-Statistic**	***p***
DEU--AHWDEU	-953.60	624.65	-1.53	0.13
ESP--AHWESP	-131.84	198.40	-0.66	0.51
FIN--AHWFIN	-404.76	684.40	-0.59	0.56
FRA--AHWFRA	-117.06	1394.69	-0.08	0.93
GRB--AHWGRB	-5225.31	416.66	-12.54	0.00
ITA--AHWITA	-461.74	465.13	-0.99	0.32
NOR--AHWNOR	-106.14	429.19	-0.25	0.81
POL--AHWPOL	-403.99	770.33	-0.52	0.60
DEU--LFDEU	36.69	21.51	1.71	0.09
ESP--LFESP	14.85	15.70	0.95	0.35
FIN--LFFIN	308.07	435.44	0.71	0.48
FRA--LFFRA	6.31	73.20	0.09	0.93
GRB--LFGRB	345.40	22.59	15.29	0.00
ITA--LFITA	37.12	34.25	1.08	0.28
NOR--LFNOR	70.34	242.11	0.29	0.77
POL--LFPOL	48.86	87.97	0.56	0.58
r^2	0.970994	Mean dependent var	318885.8	
Adjusted r^2	0.966213	S.D. dependent var	651942.9	
S.E. of regression	119835.9			

Source: Own elaboration with OECD database.

To apply an analysis, since the behavior of Pension Systems is directly related to the Labor Force size and it is independent from the Average of Hours Worked, if a labor reform is introduced to increase or decrease the average of hours worked is irrelevant regarding the pension systems' costs. However, growing the population would naturally increase labor force and therefore pension systems costs.

Table 13. Estimation for EU and Norway of pension system with heterogeneity across time

Dependent Variable: PEN?				
Method: Pooled Least Squares				
Sample: 2001 2014				
Included Observations: 14				
Cross-Sections Included: 8				
Total Pool (Unbalanced) Observations: 107				
Variable	**Coefficient**	***SE***	**t-Statistic**	***p***
AHW?--2001	-2.34	277.41	-0.01	0.99
AHW?--2002	-1.08	279.67	0.00	1.00
AHW?--2003	-4.93	281.74	-0.02	0.99
AHW?--2004	-0.07	280.80	0.00	1.00
AHW?--2005	11.06	279.31	0.04	0.97
AHW?--2006	11.92	279.95	0.04	0.97
AHW?--2007	20.84	280.72	0.07	0.94
AHW?--2008	14.97	282.50	0.05	0.96
AHW?--2009	22.84	285.34	0.08	0.94
AHW?--2010	21.64	285.31	0.08	0.94
AHW?--2011	-22.17	287.04	-0.08	0.94
AHW?--2012	-10.18	289.32	-0.04	0.97
AHW?--2013	-0.73	289.51	0.00	1.00
AHW?--2014	-25.65	288.48	-0.09	0.93
LF?--2001	9.72	20.95	0.46	0.64
LF?--2002	9.44	20.88	0.45	0.65
LF?--2003	12.41	20.81	0.60	0.55
LF?--2004	14.59	20.52	0.71	0.48
LF?--2005	12.14	19.29	0.63	0.53
LF?--2006	15.49	19.04	0.81	0.42
LF?--2007	15.97	18.98	0.84	0.40
LF?--2008	10.64	18.89	0.56	0.57
LF?--2009	13.19	18.79	0.70	0.48
LF?--2010	14.54	18.80	0.77	0.44
LF?--2011	18.45	18.87	0.98	0.33
LF?—2012	19.96	18.77	1.06	0.29
LF?—2013	21.51	18.63	1.15	0.25
LF?—2014	25.80	19.21	1.34	0.18

r^2	0.127039	Mean dependent var	318885.8
Adjusted r^2	-0.171314	S.D. dependent var	651942.9
S.E. of regression	705579.9		

Source: Own elaboration with OECD database.

FUTURE RESEARCH DIRECTIONS

A research including countries from other regions such as Asia and South-America is suitable to have a better understanding of their pension dynamics. In addition, an extension of the number of years to analyze will improve the intermediate and advanced statistical analysis.

Other directions might be to conduct the study by gender due to the increasing participation of women on the labor force and the impact of external factors to the model such as worker mobility among countries or the impact of technologies and outsourcing trends that pressure unemployment.

CONCLUSION

Average Hours Worked and Labor Force are two representative variables that explain the situation in pension systems among countries. For this study, when analyzing global pension system, it can be concluded that a higher number of AHW has a negative and significant impact on pension systems, while LF has a positive and significant impact (Table 5). A similar trend can be observed when analyzing the information across time period (Table 7): AWH showed a negative and significant impact on pension systems (only one year, 2001, the result was approaching significance) and in every year, LF presented a positive and significant effect on pension systems.

Therefore, when people work more hours on a yearly average, they tend to decrease the pension system in their country. A suggestion for the governments would be not to focus on the number of occupational hours of the people, but in increasing the labor force. As presented in Figure 1, if the population that is increasing more in employment rates consists of women, but they tend to leave the job when having children (Figure 3), then governments should create policies to offer flexible alternatives for women to keep their jobs during maternity. This suggestion is not only to offer better working conditions to women, because in a short-term point of view having people employed when they are not at full working capacity might be seen as a cost for companies, however, in the long-run is more beneficial for the entire country.

According to the results, AWH does not have a positive effect on pension systems; therefore, the hypothesis presented that suggested that having more part-time jobs (Figure 2) might affect negatively pension systems, is rejected. It is more influential having more people working than having only full-time working positions.

The conclusion of the importance of having more LF as a positive outcome for pension systems and that AHW are negative for pension systems, are consistent when analyzing the information by economic groups. In Table 8 the estimation for NAFTA, countries presented the same significant trend, however in Table 9, the trends by countries were not significant for Canada and Mexico, but they showed the same trend. The same effect is showed in Table 10 when analyzing the information by year. Not every year was significant, but the same trend of AWH and LF was obtained. A similar trend is for the EU and Norway; as showed in Tables 11 and 12, AWH affect negatively to pension systems, while LF has a positive impact. For this economic region, the indicators were not always significant, but the same trend remained. For EU, only for the years before and after the economic crisis of 2008, AWH presented a positive and significant impact on pension systems (Table 13). Further research would need to explore if the results might be different only while economic crisis and if there is a long-term implication.

In the long-run Pension Systems are directly related to the Labor Force size and indirectly related to the Average Hours Worked. This kind of relationship is present across countries as well as in a 14 year-period of time, even when heterogeneity was introduced in both types of studies. At the global glance OECD report, Pensions Systems depend in a positive way on Labor Force since each time the latter increases in one person; Pension System will increase in \$71.43 million dollars. On the other hand, a negative impact of the Average Hours Worked on Pensions Systems is corroborated since for every additional hour worked per year the Pension System will decrease in an average of \$717.28 million dollars. If heterogeneity between autonomous behaviors of PS is allowed across countries, then AHW variable explains even less the PS' dynamics while LF variable explains more because an increase in LF of one person produces an increase in \$208.58 million dollars in the PS.

At the regional glimpse, directions are validated regarding PS, AHW, and LF relationships. For instance, each additional hour worked generates a decrease of \$1,073 million dollars on the PS value. In fact, this negative impact is greater than the one performed at a global estimation, and an increase of one person in Labor Force will produce a rise of \$79.73 million dollars, when NAFTA zone is evaluated. If EU and Norway are analyzed, results show that the AHW affects negatively the PS value; on the contrary LF affects positively since for each person that increases then PS enhance in \$15.85 million dollars.

It is important to highlight that the results found in this research depend strongly on assumptions made within equation (1), on selected countries, on time period duration, on estimation methodology, and variables selection. Therefore, interpretations and recommendations are only valid under conditions above described.

REFERENCES

Augusztinovics, M. (2002). Issues in pension system design. *International Social Security Review*, *55*(1), 21–35. doi:10.1111/1468-246X.00112

De la Maisonneuve, C. (2015). Reforming the pension system to increase coverage and equity in Colombia (Working Papers No. 1235). OECD Economics Department. Paris: OECD Publishing. doi:10.1787/5js0cqrr97s4-en

Fall, F., & Bloch, D. (2014). Overcoming Vulnerabilities of Pension Systems (Working Papers No. 1133). OECD Economics Department. Paris: OECD Publishing. doi:10.1787/5jz1591prxth-en

Fedotenkov, I., & Meijdam, L. (2013). Crisis and Pension System Design in the EU: International Spillover Effects Via Factor Mobility and Trade. *De Economist*, *161*(2), 175-197. doi:10.1007/s10645-013-9207-3

French, E. (2005). The Effects of Health, Wealth, and Wages on Labour Supply and Retirement Behaviour. *The Review of Economic Studies*, *72*(2), 395–427. doi:10.1111/j.1467-937X.2005.00337.x

Giorno, C., & Adda, J. (2016). Improving the pension system and the welfare of retirees in Israel (Working Papers No. 1288). OECD Economics Department. Paris: OECD Publishing. doi:10.1787/5jm0xf1fsqvf-en

Knell, M. (2012). Increasing Life Expectancy and Pay-As-You-Go Pension Systems. *Working Papers (Oesterreichische Nationalbank)*, (179), 1-36.

Militaru, D. N. (2011). The costs of demographic and economic crises – challenges to pension system reform. *Annals Of The University Of Petrosani Economics*, *11*(4), 175–182.

Obidziński, P. (2010). On the need for prevention in the pension system on the example of the demographic reserve fund. In *Folia Oeconomica Stetinensia* (pp. 179-189). doi:10.2478/v10031-010-0012-8

OECD. (2012). Coverage of Private Pension Systems: Evidence and Policy Options. In *OECD Pensions Outlook 2012*. Paris: OECD Publishing. doi:10.1787/9789264169401-7-en

OECD. (2013). Architecture of national pension systems. In *Pensions at a Glance 2013: OECD and G20 Indicators*. OECD Publishing. doi:10.1787/pension_glance-2013-6-en

OECD. (2014A). Architecture of national pensions systems. In *OECD, IDB and The World Bank, Pensions at a Glance: Latin America and the Caribbean*. Paris: OECD Publishing. doi:10.1787/9789264224964-9-en

OECD. (2014B). Editorial: Demographic change and economic stagnation put pressure on pension systems. In *OECD Pensions Outlook 2014*. Paris: OECD Publishing. doi:10.1787/pens_outlook-2014-2-en

OECD. (2014C). *OECD Reviews of Pension Systems: Ireland*. Paris: OECD Publishing. doi:10.1787/9789264208834-en

OECD. (2014D). Hours worked (indicator). doi:10.1787/47be1c78-en

OECD. (2015A). *Pensions at a Glance 2015: OECD and G20 indicators*. Paris: OECD Publishing. doi:10.1787/pension_glance-2015-en

OECD. (2015B). Pensions statistics (Edition 2015) OECD Pensions Statistics (database). doi:10.1787/f59da966-en

OECD. (2016A). Labour Force Statistics: Summary tables. *OECD Employment and Labour Market Statistics* (database).

OECD. (2016B). Hours Worked: Average annual hours actually worked. *OECD Employment and Labour Market Statistics* (database). doi:10.1787/data-00303-en

OECD. (2016C). *OECD Reviews of Pension Systems: Mexico*. Paris: OECD Publishing. doi:10.1787/9789264245938-en

OECD. (2016D). Hours worked. In *OECD Factbook 2015-2016: Economic, Environmental and Social Statistics*. Paris: OECD Publishing. doi:10.1787/factbook-2015-54-en

Podestà, F. (2002). Recent developments in quantitative comparative methodology: The case of pooled time series cross-section analysis. *DSS Papers Soc.*, *3*(2), 5–44.

Weaver, K., & Willén, A. (2014). The Swedish pension system after twenty years: Mid-course corrections and lessons. *OECD Journal on Budgeting*, *13*(3), 1–26. doi:10.1787/budget-13-5jxx3sx58x9t

KEY TERMS AND DEFINITIONS

Defined Benefit: The pension is provided by the government as a social security benefit.

Defined Contribution: The pension depends mainly on the monetary contribution of the employers and the voluntary savings of the worker.

Hours-Worked: The average number of hours worked per person per year.

Life-Expectancy: The average age people live; it increases from advances in health and medicine.

Pay-As-You-Go: The social security of a given country begins to pay a pension to the retired worker; the amount depends on several factors and varies among countries.

Retirement: The stage when a worker ends his/her job and begins to live with a pension.

Retirement-Age: The age when a worker ends his/her job; it varies for men and women and countries have been extending this level.

APPENDIX

Table 14. Pension system for NAFTA in millions of dollars

Year	PENCAN	PENMEX	PENUSA
2001	365,144	27,187.60	7.51E+06
2002	352,501	31,515.90	6.86E+06
2003	484,290	35,736.60	8.26E+06
2004	578,234	42,779.00	9.00E+06
2005	686,689	77,203.00	9.72E+06
2006	786,329	96,665.50	1.06E+07
2007	966,116	103,622	1.12E+07
2008	673,333	90,798.80	8.70E+06
2009	879,373	107,811	9.97E+06
2010	1.05E+06	134,749	1.10E+07
2011	1.07E+06	132,381	1.10E+07
2012	1.20E+06	168,563	1.19E+07
2013	1.26E+06	181,255	1.37E+07
2014	1.30E+06	181,881	1.45E+07

Source: Own elaboration with OECD database.

Table 15. Pension system for EU in millions of dollars

Year	PENDEU	PENESP	PENFIN	PENFRA	PENGRB	PENITA	PENNOR	PENPOL
2001	67,537.80	34,513.30	60,986.00	--	1.05E+06	24,701.40	9,369.60	4,752.59
2002	77,654.20	43,465.20	74,248.00	--	1.00E+06	31,415.10	12,147.70	8,105.66
2003	99,583.60	61,239.50	99,271.80	--	1.28E+06	41,126.40	15,432.00	12,016.60
2004	116,973	75,805.60	128,328	--	1.57E+06	48,414.20	18,900.80	20,925.60
2005	112,275	77,409.80	127,350	388.121	1.71E+06	47,004.80	19,282.30	26,291.70
2006	132,659	97,120.90	156,919	1,002.24	2.20E+06	58,729.80	23,440.70	40,475.20
2007	170,371	127,306	186,957	2,063.88	2.27E+06	73,811.80	29,655.20	58,048.40
2008	165,634	108,734	156,896	2,587.17	1.41E+06	74,721.80	21,934.40	47,136.70
2009	187,938	122,558	191,702	4,321.80	1.82E+06	90,050.30	30,309.90	63,626.40
2010	187,280	112,225	197,832	5,344.80	2.02E+06	94,616.60	33,134.80	75,238.00
2011	192,912	108,247	107,936	6,469.50	2.23E+06	99,440.60	33,627.20	67,016.50
2012	221,112	114,228	119,601	8,839.98	2.53E+06	115,637	39,454.00	88,464.30
2013	236,932	127,478	135,651	11,860.30	2.81E+06	132,168	40,908.50	100,563
2014	236,204	121,585	126,446	12,505.20	2.68E+06	130,658	37,380.40	43,125.80

Source: Own elaboration with OECD database.

Table 16. Average hours worked for NAFTA

Year	AHWCAN	AHWMEX	AHWUSA
2001	1,771.00	2,285.20	1,814.00
2002	1,754.00	2,271.20	1,810.00
2003	1,740.00	2,276.50	1,800.00
2004	1,760.00	2,270.60	1,802.00
2005	1,747.00	2,280.90	1,799.00
2006	1,745.00	2,281.00	1,800.00
2007	1,741.00	2,262.30	1,797.00
2008	1,734.00	2,260.40	1,791.00
2009	1,702.00	2,252.50	1,767.00
2010	1,703.00	2,242.40	1,777.00
2011	1,700.00	2,250.20	1,786.00
2012	1,713.00	2,225.80	1,789.00
2013	1,708.00	2,236.60	1,788.00
2014	1,704.00	2,228.40	1,789.00

Source: Own elaboration with OECD database.

Table 17. Average hours worked for EU

Year	AHWDEU	AHWESP	AHWFIN	AHWFRA	AHWGRB	AHWITA	AHWNOR	AHWPOL
2001	1,441.90	1,762.50	1,723.00	1,526.00	1,705.00	1,837.80	1,429.00	1,974.00
2002	1,430.90	1,764.60	1,714.00	1,487.30	1,684.00	1,826.60	1,414.00	1,979.00
2003	1,424.80	1,755.90	1,705.00	1,484.40	1,674.00	1,815.80	1,400.70	1,984.00
2004	1,422.20	1,741.50	1,707.00	1,513.20	1,674.00	1,815.30	1,420.50	1,983.00
2005	1,411.30	1,725.60	1,697.00	1,507.40	1,673.00	1,812.10	1,422.80	1,994.00
2006	1,424.70	1,715.70	1,693.00	1,484.00	1,669.00	1,812.60	1,419.80	1,985.00
2007	1,424.40	1,703.50	1,691.00	1,500.30	1,677.00	1,818.20	1,426.00	1,976.00
2008	1,418.40	1,712.60	1,685.00	1,507.20	1,659.00	1,807.00	1,429.50	1,969.00
2009	1,372.70	1,719.70	1,661.00	1,489.10	1,651.00	1,775.70	1,406.80	1,948.00
2010	1,389.90	1,710.40	1,668.00	1,494.00	1,652.00	1,777.30	1,415.30	1,940.00
2011	1,393.10	1,716.80	1,662.00	1,496.30	1,625.00	1,773.30	1,421.10	1,938.00
2012	1,374.20	1,703.90	1,650.00	1,490.20	1,654.00	1,734.20	1,419.70	1,929.00
2013	1,362.50	1,699.20	1,643.00	1,474.30	1,669.00	1,732.90	1,408.10	1,918.00
2014	1,371.00	1,688.80	1,645.00	1,473.50	1,677.00	1,733.90	1,426.90	1,923.00

Source: Own elaboration with OECD database.

Table 18. Labor force for NAFTA measured in persons

Year	LFCAN	LFMEX	LFUSA
2001	16,094.10	38,662.60	143,734
2002	16,560.70	39,694.60	144,863
2003	16,944.20	40,061.60	146,510
2004	17,147.10	41,738.00	147,401
2005	17,292.10	41,940.80	149,320
2006	17,502.20	43,234.10	151,428
2007	17,846.50	44,063.20	153,124
2008	18,122.40	45,121.50	154,287
2009	18,250.40	45,415.60	154,142
2010	18,450.50	49,133.10	153,889
2011	18,619.60	49,482.10	153,617
2012	18,809.50	51,477.20	154,975
2013	19,037.80	51,895.90	155,389
2014	19,124.50	51,836.80	155,922

Source: Own elaboration with OECD database.

Table 19. Labor force for EU measured in persons

Year	LFDEU	LFESP	LFFIN	LFFRA	LFGRB	LFITA	LFNOR	LFPOL
2001	39,459.00	17,959.40	2,596.60	27,051.50	28,682.00	23,567.00	2,342.00	17,376.30
2002	39,413.00	18,867.40	2,600.40	27,301.80	28,945.00	23,776.00	2,361.00	17,213.00
2003	39,276.00	19,652.50	2,590.30	27,499.10	29,456.00	23,918.00	2,357.00	16,945.00
2004	39,711.00	20,286.20	2,584.30	27,642.30	29,632.70	24,048.80	2,365.00	17,025.00
2005	40,696.00	21,048.80	2,612.00	27,825.30	29,970.50	24,031.00	2,384.80	17,161.00
2006	41,206.00	21,691.60	2,638.00	28,081.30	30,540.30	24,163.50	2,429.00	16,938.00
2007	41,364.00	22,336.30	2,666.00	28,244.50	30,729.30	24,126.50	2,491.00	16,859.00
2008	41,481.00	22,966.40	2,694.00	28,221.20	31,115.80	24,512.20	2,574.00	17,011.00
2009	41,507.00	23,150.50	2,669.60	28,424.50	31,267.80	24,357.00	2,573.00	17,279.00
2010	41,495.00	23,257.70	2,661.70	28,514.90	31,394.40	24,324.80	2,588.00	17,123.00
2011	40,997.00	23,331.20	2,673.00	28,695.20	31,728.10	24,419.90	2,617.00	17,221.00
2012	41,153.00	23,345.10	2,681.00	28,983.80	31,980.70	24,990.90	2,668.00	17,340.00
2013	41,522.00	23,101.50	2,668.00	29,134.60	32,209.50	25,017.40	2,692.00	17,361.00
2014	41,779.00	22,858.20	2,671.00	--	32,513.40	25,277.80	2,717.00	17,428.00

Source: Own elaboration with OECD database.

Chapter 8
Implementing Structural Equation Modeling on Public Data

Yair Cohen
Farmingdale State University of New York, USA

Elsa-Sofia Morote
Farmingdale State University of New York, USA

ABSTRACT

The researchers used structural equation modeling (SEM) to create a model predicting fourth-grade student achievement in math by exploring the relationships among: student, household, school, and teacher factors. Public data from the New York State Education Department (NYSED) 2012–13 school report card data, NYSED fiscal reporting system, Census 2010 School District Demographics System, and 2011 Civil Right Data Collection were used from 1,263 schools in New York excluding New York City. Variables were chosen using this convenient sample and supported by our conceptual rationale. The model predicted fourth-grade math achievement with 67 percent of effect size. Household factors had strong predictive, while school attendance rate had medium predictive value for student achievement.

INTRODUCTION

President Johnson signed the Civil Rights Act in July 1964. The stated goal of the act was to outlaw discrimination and promote equality among all races. One of the results of the act was that the U.S. Congress commissioned sociologist

DOI: 10.4018/978-1-5225-3616-1.ch008

James Coleman to write a report on education equality in the U.S. Two years later, Coleman and his team published the Equality in Educational Opportunity report, also known as the Coleman report. Coleman found that there was little variation in the resources between Black and White schools. However, there was a significant difference in outcomes in reading and math between Black and White schools. He stated that these differences in education outcomes were a result of student, family, school, and teacher characteristics (Coleman, 1966). Many researchers (New York State Office of Education Performance Review, 1974; Madden, Lawson, and Sweet, 1976; Summers & Wolfe, 1976; Hughes, 1995) followed Coleman team trying to find the malleable factors that school administrators control and effect achievement. Due to those studies, the U.S. education system went through several reforms *A Nation at Risk* (1983), *No Child Left Behind Act* (2001), *Race To The Top* (2009), and *Every Student Succeeds Act* (2015). However, the gap between schools based on socioeconomic status still exists. According to New York state assessment results (NYSED Press Conference 8/19/2013), there is one-standard-deviation gap between students who live in poverty and students who come from higher socioeconomic class. This difference is equivalent to the gap that was observed by Coleman and his team in 1966.

BACKGROUND

One of the immediate effects of the Coleman report was that it led politicians to state that schools make no difference and therefore there is no need to increase school spending since it has little to no effect in terms of student achievement. Rivkin, Hanushek, and Kain (2005) found that specific school resources do actually have significant effects on student outcomes. Teacher experience, teacher level of education, and smaller class size were found to have small but significant positive impact on student achievement (Rivkin, Hanushek, & Kain, 2005).

Other researchers (Bachman, Coley, & Chase-Lansdale, 2009; Crosnoe & Wildsmith, 2011; Hampden-Thompson, 2009) found that family structure had a direct relationship with student achievement. They found that children in stably married families experienced improved academic, behavioral, and psychological well-being compared to children in stable cohabiting or single-parent families. However, part of it is rooted in the better socioeconomic circumstances of families headed by stably married parents (Bachman, Coley & Chase-Lansdale, 2009; Crosnoe & Wildsmith, 2011; Hampden-Thompson, 2009). Contradicting to that, Weisner and Garnier (1992) found in a 12-years longitudinal study that children to non-traditional families with strong commitment to their life style do better in school than traditional children.

Common Core standards for kindergarten through 3rd grade math also require students to demonstrate a greater depth of understanding than needed under the previous New York State Standards. While the old standards were often criticized for an excessive reliance on memorizing certain facts or procedures, the new standards routinely call for students to solve problems that require a strong grasp of mathematical concepts and to explain their reasoning. In New York Grade 4, instructional time should focus on three critical areas: (1) developing understanding and fluency with multi-digit multiplication, and developing understanding of dividing to find quotients involving multi-digit dividends; (2) developing an understanding of fraction equivalence, addition and subtraction of fractions with like denominators, and multiplication of fractions by whole numbers; (3) understanding that geometric figures can be analyzed and classified based on their properties, such as having parallel sides, perpendicular sides, particular angle measures, and symmetry (http://www.corestandards.org/).

The common core standards are supported by administrators, but not by the parents. There is a movement against the common core math and English language arts curricula and testing by some parents and some teachers (https://parentsagainstthecommoncore.com/status/). There are several reasons that the aforementioned groups are concerned about standardized tests. The large amounts of class time taken up, the pacing of classes, the lack of flexibility for students with special needs or academic difficulties, and the effect of low socioeconomic status (SES) has on results in high stakes tests. According to Baker and Johnston (2010) lack of home support and encouragement cause students from low SES backgrounds to experience higher level of difficulty achieving high stakes testing goals.

Amanda Eagan (2015) presented the differences between economic disadvantaged students and affluent students in eighth grade math – after the Common Core Learning Standards (CCLS). She argued that those differences have incremented after the implementation of the CCLS.

MAIN FOCUS OF THE CHAPTER

The Problem

There is a gap on the literature in understanding how student, household, school, and teacher attributes affect student achievement, and which one of them have major impact on the student performance. Understanding the factors that affect student achievement and the relationships among them will be vital to understanding how to allocate resources effectively.

The Purpose

The purpose of this study was to use public data in order to create a model that predict students' achievement by exploring the relationships among school, teacher, student, and household factors. Achievement was measured by fourth-grade student achievement in math among New York Public Schools.

Conceptual Rationale

The model for this research has four components: (household, school, teacher, and student) and their effect on student achievement.

Coleman (1966) and his colleagues reported that student educational attainment was strongly influenced by student social background, was moderately influenced by their peers, and was weakly influenced by variations in school quality (e.g., per student expenditure, class size, building size, building age, full-time librarian, free textbooks, school cafeteria, and school gymnasium). Also, teacher quality had a moderate effect on low SES student educational attainment and had a weak effect on others (Colman et al., 1966).

Mayer (1997) noted that students from low SES backgrounds scored low on standardized tests, had lower school attendance rates, and displayed more behavioral problems than did affluent children. Mayer argued that household factors influenced student achievement more than socioeconomic status.

Other researchers (Baker, Sigmon, & Nugent, 2001; Henry, 2007; Ready, 2010) argued that students who lived in single-family households were more likely to be in poverty and more likely to be absent from school than students from intact families.

Chang and Romero (2008) used the Early Childhood Longitudinal Study, Kindergarten Cohort (ECLS-K) data. They examined attendance patterns for children in grades K-3 by grade, SES, ethnicity, gender, limited English proficiency, and special education. Chang and Romero found that persistent absence in kindergarten was associated with lower academic performance in first-grade, and persistent absence in kindergarten for students in poverty predicted the lowest levels of educational achievement at the end of fifth-grade. Family circumstances were strongly related to child attendance in school. Students in families living in poverty showed greater school absence rates. This could have been a result of lack of stable, affordable housing; lack of reliable transportation; lack of nutritious food; and limited access to health care.

Ready (2010) also used the ECLS-K data. He found that students who came from low SES backgrounds had the most chronic school absenteeism. High attendance in school was highly correlated to better achievement in literacy in kindergarten and first grade, especially for low SES students (Ready, 2010).

Research Question

How do student, school, teacher, and household factors affect fourth-grade student achievement in math in NYS schools?

Factors

Student Factors

Students With Disabilities (SWD)

For the purposes of this study, students with disabilities (SWD) were defined as the percentage of students with physical and or mental impairments (NYSED, 2014). Data were retrieved from the 2012–13 New York State school report cards.

Limited English Proficiency (LEP)

For the purposes of this study, limited English proficiency (LEP) was defined as the percentage of students with limited English proficiency at a grade level (NYSED, 2014). Data were retrieved from the 2012–13 New York State school report cards.

Economically Disadvantaged (ED)

For the purposes of this study, economically disadvantaged was defined as the percentage of students who participated in, or whose family participated in, economic assistance programs (NYSED, 2014). Data were retrieved from the 2012–13 New York State school report cards.

School Factors

Attendance Rate

For the purposes of this study, the attendance rate was defined as students' annual attendance rate in school as reported in the 2012–13 New York State school report card.

Suspension Rate

For the purposes of this study, the suspension rate was defined as the percent of students suspended from school as reported in the 2012–13 New York State school report card.

Per-Student Instructional Expenditures

For the purposes of this study, per-student instructional expenditures were the 2012–13 per-student expenditures reported for each school district by NYSED. Instructional expenditures included teacher salaries, curriculum development and support instructional salaries, BOCES Boards of Cooperative Educational Services (BOCES) instructional expenditures, other instructional salaries, and other instructional expenses. Instructional expenditures were divided by the number of students in the district to establish the per-student instructional expenditure data.

School Size

For the purposes of this study, school size was defined as the student enrollment for each school reported on the 2012–13 school report cards.

Class Size

For the purposes of this study, class size was defined as the average student class size for each school as reported on the 2012–13 school report cards (NYSED, 2015).

Teacher Factors

Percentage of Novice Teachers

For the purposes of this study, percentage of novice teachers was defined as the proportion of all teachers within the school who had fewer than three years of teaching experience as reported in 2012–13 New York State school report cards (NYSED, 2015).

Teachers With Master's Plus 30 Credits or Doctorate

For the purposes of this study, teachers with masters plus 30 credits or doctorate was defined as the percentage of all teachers within the school who had a master's degree plus 30 additional credits or a doctorate degree as reported on the 2012–13 New York State school report cards (NYSED, 2015).

Teachers Not Highly Qualified

Percent of teachers who are not highly qualified as reported in the 2012–13 New York State school report card. To be highly qualified, a teacher must have at least a

Bachelor's degree, be certified to teach in the subject area or otherwise in accordance with state standards, and show subject matter competency (NYSED, 2015).

Teacher Turnover Rate

For the purposes of this study, Teacher Turnover Rate for a specified school year is the number of teachers in that school year that were not teaching in the following school year, divided by the number of teachers in the specified school year, expressed as a percentage. Teachers who in year one were reported as providing instruction in one building, but in year two were reported under the district code or another building within the same district are included in the turnover rate (NYSED, 2015).

Teacher Absences

For the purposes of this study, teacher absences were the percentage of teachers in the school who were absent more than ten days of the 2011–12 school year, excluded days missed for approved professional development.

Household Factors

Household Structure

For the purposes of this study, household structure was defined by using the 2010 census categories of Family households included a. Husband-Wife family household, and b. Single Family Household which can be Male family household or Female family household.

Household Size

For the purposes of this study, household size was defined as the number of residents in a household. The 2010 Census data provided seven options for household size, from single resident householder to seven plus resident's household.

Research Design and Methodology

The relationships between selected variables reported by NYSED school report card 2012–13 school year, NYSED fiscal reporting system, Census 2010 School District Demographics System (SDDS), and Civil Right Data Collection (CRDC) were explored in this study using path analysis, a special case of Structural Equation Modeling (SEM).

Data Collection

NYSED school report card was based on data submitted by local school district officials and the results of the state assessments. School officials were provided with an opportunity to review verification reports and make corrections to their data until the reporting deadline (NYSED, 2012). NYSED fiscal reporting system was based on data reported by school districts on their 2012-13 annual financial report to NYSED.

School District Demographics System (SDDS) enabled access to school district demographic and related geographic data not available in any other form. SDDS was developed to help community leadership, educators, researchers and analysts, and the public to access and use demographic data to understand current demographic characteristics and patterns of change better, as well as to plan for improved educational programs and opportunities (National Center of Educational Statistics, n. d.).

CRDC surveyed a representative sample of schools and districts comprising 85 percent of the students in the country. Forty-four additional data points on school characteristics and demographics from the Department of Education's Common Core of Data complemented the Civil Rights Data Collection survey (CRDC, n. d.).

A path analysis special case of SEM (Xue, 2007) was used to explore the relationships between district and school factors, teacher factors, student factors, and household factors, with endogenous variables and how these variables predict grade fourth math achievement. Each of these factors consisted of multiple dimensions.

Selection of Subjects

The related tables were merged into one Microsoft Access table, the result was 1,402 NYS public schools excluding New York City schools could be used in the research. Data were imported into SPSS and tested for a normal distribution for each of the variables. Removal of outliers yielded 1,263 schools to be included in the study (Cohen, 2015).

Sample Size

SEM requires large sample sizes, which affects sampling error. The larger the sample collected, the smaller the sampling error would be. Although the general rule of thumb was 20 cases for each free parameter, 10 was a more likely target (Kline, 2005). For this study, the confirmatory factor analysis included 16 distinct parameters, which would have required a minimum of 160–320 samples. The 1,263 schools in this study exceeded these accepted measures of minimum sample size for a SEM study with this number of parameters.

Data distribution was an issue, as the statistical tool required normal data distribution. One strategy to make non-normal data resemble normal data is by using a transformation. Data transformations are the application of a mathematical modification to the values of a variable. There are a great variety of possible data transformations, from adding constants to multiplying, squaring or raising to a power, converting to logarithmic scales, inverting and reflecting, taking the square root of the values, and even applying trigonometric transformations such as sine wave transformations. Because data transformations can alter the fundamental nature of the data, such as changing the measurement scale from interval or ratio to ordinal, and creating curvilinear relationships, complicating interpretation (Osborne, 2002), the researchers decided to remove non-normal distributed data, approximately 9% of the schools (139 schools).

Validation

To validate the model 2012-13 data were split into two by random sample. One half (631 schools) was used to create the model and the other half (632 schools) was used to test the model accuracy. In addition, the researchers validated the model using 2013-14 school year data (1450 schools excluding New York City).

Data Analysis and Findings

Demographic Analysis

NYSED assigned each school district to a category in the Need/Resource Index, which represented the district's ability to meet the needs of its students with local resources (NYSED, 2002). There were no NYC (New York City) schools in the research database because their data were not normally distributed. There were 90 high-need large city schools (Buffalo, Rochester, Syracuse, and Yonkers), 110 suburban high-need schools, 157 rural high-need schools, 605 suburban average-need schools, and 301 suburban low-need schools. The research database contained 28.3% of high-need schools, 47.5% of average-need schools, and 23.8% of low-need schools.

Creating Math Model

For creating the model, the 1,263 sample schools were sorted, assigned random numbers, and then divided into two groups. The first group contained 631 schools and was used to build the model; the second group contained 632 schools and was used to validate the model. Then using structural model technique, the model was created carefully, first by sections and then to create the entire model. In the case of variables that strongly correlated each other, the authors selected the one that correlates most with the dependent variable. Figure 1 shows the model for fourth grade math achievement in New York.

Model Results

The model shows that the percentage of Single Family Household (SFH) in a school district had a very strong inverse relationship ($r = -.83$) with the percentage of Husband-Wife Households (HWH). This suggested segregation in New York of SFH and HWH each in their districts. SFH had a positive contribution ($\beta = .37$) toward the percentage of economically disadvantaged students (ED), and negative contribution ($\beta = -.23$) to school attendance rate (AR). This suggested that school districts with high percentage of single family households had high population of economically disadvantaged students and low attendance rate in their schools.

HWH had a negative contribution ($\beta = -.48$) to ED and positive contribution ($\beta = .17$) to AR. This suggested that school districts with high percentages of husband-wife households had low population of economically disadvantaged students and high attendance rate in their schools.

Figure 1. Math model

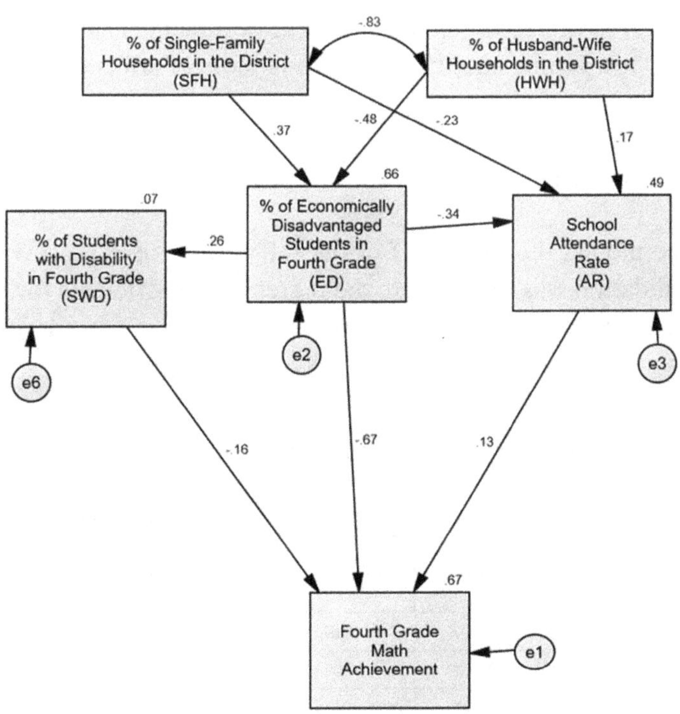

ED had a positive contribution (β =.26) to students with disabilities (SWD), a strong negative contribution (β = -.67) on fourth-grade student math achievement, and an inverse contribution (β = -.34) to attendance rate. This suggested that schools with high ED had more students with disabilities, low attendance rate, and performed low on math state exam. The model R^2 for ED was .67, indicating that 67 percent of the variance in ED was explained by SFH and HWH, showing that household structure had a strong relationship with student socioeconomic status.

AR had a positive contribution (β = .13) to fourth-grade student math achievement. This suggested that schools with high attendance rate gained high scores on math exam. The model R^2 for AR was .49, which indicated that single-family household, husband-wife household, and percentage of economically disadvantaged students in the grade explained 49 percent of the variance in attendance rate. Household structure had a strong direct and indirect relationship with student attendance rate.

SWD had an inverse contribution (β = -.16) toward fourth-grade student math achievement. This suggested that fourth grades with a high percentage of SWD experienced low fourth-grade student math achievement. The model R^2 for students with disabilities was .07, indicating that seven percent of the variance in students with disabilities was explained by ED.

The model R^2 of fourth-grade student math achievement was .67, which indicated that percentage of economically disadvantaged students in the grade, school attendance rate, and percentage of students with disabilities in the grade can explain 67 percent of the variance in fourth-grade student math achievement. The relationships from the above show how family structure had strong indirect effect mostly through ED on fourth grade math achievement.

Validating the Model

To validate the model, the other half of the full dataset (n = 632) was used. The first step in validation was to calculate the regression coefficients for fourth-grade student math achievement based on the model depicted in Figure 1. Table 1 shows the regression weights for the formula.

Table 1. Coefficient for dependent variable: math grade achievement

Model		Unstandardized Coefficients		Standardized Coefficients	t	Sig.
		B	Std. Error	Beta		
1	(Constant)	183.175	33.687		5.438	.000
	Economically Disadvantaged	-.417	.019	-.673	-21.877	.000
	Attendance Rate	1.455	.347	.127	4.194	.000
	Students with Disabilities	-.377	.055	-.161	-6.824	.000

Based on the regression weights math prediction formula was:

$Math_C = 183.175 - .417ED + 1.455AR - .377SWD$

AR=Attendance Rate*100.

To validate the model, Excel was used to compute a column calculated math based on the $Math_c$ formula. The mean of $Math_c$ column of the model population (2012-13, n = 631) was compared with calculated $Math_c$ column for the validation population (2012-13, n = 632). In addition, the researchers validated the model with 2013-14 (n-1476) and 2014-15 (n=1442) fourth grade math achievement data, the constant for these years was updated to 187.9 and 191.2 respectively. Table 2 shows the comparison results of the model and its validation.

As shown in Table 3, the Root Mean Square Error (RMSE) was calculated in order to measure the differences between the calculated model and the actual results. RMSE for the initial model was 7.71, RMSE for the first validation (n=632) was

Table 2. Initial model and validation model results comparison

	Math Model2012-13 (n = 631)	Validation 2012-13 (n = 632)	Validation 2013-14 (n=1476)	Validation 2014-15 (n=1442)
Actual Mean (AM)	300.85	301.36	303.75	306.58
Standard Deviation AM	16.10	16.31	18.73	19.32
Calculated Mean (CM)	300.81	301.69	303.65	306.54
Standard Deviation CM	13.22	13.48	13.83	14.05
Root Mean Square Error	9.18	7.57	11.05	11.59

Table 3. Math model goodness of fit (n = 631)

Model	GFI	NFI	IFI	CFI	RMSEA	λ^2/df
Math model	.988	.991	.995	.993	.077	4.758
Good Fit Range	>.95	>.95	>.95	>.95	<.08	1< & <5

GFI - Goodness of Fit Index, NFI - Normed Fit Index, IFI- Incremental Fit Index, CFI- Comparative Fit Index,

RMSEA - Root Mean Square Error of Approximation, λ^2/df - the minimum discrepancy

7.77, RMSE for the 2013-14 validation (n = 1,476) was 11.05, and RMSE for 2014-15 (n = 1,442) was 11.59 suggesting successful validation of the model. The model had good fit based on major fit measurements as shown by Table 3.

Summary

The research question was answered by using the model described in Figure 1. AMOS software was used to support SEM to find the best model for predicting fourth grade math achievement in NY. Half of the research database was used to build the model and the other half was used to validate the model, in addition the model was validated using 2013-14 and 2014-15 math results. Model validation and model goodness of fitness were successfully achieved.

The model suggested that student attendance rate in a school could be projected with medium-high accuracy (49%) using single-family household, husband-wife household, and percentage of economically disadvantaged students (ED). Household structure had the largest contribution to student attendance rate directly and indirectly through ED. This aligned with Baker et al. (2001), Black et al. (2014), Henry (2007), and Ready (2010) who claimed that household structure was correlated with SES and student absenteeism. Attendance rates as reported on the NYSED report cards were used in this study. However, it is hard to understand from this number whether the school has a real attendance issue. For example a school in which 40 percent of its students were absent 20 percent of the school year, is reporting 92 percent attendance rate. There is a need to increase the importance and awareness of attendance on all levels. This research recommends requiring schools to report the number of students with chronic absenteeism in the school report card as it is done in Georgia, Florida, Maryland, Nebraska, Oregon, and Rhode Island (Balfanz & Byrnes, 2012). Asking schools to report the number of students with chronic absenteeism would provide a better picture of the attendance challenge on the school, district, and state levels. It is also important to involve the family in the student attendance issue, as they strongly affect attendance rate.

The model suggested that SWD could be projected with weak accuracy (7%) by using ED. This phenomenon was explained by Howard et al. (2009) who suggested that the ED-SWD relationship is due to school teachers and administrators misunderstanding and prejudice of students from low SES. The fact that there was a positive relationship between SWD and ED is increasing the inequality gap between low SES schools and affluent schools as low SES schools need to allocate higher percentage of their school budget toward SWD students.

The model suggested that percentage of fourth grade economically disadvantaged students could be projected with high accuracy (66%) by using SFH and HWH. Husband-wife household and male household had the highest contributions suggesting that household structure had the strongest contribution toward student socioeconomic status. This aligned well with Mayer (1997), Toutkoushian and Curtis (2005), Cancian and Reed (2009), and DeNavas-Walt and Proctor (2014) who pointed the close relation between household type and SES. DeNavas-Walt and Proctor (2014) reported that the poverty rates in the U.S. for 2013 were 5.8 percent for husband-wife householders, 30.6 percent for families with a single-female head, and 15.9 percent for families with a single-male head. This supported the risk of poverty for single head-of-household families. Single-female heads were five times more likely live in poverty than were married couples, and single-male heads were twice as likely to live in poverty as were married couples.

The model suggested that fourth-grade student math achievement could be predicted with high accuracy (67%) using the ED, SWD, and AR. The regression formula suggested that each percent increase in attendance would result in additional point and a half in math results. However, there is a limit for improving attendance. A correct method might be to support an increase in school funds for schools with high need and low math scores by attach these funds to increase in school attendance. Future research should look at schools that perform higher in math than the projected score, analyze their teaching methodologies and strategies, school leadership, and provide recommendation for other schools.

It appears from the results of the model that school districts with high percentage of husband-wife households had direct positive effect of 17% on AR and -48% on ED, and therefore an indirect positive effect of 34% on math achievement. School districts with high percentage of single-family households had direct effect of -23% on AR and 37% on ED and therefore had indirect negative effect of 28% on math achievement.

SOLUTIONS AND RECOMMENDATIONS

School leaders should strongly address student absences. Although it is often beyond school control, it is important to educate families about the importance of school and the negative effect of absenteeism. They should also work to minimize student suspensions. High rates of student suspension cause damage to the suspended students and lower the achievement rates of the school. Schools need to find other intervention plans that will keep the student in the school. In addition, it is important that students at middle school and high school will learn about the importance of the family, its values, and the essence of good parenting. This information will provide better understanding for students about their roles as future parents, and might save the next generation from repeating mistakes.

State leaders should develop a similar formula in order to compare school performances. They also may consider instructing schools to report students with chronic absenteeism in their annual reporting.

FUTURE RESEARCH DIRECTIONS

Future research should examine the high correlation that economically disadvantaged had with achievement. The research should also examine school diversity and its effect on economically disadvantaged student achievement. In addition, future research should examine the negative correlation between single-family households and attendance rate as it was found to be a major factor related to student achievement.

CONCLUSION

According to this study, student achievement is mostly determined by the school district and the family structure of its residences. Fourth grade kids in school districts with high percentage of single-family households are at higher risk to live in poverty, higher risk for being diagnosed as students with disabilities, encountering low attendance in school, and performing low on math state exam.

REFERENCES

Bachman, H. J., Coley, R. L., & Chase-Lansdale, P. L. (2009). Is maternal marriage beneficial for low-income adolescents? *Applied Developmental Science*, *13*(4), 153–171. doi:10.1080/10888690903287633 PMID:20485456

Baker, M., & Johnston, P. (2010). The Impact of Socioeconomic Status on High Stakes Testing Reexamined. *Journal of Instructional Psychology*, *37*(3).

Baker, M., Sigmon, J., & Nugent, M. (2001). *Truancy reduction: Keeping students in school*. Washington, DC: Office of Juvenile Justice and Delinquency Prevention, U. S. Department of Justice.

Balfanz, R., & Byrnes, V. (2012). The importance of being in school: A report on absenteeism in the nation's public schools. *Education Digest: Essential Readings Condensed for Quick Review*, *78*(2), 4–9.

Black, A. T., Seder, R. C., & Kekahio, W. (2014). *Review of research on student nonenrollment and chronic absenteeism: A report for the Pacific Region*. Washington, DC: U.S. Department of Education.

Cancian, M., & Reed, D. (2009). Family structure, childbearing, and parental employment: Implications for the level and trend in poverty. *Focus (San Francisco, Calif.)*, *26*(2), 21–26.

Chang, H., & Romero, M. (2008). Present, engaged and accounted for: The critical importance of addressing chronic absence in the early grades. *National Center for Children in Poverty*. Retrieved from http://www.nccp.org/publications/pdf/text_837.pdf

Civil Rights Data Collection (CRDC). (n. d.). FAQ/User guide – Overview. Retrieved from http://ocrdata.ed.gov/Overview

Cohen, Y. (2015). Structural equation modeling to predict fourth grade student achievement.

Coleman, J. S., Cambell, E., Hobson, C., McPartland, J., Mood, A., Weinfeld, F., & York, R. (1966). *Equality of educational opportunity*. Washington, DC: U.S. Government Printing Office.

Crosnoe, R., & Wildsmith, E. (2011). Nonmarital fertility, family structure, and the early school achievement of young children from different race/ethnic and immigration groups. *Applied Developmental Science*, *15*(3), 156–170. doi:10.1080/10888691.2011.587721 PMID:21894243

DeNavas-Walt, C., & Proctor, B. D. (2014). Income and poverty in the United States - 2013. *U.S. Census –. Current Population Reports. Series P-28, Special Censuses*, (September), 60–249.

Eagan, A. (2015). How the Shift in High Stakes Testing Impacts Students of Low Socioeconomic Status in a Suburban Junior High School [Education and Human Development Master's Thesis].

Hampden-Thompson, G. (2009). Are two better than one? A comparative study of achievement gaps and family structure. *Compare: A Journal of Comparative and International Education*, *39*(4), 513–529.

Henry, K. L. (2007). Who's skipping school: Characteristics of truants in 8th and 10th grade. *The Journal of School Health*, *77*(1), 29–35. doi:10.1111/j.1746-1561.2007.00159.x PMID:17212757

Howard, T., Dresser, S., & Dunklee, D. (2009). *Poverty is not a learning disability.* Thousand Oaks, CA: Corwin Press.

Hughes, M. F. (1995). Achieving despite adversity: Why are some schools successful in spite of the obstacles they face? A study of the characteristics of effective and less effective elementary schools in West Virginia using qualitative and quantitative methods. Charleston, WV: West Virginia Education Fund. Retrieved from http://eric.ed.gov/PDFS/ED398004.pdf

Kline, R. B. (2005). *Principles and practices of structural equation modeling* (2nd ed.). New York, NY: The Guilford Press.

Madden, J. V., Lawson, D., & Sweet, D. (1976). *School effectiveness study.* Sacramento, CA: State of California Department of Education.

Mayer, S. E. (1997). *What money can't buy.* Cambridge, MA: Harvard University Press.

National Center of Educational Statistics. (n. d.). *What is school district demographics system?* Retrieved from http://nces.ed.gov/surveys/sdds/about.aspx

New York State Education Department. (2002). *Statistics for public school districts.* Retrieved from http://www.p12.nysed.gov/irs/chapter655/2002/ glossary_June_2002.htm

New York State Education Department. (2012). *New York State report cards – Data accuracy.* Retrieved from https://reportcards.nysed.gov/

New York State Education Department. (2014, May). *Reporting data for 2013–14 school year.* Retrieved from http://www.nysldstac.org/wp-content/uploads/ 2014/05/SIRS-Manual-v9.14.pdf

New York State Education Department. (2015). *Glossary of Terms - Report Cards Data.* Retrieved from http://data.nysed.gov/glossary.php?report=reportcards

New York State Education Department. (2013, August). Release of data –August 7 2013, supplemental slides. Proceedings of the New York State Education Department Press Conference. Retrieved from http://www.p12.nysed.gov/irs/pressRelease/20130807/home.html

New York State Office of Education Performance Review. (1974). *School-related factors influencing reading achievement: A case study of two inner city schools.* Office of Performance Review. Retrieved from http://www.eric.ed.gov/PDFS/ED089211.pdf

Osborn, J. (2002). Practical Research, Assessment and Evaluation Retrieved 1/24/15 from http://pareonline.net/getvn.asp?v=8&n=6

Ready, D. D. (2010). Socioeconomic disadvantage, school attendance, and early cognitive development: The differential effects of school exposure. *Sociology of Education, 83*, 271–286. doi:101177/0038040710383520

Rivikin, S. G., Hanushek, E. A., & Kain, J. F. (2005). Teachers, schools, and academic achievement. *Econometerica*, *73*(2), 417–458. doi:10.1111/j.1468-0262.2005.00584.x

Summers, A., Wolfe, B., & Columbia Univ, N. (1976). Which school resources help learning? Efficiency and equity in Philadelphia public schools. *IRCD Bulletin*, *11*(3), 1–17.

Toutkoushian, R., & Curtis, T. (2005). Effects of socioeconomic factors on public high school outcomes and rankings. *The Journal of Educational Research*, *98*(5), 259–271. doi:10.3200/JOER.98.5.259-271

U.S. Census Bureau. (2012). Households and families: 2010. 2010 Census Briefs.

Weisner, T. S., & Garnier, H. (1992). Nonconventional family life-styles and school achievement: A 12-year longitudinal study. *American Educational Research Journal*, *29*(3), 605–632. doi:10.3102/00028312029003605

Xue, Q. L. (2007). Structural Equational Models. The Johns Hopkins University. Retrieve 1.24.16 from http://ocw.jhsph.edu/courses/structuralmodels/PDFs/Lecture8.pdf

Section 3

Empirical Studies Informed by Publicly Accessible Data Sets

Chapter 9
Elementary Teachers' Math Instructional Practices, Receptivity to Change, Instructional Leadership, and Academic Optimism

Dennis D. Sullivan
Saint Joseph's College, USA

ABSTRACT

This study sought to identify the relationships among elementary teachers' instructional practices in mathematics pre- and post-Common Core Learning Standards (CCLS) implementation in relation to technological and pedagogical content knowledge (TPACK), formative assessment, reflective practice, receptivity to change, academic optimism, and instructional leadership across age, years of experience, grade level taught, and college math credits taken in high and low needs schools. Teacher responses from low and high need schools across age, years of teaching experience, grade level taught, and college math credits taken were examined with the dimensions of mathematics instructional practices to see if any relationships exist among the variables. The implementation of CCLS mathematics had an influence on elementary-school teachers' instructional practices and attitudes in both high and low needs schools. Teacher academic optimism was reported as overall higher in high needs districts, whereas teachers in low needs districts reported an increase in instructional motivation practices after the implementation of CCLS mathematics.

DOI: 10.4018/978-1-5225-3616-1.ch009

INTRODUCTION

The recently mandated education changes in New York State including high stakes testing linked to teacher and administrator performance or the Annual Professional Performance Review (APPR) and the introduction of Common Core Learning Standards (CCLS) in 2010 continue to increase the necessity to push our students to be global intellectual competitors, especially in the areas of science, technology, and math. The introduction of the CCLS has also brought under review many long-standing teaching practices.

In May of 2010, the Governor of New York signed Chapter 103 of the Laws of 2010, creating the Education Law subsection 3012-c. This legislation requires all school districts and Boards of Cooperative Educational Services (BOCES) to conduct annual, professional performance reviews of classroom teachers and building principals.

The nearly concurrent adoption of the CCLS has emphasized the incorporation of critical thinking and problem solving into all content areas. In elementary schools, the instruction of English Language Arts (ELA) and mathematical skills are no longer reserved solely for the classroom teacher. All teachers covering all subjects, from the arts to physical education, are now required to embed these concepts within their curricula and teaching practices.

State standards for education are not a new concept; since the early 1990s, many states have implemented them. By the early 2000s however, the lack of standardization and subsequent variations in the definition of student proficiency caused educational standards to become increasingly dissimilar from state to state. Between 2007 and 2009, as a result of a series of discussions by various states' education chiefs and educational researchers, the National Governors Association (NGA) and the Council of Chief State School Officers (CCSSO) made a recommendation to, "upgrade state standards by adopting a common core of internationally benchmarked standards in math and language arts for grades K-12 to ensure that all students are equipped with the necessary knowledge and skills to be globally competitive" (corestandards.org). Between 2010 and 2012, state education departments and independent reviewers examined the standards and provided feedback to the NGA and CCSSO. Once the development process had concluded in 2012, states began voluntarily adopting the CCLS, "based on their existing process for education standard adoption" (corestandards.org). The NGA and the CCSSO provide the following definition of the CCLS,

The Common Core is a set of high-quality academic standards in mathematics and English language arts/literacy (ELA). These learning goals outline what a student should know and be able to do at the end of each grade. The standards were created to ensure that all students graduate from high school with the skills and knowledge necessary to succeed in college, career, and life, regardless of where they live (ccsso.org). According to the developers, CCLS guidelines prepare students to enter a world in which colleges and businesses are demanding more than ever.

A student's elementary school experiences, both social and academic, are the foundation for their educational success. A major problem faced by university-level mathematics educators, both in content and pedagogy, is that the majority of elementary education majors have well-established attitudes towards mathematics and their ability to perform mathematical tasks, and their self-efficacy beliefs. These attitudes and beliefs may be passed on to elementary students and may act as a filter, preventing preparation for technical careers and preventing many adults from reaching economic maturity.

In light of the increasing number of transient students, the CCLS provide teachers with a consistent set of expectations for students who move into their districts and classrooms from other states. The CCLS compel teacher preparation programs to better prepare pre-service teachers for the new generation of students and the challenges they face in a global economy. In local school districts, professional development programs for veteran teachers are in place to assist in the transition to CCLS protocols (corestandards.org).

The CCLS also pose new challenges also exist for both school building and school-district leaders. As they guide their staff, students, and community members through this change, leaders face passionate arguments from both supporters and opponents of the CCLS.

The CCLS represent one of the biggest changes in educational philosophy in decades. According to Patterson (2003), organizations often feel threatened when the origin of change is external. To effectively implement the CCLS, change is necessary; school systems and teachers are no exception to Patterson's premise of resistance to change. According to Rose (2013), "under the Common Core standards, students are allowed to come up with their own alternative methods for solving problems as they make sense along the way…it's a path to understanding that teachers are usually uncomfortable with" (p. 4). Instruction in mathematics is no longer based simply on algorithmic memorizations. Instead, the CCLS encourage students to develop a deeper understanding of the fluidity of numbers and mathematical concepts.

A study conducted by Goddard, Sweetland, and Hoy in 2000 found that academic emphasis was an important element in explaining achievement in both mathematics and reading. Faculties' trust in parents and students, and academic emphasis and efficacy are key components that work together to create a positive academic environment labeled "academic optimism." The relationship among the three major components of academic optimism can be seen as fundamentally dependent upon each other and are also transactional, in that the measure of each contributes to the overall level of academic optimism.

In their 1977 study, Donady and Tobias report, "if the next generation is to acquire the necessary skills and education for entry into technology-related careers, the students must be proficient in mathematics. Mathematics is a filter to preparation for most technical careers" (p. 72). In their study on math anxiety, Malinsky, Ross, Pannells, and McJunkin (2006) report that mathematics educators have great concern that teachers' attitudes toward mathematics may influence the efficacy of their teaching.

A 2006 publication by Barlow and Reddish states, "In the discipline of mathematics, teacher practices are more influenced by beliefs about mathematical content than by beliefs about mathematical pedagogy" (p. 145). The intent of this study was to "replicate a study conducted by Frank (1990) in which she examined the beliefs in myths about mathematics held by a sample of elementary teacher candidates" (p. 150). Barlow and Reddish (2006) go on to examine how a teacher's experiences as a math student impact his/her content-related beliefs. Many teachers believe that students must "master basic mathematical facts before engaging in problem solving" (p.146). Instruction built upon this premise lacks rich mathematical experiences for students and does not spur them to develop problem-solving skills.

In their conclusions about teachers' math anxiety, Malinsky, Ross, Pannells, and McJunkin (2006) state, "Because this math anxiety may affect their own achievement and that of their future students, it is incumbent upon us as teacher educators to find ways to lessen the math anxiety of our students" (p. 279).

Wilson (2013) suggests that the CCLS emphasis on applied mathematics "has renewed interest in students' being able to solve real world problems" (p. 36). Subsequently, teachers' instructional practices need to be on the cutting edge, as they are paramount to student learning. Research published in 2014 by Cronin and Jensen shows that mathematics and related problem-solving skills form an increasingly important knowledge base for almost all professions. It is imperative for both teachers and the education system to diligently do their part to thoroughly prepare students to be competitive in the rapidly changing global marketplace.

Purpose of the Study

This study sought to identify the relationships among elementary teacher dispositions pre- and post-CCLS implementation, specifically concerning mathematics instruction, in relation to technological and pedagogical content knowledge (TPACK), receptivity to CCLS mathematics, supervisor instructional leadership, academic optimism, instructional motivation, receptivity to change, formative assessment and planning practices, and responsive instructional practices in high and low needs schools, as defined by the Needs/Resource Capacity Index.

"Academic optimism" is defined by Hoy (2012) as the explanation to the collinearity of efficacy, trust, and academic emphasis in his studies. Hoy's early goal was to find the elements within a school environment, other than socioeconomic status (SES), that fostered high achievement. The latent variable connecting efficacy and trust was optimism. A collective positive outlook affected by trust and self-efficacy, applied to the domain of academic emphasis defines academic optimism (Hoy, 2012).

Significance of the Study

This study sought to contrast elementary school teacher dispositions regarding aspects of instructional qualities and leadership in New York State public schools pre- and post-implementation of CCLS. This study was designed to examine the impact of CCLS on teaching practices and teacher attitudes towards math instruction at the elementary level. The findings of this study will help educational leaders and teachers understand the connection between effective instructional practices, leadership, and the impact of CCLS. If the education system desires to embrace the CCLS, both schools leaders and teachers need to rethink current best practices. Colleges and universities, as well as school leaders, must consider the structure of teacher preparation programs; in addition, the presentation and format of professional development for veteran teachers need to align with the skills required to meet the increased rigor of the Common Core Learning Standards.

BACKGROUND

A 1985 study by Stodolsky examined the main characteristics of math education and instructional practices in American elementary schools. Stodolsky, having completed a systematic examination of fifth-grade classrooms, found that there were vast differences in instructional practices in mathematics and social studies. Her findings show that "in contrast to other school subjects…math instruction provides students with only one route to learning: teacher explanation followed by student practice" (p. 125). Stodolsky also determined that math classes were more homogenously grouped than classes in other subject areas, and the materials used in mathematics instruction showed less variety than materials used in other content areas.

In conjunction with instructional practices, optimism and enthusiasm are two key signs of motivation, whereas pessimism and cynicism are indicators of apathy in both the teacher and the student. Pearce, Lungren, and Wince (1999) examined the effects of instructional practices on "activities, attitudes and achievement scores" (p. 82) on elementary math students. Their research shows that the learning of mathematics is related to the student's beliefs, feelings, and attitudes, and that teachers need not only to assess for conceptual comprehension but should also "routinely give attitude assessments" (p. 83) and adjust the instructional techniques and classroom environment to facilitate learning. "If teachers are to make mathematics meaningful to young students, assessing attitudes must be an important part of the development of mathematics curriculum" (p. 83).

The study by Pearce, Lungren, and Wince (1999) goes on to stress the importance of mathematics instruction that incorporates dialogue in addition to the imparting of knowledge. They emphasize that the distinction between rote and reasoning is critical: "Discussing mathematical process and procedures can improve [student] attitudes in mathematics" (p. 84).

The attitude of the student is directly related to the attitudes of the teacher. Austin, Wadlington, and Bitner (2001) considered the effects of mathematics beliefs, math anxiety, and math self-concepts on pre-service teachers. In their analysis, the Mathematics Anxiety Rating Scale (MARS), the Kulm Mathematics Self-Concept Test (KMSCT) and the Math Belief Survey Instrument (MBSI) were used "to investigate the effects of pre-service and in-service teachers' beliefs about mathematics upon their math self-concepts and levels of math anxiety" (p. 391). According to Austin, Wadlington, and Bitner (2001), "there is evidence that math-anxious elementary teachers may affect their pupils adversely. A child's attitude toward mathematics is a learned attitude that develops through math experiences, many of which take place in the elementary classroom" (p. 391). Austin, Wadlington, and Bitner (2001) based their research on evidence from Johnson's 1981 inquiry that supports the idea that some teachers may transmit their unfavorable attitudes about math to their students.

Barlow and Reddish (2006) added to this idea by replicating a 1990 study by Frank that examined pre-service elementary teachers beliefs in myths about math education and ability. They report: "How teachers approach and implement these math standards is heavily influenced by what they believe about math content and pedagogy" (p.145). The National Council of Teachers of Mathematics (NCTM) has emphasized ongoing efforts to "shift the role of the mathematics teacher from one of a giver of information to one of a facilitator of learning" (p. 146).

Barlow and Reddish (2006) further support Stodolsky's (1985) findings regarding instructional practices. They described how teachers who are less comfortable teaching math tend to devote more class time to "the memorization of mathematical rules and procedures and less time spent working to enable their students to understand mathematics and make connections within and among the mathematical concepts" (p. 155) and observed that such teachers' classes "are void of rich mathematical tasks that engage students in problem solving" (p. 146). Barlow and Reddish (2006) conclude that teacher practices are more influenced by beliefs about mathematical content than by beliefs about mathematical pedagogy, despite decades of ongoing reforms in mathematics education.

Wilkins's (2010) study investigated 490 kindergarten through fifth-grade teachers to find out their favorite teaching subjects and enjoyment of teaching different subjects. Wilkins (2010) focused on the two indicators above, favorite subject to teach and enjoyment of teaching different subjects, as a measure of attitude. Wilkins (2010) examined teacher attitude towards a given content area to see how the attitude influenced both the quantity of instructional time spent on that area and the teacher's instructional practice.

Wilkins (2010) found that "teachers with more positive attitudes towards mathematics instructions used methods of instruction that tend to promote student exploration and discovery of topics" (p. 26). Barlow and Reddish (2006) also found that "beliefs impact practices because beliefs affect how teachers see their students… how they accept ideas given to develop practice" (p. 145). Wilkins (2010) broadened these ideas, reporting that "teachers' attitudes can and do influence instructional practice. Understanding teachers' attitudes toward all subjects can provide additional information that could help explain differences in instructional practice" (p. 27). The better the teacher's attitude, the more discovery-based teaching is used, as opposed to a rules-based approach focused on memorization and getting the right answer.

Wilkins's (2010) findings show that, "in general reading was consistently ranked by teachers as the favorite subject to teach at all grade levels," whereas "math and science were consistently ranked among the least favorite subjects to teach and never ranked higher than 4th out of 6 subjects" (p. 31). Wilkins (2010) additionally revealed grade-level differences in teacher attitude toward academic content. Reading and language arts were among the favorites subjects to teach of teachers in grades K through two. Teachers in grades three to five, however, indicated that, while math may not be their favorite subject, they find teaching math to be comparatively enjoyable. These findings also suggest that different support systems may be needed to stimulate elementary teachers' instructional practices in the area of mathematics.

As the role of the teacher has evolved over the years, so, too, has the role of the administrator. The teacher role has shifted from that of a purveyor of knowledge, toward that of an academic coach or facilitator. The administrative responsibilities have grown from that of a building manager and disciplinarian to that of the leading learner in the building (Brookhart & Moss, 2013).

These role changes in require a shift in the professional relationship between teacher and administrators. Teachers no longer close their doors and run their class with little or no input from the administration, just as administrators no longer rule the building from the front office. Both are now held publicly accountable through school report cards and published assessment outcomes. This shift and increased scrutiny has changed the dynamic of the relationships between teacher and administrator, teacher and student, and teacher (or school generically) and parents.

Technological Pedagogical Content Knowledge

Guha and Leonard (2002) state that "the society in which we live is no longer industrial-based but technology based. Becoming familiar with computers...means that students will be equipped to enter a variety of job markets since no job is void of technology" (p. 41). Technology provides teachers another tool for differentiating instruction. Guha and Leonard (2002) continue that "it is important for the teachers to build the conceptual knowledge" (p. 42) and then provide explorative or remedial opportunities for students through the use of technology.

The intersection of technological knowledge (or a teacher's knowledge of how to use and create technology), pedagogical knowledge (or a teacher's knowledge of various effective teaching practices), and content knowledge (or a teacher's expertise in their given subject area) results in Technological Pedagogical Content Knowledge (TPACK) (Koehler & Mishra, 2009).

According to Koehler and Mishra (2009), "Technological pedagogical content knowledge is an understanding that emerges from interactions among content, pedagogy, and technology knowledge" (p. 66). By simultaneously integrating these three factors, expert teachers incorporate TPACK into their instruction whenever they teach (Koehler & Mishra, 2009). It is a challenge to effectively use technology in teaching. The TPACK structure suggests that a teacher must balance and successfully integrate content, pedagogy, technology, and teaching during a lesson. Teaching well with technology requires continually creating, sustaining, and re-establishing a dynamic evenness among all three components (Koehler & Mishra, 2009).

In contrast to Guha and Leonard (2002), Li and Ma (2010) found that shorter technology interventions were more effective than longer ones in promoting mathematics achievement. They conclude that the teaching method was more of factor on student achievement (Li & Ma, 2010, p. 228).

According to Cuff (2014), "from the elementary school setting to doctoral-level education, technology has become an integral part of the learning process in and out of the classroom" (p. 75). With the implementation of the CCLS and the importance of deeper understanding, a solid foundation in technological pedagogy is critical to ensure student success (Cuff, 2014). Li and Ma (2010) report that the "use of technology in mathematics education, is essential in teaching and learning..." (p. 215) and that "successful and effective use of technology for the teaching of and learning of mathematics depends upon sound teaching and learning strategies..." (p. 215).

Receptivity to Common Core Learning Standards Mathematics

A teacher's initial reaction to a change, whether it is a simple as a move to a new classroom or as encompassing as CCLS, is sometimes caused by emotion or a fear of the unknown; the lack of an adequate quantitative tool to measure receptivity to change is a factor (Waugh, 2000).

The CCLS represent one of the largest changes, both instructionally and philosophically, in education in the last fifty years. "Teacher receptivity to a vast system-wide educational change is likely to be a complex process" (Waugh, 2000, p. 355). The overall attitude of an individual teacher towards change is an important factor influencing how that teacher will adapt to the change. Waugh (2000) found that teacher receptivity to system-wide change is improved when a) there is opportunity for discussion, b) sustainability is planned, and c) there is acknowledgment that some initial confusion will occur (Waugh, 2000).

Instructional Leadership

In a time of high-stakes accountability, the pressure has never been greater for principals to excel as instructional leaders. With the recently occurring changes and political debates in education, the role of administrators continues to be redefined. The work of the principal has shifted from discipline and administrivia to a concentration on learning.

Houchens and Cabrera (2013) show that, in high-performing schools, "principals devote much of their focus to the process of teaching and learning and dedicate their efforts toward the improvement of both" (p. 56). Their study emphasizes how a principal's actions can impact both teacher professional learning and student outcomes. They define the primary roles of the school principal as possessing the "key responsibility of ensuring a guaranteed, viable curriculum through effective classroom teaching practice" (p. 58) and "to provide focused feedback on teaching practice" (p. 59).

The link between school leadership and student success continues to be underestimated (Connelly, 2014). Administrators are now being increasingly viewed as academic coaches, rather than merely building managers. The role of "coach" and the practice of academic "coaching," no matter the subject area, have added a new dimension to the teacher-administrator relationship. Holmstrom (2010) stresses the importance of administrators' participating in the professional learning communities they lead. "When administrators know what to expect in the classrooms, they also know how to help teachers develop necessary new skills that work to teach kids math" (Holmstrom, 2010, p. 62).

Academic Optimism

The concept of academic optimism is one "grounded in social cognitive theory and positive psychology that has the potential to disrupt the commonly found linkages between low socioeconomic status and low achievement" (Hoy, Tarter, and Hoy, 2006, p.444). The early goal of Hoy, et al. (2006) was to find which elements of a school environment other than socioeconomic status (SES) fostered high achievement.

Wu, Hoy, and Tarter (2013) refined the definition of academic optimism as "a collective property of schools that describes school culture in terms of the emphasis on academic achievement, the degree to which the faculty trusts parents and student, and the extent of collective efficacy of the faculty" (p. 178). This refinement resulted from a study conducted by Forsyth (2011) that more closely examined the cognitive and emotional constructs in the earlier definition provided by Hoy.

Wu, Hoy, and Tarter (2013) further emphasized the importance of trust between faculty, students, and parents as a key component of achievement and academic optimism. They predicted and proved that "collective responsibility is directly related to achievement through academic optimism" (p. 4). This collective responsibility is based on a collective trust created by the faculty's willingness to be vulnerable to the parents and the parents' being benevolent, reliable, and open with the teachers. This emphasis on academics creates a strong synergy and leads to greater student achievement (Wu, Hoy & Tarter, 2013).

Kilnic (2013) found that "the teacher sense of academic optimism was positively and significantly related to supportive, directive, and intimate school climates". Kilnic (2013) contends that the components of a collective sense of academic optimism can be applicable to the individual teacher as well. Kilnic's (2013) findings affirm, "teachers in schools with supportive, directive and intimate school climates tended to be more academically optimistic…" (p. 629). Conversely, "teachers' sense of academic optimism was positively and significantly related to directive school climate" (Kilnic, 2013, p. 630). Based on these studies and other research, academic optimism appears to be a significant factor that influences school climate, teacher practice, and student achievement.

Instructional Motivation

Instructional motivation emerged from the variable academic optimism. For the purposes of this study, instructional motivation is defined as the ability of the teacher to engage students in the content to such a level that the student is inspired to increase his/her knowledge of that content to a deeper comprehension.

As noted above, Beard, Hoy and Woolfolk-Hoy (2010) view a teacher's sense of self-efficacy as "one of the few teacher characteristics correlated with student achievement" (p. 1137). Trust is also a key element in developing positive relationships with students. When teachers create a safe and trusting environment, students are more likely to take chances and learn from their mistakes, thus the parents come to believe that the teachers are motivated by the best interest of the student (Beard, Hoy & Woolfolk-Hoy 2010).

Receptivity to Change

Michael Fullan (1985) has been studying change as process in organizations for over forty years. In a 1985 study, Fullan examined building- and district-level policies that would improve the change process in schools. Much of this study is dedicated to describing how change processes actually work, as these processes were not well-portrayed or -understood in the schools literature of the time, though such an understanding is an essential prerequisite for planning effective approaches for improvement (Fullan 1985, p. 392).

Waugh (2000) reviewed four major changes in the Australian education system that took place from 1970 to 2000. These changes affected all levels, from the United States equivalent of kindergarten through twelfth grade. Waugh (2000) asserts that teacher receptivity to change is composed of four first-order aspects. First, a teacher assesses characteristics of the change by comparison with the previous system and its practicality in one's classroom. Second, managing the change at school involves alleviation of concerns, learning about the change, and participation in decisions at one's school. Third, value for the teacher is defined by personal cost appraisal, collaboration with other teachers, and opportunities for teacher improvement. Fourth, teacher-perceived value for students represents the value for students that a teacher assigns to a particular change (Waugh, 2000).

Much of the research literature on change consists of qualitative studies using small samples of teachers and examining local or specific changes, therefore bringing the generalizability of those studies into question. A teacher's initial reaction to change, whether it is a simple as a move to new classroom or as encompassing as CCLS, is sometimes caused by emotion or a fear of the unknown; the lack of an adequate quantitative tool to measure receptivity to change is a factor (Waugh, 2000).

The act of developing skills is not sufficient to bring about instructional change if teachers are not willing to apply them persistently in the face of difficulties. Embedding professional development programs in the classroom and at the subject level, where the new learning is to eventually take place, and safeguarding regular time away from curriculum hours over the course of the school year, to reinforce collective learning, are examples of contextual conditions that the school can enforce to promote instructional change (Wilkins 2014, Wilson 2013, Leithwood & Strauss, 2009).

Formative Assessment and Planning Practices

Black and Wiliam (1998) provided evidence that formative assessment can make a difference in learning outcomes at all grade levels. They conclude that "the success of formative assessment is highly related to how teachers use it to adjust teaching... effective learning is based on active student involvement...enhanced feedback is crucial to improve outcomes...and there is a link between formative assessment and self-assessment" (p. 42). Similarly, Sadler (1989) states that "teachers use feedback to make programmatic decisions with respect to readiness, diagnosis and remediation. Students use it to monitor the strength and weaknesses of their performance..." (Sadler, 1989, p. 120).

The synthesis of research conducted by Black and Wiliam (1998) resulted in the emergence of formative assessment as an unambiguous domain of practice. The authors assert, "teachers need to know about their pupils' progress and difficulties with learning so that they can adapt their own work to meet pupils' needs" (p. 140). Although the act of teaching inherently involves levels of assessment, Black and Wiliam (1998) believe that "such assessment becomes formative assessment when the evidence is actually used to adapt the teaching to meet student needs" (p. 140).

Black and Wiliam (1998) determined that the student learning improvements elicited by formative assessment were among the largest ever reported for educational interventions, with the largest gains being realized by previously low achievers (Black and Wiliam, 1998).

They proposed that effective formative assessment involves:

1. Teachers making adjustments to teaching and learning in response to assessment evidence.
2. Students receiving feedback about their learning with advice on what they can do to improve.
3. Students' participation in the process through self-assessment. (Black and Wiliam, 1998, p. 142)

They conclude that "formative assessment is an essential component of classroom work and that its development can raise standards of achievement" (Black & Wiliam, 1998, p. 148).

Misset, Brunner, Callahan, Moon and Azano (2014) explored how teacher expectations about student ability influenced teacher's use of accelerative practices, ability grouping, and formative assessment. They report that formative assessment is a "tool that educators can use to appropriately integrate accelerative practices and ability grouping into the classroom" (Misset et al., 2014, p. 246). They see formative assessment as "assessment for learning within a unit of study where outcomes guide instruction without associated rigid quantifiers such as grades" (Misset et al, 2014, p. 249).

According to Levey (2015), "responsive teaching occurs when teachers respond to formative assessment as a diagnostic tool that guides them in making changes in what they do and how they see learning occurring in their classroom. Their analysis of formative assessments helps them redesign their own teaching" (p. 35).

Reflective Practice

Reflective practice is a way for teachers to gather information about their performance and make informed decisions about how to apply that information to their instruction. It is not a solitary or casual exercise; rather, it is an ongoing process of shared feedback, dispositions, and intentional acts of improvement (Osterman & Kottkamp, 1993). In their extensive writings on reflective practice, Osterman and Kottkamp (1993) propose an approach to reflective thinking as a process of professional development. While often confused with reflection, reflective practice is neither an independent nor a meditative process. Osterman and Kottkamp (1993) describe reflective practice as a "challenging, demanding, trying process that is most successful as a collaborative effort," and they view reflective practice as a "means by which practitioners can develop a greater level of self-awareness about the nature and impact of their performance" (p. 2).

Osterman and Kottkamp (1993) lay out the concept of reflective practice in their experiential learning cycle that shows a continuous loop that links together concrete experience, observation and analysis, abstract reconceptualization, and active experimentation as four stages of a cyclical process.

MAIN FOCUS OF THE CHAPTER

This purpose of this study was to identify the relationships among elementary teacher practices pre- and post-implementation of the Common Core Learning Standards (CCLS) in relation to instructional practices including technological pedagogical and content knowledge (TPACK), receptivity to Common Core Learning Standards mathematics, instructional leadership, academic optimism, instructional motivation, receptivity to change, formative assessment and planning practices, and responsive instructional practices across age, years of experience, grade level taught, and college math credits taken in high and low needs schools.

Teacher responses from low and high need schools (based on the Need/Resource Capacity Categories) age, years of experience, grade level taught, and college math credits taken were examined against the dimensions of instructional practices including TPACK, receptivity to Common Core Learning Standards Mathematics, instructional leadership, academic optimism, instructional motivation, receptivity to change, formative assessment and planning practices, and responsive instructional practices to see if any relationships exist among the variables.

Three high need/resource capacity urban/suburban school districts elementary schools were compared to five low need/resource capacity school districts elementary schools. The student enrollment and number of teachers employed in each district and building were considered in the analysis of data.

Information regarding the selection of subjects and data gathering techniques is presented in this chapter. In addition, a description of the questionnaire utilized in this study is explained in this chapter. The research question guiding this study was, "What relationships exist among elementary teacher characteristics of mathematics instructional practices including technological and pedagogical content knowledge (TPACK), receptivity to CCLS mathematics, supervisor instructional leadership academic optimism, instructional motivation, receptivity to change, formative assessment and planning practices, and responsive instructional practices post-CCLS implementation across age, years of experience, grade level taught and college math credits taken in high and low need schools?"

Selection of Subjects

From the selected schools, elementary-school teachers responsible for mathematics instruction were invited to participate in a survey to collect data for this study. Subjects were selected from a purposeful sample of public elementary schools based on the school districts rating as high needs urban/suburban or low needs according to the Needs/Resource Capacity Categories List. According to New York State Education Department, the Need/Resource Capacity (N/RC) index is a ratio of the estimated poverty percentage (expressed in standard score form) to the Combined Wealth Ratio (expressed in standard score form). Tables 1 and 2 list the selected school districts.

A district with both estimated poverty and Combined Wealth Ratio equal to the State average would have a need/resource capacity index (N/RC) of 1.0. All districts at or above the 70th percentile (1.1835) that have at least 100 students per square mile or an enrollment greater than 2,500 and more than 50 students per square mile are categorized as High N/RC Urban-Suburban Districts. Districts are categorized as Low N/RC Districts if they are below the 20th percentile (0.770) on the index.

The size of the school is taken from the 2014 New York State report card data and rounded to the nearest 50. Teacher demographic information, such as age, years of experience, and number of college mathematics credits taken, was used in this study to contrast teachers in high and low N/RC districts.

Table 1. List of high needs/resource capacity schools

District Code	Total K-6 Schools	School Code	School Grades	# Of Teachers
H.1	3	H.1.1	PK-K	17
		H.1.2	1-3	41
		H.1.3	4-6	45
H.2	2	H.2.1	K-2	30
		H.2.2	3-5	35
H.3	4	H.3.1	K	50
		H.3.2	1-2	35
		H.3.3	3-5	35
		H.3.4	3-5	35
Total Teachers				358

Table 2. List of low need/resource capacity schools

District Code	Total K-6 Schools	School Code	School Grades	# Of Teachers
L.1	2	L.1.1	K-3	19
		L.1.2	3-6	31
L.2	1	L.2.1	K-5	85
L.3	1	L.3.1	K-6	36
L.4	1	L.4.1	K-6	22
L.5	1	L.5.1	K-5	45
Total Teachers				238

Data Gathering Techniques

A survey instrument was developed to obtain information regarding demographics and teacher description of academic optimism; technological and pedagogical content knowledge (TPACK), formative assessment, reflective practice, receptivity to change, and instructional leadership. The researcher administered the survey to the elementary teachers via internet-based software (Google Forms). Each email contained an invitation to participate, and a link to the survey (via Google Forms), as well as a consent letter guaranteeing anonymity; the email also outlined the process and stated that participation in the study was voluntary.

Survey Instrument

Section one consisted of demographics questions created to collect data on the current age of the respondent, number of years teaching, college math credits taken, and whether or not the respondent was teaching prior to the implementation of the Common Core Learning Standards.

Section two consisted of 50 questions that asked participants to focus their responses while considering their experiences pre- and post-Common Core Learning Standards specifically in the areas of academic optimism, technological and pedagogical content knowledge, formative assessment, reflective practice, receptivity to change, and instructional leadership. This section was comprised of 8 questions reflective of academic optimism, 7 questions reflective of technological pedagogical content knowledge, 10 questions reflective of formative assessment, 8 questions reflective of reflective practice, 7 questions reflective of instructional leadership, and 10 questions reflective of receptivity to change. Respondents were asked to answer each question using a Likert Scale of 1-5, where (1) = Strongly Disagree; (2) = Disagree; (3) = Slightly Agree; (4) = Agree; and (5) = Strongly Agree while considering their answers from both a pre- and post-Common Core Learning Standards perspective.

The survey instrument was designed to measure the qualities exhibited by instructional practices including technological and pedagogical content knowledge (TPACK), formative assessment, reflective practice, receptivity to change, academic optimism, and instructional leadership.

Data Collection Procedures

Respondents were sent an email that linked to a survey created with Google Forms. Respondents in schools that are designated as low need and high need, according to the New York State Needs Resource Capacity Index, were sent links to separate surveys that were coded by the researcher as being applicable to the school type. None of the respondents from either category were aware of a coding or difference in the completion of their survey.

All areas of the online survey maintained the anonymity of the respondents and the school districts in which they are employed.

The study was planned for distribution to 20 elementary schools. All schools were solicited for responses via email, yielding 61 useable surveys. There were 30 respondents in the high needs resource capacity group and 31 respondents in the low needs resource capacity group.

Demographic Analysis

The participants in this study consisted of elementary-school teachers responsible for mathematics instruction from seven school districts in New York State. The criterion for selection was based on the New York State Needs Resource Capacity Index. Five hundred ninety-six surveys were distributed via email and 61 surveys were returned for a return rate of 10.23 percent. From the 61 useable surveys, there were 31 respondents in Group 1, representing High Needs Resource Capacity Districts, and 30 respondents from Group 2, representing Low Needs Resource Capacity Districts.

Results

A Pearson correlation analysis was applied to investigate the binary relationships among the variables. Correlation coefficients were computed using the Pearson Product Moment correlation analysis to determine statistically significant relationships among TPACK, supervisor instructional leadership, academic optimism, instructional motivation, receptivity to change, planning and formative assessment practices, and responsive instructional practices in both high and low needs schools. In the analysis of high needs districts, 16 of the 55 correlations were reported as significant. In the low needs districts 13 of the 55 correlations were reported as significant.

The variable receptivity to CCLS mathematics had a direct, strong relationship with the variable academic optimism ($r = .510$, $p < .01$). Receptivity to CCLS mathematics describes 26.0 percent of the variance in academic optimism. The variable instructional motivation had a direct, strong relationship with the variable academic optimism ($r = .723$, $p < .01$). Instructional motivation described 52.2 percent of the variance in academic optimism. The variable receptivity to change had a direct, moderate relationship with the variable academic optimism ($r = .465$, $p < .01$). The variable receptivity to change describes 21.6 percent of the variance in academic optimism. The variable formative assessment practices had a direct, moderate relationship with academic ($r = .442$, $p < .05$). The variable formative assessment practices described 19.5 percent of the variance in academic optimism.

The variable instructional leadership had a direct, strong relationship to the variable receptivity to CCLS mathematics ($r = .533$, $p < .01$). The variable instructional leadership described 30.5 percent of the variance in the variable receptivity to CCLS mathematics. The variable instructional motivation had a direct, moderate relationship to the variable receptivity to CCLS mathematics ($r = .467$, $p < .01$). The variable instructional leadership described 21.8 percent of the variance in the variable receptivity to CCLS mathematics. The variable receptivity to change had a direct, moderate relationship to the variable receptivity to CCLS mathematics ($r = .418, p < .05$). The variable receptivity to change described 17.4 percent of the variance in the variable receptivity to CCLS mathematics. The variable formative assessment practices had a direct, strong relationship to the variable receptivity to CCLS mathematics ($r = .607, p < .01$). The variable formative assessment practices described 36.8 percent of the variance in the variable receptivity to CCLS mathematics. The variable responsive instructional practices had a direct, strong relationship to the variable receptivity to CCLS mathematics ($r = .562, p < .01$). The variable responsive instructional practice described 31.5 percent of the variance in the variable receptivity to CCLS mathematics.

The variable receptivity to change had a direct, moderate relationship to the variable instructional leadership ($r = .434, p < .05$). The variable receptivity to change described 18.8 percent of the variance in the variable instructional leadership. The variable receptivity to change had a direct, moderate relationship to the variable instructional motivation ($r = .461, p < .05$). The variable receptivity to change described 21.2 percent of the variance in the variable instructional motivation.

The variable responsive instructional practices had a direct, moderate relationship to the variable instructional motivation ($r = .463, p < .01$). The variable responsive instructional practices described 21.4 percent of the variance for instructional motivation. The variable responsive instructional practices had a direct, moderate relationship to the variable formative assessment practices ($r = .477, p < .01$). The variable responsive instructional practices described 22.7 percent of the variance in the variable formative assessment practices.

The variable receptivity to CCLS mathematics had a direct, strong relationship to the variable TPACK (r = .661, $p < .01$). The variable receptivity to CCLS mathematics described 46.3 percent of the variance for the variable TPACK. The variable instructional leadership had a direct, strong relationship to the variable TPACK (r = .513, $p < .01$). The variable instructional leadership described 26.3 percent of the variance for the variable TPACK. The variable instructional motivation had a direct, strong relationship to the variable TPACK (r = .592, $p < .01$). The variable instructional motivation described 35.0 percent of the variance in the variable TPACK. The variable receptivity to change had a direct, moderate relationship to the variable TPACK (r = .615, $p < .01$). The variable receptivity to change described 37.8 percent of the variance for the variable TPACK. The variable formative assessment had a direct, moderate relationship to the variable TPACK (r = .379, $p < .05$). The variable formative assessment described 14.3 percent of the variance in the variable TPACK.

Table 3. Pearson product moment correlation high needs schools

		AO	TPCK	RCCM	IL	IM	RC	FA	RP	AGE	YT
TPCK	r	.009									
	r^2	.000									
	N	31									
RCCM	r	.510**	-.010								
	r^2	.260	.000								
	N	31	31								
IL	r	.293	-.035	.553**							
	r^2	.085	.001	.305							
	N	31	31	31							
IM	r	.723**	.204	.467**	.326						
	r^2	.522	.041	.218	.106						
	N	31	31	31	31						
RC	r	.465**	.048	.418*	.434*	.461*					
	r^2	.216	.002	.174	.188	.212					
	N	30	30	30	30	30					
FA	r	.442*	.265	.607**	.361*	.324	.284				
	r^2	.195	.070	.368	.130	.104	.080				
	N	31	31	31	31	31	30				
RP	r	.348	.127	.562**	.251	.463**	.231	.477**			
	r^2	.121	.016	.315	.063	.214	.053	.227			
	N	31	31	31	31	31	30	31			
AGE	r	.197	-.347	.196	-.038	.157	.124	-.199	.008		
	r^2	.038	.120	.038	.001	.024	.015	.039	.000		
	N	31	31	31	31	31	30	31	31		
YT	r	.166	-.178	.170	-.015	.123	.001	-.166	-.066	.783**	
	r^2	.027	.031	.028	.000	.015	.000	.027	.004	.613	
	N	31	31	31	31	31	30	31	31	31	
TMC	r	.040	.012	-.166	-.171	.231	.141	.142	-.258	.260	.493*
	r^2	.001	.000	.027	.029	.053	.019	.020	.066	.067	.243
	N	25	25	25	25	25	24	25	25	25	25

Note. * = $p < .05$, ** = $p < .01$ (2 – tailed). TPCK = Technological and pedagogical content knowledge, RCCM = Receptivity to CCLS mathematics, IL = Instructional leadership, AO = Academic optimism, IM = Instructional Motivation, RC = Receptivity to change, FA = Formative assessment and planning practices, RP = Responsive instructional practices, YT = Years teaching, TMC = Total math credits taken

The variable instructional motivation had a direct, strong relationship to the variable receptivity to CCLS mathematics (r = .692, $p < .01$). The variable instructional motivation described 47.8 percent of the variance for the variable receptivity to CCLS mathematics. The variable receptivity to change had a direct, strong relationship to the variable receptivity to CCLS mathematics (r = .625, $p < .01$). The variable receptivity to change described 39.0 percent of the variance for the variable receptivity to CCLS mathematics. The variable formative assessment had a direct, moderate relationship to the variable receptivity to CCLS mathematics (r = .449, $p < .05$). The variable formative assessment described 20.1 percent of the variance of the variable receptivity to CCLS mathematics.

The variable receptivity to change had a direct, strong relationship to the variable instructional leadership (r = .508, $p < .01$). The variable receptivity to change described 25.8 percent of the variance in the variable instructional leadership. The variable formative assessment had a direct, strong relationship to the variable instructional leadership (r = .537, $p < .01$). The variable formative assessment described 28.8 percent of the variance for the variable instructional leadership. The variable receptivity to change had a direct, strong relationship to the variable instructional motivation (r = .591, $p < .01$). The variable receptivity to change described 34.9 percent of the variance for the variable instructional motivation. The variable receptivity to change had a direct, moderate relationship to the variable formative assessment (r = .494, $p < .01$). The variable receptivity to change described 24.4 percent of the variance in the variable formative assessment.

The concept of academic optimism is "grounded in social cognitive theory and positive psychology that has the potential to disrupt the commonly found linkages between low socioeconomic status and low achievement" (Hoy, Tarter, & Hoy, 2006, p.444). The early goal of Hoy, et al. (2006) was to find the elements within a school environment other than socioeconomic status (SES) that fostered high achievement.

The present study has reinforced these findings by Hoy (2006) and his decades-long research on academic optimism. The academic optimism of teachers in the high needs districts in this study showed a relationship to receptivity to CCLS mathematics, instructional motivation, receptivity to change, and formative assessment and planning practices. Conversely, the academic optimism of teachers in low needs districts shows no significant relationship to any of the variables.

The relationship between academic optimism and receptivity to CCLS mathematics, receptivity to change, and instructional motivation is particularly noteworthy, in that these variables are all indicative of a growth mindset that is based more on trust and motivation.

In the low needs districts, TPACK showed the most relationships to the variables receptivity to CCLS mathematics, instructional leadership, instructional motivation, receptivity to change, and formative assessment and planning practices. This indicates

Table 4. Pearson product moment correlation low needs schools

		AO	TPCK	RCCM	IL	IM	RC	FA	RP	AGE	YT
TPCK	r	.111									
	r^2	.012									
	N	30									
RCCM	r	.054	.661**								
	r^2	.002	.436								
	N	30	30								
IL	r	-.162	.513**	.173							
	r^2	.026	.263	.029							
	N	30	30	30							
IM	r	.087	.592**	.692**	.264						
	r^2	.007	.350	.478	.069						
	N	30	30	30	30						
RC	r	-.155	.615**	.625**	.508**	.591**					
	r^2	.024	.378	.390	.258	.349					
	N	30	30	30	30	30					
FA	r	.124	.379*	.449*	.537**	.240	.494**				
	r^2	.015	.143	.201	.288	.057	.244				
	N	30	30	30	30	30	30				
RP	r	-.078	-.034	.009	.050	.111	-.107	.294			
	r^2	.006	.001	.000	.002	.012	.011	.086			
	N	30	30	30	30	30	30	30			
AGE	r	.232	.156	-.038	-.051	-.121	-.033	-.110	-.187		
	r^2	.053	.024	.001	.002	.014	.001	.012	.034		
	N	30	30	30	30	30	30	30	30		
YT	r	.186	.175	-.027	.045	-.092	-.069	.041	.220	.801**	
	r^2	.034	.030	.000	.002	.008	.004	.001	.048	.641	
	N	30	30	30	30	30	30	30	30	30	
TMC	r	-.041	.051	-.159	.132	.199	-.025	-.104	-.076	.286	.224
	r^2	.001	.002	.025	.017	.039	.000	.010	.005	.081	.050
	N	23	23	23	23	23	23	23	23	23	23

Note. * = $p < .05$, ** = $p < .01$ (2 – tailed). TPCK = Technological and pedagogical content knowledge, RCCM = Receptivity to CCLS mathematics, IL = Instructional leadership, AO = Academic optimism, IM = Instructional Motivation, RC = Receptivity to change, FA = Formative assessment and planning practices, RP = Responsive instructional practices, YT = Years teaching, TMC = Total math credits taken that teachers that show a higher rating in TPACK also tend to also rate higher in instructional motivation and formative assessment.

Guha and Leonard (2002) assert "teachers have a wide range of possibilities when it comes to integrating the use of computers into teaching math on the elementary level" (p. 41). In their review of the literature, they showed that the difference of the teachers' beliefs about technology influenced extent to which they used technology in classroom settings (p. 41). They conclude that the use of technology during mathematics instruction at the elementary level helps to develop the minds of students and has the potential to engross them for longer periods and possibly change their attitudes toward and abilities in mathematics (Guha & Leonard, 2002, p. 43).

In low needs schools, the variable receptivity to CCLS mathematics had a direct, strong relationship to the variable TPACK ($r = .661, p < .01$). The variable receptivity to CCLS mathematics described 46.3 percent of the variance for the variable TPACK. The variable instructional leadership had a direct, strong relationship to the variable TPACK ($r = .513, p < .01$). The variable instructional leadership described 26.3 percent of the variance for the variable TPACK. The variable instructional motivation had a direct, strong relationship to the variable TPACK ($r = .592, p < .01$). The variable instructional motivation described 35.0 percent of the variance in the variable TPACK. The variable receptivity to change had a direct, moderate relationship to the variable TPACK ($r = .615, p < .01$). The variable receptivity to change described 37.8 percent of the variance for the variable TPACK. The variable formative assessment had a direct, moderate relationship to the variable TPACK ($r = .379, p < .05$). The variable formative assessment described 14.3 percent of the variance in the variable TPACK.

The variable instructional motivation had a direct, strong relationship to the variable receptivity to CCLS mathematics ($r = .692, p < .01$). The variable instructional motivation described 47.8 percent of the variance for the variable receptivity to CCLS mathematics. The variable receptivity to change had a direct, strong relationship to the variable receptivity to CCLS mathematics ($r = .625, p < .01$). The variable receptivity to change described 39.0 percent of the variance for the variable receptivity to CCLS mathematics. The variable formative assessment had a direct, moderate relationship to the variable receptivity to CCLS mathematics ($r = .449, p < .05$). The variable formative assessment described 20.1 percent of the variance of the variable receptivity to CCLS mathematics.

The variable receptivity to change had a direct, strong relationship to the variable instructional leadership ($r = .508, p < .01$). The variable receptivity to change described 25.8 percent of the variance in the variable instructional leadership. The variable formative assessment had a direct, strong relationship to the variable instructional leadership (r = .537, $p < .01$). The variable formative assessment described 28.8 percent of the variance for the variable instructional leadership. The variable receptivity to change had a direct, strong relationship to the variable instructional motivation (r = .591, $p < .01$). The variable receptivity to change described 34.9 percent of the variance for the variable instructional motivation. The variable receptivity to change had a direct, moderate relationship to the variable formative assessment (r = .494, $p < .01$). The variable receptivity to change described 24.4 percent of the variance in the variable formative assessment. Unlike the high need schools, teachers in the low needs schools reported that academic optimism does not have a strong relationship with the other variables. In fact, academic knowledge and technical skill with instructional technology has the greatest relationship with the other variables in low need schools.

In the high needs districts, academic optimism was strongly related to receptivity to CCLs mathematics and instructional motivation. In low needs districts, academic optimism did not play as important a role as TPACK, instructional leadership, or instructional motivation did, as these latter three had a strong relationship to receptivity to CCLS mathematics.

In the high need schools; academic optimism is a critical variable. In the low need schools, technical instructional skills and the use of technology and content knowledge (TPACK) are more highly related to effective teaching and leadership. This disparity again brings to light a longstanding dilemma that U.S. courts have addressed with mixed results in many other cases over the last century that attempted to create equitable educational opportunities for all students. Although there has been progress in many areas within the education system, the specific variables that guide educators towards excellence in teaching and best practices regarding curriculum (and provide answers to decades-old questions) continue to be elusive and controversial.

FUTURE RESEARCH DIRECTIONS

To provide future research with the appropriate guidance, several suggestions are recommended. Future researchers should expand their data collection to more schools. This research was limited to only seven school districts, due in part to some districts' unwillingness to participate in light of the current, public debates on CCLS, testing, and teacher-performance rating.

Future researchers should focus on the possibility of an Annual Professional Performance Review (APPR) effect on teacher receptivity to CCLS. In the early

2000s, New York State eliminated the fifth grade social studies test, in an effort to reduce testing. Teachers were upset because they felt the state government had deemed this subject no longer valuable enough to be tested. At the time, teachers were, in fact, in favor of testing students. Now that the test scores are tied to teacher evaluations, there is an outcry among teachers that students are over-tested.

Future researchers should consider replicating this study using other content areas in addition to mathematics. Additionally, expanding the study to include more grade levels would offer further insight into the effects of CCLS on instruction. Examining other subject areas and grade levels might also help to indicate a relationship to APPR, since some teachers are disproportionately affected by it.

Future researchers should replicate this study using a larger sample size with a similar design and survey instrument. Increasing the number of respondents and respondent locations would improve the study's generalizability. The survey instrument should also be carefully reviewed prior to reuse. The factor analysis, and specifically Table 3.4, showing items deleted from the survey should be a guide to restructuring the survey for future use.

A qualitative study examining academic optimism and instructional motivation would prove useful in further exploration of these two key variables. As stated above, these are important variables, not only for a student's academic success, but also for the long-term efficacy of teachers. This qualitative approach could also include an observational component focused on how instruction varies among teachers in different subject areas and grade levels, as related to CCLS.

A study that examines student and family perceptions of CCLS, and how the CCLS changes impacted student-family relationships and family-school relationships, would greatly add to the body of knowledge on CCLS.

CCLS also influences the world of higher education, especially teacher preparation programs. A study could be conducted to examine the changes in teacher preparation programs pre- and post-CCLS and how political debates regarding CCLS have influenced higher-education teacher programs.

CONCLUSION

The implementation of CCLS mathematics had an influence on elementary-school teachers' instructional practices and attitudes in both high and low needs schools. Teachers' academic optimism was reported at a higher overall level in high needs districts, whereas teachers in low needs districts reported an increase in instructional motivation practices after the implementation of CCLS mathematics.

Educational leaders should be mindful of this finding when examining the culture and instructional practices in their buildings and districts. Academic optimism and instructional motivation tend to not be easily measured quantitatively but are important influences on both student achievement and the long-term success and efficacy of the teacher. Administrators should encourage and model instructional motivation practices, while keeping in mind that individual teachers will adapt the practices in different ways. Teaching is an art and therefore not easily quantitatively measured. As in other real-world settings, different individuals are drawn to each other for reasons not necessarily apparent to themselves or others.

The mathematical content knowledge of a subject and use of technology for instruction were important elements related to all other variables in low need schools. Content knowledge and technological instructional skills should be considered more frequently in the placement of teachers in particular grades.

Instructional leaders in high needs districts were perceived to be more exert greater influence on teachers' feelings towards CCLS mathematics. Instructional leaders in low needs districts should consider the importance and benefits of more frequent classroom visits and increased dialogue with their teachers about CCLS mathematics instruction.

Educational leadership programs should also consider their roles in preparing aspiring administrators. This study showed that teachers in both high and low needs districts felt their administrators were less knowledgeable about curriculum and instructional practices post CCLS. The role of the school administrator is now more multifaceted than in the past. District and building leaders need to be more than just managers of the day-to-day operations, they need to be true instructional leaders. The internship process in administrative programs must consider requiring more time spent on instructional leadership experiences than on mundane management tasks.

Teacher-preparation programs should increase the number of math credits required for elementary teaching candidates. The more comfortable and fluent teachers are with mathematics and mathematical concepts, the more they can be aware of and respond to the needs of their students, and avoid projecting their own math anxieties onto students. Having a deeper knowledge of mathematics content and concepts will make teachers more confident in their instruction.

Change is a constant in education. The content, organizational structure, and roles and responsibilities of schools are vastly different than they were a generation ago and will most likely be vastly different a generation from now. While schools have a responsibility to pass on the lessons and traditions of our society, teachers must be receptive to and aware of the local and global changes in knowledge and technology to properly prepare their students for the world. School leaders need to acquire more skills in the development of teacher receptivity to change and academic optimism.

Educators are preparing students for jobs that do not yet exist. Due in large part to technology, the world is smaller than it ever has been and it is more difficult to predict what kind of future will our students will face. Teachers have as much of a responsibility to ingrain in them the lessons of the past as they do to prepare them to see and understand the changes and opportunities the future has in store for them. To succeed in this endeavor, educators must model for students what receptivity to change looks like and refrain from rote adherence to traditions and methods of the past.

REFERENCES

Austin, S., Wadlington, E., & Bitner, J. (2001). Effect of beliefs about mathematics on math anxiety and self-concept in elementary teachers. *Education, 112*(3), 390–396.

Barlow, A. T., & Reddish, J. M. (2006). Mathematical myths: Teacher candidates' beliefs and the implications for teacher educators. *Teacher Educator, 41*(3), 145–157. doi:10.1080/08878730609555380

Beard, K. S., Hoy, W. K., & Woolfhook-Hoy, A. (2010). Academic optimism of individual teachers: Confirming a new construct. *Teaching and Teacher Education, 26*(5), 1136–1144. doi:10.1016/j.tate.2010.02.003

Black, P., & Wiliam, D. (1998). Inside the black box: Raising standards through classroom assessment. *Phi Delta Kappan*, 92(1), 139–148.

Brookhart, S. M., & Moss, C. M. (2013, May). Leading by learning. *Phi Delta Kappan, 94*(8), 13-17.

Common Core State Standards Initiative. (2015, July 1). Retrieved from http;//www.corestandards.org

Connelly, G. (2014). Where the buck stops. *Principal*, May/June, 56–57.

Cronin, J., & Jensen, N. (2104, September). The phantom collapse of student achievement in New York. *Phi Delta Kappan, 96*(2), 60-66.

Cuff, E. (2014). The effects and importance of technology in the research process. *Journal of Educational Technology Systems, 94*(3), 75–97. doi:10.2190/ET.43.1.f

Donady, B., & Tobias, S. (1977, November). Math Anxiety. *Teacher, 95*(3), 71-74.

Fullan, M. (1985). Change process and strategies at the local level. *The Elementary School Journal, 85*(3), 391–421. doi:10.1086/461411

Goddard, R. D., Sweetland, S. R., & Hoy, W. K. (2000). Academic emphasis of urban elementary schools and student achievement in reading and mathematics: A multilevel analysis. *Educational Administration Quarterly*, *36*(5), 683–702. doi:10.1177/00131610021969164

Guha, S., & Leonard, J. (2002, January/February). Motivation in elementary mathematics: How students and teachers benefit from computers. *TechTrends*, *46*(1), 40–43. doi:10.1007/BF02772036

Holmstrom, A. (2010). District finds the right equation to improve math instruction. *Journal of Staff Development*, 31(6), 58–62.

Houchens, G., & Cabrera, J. (2013). Preparing principals for instructional leadership: Integrating the common core standards-research. *Kentucky Journal of Excellence in College Teaching and Learning*, *11*(1), 56-62.

Hoy, W. (2012). School characteristics that make a difference for the achievement of all students: A 40-year odyssey. *Journal of Educational Administration*, *50*(1), 76-97.

Hoy, W. K., Tarter, J. C., & Hoy, A. W. (2006). Academic optimism of schools: A force for student achievement. *American Educational Research Journal*, *43*(3), 425–446. doi:10.3102/00028312043003425

Kılınç, A. Ç. (2013). The relationship between individual teacher academic optimism and school climate. *Journal of Educational Sciences*, *1*(5), 621-634.

Koehler, M. J., & Mishra, P. (2009). What is technological pedagogical content knowledge? *Contemporary Issues in Technology & Teacher Education*, 9(1), 60–70.

Leithwood, K., & Strauss, T. (2009, Spring). Turnaround schools: Leadership lessons. *Education Canada*, 49(2), 26–29.

Levey, E. K. (2015, July 1). *Teacher attitudes on personal teaching efficacy and responsive teaching, and principal leadership behaviors in the areas of leader social relationships, leadership/goal setting, and collaboration for learning in low wealth, low and high achieving middles.* Dowling.edu. Retrieved from http;//0-search.proquest.com/library.dowling.edu/docview/1503738159?=10549

Li, Q., & Ma, X. (2010). A meta-analysis of the effects of computer technology on school students' mathematics learning. *Educational Psychology Review*, *22*(3), 215–243. doi:10.1007/s10648-010-9125-8

Malinsky, M., Ross, A., Pannells, T., & McJunkin, M. (2006). Math anxiety in pre-service elementary school teachers. *Education*, 127(2), 274–279.

Missett, T. C., Brunner, M. M., Callahan, C. M., Moon, T. R., & Azano, A. P. (2014). Exploring teacher beliefs and use acceleration, ability grouping, and formative assessment. *Journal for the Education of the Gifted*, *37*(3), 245–268. doi:10.1177/0162353214541326

Osterman, K. F., & Kottkamp, R. B. (1993). *Reflective Practice for Educators: Improving Schooloing Through Professional Development*. Newbury Park, CA: Corwin Press.

Patterson, J. (2003). *Coming Even Cleaner About Change*. Lanham, MD: Rowman & Littlefield Publishers, Inc.

Pearce, K. L., Lungren, M., & Wince, A. (1998). The effects of curriculum practices on first graders' attitudes, activity preferences, and achievements in mathematics. *Education*, 1998, 82–90.

Rose, M. (2013). The core of the matter. *American Teacher*, May/June, 4-5.

Sadler, D. R. (1998). Formative assessment and the design of instructional systems. *Instructional Science*, 18(2), 119–140.

Stodolksy, S. S. (1985). Telling Math: Origins of math aversion and anxiety. *Educational Psychologist*, 20(3), 125–133.

Waugh, R. F. (2000). Towards a model of teacher receptivity to planned system-wide educational change in a centrally controlled system. *Journal of Educational Administration*, *38*(4), 350–367. doi:10.1108/09578230010373615

Wilkins, D. (2014). Planning for a future you can't predict. *American School & University*, November, 201–203.

Wilkins, J. L. (2010). Elementary School Teachers Attitudes Toward Different Subjects. *Teacher Educator*, *45*(1), 23–36. doi:10.1080/08878730903386856

Wilson, G. L. (2013, September/October). The math frame reaching common core heights for students who struggle. *Teaching Exceptional Children*, *46*(1), 36–46. doi:10.1177/004005991304600105

Wu, J. H., Hoy, W. K., & Tarter, J. C. (2013). Enabling school structure, collective responsibility, and a culture of academic optimism. *Journal of Educational Administration*, *51*(2), 176–193. doi:10.1108/09578231311304698

APPENDIX: TEACHER SURVEY

Directions: Complete the questionnaire below as well as the attached survey. All information will be kept confidential and anonymous (adapted from Kennedy, 2014).

Part I: Demographics

Please check the appropriate box:

1. I currently teach mathematics at the elementary level.
   (_____) YES
   (_____) NO
2. My current age is:
   - 20-29
   - 30-39
   - 40-49
   - 50-59
   - 60 or over
3. I have been teaching for the following number of years: _______________
4. My gender is: (_____) Male (_____) Female
5. I have taken the following number of credits specifically in Mathematics content courses:
   Undergraduate: _____
   Graduate: _____
   Professional Development: _____
6. Did you teach prior to the implementation of the Common Core Learning Standards (2011)?
   (_____) YES
   (_____) NO

If you answered NO to this item you may stop at this point.

Part II

Directions: Using the key below, please identify the answer that best fits your experience. Consider your experience for each item both (pre) before the 2011-2012 school year and after (post) implementation of Common Core Learning Standards (From the 2012-2013 school year until now). Please do not consider APPR while responding to this survey.

1. Strongly Disagree
2. Disagree
3. Slightly Agree
4. Agree
5. Strongly Agree.

Table 5.

Item #	Pre 2011-2012						Current School Year				
1	1	2	3	4	5	I get my students to be honest with me.	1	2	3	4	5
2	1	2	3	4	5	I get my students to trust me.	1	2	3	4	5
3	1	2	3	4	5	I get my students to achieve academically.	1	2	3	4	5
4	1	2	3	4	5	I get my students to do challenging work.	1	2	3	4	5
5	1	2	3	4	5	I get my students to attain high academic goals.	1	2	3	4	5
6	1	2	3	4	5	I get my students who show low interest in schoolwork to engage in challenging discoveries.	1	2	3	4	5
7	1	2	3	4	5	I get my students to believe they will do well in school.	1	2	3	4	5
8	1	2	3	4	5	I get my students to meet rigorous academic benchmarks.	1	2	3	4	5
9	1	2	3	4	5	I can teach lessons that appropriately combine mathematics and technology.	1	2	3	4	5
10	1	2	3	4	5	I can select technologies to use in my classroom to help students visualize math principles.	1	2	3	4	5
11	1	2	3	4	5	I can choose technologies that lead to student mastery of math concepts.	1	2	3	4	5
12	1	2	3	4	5	I can choose technologies that allow students to see a variety of ways to solve a problem.	1	2	3	4	5
13	1	2	3	4	5	I can select technologies that require students to apply mathematical concepts to solve a problem.	1	2	3	4	5
14	1	2	3	4	5	I can use a wide range of technologies to differentiate math instruction.	1	2	3	4	5
15	1	2	3	4	5	I can use a wide range of technologies that expose students to misconceptions about math.	1	2	3	4	5

continued on following page

Table 5. Continued

Item #	Pre 2011-2012						Current School Year				
16	1	2	3	4	5	I teach in such a way that students show their understanding.	1	2	3	4	5
17	1	2	3	4	5	I teach in such a way that I can change my teaching methods during a lesson.	1	2	3	4	5
18	1	2	3	4	5	I teach with opportunities for students to assess their own learning.	1	2	3	4	5
19	1	2	3	4	5	I teach so that prior to giving any test or quiz I show my students a grading rubric about how they will be graded.	1	2	3	4	5
20	1	2	3	4	5	I teach so that I am always aware of each student's daily progress toward mastery of mathematics concepts being taught	1	2	3	4	5
21	1	2	3	4	5	I teach so that specific feedback for my students is written in language they comprehend.	1	2	3	4	5
22	1	2	3	4	5	I teach in ways that allow students the opportunity to make corrections.	1	2	3	4	5
23	1	2	3	4	5	I teach so that my students analyze each other's work using rubrics.	1	2	3	4	5
24	1	2	3	4	5	I teach using frequent formative assessments to adjust daily instruction.	1	2	3	4	5
25	1	2	3	4	5	I teach and change the pacing of a lesson or unit based upon student feedback.	1	2	3	4	5
26	1	2	3	4	5	I find that I often reflect on how my students react to my current teaching practices.	1	2	3	4	5
27	1	2	3	4	5	I find that when I am planning a lesson, I ask myself what current research in education about teaching might be useful.	1	2	3	4	5
28	1	2	3	4	5	I find that I often write myself notes to revise my teaching methods.	1	2	3	4	5
29	1	2	3	4	5	I find that I often ask myself how my teaching will facilitate learning mathematics concepts.	1	2	3	4	5
30	1	2	3	4	5	I find that teaching is an adaptive process that requires self-reflection.	1	2	3	4	5
31	1	2	3	4	5	I find that after a discussion about teaching methods with my colleagues, I ask myself how I could improve my teaching.	1	2	3	4	5
32	1	2	3	4	5	I find that when I am trying to help the least motivated student, I ask myself what I could do differently.	1	2	3	4	5
33	1	2	3	4	5	I find that if my students do poorly on a test, I ask myself how I could have taught differently.	1	2	3	4	5
34	1	2	3	4	5	My principal or chairperson clearly defines expectations for instructional practices about mathematics.	1	2	3	4	5

continued on following page

Table 5. Continued

Item #	Pre 2011-2012						Current School Year				
35	1	2	3	4	5	My principal or chairperson regularly discusses instructional issues with me.	1	2	3	4	5
36	1	2	3	4	5	My principal or chairperson regularly observes my classroom instruction.	1	2	3	4	5
37	1	2	3	4	5	My principal or chairperson regularly attends teacher meetings where teachers analyze their students' performance.	1	2	3	4	5
38	1	2	3	4	5	My principal or chairperson regularly makes suggestions to improve classroom behavior or classroom management.	1	2	3	4	5
39	1	2	3	4	5	My principal or chairperson is knowledgeable about curriculum and instruction.	1	2	3	4	5
40	1	2	3	4	5	My principal or chairperson regularly seeks teachers' feedback about student progress.	1	2	3	4	5
41	1	2	3	4	5	I believe most curriculum changes in mathematics are valuable.	1	2	3	4	5
42	1	2	3	4	5	I believe curriculum in mathematics does not need to be changed.	1	2	3	4	5
43	1	2	3	4	5	I believe I am open to curriculum changes in mathematics when my instructional leaders or colleagues suggest them.	1	2	3	4	5
44	1	2	3	4	5	I believe I am open to curriculum changes in mathematics when administrators mandate them.	1	2	3	4	5
45	1	2	3	4	5	I believe most curriculum changes in mathematics improve my students' opportunity to learn.	1	2	3	4	5
46	1	2	3	4	5	I believe that once an effective curriculum in mathematics is implemented, it should not be changed.	1	2	3	4	5
47	1	2	3	4	5	I believe every elementary mathematics teachers should introduce Algebraic concepts such as applying properties of operations.	1	2	3	4	5
48	1	2	3	4	5	I believe every elementary mathematics teachers should introduce Numbers and operations in base ten such as place value and fractions.	1	2	3	4	5
49	1	2	3	4	5	I believe every elementary mathematics teachers should introduce Measurement and Data such as time and money concepts.	1	2	3	4	5
50	1	2	3	4	5	I believe every elementary mathematics teachers should introduce Geometry concepts such as working with shapes and angles.	1	2	3	4	5
51	The concurrent implementation of the CCLS and APPR influenced my feelings regarding the academic value of the CCLS.						1	2	3	4	5

Chapter 10
What Are the Relationships Between Poverty, Attendance, Teacher Evaluations, and High School Graduation Rates?

Kenneth Forman
Stony Brook University, USA

Craig Markson
Stony Brook University, USA

ABSTRACT

The focus of this study was to examine the relationships among poverty, attendance rates, the New York State's Annual Professional Performance Review (APPR) teacher evaluation system, and student achievement. The setting of this study was high schools from New York State's Nassau and Suffolk counties, a suburban region of New York City. The results of this study showed that poverty had a strong negative correlation with graduation rates from the Regents Diploma, accounting for 31.02 percent of the variance. However, the negative impact that poverty had on the graduation rates from the Regents Diploma with Advanced Designation more than doubled. While high school student attendance rates had a weak, but statistically significant, positive correlation with Regents Diploma graduation rates, the positive correlation more than tripled with the Regents Diploma with Advanced Designation graduation rates. The New York State teacher evaluation system did not have the desired effect on student achievement.

DOI: 10.4018/978-1-5225-3616-1.ch010

INTRODUCTION

The chapter deals with using public data available on the Internet as a vehicle to strategically facilitate school and/or district improvement while concomitantly supporting student achievement. A variety of public domain websites provide information about school and district achievement across the country. States have a reporting responsibility under federal education law to make public information about their schools' achievement. Therefore, a variety of information is available to the consumer regarding performance, graduation and related factors. The New York State Education Department demonstrated its commitment to transparency by making data about its schools public and easy to use by establishing a public data site where "all interested parties can better be informed as they work to advance student achievement" ("New York State Education Department Data Site," n.d.). The public data site provides information about 733 public and charter school districts across New York State, which includes 2,649,039 students and 207,369 educators. The information provided is categorized student data and school data. Under student data, English Language Arts and Mathematics achievement is provided for grades 3-8, while school data includes each school's report card. The school report card provides such information as: School Profile (enrollment & free/reduced lunch), Outcomes (high school completion & post-secondary plan for completers), Additional Assessment Information (achievement in English Language Arts, Mathematics & Science including English Language Learner student information, National Assessment of Educational Progress, high school cohort data, Regents examination results, competency test results, and English as a Second Language achievement test results), and Accountability Data (elementary & middle level achievement in English Language Arts, Mathematics & Science, secondary achievement in English Language Arts and Mathematics, and graduation rate).

By providing access to information via the public data site, the New York State education governing body, the Board of Regents, believes that this broadband of information will positively raise learning standards for all students. Furthermore, the Regents contend that knowledge gained from the Report Card on a school's or district's strengths and weaknesses can be used to improve instruction and services to students ("New York State Education Department Data Site," n.d.).

The objectives for this chapter are:

- To examine the use of public data provided, in particular, from the New York State Education Department.
- To evaluate the use of this data in understanding its relationship to student achievement and school improvement.

BACKGROUND

Poverty

Futscher (2013) examined educational programs and achievement levels of high and low wealth districts. The researcher found evidence of inequity and suggested that poverty was the cause for poor performance.

In 1990, more than 30 percent of children living in urban locations were in poverty which was more than twice the percentage of students living in poverty (13 percent) in the suburbs surrounding these urban locations (Lippman, Burns, & McArthur, 1996). Similar studies indicated a strong relationship between poverty and student achievement levels in schools (Kiser, 2007). In addition to a high concentration of poverty in urban locations, these schools were more likely to serve students from ethnic or racial minorities and students whose language background was not English (Jacobs, 2011).

A student's background (family support, resources, and socioeconomic status) has been shown to have a substantial effect on a student's academic achievement. Lippman et al. (1996) found a number of background traits in which urban schools and students were disadvantaged:

- Fewer students in two-parent family
- More single parents
- Fewer parents completed college
- More students changing schools more often
- Fewer parents who expect child to complete college
- Fewer parents who talk to child about school
- Fewer school sports offerings (fewer than suburban, equal to rural)
- Fewer students participating in sports
- Fewer students participating in the labor force

Poverty also has a significant relationship between school completion and college enrollment (Duncan, Yeung, Brooks-Gunn, & Smith, 1998). Using a variety of models, Duncan et al. (1998) found that: (a) family income levels had strong associations with achievement and ability related outcomes; (b) the stage in a child's development when the poverty occurred was significant; and, (c) the impact of family income was significantly higher for those children in low-income families than those from high-income families. When poverty occurred during the early years of a child's development, it mattered more for achievement than for behavior and habit forming.

When poverty occurred later in a child's development, the largest impact was in college enrollment. However, when a family's income increased later in a child's development, they were just as likely to enroll in college as the children from families who had never been in poverty (Duncan et al., 1998).

While the suburbs have become far more diverse economically, socially, and racially, the research on suburban poverty was extremely lacking. Suburban poverty was most frequently researched as a point of comparison to urban and rural poverty (Fan & Chen, 1998). Murphy found that there was some evidence that poverty increased in suburban areas over the past decades (Murphy, 2007). He indicated that from 1990 to 2000, the number of people living below the poverty line in American suburbs rose 21 percent, but rose only 8 percent in cities. The increase in suburban poverty was more severe in the United States Northeast, where suburbs tended to be older and once housed manufacturing (Murphy, 2007).

Lonneville (2014) found there were a variety of school district characteristics that were related to student achievement levels. Additional research established that financial factors, student factors, teacher factors, and outside factors all had a relationship to student achievement levels in school districts (Burke & Sass, 2008; Hanushek & Lindseth, 2009). Forman and Markson (2015, 2016) found that poverty had a strong negative correlation with performance on the New York State English Language Arts (ELA) and Mathematics assessments among students in grades 3-8. As poverty went up, performance on the state assessments went down. Poverty accounted for over 60 percent of the variance on student performance on both state assessments.

Perry and McConney (2010) found that an increase in the average socioeconomic status of a school led to increasing student achievement levels. Van Ewijk and Sleegers (2010) performed a meta-analysis that looked at 30 different studies on socioeconomic status and student achievement levels and determined that while the measure of socioeconomic status varied from study to study, peer socioeconomic status had a strong correlation with student achievement levels. Essentially, the higher the socioeconomic status of a school, the higher the student achievement levels.

Desimone (1999) concluded that a student's background was a key component of student achievement in school. Boggs (2011) found while there have been notable "pockets" of success and innovative initiatives, it was clear that most educational reforms have failed to make a noticeable dent in the academic performance of the vast majority of American school children, particularly ethnic minorities and children living in poverty. Additionally, the researcher found that the single most powerful intervention with the capability of arresting the negative outcomes of poverty was educational completion (Boggs, 2011).

Attendance

The largest variable that was almost solely within control of students or guardians was student attendance in school. At the most basic level, when a student was absent, whether through legal or illegal absence, they could not be learning in the class (Lonneville, 2014). Several other studies reported by Lonneville (2014) have shown a relationship between student achievement and higher attendance rates. These studies indicated that as student attendance rates decreased, student achievement levels decreased.

McBride (2009) provided administrators with relevant information regarding the negative influences that absenteeism had on overall stability of public schools. The participating schools in this study were 30 high schools in a school district in Texas. This study also provided data on the impact absenteeism had on student dropout rates, which had a negative relationship with the future economic success of students as well as the entire economy.

Nichols (2003) found a clear indicator of potential academic failure centered on the high rate of yearly school absences for students who struggle academically. A pattern of poor school attendance was evident by the sixth grade year with most failing students averaging more than ten absences per year throughout their school careers. Unfortunately, the rate of absences for these students continued to increase. There were strong correlations among poor English and mathematics achievement and high rates of school absence in early and later years established a clear pattern of "school discontinuity" or disengagement that was predictive of future school failure. Nichols found for each graduating class, low-income students averaged three to four more absences per year than higher income students who also failed to meet state proficiencies. This pattern of poor school attendance, particularly for low-income students, began early in their educational careers and in some cases, approached an average of eighteen to twenty absences per year by the tenth grade (Nichols, 2003).

MacIver and Groginksy (2011) found that high school graduation rates depended on what happened in individual schools and classrooms. Prior attendance levels and academic readiness of the entering 9th grade largely determined high school graduation rates. Furthermore, students who dropped out had problems in attendance, behavior, and course performance.

Teacher Effectiveness

Most school reform efforts have focused on school programs and curricula as the means to improve student performance. More recent evaluation efforts have focused on teacher accountability. The research indicated that children could be adversely affected from ineffective teaching for up to two years (Mangiante, 2011; Stronge, Ward, Tucker, & Hindman, 2012; Tucker & Stronge, 2005). Conversely, looking at teacher effectiveness where there were good teacher ratings, Rivkin, Hanushek, Markman, and Kain (2003) reinforced that having a high-quality teacher could substantially offset or even eliminate the disadvantage of low socio-economic background. Wong and Wong (2010) added that the only way to improve student achievement was through well-prepared teachers who delivered effective instruction. They defined teacher effectiveness as the ability to produce student learning, growth, and achievement. According to Stronge et al. (2012), the purpose of teacher evaluation was to use data to inform instruction and to enable teachers to hone their skills. Moreover, evidence suggested that the ability to improve instructional practices of marginal teachers raised levels of student achievement when implemented appropriately (Tucker & Stronge, 2005).

Components of teacher evaluation systems most commonly included: professional teaching standards, evidence of teacher practice and student learning, an annual process, well trained and knowledgeable evaluators, informative feedback to teachers, professional development opportunities provided for improvement, clear articulated differentiation among ratings, documentation of student growth, multiple measures, transparency, resources to support implementation, collaboration with teachers' bargaining units, and clear and rigorous expectations (Marzano, Toth, & Schooling, 2012). The New York State Annual Professional Performance Review law incorporated many of the above components. As part of the New York State teacher evaluation system, teachers received scores based on student performance on state and local assessments. Those scores led to one of four rankings: Highly-Effective, Effective, Developing or Ineffective (HEDI). It was also noteworthy, that 96% of New York State teachers have been evaluated as "effective or "highly effective" during the 2013-2014 school year ("New York State Education Department Data Site," n.d.). Scores from future years have been embargoed by the State Education Department.

High School Graduation

Schiller and Muller (2000) found that students' probabilities of graduating from high school were associated with states' testing policies. Widespread and frequent testing was found to be positively associated with students' greater likelihood of earning a high school diploma. How testing was used to evaluate students and schools also appeared to be associated with teachers' influence on whether students earn a diploma, although the relationships were weaker and differed depending on whether students or schools were being held accountable for students' progress. Linking test performance to consequences for students mitigated the negative relationship between students' SES and graduation. Furthermore, it weakened the relationship between teachers' low expectations and earning a diploma (Schiller & Muller, 2000).

Hernandez (2011) confirmed this link in the first national study to calculate high school graduation rates for children at different reading skill levels and with different poverty rates. Results of a longitudinal study of nearly 4,000 students found that those who did not read proficiently by third grade were four times more likely to leave school without a diploma than proficient readers. While struggling readers accounted for about a third of the students, they represented more than three-fifths of those who eventually dropped out or failed to graduate on time. One in six children who were not reading proficiently in third grade did not graduate from high school on time, a rate four times greater than that for proficient readers. The rates were highest for the low, below-basic readers: 23 percent of these children dropped out or failed to finish high school on time, compared to nine percent of children with basic reading skills and 4 percent of proficient readers. Overall, 22 percent of children who lived in poverty did not graduate from high school. That rose to 32 percent for students spending more than half of their childhood in poverty. For children who were poor for at least a year and were not reading proficiently in third grade, the proportion that did not finish high school rose to 26 percent. That's more than six times the rate for all proficient readers. The rate was highest for poor Black and Hispanic students, at 31 and 33 percent respectively. Even among poor children who were proficient readers in third grade, eleven percent still didn't finish high school. Graduation rates for Black and Hispanic students who were not proficient readers in third grade lagged far behind those for White students with the same reading skills. This study also showed that poverty had a powerful influence on graduation rates; the combined effect of reading poorly and living in poverty put these children in double jeopardy (Hernandez, 2011).

New York State High School Diploma Types: Regents vs. Regents with Advanced Designation

There were two types of diplomas issued to students graduating from high schools in New York State, inclusive of Long Island high schools: Regents Diploma and Regents Diploma with Advanced Designation. The passing of five Regents examinations with a score of 65 or better was required for a Regents Diploma: English Language Arts (ELA); any mathematics examination (Algebra I, Geometry, or Algebra II/Trigonometry); any social studies exam (Global History and Geography or U.S. History and Government); any science examination (Living Environment, Chemistry, Earth Science, or Physics); any additional Regents examination or assessment approved by the state for this purpose ("NYSED/P-12 /Part 100 Regulations/100.5 Diploma Requirements," n.d.).

It was more rigorous to achieve a Regents Diploma with Advanced Designation. Passing eight of the following Regents examinations with a score of 65 or better was required for a Regents Diploma with Advanced Designation: English Language Arts (ELA); three mathematics examinations (Algebra I, Geometry, and Algebra II/ Trigonometry); any social studies examination (Global History and Geography or U.S. History and Government); two science examinations (Living Environment and one of the following: Chemistry, Earth Science, or Physics); any additional Regents exam or assessment approved by the state for this purpose. In addition, there was a LOTE requirement, that is, completion of a two-year course of study in a Language Other Than English. Students that graduated with a Regents Diploma with Advanced Designation had a distinct advantage for college admission, especially in the State University of New York college system ("Benefits of an Advanced Regents Diploma - Guidance Resources," n.d.).

MAIN FOCUS OF THE CHAPTER

In a recent study, *Is "Effective" the New "Ineffective": A Crisis with the New York State Teacher Evaluation System*, Forman and Markson (2015) examined the relationship among New York State's teacher evaluation system Annual Professional Performance Review (APPR), poverty, attendance, per pupil spending, and academic achievement from 110 school districts, over 30,000 educators and over 60,000 students from Nassau and Suffolk counties in New York State excepting fifteen school districts because their teacher population was less than 50 (Forman & Markson, 2015). The researchers found a weak to conflicting correlation among teacher evaluations and student achievement. The percent of teachers rated "highly effective" had a statistically significant and positive correlation with student achievement on the New York State English Language Arts (ELA) and Mathematics Assessments for grades three through eight. School districts' percent of teachers rated "effective" had a negative correlation with student achievement. As the percent of teachers rated "effective" went up, student performance on the state assessments went down. The "developing" rating did not have a statistically significant relationship with ELA and Mathematics assessments. The "ineffective" rating had a statistically significant and negative correlation with the ELA and Mathematics assessment results. What was surprising was the inverse relationship that the "effective" category had with the student achievement success rates, Level 3 and 4 (on-grade and above). With only 11 school districts reporting "ineffective" and the inverse relationship that "effective" had with student achievement, "effective" has become the new "ineffective" (Forman & Markson, 2015). One of the most important conclusions of this study was that the real crisis with the New York State teacher evaluation system overshadows the most important problem of poverty and its harmful effects on student achievement. The correlation analyses also revealed that as poverty went up, attendance rates went down (Forman & Markson, 2015).

The dependent variables that measured student achievement in the Forman and Markson (2015) study were student performance on the English Language Arts and Mathematics state assessments. However, other studies have challenged the efficacy of state assessments as well as disputed the relationships among graduation rates, other measures of student achievement, and performance on state assessments (Govan, 2013). Polikoff, Porter, and Smithson (2011) found state assessments to be not properly aligned with the school curriculum. As such, they argued that it would not be appropriate to use student performance on state assessments to evaluate teachers. Therefore, the focus of this chapter is the examination of the relationships among poverty, attendance, teacher evaluations, and high school graduation rates.

Data Sources

The primary source of data for this study was the New York State Education Department's Data Site (2016). Data on 111 high schools located in Nassau and Suffolk Counties, New York were included in this study. On each high school, the following data were collected: (a) the percent of students collecting free and reduced lunch; (b) the percent of average daily student attendance; (c) the APPR teacher rating percentages; (d) the percent of students receiving a Regents Diploma; and (e) the percent of students receiving a Regents Diploma with Advanced Designation. The data were from the 2013 to 2014 school year.

Method

High school graduation rates were used to measure student achievement in each of the 111 high schools included in this study. The dependent variable was student achievement and was measured by the percent of high school students receiving a New York State High School Regents Diploma and a Regents Diploma with Advanced Designation. It should be noted that the Regents Diploma percentages also included students receiving the Regents Diplomas with Advanced Designation, whereas the Regents Diploma with Advanced Designation percentages only included students graduating with the Regents Diplomas with Advanced Designation.

Among the independent variables, poverty was calculated by the percent of high school students receiving free and reduced lunch. Attendance was determined by the percent of average daily attendance for each school. Teacher performance was assessed by the percent of teachers rated on each category on the high school's

Annual Professional Performance Review: Level 4 - "highly effective," Level 3 - "effective," Level 2 - "developing," and Level 1 - "ineffective."

Two correlation analyses were carried out to determine if poverty, attendance, and teacher evaluation ratings were related to graduation rates. A Pearson Product-Moment correlation analysis, with a two-tailed test of significance with alpha set at .05, was used to analyze the relationships among the variables.

Results

Table 1 illustrates the results for the correlations with the percent of high school students who received a Regents Diploma. The percent of high school students receiving free and reduced lunch had a statistically significant relationship with the percent of students obtaining a Regents Diploma. There was an inverse relationship, accounting for 31.02 percent of the variance: as the percent of students receiving free and reduced lunch increased, the percent of students obtaining a Regents Diploma substantially decreased. The attendance rate had a statistically significant relationship with the Regents Diploma graduation rate. Attendance had a positive correlation, accounting for 7.78 percent of the variance on the percent of students obtaining a Regents Diploma. Additionally, and noteworthy, the percent of teachers rated "highly effective" had a statistically significant and positive correlation with Regents Diploma graduation rates, accounting for 11.7 percent of the variance. The "effective" APPR rating also had a statistically significant but inverse relationship with the student graduation rates with a Regents Diploma, accounting for 8.9 percent of the variance. As the percent of high school teachers rated "effective" went up, graduation rates went down.

The "developing" teacher rating did not have a statistically significant relationship with Regents Diploma graduation rates, $p > .05$. Finally, the "ineffective" APPR rating had a statistically significant and inverse relationship with Regent graduation rates, accounting for 45.43 percent of the variance.

Table 2 illustrates the results for the correlations with the percent of high school students who received a Regents Diploma with Advanced Designation.

The percent of students receiving free and reduced lunch had a statistically significant relationship with the percent of students graduating with a Regents Diploma with Advanced Designation. There was an inverse relationship, accounting for 66.26 percent of the variance: as the percent of students receiving free and reduced lunch increased, the percent of graduates with Advanced Diplomas decreased. The attendance rate also had a statistically significant relationship with the Regents Diploma with Advanced Designation graduation rates. Here, there was a positive

What Are the Relationships?

Table 1. Correlations with Regents Diploma (N = 111)

		Regents Diploma	Free and Reduced Lunch	Attendance Rate	Highly Effective APPR	Effective APPR	Ineffective APPR
Free and Reduced Lunch	r	-0.557**					
	r^2	31.02%					
	p	0.000					
	N	110					
Attendance Rate	r	0.279**	-0.426**				
	r^2	7.78%	18.15%				
	p	0.003	0.000				
	N	110	109				
Highly Effective APPR	r	0.342**	-0.406**	0.195*			
	r^2	11.70%	16.48%	3.80%			
	p	0.000	0.000	0.049			
	N	104	103	103			
Effective APPR	r	-0.299**	0.368**	-0.15	-0.978**		
	r^2	8.94%	13.54%	2.25%	95.65%		
	p	0.002	0.000	0.132	0.000		
	N	104	103	103	104		
Developing APPR	r	-0.102	0.013	-0.298	-0.415*	0.143	
	r^2	1.04%	0.02%	8.88%	17.22%	2.04%	
	p	0.637	0.95	0.157	0.044	0.505	
	N	24	24	24	24	24	
Ineffective APPR	r	-0.674*	0.376	0.031	0.282	-0.591	0.168
	r^2	45.43%	14.14%	0.10%	7.95%	34.93%	2.82%
	p	0.046	0.319	0.936	0.463	0.093	0.691
	N	9	9	9	9	9	8

** Correlation is significant at the 0.01 level (2-tailed).
* Correlation is significant at the 0.05 level (2-tailed).

correlation, accounting for 27.56 percent of the variance with the Regents Diploma with Advanced Designation graduation rates. The percent of high school teachers rated "highly effective" had a statistically significant and positive correlation with students obtaining a Regents Diploma with Advanced Designation, accounting for 19.71 percent of the variance. The "effective" teacher rating also had a statistically

Table 2. Correlations with Regents Diploma with Advanced Designation (N = 111)

		Regents Diploma w/ Adv. Designation	Free and Reduced Lunch	Attendance Rate	Highly Effective APPR	Effective APPR	Ineffective APPR
Free and Reduced Lunch	r	-0.814**					
	r^2	66.26%					
	p	0.00					
	N	110					
Attendance Rate	r	0.525**	-0.426**				
	r^2	27.56%	18.15%				
	p	0.00	0.00				
	N	110	109				
Highly Effective APPR	r	0.444**	-0.406**	0.195*			
	r^2	19.71%	16.48%	3.80%			
	p	0.00	0.00	0.049			
	N	104	103	103			
Effective APPR	r	-0.396**	0.368**	-0.15	-0.978**		
	r^2	15.68%	13.54%	2.25%	95.65%		
	p	0.00	0.00	0.132	0.00		
	N	104	103	103	104		
Developing APPR	r	-0.193	0.013	-0.298	-0.415*	0.143	
	r^2	3.72%	0.02%	8.88%	17.22%	2.04%	
	p	0.365	0.95	0.157	0.044	0.505	
	N	24	24	24	24	24	
Ineffective APPR	r	-0.441	0.376	0.031	0.282	-0.591	0.168
	r^2	19.45%	14.14%	0.10%	7.95%	34.93%	2.82%
	p	0.235	0.319	0.936	0.463	0.093	0.691
	N	9	9	9	9	9	8

** Correlation is significant at the 0.01 level (2-tailed).

* Correlation is significant at the 0.05 level (2-tailed).

significant but negative correlation with the Regents Diploma with Advanced Designation graduation rates, accounting for 15.68 percent of the variance. The "developing" APPR rating did not have a statistically significant relationship with the Regents Diploma with Advanced Designation, $p > .05$. Similarly, the "ineffective" APPR rating did not have a statistically significant relationship with the Regents Diploma with Advanced Designation, $p > .05$.

SOLUTIONS AND RECOMMENDATIONS

The results of this study showed that the New York State APPR teacher evaluation system did not have the desired impact on student achievement. For example, the percent of teachers rated "effective" put downward pressure on student achievement, as measured by the percent of high school students obtaining the Regents Diploma and the Regents Diploma with Advanced Designation. Obviously, this was not the desired outcome among "effective" teachers. As expected, the percent of teachers rated "ineffective" put strong downward pressure on graduation rates for the Regents Diploma. However, with only 11 of 111 high schools having any percentage reporting of teachers in the "ineffective" category, the variable was not a viable statistic. Furthermore, the "ineffective" teacher rating did not have a statistically significant relationship with the Regents Diploma with Advanced Designation graduation rates, $p > .05$. The "highly effective" teacher rating had a strong inverse relationship with the "effective" rating, where one would expect such a relationship to exist among "highly effective" and "ineffective" teachers. This was probably indicative of the over-reporting of teachers in the "highly effective" and "effective" categories and underreporting of teachers in "developing" and "ineffective" categories, which skewed the data. These findings were consistent with the findings of prior studies by Forman and Markson (2015, 2016), which measured student achievement by student performance on the New York State English Language Arts and Mathematics assessments.

Poverty had the strongest relationship with student achievement and it was negatively correlated. Among obtainment of the Regents and Regents Diplomas with Advanced Designation, poverty accounted for 31.02 and 66.26 percent of the variance respectively. The strength of this relationship more than doubled when comparing the relationship of poverty with the Regents and Regents Diplomas with Advanced Designation. The strength of the relationship among attendance rates and graduation rates more than tripled on the obtainment of the Regents Diploma with Advanced Designation. As attendance rates went up, so did the graduation rates. Poverty also had a statistically significant and inverse relationship with attendance rates.

The results of this study showed that poverty was the big lever in the educational system that moved student achievement and these results were consistent with prior studies by Forman and Markson (2015, 2016). Furthermore, teacher evaluations had weak, conflicting, and no statistically significant relationships with student achievement. These results were also consistent with prior studies by Forman and Markson (2015, 2016).

If the results of this study remain similar to the findings of future studies, educational leaders should revise how teacher evaluations are designed and implemented. An effective teacher evaluation system should have a strong and consistent correlation with student achievement. Most importantly, the greatest amount of time, energy, and resources should be spent researching, designing, and implementing programs that reduce the negative effects that poverty has on graduation rates as well as student achievement.

FUTURE RESEARCH DIRECTIONS

Poverty was an important variable in this study. However, it was measured simply by the percent of students collecting free and reduced lunch. Future studies should aim for a deeper understanding of the various characteristics of poverty and which of these characteristics have the greatest impact on student achievement. In order to better serve students living in poverty, there is certainly a need for a much more detailed understanding of their backgrounds. Future research should also examine the most successful programs that improve student attendance or perhaps utilize online technology to promote learning while students are absent from school.

CONCLUSION

The main focus of this chapter was to analyze data from the New York State Education Department's public data website and identify which variables had the strongest relationships with student achievement, as measured by high school graduation rates ("New York State Education Department Data Site," n.d.). The variables indentified as having the strongest relationships with student achievement would serve as the basis for making recommendations for school improvement. Student poverty and attendance rates had the strongest relationships with high school graduation. New York State's APPR teacher evaluation rating system did not have the desired outcomes, as teachers rated "effective" drove graduation rates down. Therefore, the New York State Education Department should promote initiatives that lessen the negative impact that poverty has on student achievement and programs that improve student attendance. The APPR teacher evaluation system should be restructured.

REFERENCES

Benefits of an Advanced Regents Diploma – Guidance Resources. (n. d.). Retrieved May 7, 2016, from http://www.hphsnyc.org/apps/pages/index.jsp?uREC_ID=246434&type=d&pREC_ID=568540

Boggs, O. (2011). The rise of childhood poverty in Georgia: Implications for public school planning and pedagogy.

Burke, M. A., & Sass, T. (2008). *Classroom peer effects and student achievement.* National Center for Analysis of Longitudinal Data in Education Research.

Desimone, L. (1999). Linking parent involvement with student achievement: Do race and income matter? *The Journal of Educational Research, 93*(1), 11–30. doi:10.1080/00220679909597625

Diploma Requirements. (n. d.). Retrieved May 7, 2016, from http://www.p12.nysed.gov/part100/pages/1005.html

Duncan, G. J., Yeung, W. J., Brooks-Gunn, J., & Smith, J. R. (1998). How much does childhood poverty affect the life chances of children? *American Sociological Review, 63*(3), 406–423. doi:10.2307/2657556

Fan, X., & Chen, M. J. (1998). Academic achievement of rural school students: A multi-year comparison with their peers in suburban and urban schools.

Forman, K., & Markson, C. (2015). Is "effective" the new "ineffective"? A crisis with the New York State teacher evaluation system. *Journal for Leadership and Instruction, 14*(2), 5–11.

Forman, K. & Markson, C. (2016, May). The efficacy of teacher evaluations in New York City: A tale of two districts. *New York Academy of Public Education, 5.*

Futscher, M. R. (2013). Principals' perceptions about the impact of the New York State Annual Professional Performance Review legislation on the instructional practices of New York public schools. *Dissertations Abstracts International Section A, 75.*

Govan, C. J. (2013, January 1). *Observing the academic performance and student graduation rates of grade 8 students who failed Texas State Assessments.* Retrieved from http://www.proquest.com/en-US/products/dissertations/individuals.shtml)

Hanushek, E., & Lindseth, A. (2009). *Schoolhouses, courthouses, and statehouses: Solving the funding-achievement puzzle in America's public schools.* Princeton University Press. doi:10.1515/9781400830251

Hernandez, D. J. (2011). *Double Jeopardy: How third-grade reading skills and poverty influence high school graduation.* The Anne E. Casey Foundation.

Jacobs, N. (2011). Understanding school choice: Location as a determinant of charter school racial, economic, and linguistic segregation. *Education and Urban Society.*

Kiser, L. J. (2007). Protecting children from the dangers of urban poverty. *Clinical Psychology Review, 27*(2), 211–225. doi:10.1016/j.cpr.2006.07.004 PMID:16979274

Lippman, L., Burns, S., & McArthur, E. (1996). *Urban schools: the challenge of location and poverty*. Washington, DC: United States Department of Education.

Lonneville, J. (2014, April). Why some school districts outperform others: A mixed methods study on poverty, student performance on the New York State school assessments, and school district funding across rural, suburban, and urban school districts [Doctoral Dissertation]. Niagara University.

MacIver, M. A., & Groginsky, S. (2011). Working statewide to boost graduation rates. *Phi Delta Kappan, 92*(5), 16–20. doi:10.1177/003172171109200505

Mangiante, E. M. S. (2011). Teachers matter: Measures of teacher effectiveness in low-income minority schools. *Educational Assessment, Evaluation and Accountability, 23*(1), 41–63. doi:10.1007/s11092-010-9107-x

Marzano, R., Toth, M., & Schooling, P. (2012). *Examining the role of teacher evaluation in student achievement: Contemporary research base for the Marzano causal teacher evaluation model* (White paper). Retrieved May 1, 2016 from http://www.marzanocenter.com/files/MC_White_Paper_20120424.pdf

McBride, S. K. (2009, January 1). The relationship of selected academic and educational factors on student attendance.

McMillan, J. H. (2012). *Educational research: Fundamentals for the consumer* (6th ed.). New York: Longman.

Murphy, A. K. (2007). The suburban ghetto: The legacy of Herbert Gans in understanding the experience of poverty in recently impoverished American suburbs. *City & Community, 6*(1), 21–37. doi:10.1111/j.1540-6040.2007.00196.x

New York State Education Department Data Site. (n. d.). Retrieved May 13, 2016, from http://data.nysed.gov/ NYSED/P-12 /Part 100 Regulations/100.5

Nichols, J. D. (2003). Prediction Indicators for Students Failing the State of Indiana High School Graduation Exam. *Preventing School Failure, 47*(3), 112–120. doi:10.1080/10459880309604439

Oliveras, Y. (2014). *The empirical relationship between administrator ratings of teacher effectiveness and student achievement on the State of Texas assessments of academic readiness.*

Perry, L., & McConney, A. (2010). Does the SES of the school matter? An examination of socioeconomic status and student achievement using PISA 2003. *Teachers College Record, 112*(4), 7–8.

Polikoff, M. S., Porter, A. C., & Smithson, J. (2011). How well aligned are state assessments of student achievement with state content standards? *American Educational Research Journal, 48*(4), 965–995. doi:10.3102/0002831211410684

Rivkin, S. G., Hanushek, J. F., Markman, J. M., & Kain, J. F. (2003). Does peer ability affect student achievement? *Journal of Applied Econometrics, 18*(5), 527–544. doi:10.1002/jae.741

Schiller, K. & Muller, C. (2000). External examinations and accountability, educational expectations, and high school graduation. *American Journal of Education, 108*.

Stronge, J. H., Ward, T. J., Tucker, P. D., & Hindman, J. L. (2012). What is the relationship between teacher quality and student achievement? An exploratory study. *Journal of Personnel Evaluation in Education, 20*(3-4), 165–184. doi:10.1007/s11092-008-9053-z

Tucker, P. D., & Stronge, J. H. (2005). *Linking teacher evaluation and student learning*. Alexandria, VA: Association for Supervision and Curriculum Development.

Van Ewijk, R., & Sleegers, P. (2010). The effect of peer socioeconomic status on student achievement: A meta-analysis. *Educational Research Review, 5*(2), 134–150. doi:10.1016/j.edurev.2010.02.001

Wong, H., & Wong, R. (2010, November). *Developing and retaining effective teachers and principals*. Retrieved May 22, 2016 from http://www.oswego.edu/Documents/project_smart/Summer Institute/Developing and Retaining.pdf

KEY TERMS AND DEFINITIONS

Annual Professional Performance Review (APPR) Teacher Evaluation System: The New York State law which requires teacher and principal evaluation on an annual basis and receive a rating of either "highly effective," "effective," "developing," or "ineffective" (HEDI).

Attendance: The record of students present in school calculated as a percentage based on the high school's total possible student attendance divided by the actual attendance during an entire school year.

Data.NYSED.gov: The New York State Education Department's (NYSED) data website which was utilized as the source of the data for this study. The website contains reporting on 733 school districts, 4,469 public schools, and 300 charter schools, so that interested parties can be better informed on how to advance student achievement.

High School Graduation Rate: The percent of students, by high school, receiving a Regents Diploma or Regents Diploma with Advanced Designation. The percent of students obtaining a Regents Diploma also includes those that obtained the Regents Diploma with Advanced Designation.

Poverty: The percent of high school students receiving free and/or reduced lunch.

Regents Diploma: The high school diploma obtained by passing of five Regents examinations with a score of 65 or better, and in addition to 22 credits of coursework.

Regents Diploma With Advanced Designation: The high school diploma obtained by passing eight Regents examinations with a score of 65 or better and completion of a two year course of study in a Language Other Than English.

Student Achievement: Student achievement is defined by the number of Regents exams passed annually starting in the year of student entry into grade 9 and is measured by the percent of high school students who graduated with New York State Regents Diploma and Regents Diploma with Advanced Designation.

Chapter 11
Effects of Annual Professional Performance Review on Teacher Efficacy, Instructional Practices, and Professional Development

Erica Murphy-Jessen
Huntington Union Free School District, USA

ABSTRACT

The purpose of this study was to examine the effects of new Annual Professional Performance Review (APPR) legislation on professional development, instructional practices, and teacher efficacy. Additionally, teacher perceptions of the impact of new APPR standards on the disability classification rate in their school districts were examined. A mixed-method survey was conducted comparing two Average Needs, public school districts, in New York. Although similar student demographics were reported, the disability classification rate in District 1 was above the state the average and District 2 below the state average. The results of this study revealed that the implementation of APPR legislation significantly affected teacher's perceptions of professional development, instructional practices, and teacher efficacy. Professional development proved to be of high importance for all teachers in both districts. However, there was little consensus about the effects of APPR on the disability classification rates.

DOI: 10.4018/978-1-5225-3616-1.ch011

INTRODUCTION

In the United States over the past 50 years the issue of civil rights has permeated not only our society but also our educational institutions. The theoretical underpinnings of this study are guided by the United States values of life, liberty, and equality [in education] (Turnbull, 2012). Some researchers and educators believe that the purpose of education is to give young people the knowledge and training to further advance in our society (Galston, 2001). As the population changes over time so do societal and cultural values and norms, which impact our educational system. Federal, state and local laws mandate school districts to educate students with disabilities in the least restrictive environment (LRE), prohibit discrimination of individuals based on a cognitive, academic or behavioral disability, and permit procedural safeguards for parents. However, evidence in the literature does not support a transformation of these political policies into classroom practices (Turnbull, 2012). Luanna H. Meyer (2012) added that "we" as a society have a long way to go in terms of rights for people with disabilities" (p.222). Many school districts continue to struggle to address LRE mandates and meet the needs of students with disabilities, and the path that leads towards the goal of achieving the highest learning potential for all students, seems no less evasive. Despite policy makers' attempts, research and experience have shown that there is no one magical solution. As Luke (2012) said "school reform is by necessity a messy, complex, local and longitudinally drawn-out process... sustainable gains in achievement take time, as does cultural change" (p.10).

This chapter reviews the most recent changes made to the educational environment by policy makers. This chapter compares teacher's perspectives about the effects of new Annual Professional Performance Review (APPR) on professional development, instructional practices, differentiated professional development, teacher efficacy and the disability classification rates in two different school districts.

BACKGROUND

In 2002, The No Child Left Behind (NCLB) law called for higher accountability system-wide. NCLB attempted to improve student learning by holding teachers and building principals accountable for student test scores. Students' success would be measured using high-stakes standardized testing and a goal was set that all students would achieve 100% mastery in English Language Arts (ELA) and Mathematics by 2014 thereby closing the achievement gap (nysed.gov; Hirsh, 2005, p.38). Following this legislation, pressure and anxiety heightened among many educators, as public school districts attempted to raise students' test scores, meet annual yearly progress (AYP) standards, and avoid punishment by the state (Meier et al., 2004). NCLB also emphasized the importance of educating students with disabilities in the Least Restrictive Environment (LRE) to the greatest extent possible with their non-disabled peers. According to the Least Restrictive Environment Policy Paper, posted on www.p12.nysed.gov (1998), "students with and without disabilities need to learn to interact and develop interdependent relationships so that, as adults, they can successfully participate in a society that values full participation in the economic, political, social, cultural and educational mainstream of American society" (Section III, para. 1).

Many believe that in retrospect, the goals set forth by NCLB policy makers, have failed (Meier et al., 2004 & Starnes, 2011). According to Luke (2012) this legislation has been criticized as a "test and punish policy" (Lessler, 2010). Since the enactment of NCLB, the amount of time students spend during the school day taking standardized tests and preparing for those tests has increased significantly (Jones et al., 1999). As the focus in the classroom has increasingly become about improving test scores researchers such as Darling-Hammond (1999) are beginning to "wonder if the pressure to pass these high stakes tests creates artificial test scores, or [is] accurately measuring student growth" (p. 17). Some researchers, such as Nichols, Glass, and Berliner (2006) have gone as far as to argue that "high-stakes testing is corrupting U.S. schools and has numerous negative effects on youngsters…" (p. 2). They added that when "high stakes testing is attached to performance, there will be some form of distortion to the measurement system" (Lessler, 2010, p. 2). Another problem with the success of NCLB is that teachers, parents, and stakeholders have had no voice in policy decisions (Jones, et al., 1999; Ambrosio, 2013).

NCLB legislation brought to light serious issues of disproportionality across various demographics, many program inequalities across New York State, and at times revealed counterproductive educational policies and practices (McTighe & Brown, 2005). In fact, schools in urban areas that serve numerous students with a low socioeconomic status and schools with high populations of minorities face the most challenges and the highest expectations to improve test scores (Meier et al., 2004). These teachers and administrators face more accountability, more pressure, and a higher likelihood of demoralized staff and faculty. The high-stakes testing solution to improve educational outcomes and "close the gap" has done the exact opposite and creates "a host of collateral and unintended negative effects" (Luke 2012, p. 9). As 2014 came and went, so did the dream of meeting the goal of 100% mastery for all students in ELA and Math in most districts across the United States.

Luke (2012) and others (Jones et al., 1999; Starnes, 2011 & Von Der Embse & Hasson, 2012) concluded from a plethora of international research, spanning over decades, that high-stakes testing has not demonstrated the improved educational outcomes for students. Educators must find a way to incorporate theories such as the theory of multiple intelligence, and differentiated instruction, into their instructional practices in the new high-stakes testing environment, in a way that all students can benefit and produce successful outcomes. As the pressures increase, William Sterrett and Nathan Bond (2012) urge educators to respond to challenges in public schools such as the rising cost of education, increased expectations, and accountability standards. They recommend that as the needs of our students increase and as economic restraints tighten, educators need to focus on three key priorities. These priorities include a strengthening of relationships among stakeholders that foster communication, the preservation of professional development programs, which keep teachers moving forward towards continued achievement, and clear communication of the realities and challenges educators face today (p. 54). Research shows that professional development sessions must be ongoing and provide useful information that is easily transferrable into classroom practices (Mouza, 2006; Jacobs et al., 2009; nysed.gov., 2016; engageny.gov., 2016)

MAIN FOCUS OF THE CHAPTER

The most recent legislation that affects the field of education is the new Annual Professional Performance Review (APPR) for classroom teachers and building principals. APPR law was implemented beginning in the 2012-2013 school year and demanded higher levels of accountability from educators, as well as improved teacher and principal evaluation standards. This law has created an environment of fear and distrust for many educators. Teacher confidence has been shaken as is evidenced by a swarm of controversial information shared in social media forums, newspapers, community based movements to opt out of these tests, and public complaints from parents, administrator and teacher unions (NYSUT, 2016; nysed.gov., 2016). Teacher efficacy, in K-12 schools, has been negatively affected as teachers become more concerned with the possibility of losing their jobs especially those educating the neediest students. Instructional practices continue to change as a result of the APPR policies, and more educators report that teaching has become mostly about test preparation and test scores (Meier et al., 2004), which are now tied to their livelihood. Additionally, the manner in which districts provide professional development and its content must also change dramatically to meet federal, state and local standards.

The purpose of this study was to examine the effects of APPR legislation on professional development, instructional practices, differentiated professional development, and teacher efficacy. Additionally, teacher perceptions regarding the impact of APPR standards on the disability classification rate was examined. A mixed-method case study was conducted which compared two public school districts, with similar demographics, but differing disability classification rates (one above the state average and one below the state average) in the New York State.

Statement of the Problem and Research Questions

How do general education teachers and teachers of students with disabilities in two school districts perceive the effects of APPR on professional development, instructional practices, differentiated professional development, and teacher efficacy and the disability classification rate? Further, the following questions were included in the original study:

- Is there a difference, pre and post APPR, in general education teachers' and teachers of students with disabilities' perceptions of professional development, instructional practices, differentiated professional development, and teacher efficacy?
- What are the relationships among perceptions of professional development, instructional practices, differentiated professional development, and teacher efficacy and grade level taught in each school district?
- How do general education teachers and teachers of students with disabilities in two districts describe the effect of APPR on the disability classification rates?

Significance of the Study

Results of this study can be used to make necessary changes within educational institutions, add to the current body of research that guides educators, and improve the quality teacher professional development. Specifically, teachers can use the results of this study to improve their understanding of teacher efficacy and instructional practices as they relate to educating students with disabilities in the least restrictive environment. Administrators should use the results of this study to examine teachers' perceptions of the type and quality of professional development opportunities that are offered to improve the quality of professional development in their district, and ensure proper implementation of these strategies into the classroom setting. Further, the results of this study should be used to re-examine instructional practices used with students with disabilities and how disability classification rates in public school districts can be decreased.

Limitation of the study

This study is limited to two similarly performing; moderate needs public school districts, with similar demographics in New York State. The results of this study rely on teachers' perceptions, and retrospective reflections of the impact of state mandates on the variables.

ISSUES, CONTROVERSIES, PROBLEMS

Many researchers, educators, and advocates believe that "in the decade since NCLB was passed, this law has had no measurable or positive impact on the achievement gap and little to no effect on students' academic performance over time (Nichols, Glass, & Berliner, 2006, cited in Nichols & Valenzuela, p.154). Further, many believe that "high stakes testing changes school cultures and instructional practices in ways that are obvious to students" (Nichols & Valenzuela, p. 155). Student, teacher, and administrator stress has heightened and now seems to be focused on improving test scores rather than educational opportunities for students, leading to overall successful outcomes. Nichols and Valenzuela (2013) concluded that "the punitive meritocratic ideology that high stakes tests embody, classifies children as winners or losers, undermining what should be a sense of belonging and intrinsic value for learning... high stakes testing exacerbates stratification processes and undermines the quality of the nations' schools and classrooms generally" (p. 156). They recommend that teachers resist implementing a test-dominated culture of instruction and embrace principles of inclusivity, multiculturalism, and autonomy [and]...at the very least "teachers need to be mindful of the potential effects of their instructional practice- especially if that practice is laden with test-based messages and pressures...teachers must work towards providing their students an asset-based, diversity-conscious educational experience that fosters a love of learning, self, family, and community (p. 157). School administrators must focus on professional development to help teachers foster these valuable educational opportunities that help students become successful after graduating high school and continue as long-long learners. Professional development can help level the playing field for educators with varying qualifications across the country and close achievement gaps. However, professional development must be differentiated to the needs of the teachers, students, culture, and community as a whole. Teachers must learn to utilize best practices when working with students with and without disabilities inclusive of differentiated instruction, multiple intelligences theory and multicultural diversity. If linked to the culture and vision of the school, as an ongoing experience, professional development can transform a school culture (Sparks, 2003; Hirsh, 2005; Schubert, 2007).

Data Sources

Public school general education teachers and teachers of students with disabilities, teaching grades K-12 were chosen as participants for this study via purposeful convenience sampling. Two public school districts were chosen, as a comparison, because they were both classified as moderate need school districts, as per the Need/Resource Capacity Categories Index published in 2009-2010, educated students with similar demographics and were both situated in similar suburban areas of New York State. As per the New York State Report Card, 2013-2014, school district one has a higher disability classification rate than the state average of 13.2 percent, and the other district has a lower disability classification rate than the state average. Data were gathered from the New York State website https://data.nysed.gov/, a publicly accessible site via the Internet.

According to www.p12.NYSED.gov, disability classification rates in New York State have fluctuated in the past ten years among various districts. The disability classification rate has steadily increased in District 1 from about ten percent to about 14 percent, jumping about two percentage points since the implementation of APPR. Conversely, in school District 2 the disability classification rate has steadily decreased in the past nine years. In District 2 this rate fluctuated and at one point was as high as 15 percent, but has decreased from almost 13 percent to about ten percent, since the implementation of APPR. Previous New York State guidelines dictated that the average disability classification rate should remain at or below a 12 percent threshold in each school district. However, in the past nine years the state average pierced through the 12 percent disability classification rate mandate and steadily increased up to 14.3 percent as recently reported on the 2014-2015 state report cards. The state average has increased approximately one and a half percentage points since the implementation of APPR in 2012.

School district's enrollment data collected as part of NYSED's Student Information Repository System (SIRS), on "Basic Educational Data System (BEDS) day" for the 2014-2015 school year reports total enrollment, percent of students by ethnic origin and data for the following subgroups: limited English proficiency, students with disabilities and economically disadvantaged, as well as percent of students receiving free or reduced lunch and graduation rates. Both districts report a total student enrollment between 2,000 and 4,500; the student populations reported a somewhat even split between male and female students. Both districts report that the ethnic origin of students is approximately 45 percent White, 50 percent Hispanic/ Latino and less than ten percent African American, Asian, and multi-racial. Neither district reports a Native American population. Both districts report that approximately 20 percent of students are English Language Learners, and 10-15 percent of students are students with disabilities. Almost 50 percent of the populations in both school districts are classified as economically disadvantaged and more than 35 percent of students receive free lunch and less than ten percent of students are qualified for the reduced lunch program. According to the 2014-2015 New York State Report Card District 1 reports an 88 percent graduation rate within four years, and 93 percent within five years, while District 2 reports an 90 percent overall graduation rate and 92 percent five year graduation rate.

The most recently reported fiscal supplement (2013-2014) showed that both districts spent an average of more than $22,000 per pupil. Both districts spent around $12,000 per pupil on general education students; however, District 1 spent more than $42,000 on students with disabilities compared to the less than 40,000 that District 2 spent on students with disabilities per pupil.

Educator performance as measured by the *Annual Professional Performance Review (APPR): Overall Composite Rating,* posted on www.data.nysed.gov/glossary, is also included in the NYS Report Card Data and is defined as follows:

This rating is provided to NYSED by districts, BOCES, and charters. Each classroom teacher and building principal must receive an overall rating of Highly Effective, Effective, Developing, or Ineffective (HEDI) based on a single composite effectiveness score that is calculated based on the scores received by the teacher or principal in each of the three subcomponents (State Growth or Other Comparable Measures, Locally-Selected Measures of Student Achievement, and Other Measures of Educator Effectiveness).

The scoring ranges for each Overall Composite Rating are as follows and are set by statute: Highly Effective (91-100), Effective (75-90), Developing (65-74), and Ineffective (0-64) [see Education Law §3012-c(2)(a)(2)]. For the 2013-2014 school year and thereafter, the Commissioner will review the scoring ranges annually before the start of each school year and recommend any changes to the Board of Regents [§3012-c(2)(a)(7)].

In the 2013-2014 school year, Annual Professional Performance Review Ratings indicate that both districts employ 150-350 educators. In both districts, 98 percent of teachers were categorized as Effective or Highly Effective in overall composite ratings. Two percent of educators were classified as developing or ineffective in their overall composite ratings.

Data Gathering Techniques

After gaining permission from the Institutional Review Board (IRB) from the degree granting institution, a survey was emailed along with a Google-form attachment and a cover letter ensuring anonymity and any potential risk of harm. Participants responded to demographic questions about their gender, certification type, grade level taught, years teaching as well as the type and number of professional development hours taken. Participants were asked to respond to 21 items using a 5-point Likert scale, and two open-ended questions. Survey items and the open-ended questions were used to gather information about teachers' perceptions of professional development, instructional practices, differentiated professional development, and teacher efficacy pre and post APPR as well as their perceptions of the impact of

Response to Intervention (RTI) and APPR legislation on the disability classification rate in their respective districts.

Participants selected included general education teachers and teachers of students with disabilities working with students in grades K-12. All teachers that met the criteria were emailed a cover letter explaining the possible risk of harm and ensuring their confidentiality if they choose to participate in the survey.

Instrumentation

The survey consisted of three sections. Part I consisted of demographic information. The demographics that were addressed are gender, years of teaching experience, type of teaching certification; content/grade level teaching, and number of professional development hours taken in the areas of Multiple Intelligences (MI), Differentiated Instruction (DI), Students with Disabilities (SWD), Annual Professional Performance Review (APPR), Common Core Learning Standards (CCLS) and Response to Intervention (RTI). Part II consisted of 21 items that were developed using a combination of items from La Melza's scale (2003) and the *Teacher Efficacy Scale* established by Sherri Gibson, Ph.D. in 1983. Teachers responded to survey items using a 5-point Likert agreement scale (strongly agree, agree, slightly agree, disagree, and strongly disagree). Part III included two open-ended question, which asked teachers to describe their perception of the relationship between response to intervention (RTI), which is mandated by New York State for reading in grades K-4, and APPR, mandated by federal law for all classroom teachers and building principals on the disability classification rate in their district. Table 1 displays item numbers and the research sources used to develop the survey.

Table 1 shows the item numbers that align with each variable in this study. Teacher efficacy items were chosen and modified from Sherri Gibson's (1983) *Teacher Efficacy Scale* and a modified version of Joseph LaMelza's (2003) survey. Instructional practices and differentiated professional development items were adapted and modified from Tomlinson (1985) and Gardner (1983) resources. Instructional practices and quality professional development items were chosen based on the literature regarding best teaching practices and guidance offered to teachers from the engagey.org website. Quality professional development items were adapted from multiple sources and modified. Other sources related to quality professional development include LaMelza's (2003) study, and guidance from New York State through engageny.org. Research regarding the effects of RTI and APPR on disability classification rates was guided by Hoover (2010) and information provided by the New York State Department of Education via nysed.gov.

Table 1. Survey instrument items

Variables	Items	# of Items	Score Range	Sources
Demographics	A, B, C, D, E, F, G, H, I, J, K	11		
Teacher efficacy	1, 2, 3, 4, 5, 6, 7, 8, 9	9	9-45	Gibson (1983) Bandura (1977, 1982)
Instructional Practices & Differentiated Professional Development	10, 11, 12, 13, 14, 15, 16	7	7-35	Gardner (1983) Tomlinson (1985)
Quality Professional Development	17, 18, 19, 20 21, 22, 23	7	7-35	Bellanca (1998) Hirsh (2005) Mouza (2006)
RTI effect on disability classification rate	24	1		Hoover (2010)
APPR effect on disability classification rate	25	1		NYSED.gov

This study was planned for distribution to two school districts. All teachers in both schools were solicited for responses via email (n = 505), yielding 140 usable surveys. There were 81 respondents from District 1 (higher disability classification rate than state average), and 60 respondents from District 2 (lower than state average disability classification rate). Both schools are classified, as moderate needs schools according to the New York State Needs/ Resource Capacity index.

A group of five teachers were selected to jury the survey items for content validity. This jury reviewed the definitions of terms and rated each item in the survey for content clarity. The jurors were asked to assign each survey item to the corresponding variable as indicated by the definition. Review of the jury responses ensured that there was at least 80 percent agreement among teachers regarding the measure of each item.

Results

After identifying 140 useable surveys based on the satisfactory completion of the survey by respondents, a factor analysis was performed to gain a sharper distinction among the proposed variables used to determine the effects of APPR on professional development, instructional practices, differentiated professional development, and teacher efficacy. The 21 items from the survey were subjected to a factor analysis using the data from the 140 respondents and analyzed using Principal Component Analysis extraction method and Varimax with the Kaiser Normalization rotation method. This rotation method yielded four interpretable variables. The factor analysis performed determined that the professional development variable needed to be split into two separate variables: Professional Development and Differentiated Professional Development. The reliability analysis was performed, and the strength of the Cronbach Alpha for each factor confirmed the reliability of all four variables. A content analysis was performed to identify the perceptions of teachers in regard to the effects of APPR on disability classification rates in their respective districts.

Research Question 1: Is there a difference, pre and post APPR, in general education teachers and teachers of students with disabilities' perceptions of professional development, instructional practices, differentiated professional development and teacher efficacy?

Tables 2, 3, and 4 display the results of a two-way repeated measures analysis of variance (ANOVA) to evaluate the effects of the impact of professional development pre and post APPR on general education teachers and teachers of students with disabilities. The means and standard deviations for professional development pre and post APPR for general education teachers and teachers of students with disabilities are presented in Table 2. The ANOVA indicated no significant differences pre and post APPR for general education teacher and teachers of students with disabilities' perceptions of professional development. Wilks Lambda = .98, $F(1,138) = 2.330$, $p = .129$. The ANOVA indicated that there was also no significant interaction between professional development pre and post APPR and student population taught (general education teachers and teachers of students with disabilities), Wilks Lambda = .99, $F(1, 138) = 3.096$, $p = .287$.

Tables 5, 6, and 7 display the results of a two-way repeated measures analysis of variance (ANOVA) that was conducted to evaluate the effects of the impact of instructional practices pre and post APPR on general education teachers and teachers of students with disabilities. The means and standard deviations for instructional practices pre and post APPR for general education teachers and teachers of students

Table 2. Descriptive statistics: professional development for student population taught

Student Population Taught		*M*	*SD*	*N*
PD Pre-APPR	General Education	16.49	4.16	94
	Special Education	15.93	4.18	46
	Total	16.31	4.16	140
PD Post-APPR	General Education	16.39	3.99	94
	Special Education	15.39	4.06	46
	Total	16.06	4.03	140

Table 3. Test of within-subjects effects: professional development for student population taught

Source		Type III Sum of Squares	Df	Mean Square	F	*p*
PD	Greenhouse-Geisser	6.310	1.000	6.310	2.330	.129
PD * student pop. taught	Greenhouse-Geisser	3.096	1.000	3.096	1.143	.287
Error (PD)	Greenhouse-Geisser	373.776	138.000	2.709		

Table 4. Test of between-subjects effects: professional development for student population taught

Source	Type III Sum of Squares	df	Mean Square	F	*p*
Intercept	63667.875	1	63667.875	2068.350	.000
Student population taught	37.432	1	37.432	1.216	.272
Error	4247.911	138	30.782		

Table 5. Descriptive statistics: instructional practices for student population taught

Student Population Taught		*M*	*SD*	*N*
IP Pre-APPR	General Education	24.47	3.43	94
	Special Education	25.76	3.16	46
	Total	24.89	3.39	140
IP Post-APPR	General Education	22.66	4.01	94
	Special Education	22.41	4.72	46
	Total	22.58	4.24	140

Table 6. Test of within-subjects effects: instructional practices for student population taught

Source		Type III Sum of Squares	Df	Mean Square	F	P
IP	Greenhouse-Geisser	410.592	1.000	410.592	58.145	.000
IP* student pop. taught	Greenhouse-Geisser	36.592	1.000	36.592	5.182	.024
Error (IP)	Greenhouse-Geisser	974.494	138.000	7.062		

Table 7. Test of between-subjects effects: instructional practices for student population taught

Source	Type III Sum of Squares	df	Mean Square	F	*p*
Intercept	140258.047	1	140258.047	6309.819	.000
Student population taught	16.904	1	16.904	.760	.385
Error	3067.538	138	22.229		

with disabilities are presented in Table 5. The ANOVA indicated a significant difference pre and post APPR for the variable instructional practices, Wilks' lambda, = .704 $F(1, 138) = 58.145, p = .000$. There was also a significant interaction between instructional practices and student population taught (general education teachers and teachers of students with disabilities), Wilks' lambda = .964 $F(1, 138) = 5.182$, $p = .024$. The data showed that the mean scores for both general education teachers and teachers of students with disabilities were significantly higher pre APPR than post APPR.

Tables 8, 9, and 10 display the results of a two-way repeated measures ANOVA that was conducted to evaluate the effects of the impact of differentiated professional development pre and post APPR on general education teachers and teachers of students with disabilities. The means and standard deviations for differentiated professional development pre and post APPR for general education teachers and teachers of students with disabilities are presented in Table 8. The ANOVA indicated a significant difference pre and post APPR for the variable differentiated professional development, Wilks' lambda, = .946, $F(1, 138) = 7.28$, $p = .006$. There was not significant interaction between differentiated professional development pre and post APPR and student population taught (general education teachers and teachers of students with disabilities), Wilks' lambda = . 978 $F(1, 138) = 3.067, p = .082$. The

Table 8. Descriptive statistics: differentiated professional development for student population taught

Student Population Taught		*M*	*SD*	*N*
DPD Pre-APPR	General Education	6.33	1.79	94
	Special Education	6.65	1.93	46
	Total	6.44	1.84	140
DPD Post-APPR	General Education	6.2	1.72	94
	Special Education	6.20	2.07	46
	Total	6.21	1.83	140

Table 9. Test of within-subjects effects: differentiated professional development for student population taught

Source		Type III Sum of Squares	df	Mean Square	F	*p*
DPD	Greenhouse-Geisser	4.893	1.000	4.893	7.928	.006
DPD * student pop. taught	Greenhouse-Geisser	1.893	1.000	1.893	3.067	.082
Error (DPD)	Greenhouse-Geisser	85.175	138.000	.617		

Table 10. Test of between-subjects effects: differentiated professional development for student population taught

Source	Type III Sum of Squares	df	Mean Square	F	*p*
Intercept	9963.912	1	9963.912	1622.281	.000
Student population taught	1.341	1	1.341	.218	.641
Error	847.584	138	6.142		

data showed that the mean scores for both general education teachers and teachers of students with disabilities were significantly higher pre APPR than post APPR.

Tables 11, 12, and 13 display the results of a two-way repeated measures ANOVA that was conducted to evaluate the effects of the impact of teacher efficacy pre and post APPR on general education teachers and teachers of students with disabilities. The means and standard deviations for teacher efficacy pre and post APPR for general education teachers and teachers of students with disabilities are presented in Table 11. The ANOVA indicated a significant difference pre and post APPR for the variable teacher efficacy, Wilks' lambda, = .953, $F(1, 138) = 6.813$, $p = .010$. There was not significant interaction between teacher efficacy pre and post APPR

Table 11. Descriptive statistics: teacher efficacy for student population taught

Student Population Taught		*M*	*SD*	*N*
TE Pre-APPR	General Education	14.79	2.22	94
	Special Education	14.87	2.35	46
	Total	14.81	2.26	140
TE Post-APPR	General Education	14.32	2.51	94
	Special Education	14.41	2.89	46
	Total	14.35	2.63	140

Table 12. Test of within-subjects effects: teacher efficacy for student population taught

Source		Type III Sum of Squares	df	Mean Square	F	*p*
TE	Greenhouse-Geisser	13.202	1.000	13.202	6.813	.010
TE* Student pop. taught	Greenhouse-Geisser	.002	1.000	.002	.001	.974
Error (TE)	Greenhouse-Geisser	267.409	138.000	1.938		

Table 13. Test of between-subjects effects: teacher efficacy for student population taught

Source	Type III Sum of Squares	df	Mean Square	F	*p*
Intercept	52648.937	1	52648.937	5185.491	.000
Student pop. taught	.480	1	.480	.047	.828
Error	1401.131	138	10.153		

and student population taught (general education teachers and teachers of students with disabilities), Wilks' lambda = 1.00 $F(1, 138) = .001, p = .974$. The data showed that the mean scores for both general education teachers and teachers of students with disabilities were significantly higher pre APPR than post APPR.

Research Question 2: What are the relationships among perceptions of professional development, instructional practices, differentiated professional development and teacher efficacy and grade level taught in each school district?

Correlation data are displayed in Table 14. Professional development had a direct moderate relationship with instructional practices (r = .491, p = .01), and professional development described 24.1 percent of the variance in instructional practices. Professional development also had a direct relationship with differentiated professional development (moderate strength) and teacher efficacy (weak strength). Professional development described 19.4 percent and 5.6 percent of the variance in differentiated professional development and teacher efficacy respectively.

Instructional practices had a moderate relationship with differentiated professional development (r = . 456, p = . 01). Instructional practices described 20.8 percent of the variance in differentiated professional development. Instructional practices had a direct moderate relationship with teacher efficacy (r = .378, p = .01) and accounted for 14.3 percent of the variance for teacher efficacy. Instructional practices had an

Table 14. Pearson product moment correlation table

		PD	IP	DPD	TE
IP	r	.491**			
	r^2	.241			
	N	140			
DPD	r	.441**	.456**		
	r^2	.194	.208		
	N	140	140		
TE	r	.237**	.378**	.207*	
	r^2	.056	.143	.043	
	N	140	140	140	
GL	r	-.081	-.229**	-.221**	.080
	r^2	.007	.053	.049	.006
	N	137	137	137	137

**. Correlation is significant at the 0.01 level (2-tailed).

*. Correlation is significant at the 0.05 level (2-tailed).

IP = Instructional Practice, DPD = Differentiated Professional Development, TE = Teacher Efficacy, GL = Grade Level Taught

inverse weak relationship with grade level taught (r = -.229, p = .01) and accounted for 5.3 percent of the variance with grade level taught.

Differentiated professional development had a direct, weak relationship with teacher efficacy (r = .207, p = .05) and accounted for 4.3 percent of the variance with teacher efficacy. Differentiated professional development had a weak, inverse relationship with grade level taught (r = -.221, p = .05) and accounted for 4.9 percent of the variance for grade level taught.

Research Question 3: How do general education teachers and teachers of students with disabilities in two districts describe the effect of APPR on the disability classification rates?

One hundred and forty surveys (80 from District 1 and 60 from District 2) were analyzed to identify teacher perceptions of the effects of APPR on the disability classification rate in their districts. Twenty-seven (34%) teachers from District 1 and 37 (62%) teachers from District 2 did not respond to this item on the survey. Data are displayed in Table 15.

Table 15. Content analysis: APPR effect on disability classification rate

	District 1 (N = 80)	District 2 (N = 60)
No answer	27 (34%)	37 (62%)
Don't know/ not sure	15 (18.75%)	4 (6.67%)
No change	9 (11.25%)	10 (16.67%)
Decrease/ delay in DCR	6 (7.5%)	3 (5%)
Builds awareness/ helps students	3 (3.75%)	1 (1.67%)
Teachers frustrated/ nothing matters	6 (7.5%)	2 (3.3%)
Parent referrals increased	4 (5%)	0
Increase in DCR	10 (12.5%)	3 (5%)

Fifteen (17.5%) participants stated they did not know or were unsure of any effects resulting in the new APPR standards of evaluation of the disability classification rate. One teacher stated that they did not have any knowledge about the classification rates.

In District 1, nine (11.25%) participants, and in District 2 ten (16.6%) participants reported no observable change in classification rates. One general education teacher stated, "I don't think it has a bearing, does it? I would hope not" and others concurred but stated that they did not have enough data to support an answer either way. Another general education teacher commented, "I am not aware of any effect it has. My perception is that it hasn't had any influence." From District 2, a general education teacher stated, "I do not think that APPR has affected the rate of classification of students in my district at all. I think we classify students as needed and it has nothing to do with APPR." Another general education teacher commented, "I do not think APPR has affected this rate. Teachers still teach the way they do." Another teacher stated, "I think it has no effect. Most teachers I know think of kids' needs first. They do not think of the numbers or what the district may consider to be too many referrals. We have a complex population of children with a lot of diverse needs…."

Six (7.5%) teachers from District 1 responded that the effects of APPR have led to a decrease or delay in classification for students. One general education teacher stated, "I believe that APPR has led to a decrease in the referral process. I think we are looking at data more closely and only referring students who have showed a trend of not making progress when provided various interventions." Other teachers expressed that APPR has led to a delay in classifying students and made it "…more difficult to get children necessary services." A different general education teacher commented, "…the state seems to put in place any obstacle to delay a student from getting tested or services…" Many teachers also expressed concern about disproportionate numbers of referrals for students newly acquiring the English language, and minorities. A special education teacher stated, "The gap in general education setting has increased…as a result of a decrease in student referrals." Another special education teacher commented "It seems like more students are failing and being brought up to IST because of the rigor and high expectations to meet state assessments and standards. But, the district is tying to minimize the numbers of referrals."

In District 2, three (5%) of teachers stated that APPR has decreased the number of student's referred to special education. A general education teacher commented, "It has affected it greatly! No student is ever classified now!" Another general education teacher mirrored this sentiment,

It has prevented students who are in need of those services from getting them as quickly as they need them. It has lessened the amount of classified students tremendously and has turned many teachers away from collecting the data and doing the work in order to bring a child up to the team.

Three teachers (3.75%) from District 1, and one teacher (1.67%) from District 2 commented that APPR has enabled them to more effectively help students by highlighting those who are struggling. One special education teacher commented, that APPR has "…heightened awareness and focus on identifying students with disabilities and providing remedial support", which was supported by other participant statements that progress monitoring has improved teacher awareness about the different needs of students. A different special education teacher agreed but expressed frustration stating, "I think teachers have developed a greater awareness of the different needs of their students. [However] one of the greatest flaws is the lack of support."

Six teachers (7.5%) from District 1 expressed frustration with the effects of the new APPR system. One general education teacher expressed that Instructional Support Team (IST) and Committee on Special Education (CSE) meetings can be a good avenue to getting help and support when a student is struggling in class however, "…[complex] explanations, lack of time, scores/accountability and lack of expertise often lead teachers to frustration/ overwhelmed and away from what could potentially be done within the classroom prior to referral." Most teachers, who responded similarly, feel that paperwork is presented as a barrier to classification for students in need. One general education teacher articulated that many strategies are presented and meetings are held to discuss the strategies but "Teachers feel it's too much paperwork, so they don't do it." This teacher added that "…this [process] continues, and many students don't get tested for months or years later. Teachers find this frustrating!" Another general education teacher added many "people do not want to teach special ed." anymore. A special education teacher concurred, "…the process angers teachers more, but I don't think it has moved students through any quicker. I think that teachers write some kids off because there is no way they will pass" supporting the general notion that APPR has hindered student success. One general education teacher commented, "I think teachers are freaking about APPR and instead of trying to differentiate and work a little harder in the classroom to help struggling learners succeed, it's easier to say the student should have special education services…" that teacher added "…we do not want a bad rating attached to our names, so I think it's easier to say a child should be referred to Special Education."

In District 2, two (3.3%) of respondents expressed frustration with the way the APPR system has affected students and teachers. One general education teacher stated, "I would say it has affected the district by lower scores due to students not receiving the time and service they need." A different general education teacher stated,

There has definitely been increased emphasis on testing struggling students to see if they qualify for classification. Absent classification, we aggressively enroll students in mandatory AIS [academic support] classes. Everything is being driven by the assessments. This reinforces an overly simplistic view of student achievement where the students are empty vessels and it's the teacher's job to fill them with knowledge, akin to pouring water into an empty glass. It follows then, it students aren't succeeding it must be because teachers don't know how to pour. It is an enormously demeaning and frustrating set of circumstances.

In District 1, four special education teachers (5%) agreed that parent push back due to high-stakes testing is the cause of increasing number of students being referred to special education. One of the special education teachers stated, "I think that APPR has affected the rate of parent referrals within the district which puts stress on the individuals implementing the evaluations driven by parent request." Two other special education teachers responded similarly by stating that high stakes testing has led to an increase in parent referrals in order to secure "…the testing accommodations that come along with special education services…" for students struggling with curriculum content.

Ten teachers (12.5%) from District 1 and three teachers (5%) from District 2 responded that they felt APPR has led to an increase in the number of students being referred to and classified with a disability. Several teachers agreed that the new curriculum content and higher expectations have led to increases in the level of stress in students and teachers and as a result the number of students being classified has increased. One general education teacher stated, "I think it would be an increase. The content is more difficult and a result, borderline students are getting lost. We are very unrealistic in our expectations of students in math." Another general education teacher added, "I believe that the rate of referrals has increased since the implementation of APPR. More students are required to produce above what they are able to do. This in turn leads to an escalation of already underlying academic and behavioral issues." Another teacher stated that there has definitely been increased emphasis on testing struggling students to see of they qualify for classification..." due to the increased curriculum expectations. A special education teacher also said, "...students are experiencing more stress and anxiety, which leads to attempts to get them classified as special needs students." In District 2, a general education teacher stated "Children who have difficulty learning the rigorous new content are not more likely to be referred to special education or response to intervention whereas in the past we would have given the children additional time to develop." A different general education teacher felt that although "...the rate has gone up and students are given more testing accommodations [they are] put into math labs and AIS classes at a higher rate than in the past."

Some teachers' remarks pointed out teacher frustration with the APPR system as it affects students. One special education teacher stated the belief the district has seen an "...increase [in referrals] as a result of teachers being overly concerned over their student's test scores." Three respondents agreed that teachers are feeling more stress and it's easier to "...push harder to get a student the services they deserve..." and believe that "...teachers are seeing students not performing as they are expected and are referring [students to special education] quicker."

In summary, the majority of participants (42% or 41% respectively) either did not answer the question or did not know about the effects of APPR on the disability classification rate in their district and reported they did not have data to support any observable change. More teachers, in District 1 felt that APPR had led to an increase in the disability classification rate. In District 2 an equal number of teachers (three or 5%) believed the rates of classification had increased or decreased. General education and special education teachers who commented the most stated that the processes in place hindered their ability to help students and provide necessary support for academic success.

CONCLUSION

General Education Teachers and Teachers of Students With Disabilities' Perspectives

A two-way repeated measures Analysis of Variance (ANOVA) was conducted to evaluate differences between general education teachers and teachers of students with disabilities on each of the variables. In the area of professional development, results indicated no significant difference pre and post APPR or any interaction. There was, however, a significant difference pre and post APPR for the variable instructional practices and the interaction between student population taught and instructional practices. There were significant results pre and post APPR on the variables differentiated professional development and teacher efficacy. There was not a significant result for the interaction between student population taught and differentiated professional development or teacher efficacy. Overall, general education teachers and teachers of students with disabilities reported their differentiated professional development experiences were similiarly affected by APPR. Regarding instructional practices, general education teachers and teachers of students with disabilities were affected differently pre and post APPR.

The new APPR standards changed teachers' perceptions of instructional practices of both general education teachers and teachers of students with disabilities. This indicates that high-stakes testing and accountability linked to teachers' APPR composite scores affected the way teachers were able to teach. Howard Gardner's *Theory of Multiple* Intelligences is one theory that can offer teachers, especially those serving a diverse student population, a guide for success. His theory helps teachers in a variety of ways to understand the learning styles of their individual students and helps with the design of curriculum and assessments.

Further, the practice of differentiated instruction, first introduced by Tomlinson in 1985, offered teachers a diverse way of thinking about student learning. According to Taffe et al. (2012) teachers who differentiated their instruction demonstrated a deeper understanding of the content materials and evidence-based practices used to improve instruction. General education teachers and teachers of students with disabilities must work to carefully develop a deep understanding of the needs of their students and carefully monitor their progress towards instructional goals. Finally, teachers who were able to effectively differentiate their instruction demonstrated the ability to use given materials in a flexible manner, to emphasize the key elements of the curriculum and to develop systems and routines that support differentiated classroom practices.

Differentiated professional development also changed as a result of APPR. Differentiated professional development that is specifically focused on Gardner's theories, for example, can be utilized to improve classroom practices and student outcomes. His research can be used to show educators that "teaching for intelligence is a never-ending challenge as well as an infinite opportunity to help all children become active, engaged and successful learners [further]...teaching is more than just sharing of information and testing for recall... teaching is [a] strategic act of engagement" (Bellanca, 1998, p.4). Gardner's theories have helped educators since the 1980s expand their perceptions about student learning needs and abilities (infed.org). Professional development must also be differentiated to meet the needs of teachers working with students with and without disabilities, and provide teachers with ongoing opportunities to improve their skills and work collaboratively. Jacobs, Gregory, Hoppey, and Yendol-Hoppy, D. (2009) conducted a study which adds to this body of research and concluded "it is essential for teachers [today] to utilize data to inform their instruction in the classroom" (p.52).

Relationship Between Professional Development, Instructional Practices, Differentiated Professional Development, and Teacher Efficacy

A Pearson Product Moment correlation analysis was conducted to evaluate the relationships between the variables professional development, instructional practices, differentiated professional development, teacher efficacy, and grade level taught. Significant direct moderate strength relationships were found between professional development and instructional practices, professional development and differentiated professional development, and instructional practices and differentiated professional development. Direct moderate to weak relationships were found between instructional practices, professional development, differentiated professional development, and teacher efficacy. An inverse but weak relationship was found between grade level taught and instructional practices as well as differentiated professional development. Overall, these results suggest that professional development is correlated with instructional practices, differentiated professional development and teacher efficacy. Additionally, grade level taught and instructional practices and differentiated professional development are negatively correlated. The impact of this study indicates that dsitrict leaders need to carefully plan their professional development opportunities, to improve teacher's sense of efficacy based on the grade level taught by teachers which will improve their instructional practices in the long-run.

Researchers including Haycock (1998) and Hirsh (2005) reported that most teachers would engage in valuable professional development experiences if they believed their efforts would lead to student improvement. Mr. Harry Wong (2012) encouraged educational leaders to begin training new staff through professional development opportunities the week before they begin teaching, to establish a successful transition. He stated that intensive new-teacher professional development is a process and should continue through the first few years. Ruppar et al. (2015) found that some teachers reported they did not feel their teacher preparation programs gave them the confidence or skills to teach students with disabilities, especially literacy. These teachers sought out quality professional development opportunities and reported significant changes the way they perceived the students' abilities, which facilitated better teaching.

Park, Roberts, and Stodden (2012) designed a three-day professional development workshop opportunity for staff working with students with disabilities. The intention of this training was to enhance the staff's competence in meeting the needs of diverse learners and help facilitate the development of more "positive attitudes towards students with disabilities (SWD) as valued learners" (p. 378). The workshop helped teachers develop higher levels of self-efficacy and more positive attitudes. Faculty members were able to create their own learning communities and design effective accommodations. Park et al. (2012) concluded that the training was a success and that "short term effects can be sustained over time" (p.382), with "continued direct support, technical assistance, and provision of more resources…in order to sustain the momentum gained from the training" (p.382). The research demonstrated that professional development, when run properly, increases a teacher's sense of teaching efficacy and ability to use differentiated instruction to increase a student's learning outcomes at all grade levels.

Perspectives of the Effect of APPR on Disability Classification Rate

A Content analysis was conducted to uncover teachers' overall perceptions of the effects of APPR on the disability classification rate in two districts. In District 1, 34 percent of participants and 62 percent of participants in District 2 chose not to respond to this question.

In District 1, with a high disability classification rate, the majority of teachers who responded said they did not know if APPR affected the disability classification rate. The next most frequent response indicated that the disability classification rate had increased followed by no change observed. Eight percent of teachers in District 1 reported a decrease in disability classification rate and eight percent indicated they were frustrated with the processes involved in helping students receive special education services. Parent involvement and requests for special education referrals, due to the increased emphasis on testing, was reported by five percent of participants. Conversely, four percent of participants responded that the new APPR system increased the level of teacher awareness and helped kids become more successful.

In District 2, with a lower disability classification rate, most teachers reported no observable change in disability classification rate followed by seven percent who indicated that they did not know or have data to support an answer either way. Increases and decreases in disability classification rate were reported by five percent of participants in both areas. Only three percent of teachers reported they were frustrated the effects of APPR on students, and three percent of participants reported it increased awareness and helped students.

Fullan (1996) encouraged educators to consider that "policies are essential catalysts" for change. He believes that if a vision is set, and educators view change as a process, not an event, they can learn from mistakes and collaboratively build a successful environment. Other researchers such as Udall and Rugen (1997) showed that it is imperative for school district leaders to be creative and find effective ways of continuously educating their staff in meaningful ways by engaging "teachers as learners" to facilitate deep connections.

Aron and Loprest (2012) stated that federal law was intended to lessen the issues of disproportionality but instead highlighted the many inadequacies of special education programming. They also connected the issue of disproportionate representation in special education classes of students in certain subgroups including race, gender and ethnicity directly to IDEA. Teacher efficacy, which influences teacher confidence, and the perceived ability to work with diverse students, can be negatively influenced by political policy. Political pressures, and state agencies can interfere with the educational process (Raines, Dever, Kamphaus, & Roach, 2012). Podell and Soodak (1993) found that "teachers' beliefs in their own effectiveness and the biases they hold can influence their tendencies to make referrals" (p. 252).

FUTURE RESEARCH DIRECTIONS

It is recommended that future research evaluate the rising costs of special education services within the diminishing tax cap demands, as well as the methodology behind high stakes accountability.

Further research should explore the comorbid impact of APPR and the Common Core Learning Standards on student success and the opportunities available for differentiated instruction within the confines of a federally constructed, scripted curriculum.

Further research should explore an in-depth look at the variable differentiated professional development, as it related to both differentiated instruction for educators and professional development for administrators.

REFERENCES

Ambrosio, J. (2013). Changing the subject: Neoliberalism and accountability in public education. *Educational Studies, 49*(4), 316–333. doi:10.1080/00131946.2013.783835

Aron, L., & Loprest, P. (2012). Disability and the education system. *The Future of Children, 22*(1), 97–122. doi:10.1353/foc.2012.0007 PMID:22550687

Bellanca, J. (1998, May). Teaching for intelligence: in search of best practices. *Phi Delta kappan, 79*(9).

Fullan, M. (1996). Professional culture and educational change. *School Psychology Review, 25*(4), 496–500.

Galston, W. A. (2001). Political knowledge, political engagement, and civic education. *Annual Review of Political Science, 4*(1), 217–234. doi:10.1146/annurev.polisci.4.1.217

Gardner, H. (1983). *Frames of Mind: Theory of multiple intelligences*. New York: Basic Books.

Gibson, S., & Dembo, M. H. (1984). Teacher efficacy: A construct validation. *Journal of Educational Psychology, 76*(4), 569–582. doi:10.1037/0022-0663.76.4.569

Haycock, K. (1998). Good teaching matters... A lot. *Organization of American Historians, 13*(1), 61–66.

Hirsh, S. (2005). Professional development and closing the achievement gap. *Theory into Practice, 44*(1), 38–44. doi:10.1207/s15430421tip4401_6

Hoover, J. J. (2010). Special Education Eligibility Decision Making in Response to Intervention Models. *Theory into Practice, 49*(4), 289–296. doi:10.1080/00405841.2010.510752

Jacobs, J., Gregory, A., Hoppey, D., & Yendol-Hoppey, D. (2009). Data literacy: Understanding teachers data use in a context of accountability and response to intervention. *Action in Teacher Education, 31*(3), 41–55. doi:10.1080/01626620.2009.10463527

Jones, M. G., Jones, B. D., Hardin, B., Chapman, L., Yarbrough, T., & Davis, M. (1999). The impact of high-stakes testing on teachers and students in North Carolina. *Phi Delta Kappan*, 199–203.

LaMelza, J. (2003). High school resource room teacher attitudes towards the 1997 amendments to the Individuals with Disabilities Education Act and its influence on their instructional practices [Doctoral dissertation].

Lessler, K. J. (2010). High-stakes and non-stakes testing states and the transfer of knowledge to students' advanced placement test, advanced placement U.S. history test and SAT exam scores [Doctoral dissertation].

Luke, A. (2012). After the testing: Taking reading and writing into the world. *Journal of Adolescent & Adult Literacy*, *56*(1), 8–13. doi:10.1002/JAAL.00095

McTighe, J., & Brown, J. L. (2005). Differentiated instruction and educational standards: Is detente possible? *Theory into Practice*, *44*(3), 234–244. doi:10.1207/s15430421tip4403_8

Meier, D., Kohn, A., Darling-Hammond, L., Sizer, T. R., & Wood, G. (2004). Many children left behind (D. Meier, & G. Wood, Eds.). Boston, MA: Beacon Press.

Meyer, L. H. (2012). Freedom, fairness, and justice: What now for severe disabilities?: A response to Turnbull. *Research and Practice for Persons with Severe Disabilities*, *37*(3), 220–223. doi:10.2511/027494812804153480

Mouza, C. (2006). Linking professional development to teacher learning and practice: A multi-case study analysis of urban teachers. *Journal of Educational Computing Research*, *34*(4), 405–440. doi:10.2190/2218-567J-65P8-7J72

New York State Department of Education. (2014). Guidance on New York State's annual professional performance review for teachers and principals to Implement education law §3012-c and the commissioner's regulations, 1-166.

Nichols, S. L., Glass, S. L., & Berliner, G. V. (2006). High-stakes testing and student achievement: Does accountability pressure increase student learning? (S. Dorn, Ed.). Education Policy Analysis Archives, 14 (1), 1-180.

Nichols, S. L., & Valenzuela, A. (2013). Education policy and youth: Effects of policy on practice. *Theory into Practice*, *52*(3), 152–159. doi:10.1080/00405841.2013.804306

Park, H. J., Roberts, K. D., & Stodden, R. Faculty perspectives on professional development to improve efficacy when teaching students with disabilities. *Journal of Post Secondary Education and Disability, 25*(4), 377-383.

Podell, D. M., & Soodak, L. C. (1993). Teacher efficacy and bias in special education referrals. *The Journal of Educational Research, 86*(4), 247–253. doi:10.1080/00220671.1993.9941836

Raines, T., Dever, B., Kamphaus, R., & Roach, A. (2012). Universal screening for behavioral and emotional risk: A promising method for reducing disproportionate placement in special education. *The Journal of Negro Education, 81*(3), 283–296. doi:10.7709/jnegroeducation.81.3.0283

Ruppar, A. L., Gaffney, J. S., & Dymond, S. K. (2012). Influences on teachers' decisions about literacy for secondary students with severe disabilities. *Exceptional Children, 81*(2), 2 09-226.

Schubert, J. (2007). Transformation through staff development. *Reclaiming Children and Youth, 16*(3), 53–55.

Sparks, D. (2003). We care, therefore they learn. *National Staff Development Council, 24*(4), 42–47.

Starnes, B. A. (2011). *Change, Sputnik, and Fast Food. Phi Delta Kappan, 92*(7), 72–73.

Sterrett, W., & Bond, N. (2012). Beyond tough choices: Prioritizing and preserving education in times of cuts and layoffs. *Kappa Delta Pi Record, 48*(2), 52–54. doi:10.1080/00228958.2012.680380

Taffe, S. W., Laster, B. P., Broach, L., Marinak, B., McDonald Connor, C., & Walker-Dalhouse, D. (2012). Differentiated instruction: Making informed teacher decisions. *The Reading Teacher, 66*(4), 303–314. doi:10.1002/TRTR.01126

Tomlinson, C. A. (1999). Mapping a route toward differentiated instruction. *Educational Leadership, 57*(1), 12–16.

Turnbull, R. H. (2012). "Free at last": Kennedy, King, and the meaning of liberty in the disability movement (M. Agran, Ed.). Research & Practice for Persons with Severe Disabilities, 37(3), 210-216.

Wong, H., & Wong, R. T. (2004). *The First Days of School.* Mountain View, CA, USA: Harry K. Wong Publications, Inc.

KEY TERMS AND DEFINITIONS

Annual Professional Performance Review (APPR): A law, which mandated the use of a research-based rubric to measure classroom teacher and building principal effectiveness. The rubric provides an overall composite score based on student results of high-stakes standardized tests, and other measures for all teachers and building principals.

Differentiated Professional Development (DPD): Specified practices of professional development focused on techniques to improve student-learning outcomes, take into account the learning styles of the faculty and enable teachers to transport these strategies into classroom practices.

Disability Classification Rate (DCR): The ratio of the count of school-age students with disabilities (ages 4-21) to the total enrollment of all school-age students in the school district including students who are parentally placed in nonpublic schools located in the school district. Data are drawn from the Student Inventory Reporting System and from the Basic Education Data System (BEDS)" www.data. NYSED.gov/glossary.

High-Stakes accountability (HAS): Teachers and building principals are evaluated based on student's high stakes standardized test scores. Incentives to improve accountability include rewards for high achieving school and by "imposing stiff sanctions on low performing schools" (Malen & Rice, 2005, p. 1).

Instructional Practices (IP): Describes what educators do in the classroom and how they do it on a daily basis to improve student learning. These include research-based theories, best practices, and specific learning techniques that engage students in the learning process.

Professional Development (PD): The process used by school district administrators to inform and guide faculty members regarding the goals and vision of the district, changes in legal requirements, curriculum changes, best instructional theories and other practices that facilitate student learning.

Teacher Efficacy (TE): A teacher's beliefs and perceptions about their abilities and the conviction that one can successfully bring about the desired outcome in one's students (Gibson & Dembo, 1984).

Chapter 12
Hiring Practices, Uses of Social Media, and Teacher Retention Differences

Bridgette Waite
Dowling College, USA

Elsa-Sofia Morote
Farmingdale State University of New York, USA

ABSTRACT

This study assesses the differences between teacher retention rate and human resource (HR) managers' hiring practices, self-efficacy. Their use of social media websites (Facebook, LinkedIn, and Twitter) for hiring was evaluated. Turnover of teachers with fewer than 5 years of experience was gathered from New York State Education Department (NYSED) database. New York State schools were separated by high and low teacher retention rates. A Likert Scale Survey with one open ended question was sent to school districts HR managers. An independent sample t test was used to determine the differences between high and low teacher retention rates. A content analysis is presented using the responses to the open-ended question. Findings indicated that less than half of the HR managers used social media in the hiring process. No significant differences between teacher retention rates, HR managers' practices, and HR self-efficacy was found.

DOI: 10.4018/978-1-5225-3616-1.ch012

INTRODUCTION

Human resource (HR) managers faced new challenges in hiring practices. As paradigms changed, the characteristics affecting human resource management also had to be revised (Lipiec, 2001). According to Van Iddekinge, Lanivich, Roth, and Junco (2013), the Internet had a profound effect on the way organizations recruited and selected employees. The Internet served to broaden networks, helped communicate more efficiently, and accomplished undertakings more proficiently. It influenced the hiring practices that organizations implemented. It allowed organizations to reach more applicants via popular job sites and made applicant information more accessible. The widespread use of social media such as Facebook, Twitter, and LinkedIn revolutionized communication, both personally and professionally. The phenomenon of social networking websites (SNWs) on the Internet exploded in the mainstream (Kluemper & Rosen, 2009). One of the major contributors to change in the workplace was the accelerated use of the Internet (Cascio & Agunis, 2005).

HR managers used a vast amount of personal information on social media websites as a source for recruiting and making hiring decisions. Then recent reports suggested that many organizations were using the Internet to search for information about job applicants (Preston, 2011). Both job seekers and recruiters found places to connect on the Internet. The new openness and freer flow of information affected the employment process. Per Daniel (2012), social media became an increasingly useful tool for HR managers and understanding its benefits and limitations was crucial for future success. Given the advances in technology and the effect it could have on an organization, it was essential for research to examine how the use of the Internet in the recruiting, hiring, and selection process affected HR managers.

For a majority of recruiters, LinkedIn, Twitter, Facebook, and employee referrals officially surpassed job boards as the preferred way to acquire talent (Brotherton, 2012). Increasingly more companies boosted their recruiting efforts by investing in social media to reach job candidates, according to Jobvite, a recruiting platform for the social web. A recent Jobvite survey (2013) of 800 U.S. based HR professionals, more than half (55 percent) planned to increase their budget for social network recruiting. LinkedIn was on the list for 87 percent of companies, up from 78 percent in 2010; 55 percent used Facebook, and 47 percent were using Twitter. According to Jobvite, in the first 6 months of 2011, 73 percent of social hires came from LinkedIn, 20 percent from Facebook, and 7 percent from Twitter. The effect of social media in recruitment and hiring and the emerging issues and their implications for HR managers were examined in this study. The questions of self-efficacy and the extent to which HR managers' beliefs in their own abilities to complete tasks were affected were also examined. Additionally, the differences between hiring practices and social media use and teacher retention were examined.

BACKGROUND

The purpose of this quantitative study was to assess the differences between HR managers' self-efficacy and the retention levels in their districts (low versus high) and their use of social media websites—specifically Facebook, LinkedIn, and Twitter—for recruitment, selection, and hiring.

How do human resource managers in school districts with high and low retention rates differ in their use of the three social media dimensions of self-efficacy, recruiting, and hiring and selection?

It was a widely-held view that an organization's human resources were its most important assets and among the resources an organization had, might have offered the only non-imitative competitive edge (Pfeiffer, 1994). Therefore, an organization's ability to attract and retain capable employees might have been the single most important determinant of organizational effectiveness. The recruitment function played a critical role in enhancing organizational survival and success. Finn and Singh (2003) examined the effect of information technology on the recruitment function of organizations. They sought to outline the extent to which information technology had been used in recruitment and examine the effect of information technology on recruitment in terms of its effect on people, processes, and organizational structures: "As a filtering mechanism in the selection process, the recruitment function was one of the most important areas of human resource management" (Finn & Singh, 2003, p. 396). The recruitment process began with the identification of a vacancy, was followed by an analysis of the skills needed, and continued with an advertisement of the position, both internally and externally. Many organizations had begun to use innovative information technology methods to complement the traditional sources, such as employee referrals, newspaper and other print media ads, employment agencies, search firms, college recruiting, and job fairs.

There are several advantages in using advanced information technology to recruit. In a survey of 311 HR managers and 244 independent recruiters, respondents identified the following as the most important reasons, in descending order, for using information technology. At the top of the list was access to more candidates, followed by improved ability to target specific audiences, reduced cost of placing job postings, speed, absence of intermediaries, convenience, wide distribution of postings, quality of candidates, less paperwork, better resume management, and better service (Kay, 2000). Finn and Singh (2003) noted that because of such benefits, organizations were increasingly turning to information technology methods to enhance the recruitment function. A review of the literature revealed that increased use of information technology in recruitment was having a fundamental effect on all aspects of organizations' recruitment functions, including their HR personnel involved (the recruiters themselves). The use of information technology appeared to be leading to a transformation in recruiters needed skill set. With the implementation of advanced information technology systems, HR managers had to learn and even master the new technologies to perform their jobs effectively. This led to a retraining of HR managers and recruiting staff, which resulted in more technology-oriented recruiting HR departments and better service to stakeholders. The upgrading of HR personnel skills was leading to a transformation of the HR department itself. Snell, Pedigo, and Krawiec argued, "As informational technology changes operations within HR, it simultaneously recasts HR from solely an administrative function to one that is more oriented toward technical/professional expertise" (Snell, Pedigo, & Krawiec, 1995, p.162). The question was not whether institutions should use social media, but rather how they could use technology in their recruiting in a way that benefited other activities in their recruiting, selection, and hiring practices.

Important motivating behaviors for joining social networking sites were building relationships with people separated by geographic boundaries and others who had similar interests, and increasing personal visibility. HR personnel were beginning to access these sites to find posted personal information to use in making their hiring decisions (Jones & Behling, 2010). Some companies were giving considerable weight to information found on these sites in the employment process (Lorenz, 2009). The implications of this occurrence were explored in a paper written by Jones and Behling (2010), in which they conducted a review of what and how some employers used information available via social networking sites, including ethical, personal, security, and legal issues associated with using and accessing social networks. Jones and Behling detailed that in a 2009 CareerBuilder survey, 45 percent of employers reported using social networking sites to screen candidates; 35 percent found content that caused them not to hire the candidates. The same surveys also listed numerous reasons why employers ended up hiring candidates. The authors asserted, "Millions of people are interacting with others and posting information which they may believe is private and personal, only to find that access of this information may not be as restricted as they believe" (p. 591).

Social network websites were used because they were quick and cheap (Davidson et al., 2012; Slovensky & Ross, 2012). More specifically, only 17 percent of HR managers believed it took too much time and effort to screen social network websites in relation to the information gained. Sixty-three percent of those HR managers who used SNW screening indicated that this approach took little time and effort in relation to the information gained via social network website screening (SHRM, 2011). It was incumbent on HR departments to obtain as much information as possible about a candidate to avoid negligent hiring (Woska, 2007).

Aspiridis, Kazantzi, and Kyriakou (2013) investigated the opportunity to use social networking sites as an additional tool to advance in a modern world of HR. They asserted that the last few years' research had addressed the effect of social media in HR management and particularly, the effectiveness of the functions of attracting, selecting, and recruiting candidates. Social media sites such as Facebook, LinkedIn, and Twitter were used for recruitment, career advancement motivation, and employability evaluation. The way in which this relationship was viewed by potential and current employees as well as companies' HR departments and the emergence and application of all these in Greece was the scope of Aspiridis, Kazantzi, and Kyriakou's research. They conducted an exploratory study to examine the possibility of connecting the recruitment process and selection of social networking and determined whether this modern approach towards the current traditional way was effective (Rontaos & Repanis, 2006).

The methodology used in the Aspiridis, Kazantzi, and Kyriakou (2013) research was based on structured questionnaires administered via electronic mail (e-mail), which consisted of open-ended and multiple-choice (closed) questions. The questionnaires were administered to different age groups (18 and above) and different educational levels and occupations to cover all sides of the spectrum. In addition, a review of the academic literature was performed. The research findings indicated that the use of social media to attract and select candidates was being used to make a global pool of prospective employees. Moreover, prospective employers could eliminate distance and cost, as candidate selection could be made from anywhere in the world. Social networking sites were a tool for faster immediate job search for candidates by seeking key words; they could locate the desired job. HR managers could target audiences and define the types of people they were trying to attract.

In an Internet-rich world, networking with potential employers through social media sites could have helped pre-service and new teachers connect with experienced teachers, learn about potential job openings, and engage in professional conversations. By using social media sites to follow trends in education, pre-service teachers were able to stay current on educational policies and identify where they would like to begin their careers. Sites such as LinkedIn, Facebook and Twitter allowed people to post relevant news articles and other educational information. In addition, many national education organizations maintained pages on Facebook and other social media sites, connecting subscribers with specific sites that aligned with their own interests. Novice teachers could upload electronic portfolios, resumes, or artifacts demonstrating successful student teaching.

This quantitative study was conducted to address this important issue. The research focus was the use of Facebook, LinkedIn, and Twitter. Bickley and Kwok (2011) conducted a study of 430 employees. LinkedIn and Facebook use was the highest among employees aged 26 to 45. Employers, who used LinkedIn and Facebook in this study, had a higher potential of reaching young professionals in the work force. Social media was effective in targeting enthusiastic and interested job applicants (Bickley & Kwok, 2011). The Society for Human Resource Management (SHRM) (2013) reported that the use of the top three social media networks—Facebook, LinkedIn, and Twitter—was increasing in the recruitment and selection process. The use of social media had evolved into a more complex process of attracting top candidates. Social media had become a strategic tool in the recruitment and selection process to reach candidates (p.1). Griffin and Lake (2012) stated "While the literature in the business, psychology, and pharmacy fields shows initial investigations of the impact of social networking sites 'information on hiring decisions, this area has not been investigated in the field of education." There was a lack of available scholarly research around HR managers 'use of social networking websites in the employment process in public schools. The research findings in this study were expected to provide useful information regarding how human resource managers in New York State public schools use of social media as a recruiting, hiring and selection tool, self-efficacy and its effect on teacher retention. The research indicated whether further research into HR managers' use of data from social networking websites in hiring decisions was warranted. Finally, the results of this study might have helped to address this important issue and identify the effectiveness that might have existed.

MAIN FOCUS OF THE CHAPTER

Research Design and Methodology

The purpose of this quantitative study was to assess the relationship between Human resource (HR) managers' self-efficacy and the retention level of teachers' in their district (low versus high) and their use of social networking websites (SNWs), specifically Facebook, LinkedIn, and Twitter. The research examined the use of social media as a tool for identifying and hiring job candidates. Additionally, it centered on SNWs as a tool for screening job candidates. The study determined the effectiveness of the use of these networks when making hiring decisions.

Measuring Retention Rates

The turnover rate of teachers with fewer than five years of experience from NYS School Districts was gathered from the New York State Education Department (NYSED) database. The New York State Education Department is part of the State University of New York (SUNY) is one of the most complete, interconnected systems of educational services in the United States. The mission of this department is to raise the knowledge, skill, and opportunity of all the people in New York. Data in the report cards were submitted by local school district officials.

The document from which the information was extracted included the tables contained in the school report card (SRC) (2013), in which data about performance of designated subgroups were reported by total public schools (aggregated data for all districts and charter schools), county (aggregated data for all districts and charter schools in the county), needs-to-resource capacity (NRC), district, and public schools. To ensure student confidentiality, NYSED did not publish data for groups with fewer than five students or data that might have allowed readers to determine the performance of such groups easily.

Seven hundred and twenty-three school districts in New York State were identified. The mean turnover rate during the first five years was 22.98 percent (median = 22). The high turnover school districts M+ SD = 38.1 percent and higher. One hundred and seventeen schools were in this range. Low turnover school districts M – SD = 7 percent and below. One hundred and thirty-four school districts were identified. 38 responses.

Selection of Subjects

HR managers from New York State school districts selected were invited to participate in a survey to collect data for this study. Respondents were contacted by phone and by email that linked to an online survey that was completed online. Respondents in schools that were designated as low retention and high retention were sent different emails, respectively, and were linked to different surveys that were coded to the researcher as being applicable to either low retention or high retention, as appropriate. Respondents from both categories were not aware of any coding or differences in the completion of their survey.

All aspects of the online survey maintained anonymity of the respondents and the school districts to which they were employed. Respondents were able to choose, upon completion of the online survey to volunteer their email address for a raffle to be conducted later. Respondents could use their personal email address for the purpose of the raffle.

For this study, the data from the NYSED school report cards were downloaded. Data showing the turnover rate of teachers with fewer than five years of experience was accessed to determine school districts with high and low teacher turnover rates.

To measure HR managers' self-efficacy, their levels of use of social media in recruiting and selection, and retention of teachers, a questionnaire (Waite, 2015) was distributed by email to 250 New York State HR managers in the fall of 2014. A link to the questionnaire was sent to the participants in each identified group. To ensure that all the HR managers were in the designated high retention or low retention groupings, a separate survey link was provided. Permission was granted by the Dowling College Institutional Review Board prior to survey distribution.

Survey Instrument

The survey instrument was constructed in three parts. Part I of the instrument included demographic information related to the positions of the respondent in their school district, gender, and years of experience. In addition, in Part I of the questionnaire, respondents reported their social media use by responding to four yes or no questions. Respondents were asked to report which SNWs they found useful for hiring. The response was measured using not useful, slightly useful, somewhat useful, useful, and very useful. To measure the use of social media as a tool for recruitment by HR managers, statements were developed based on the Society for Human Resource Management poll (SHRM) (2011). Questions were modified from a survey conducted by the SHRM (2011). SHRM conducted a series of surveys of workers in the employment or recruiting job function about the use of SNWs in recruiting and screening job candidates. The final three questions were based on the research of Davidson et al. (2011). The range of allowed responses was *1 = strongly agree, 2 = agree, 3 = slightly agree, 4 = disagree, and 5 = strongly disagree.*

To measure the use of social media for screening and selection, 15 statements were developed. Three were based on the research by Davidson et al. (2011). Statements 24 and 25 were based on the research of Van Iddekinge et al. (2013). Statements 26 through 29 were taken from a survey (Swallow, 2011). For social media monitoring service, Repplier (2011) surveyed more than 30 hiring professionals to determine when and how job recruiters screened job candidates on different social networks. Additional statements were developed based on experience. The range of potential responses *was 1 = strongly agree, 2 = agree, 3 = slightly agree, 4 = disagree, and 5 = strongly disagree.*

The participants reported usefulness of SNWs LinkedIn, Twitter, Facebook and others were measured using a 5-point Likert scale: *5 = not useful, 4 = slightly useful, 3 = somewhat useful, 2 = useful, 1 = very useful.*

Statements from a Jobvite Social Recruiting Survey (2013) were modified to measure the benefits of the use of social media. The results of the survey showed how recruiters were leveraging social recruiting in addition to whether they were using it.

To measure self-efficacy, HR managers responded to 10 statements in the fourth section of the survey. This section was based on 10 statements from the general self-efficacy scale (GSE) created by Schwarzer and Jersalem (1992). The construct of perceived self-efficacy reflected an optimistic self-belief (Schwarzer, 1992). In samples from 23 nations, Cronbach's alphas ranged from .76 to .90, with the majority in the high 80s. The scale was unidimensional. This was the belief that one was able to perform a novel or difficult task, possibly having to cope with adversity in various domains of human functioning. The HR managers evaluated the

10 statements on a 5-point Likert scale about their perceived self-efficacy relating to their job performance. The scale was *1 = strongly agree, 2 = agree, 3 = slightly agree, 4 = disagree, and 5 = strongly disagree*. To see the entire survey, go to Waite (2005, page x)

To measure teacher retention, an open-ended question was constructed based on the research of Ingersoll (2004). For this study, Ingersoll's research was used as a guide in defining turnover as the departure of teachers from their teaching jobs in schools. New York State school district teacher turnover rate after five years was used.

Construct Validity

The survey instrument was administered to HR administrators. Forty-nine respondents completed the questionnaire. A factor analysis of the survey responses was conducted to evaluate the underlying structure of the responses to determine whether they supported the four variables initially identified. Recruitment, screening and selection, self-efficacy, and social media benefits were subjected to a factor analysis.

Eight of the 12 items examined recruitment from the findings of Davis et al. (2011). The results determined that four of the 12 items did not appropriately measure the variables according to their definitions. One of the 12 measured social media benefits, and three of the 12, measured screening. Two items were removed because the results determined that the items did not appropriately measure the variables per their definitions. One was from the area that measured social media benefits and the other was from the area that measured screening. Additionally, one of the 15 items that measured screening was reassigned to recruitment. One of the six items that measured social media benefits was reassigned to recruitment.

Because of the factor analysis and scree plot, an additional variable emerged. Screening became an independent variable. Four of the 15 items for screening and selection were reassigned to Screening. One of the 11 items from Screening was reassigned to Social Media Benefits. Three of the 10 items from Recruitment were reassigned to Screening.

One of the 10 items from Self-Efficacy and one of the six items measuring Social Media Benefits were delineated. Table 1.0 reports the deleted items after the factor analysis was conducted. The factor analysis decreased the number of items from 50 to 48. Table 1.0 presents the refined survey dimensions, items, score range, and reliability.

The survey was adjusted to combine agree and slightly agree as one item. If the respondents selected agree or slightly agree, it was ranked as a number 3 in the Likert scale. The 5-point Likert scale was converted to a 4-point scale. Table 1.0 reflected the change including the change in the range for each variable.

Table 1. Revised survey dimensions, items, score ranges, and reliability

	Items	# of Items	Range	Reliability
Demographics	1, 2, 3, 4	4		
Hiring	46,47,48,49	4		
Independent Variables				
Screening	8, 9, 11, 15, 16, 17, 18, 19, 24, 25, 27, 28	12	12 – 48	.940
Self-Efficacy	30, 32, 33, 34, 35, 36, 37, 38, 39	9	9 – 36	.916
Recruitment	5, 6, 7, 10, 12, 13, 45, 26	8	8 – 32	.897
Selection	20, 21, 22, 23	4	4 – 16	.977
Social Media Benefits	14, 41, 42, 43, 44, 29	6	6 – 24	.795
Dependent Variable				
Retention	50			

Waite, 2015, p 60.

SOLUTIONS AND RECOMMENDATIONS

How do human resource managers in school districts with high and low retention rates differ in their use of the three social media dimensions of self-efficacy, recruiting, and hiring and selection and in their perception of benefits of social media?

Quantitative Analysis

Descriptive statistics and independent samples t-tests were used to address this research question are presented in Table 2. The means, standard deviations, and results of the t tests were provided in Table 3.1. There were no significant differences found in the use of social media in Recruitment between HR managers in low retention districts (M = 17.50, SD= 4.08) and high retention districts (M = 15.64, SD = 4.18), t(32) = 1.29, p = .205. There were no significant differences found in the use of social media in Screening between HR managers in low retention districts (M = 27.43, SD = 7.10) and high retention districts (M= 25.75, SD = 7.50), t(35) = .696, p = .491. There were no significant differences found in Selection among HR managers in low retention districts (M = 9.14, SD = 2.78) and high retention districts (M = 8.94, SD = 3.28), t(35) = .206, p = .838. There were also no differences in perception of Social Media Benefits among HR managers' in low retention 77 districts (M = 16.70, SD = 2.05) and high retention districts (M = 15.79, SD= 3.56), t(32)= .949, p = .350. Finally, there were no differences in Self-Efficacy among HR managers in low retention districts (M = 29.79, SD = 3.66) and high retention districts (M= 29.71, SD = 3.27), t(31) = .061, p = .952.

Table 2. Descriptive statistics and t test for high and low retention rate school districts in their use of social media networks

Variable		*n*	Range	*M*	*SD*	*t*	*df*	*p*
Recruitment	Low High	20 14	8-32 8-32	17.50 15.64	4.08 4.18	1.292	32	.205
Screening	Low High	21 16	12-48 12-48	27.42 25.75	7.09 7.49	0.696	35	.491
Selection	Low High	21 16	4-16 4-16	9.14 8.93	2.78 3.27	0.206	35	.838
Self-Efficacy	Low High	19 14	9-36 9-36	29.78 29.71	3.66 3.26	0.061	31	.952
Social Media Benefits	Low High	20 14	6-24 6-24	16.70 15.79	2.05 3.55	0.949	32	.350

Waite, 2015 p.77.

These results indicated that there were no differences among the HR managers in high and low retention districts in their use of social media in hiring, selecting, and recruiting district employees, their perception of social media as a benefit in their work and in their self-efficacy.

Qualitative Analysis

Qualitative analyses explored the emergent themes, patterns, and discrepancies among HR managers' responses to the open-ended question, "How do you think hiring practices using/not using social media affect teacher retention?" HR managers' commentaries offered another set of data; "qualitative inquiry assists researchers in expanding their understanding and explanations of real life phenomena" (Beard, 2009, p. 47). This question came after question 49 of the survey. Table 3 presents the emergent themes and patterns as reported by HR managers.

By giving them the opportunity to express themselves allowed human resource managers to discuss their beliefs regarding social media's utility in hiring practices and teacher retention. Responses were in a narrative format. A descriptive analysis of themes and patterns was used to extract more data from respondents. The themes that emerged from the HR managers' responses were social media use, social media benefits, social media use in relationship to retention, and social media in relationship to recruitment.

The first theme identified was the non-use of social media in the hiring process. HR managers (28 percent) indicated that they did not use social media in the hiring process. In addition, they did not think it was useful. More specifically, one of the respondents stated, "I don't believe that I would ever, in the Public-School System,

Table 3. Themes, patterns, and discrepancies: human resource managers social media use influence teacher retention

Themes That Emerged for Social Media Use	Themes That Emerged for Social Media Benefits
• We have not found the need to use social media for hiring yet. We do not use social media at all (28%) • With the growing use of social media, I can see moving in that direction in the future (7%)	• Social media may provide additional information regarding a potential applicant it can provide greater insight into a candidate's background, tenure, professionalism, and as to their job interest (10%) • Social media is a tool used to receive high return of applicants (7%) • The information obtained through social media is subjective and must be verified (3%)
Themes that emerged for social media use in relationship to retention	Themes that emerged for the use of social media in relationship to recruitment
• Teacher retention is not directly affected using social media in the hiring process (21%) • Too early to tell if the use of social media would provide details of a potential candidate that will assist in determining teacher retention rates (7%)	• It is more involved in recruitment (7%) • We on occasion post openings on our Facebook page (7%) • We make little use of social media for recruiting or hiring purposes (3%)

use Facebook or Twitter in the hiring process." Overall, the patterns were consistent except for 7 percent of the HR managers who reported growing use of social media, "it will probably come to that in the future." Another supported that statement by responding, "I can see moving in that direction in the future." An interesting finding was that 3 percent indicated that social media was subjective and needed to be verified.

A second theme that emerged was the benefit of using social media. The pattern that emerged by the responding HR managers was that social media might provide additional information regarding a potential applicant (10 percent). Respondents reported that social media "can provide greater insight into a candidate's background, tenure, professionalism and as to their job interest." It was also reported that, "You can see how they felt or behaved at previous employment." Additionally, seven percent of the respondents stated, "the use of social media increases the responses to an ad" and "social media is used to receive high return of applicants." Finally, three percent of the HR managers asserted that the "the information obtained through social media is subjective and must be verified."

The third theme that emerged related to how HR managers believed their hiring practices and social media use influenced teacher retention. The majority (21 percent) of HR managers reported that they did not think retention was directly affected using social media in the hiring process. Several respondents felt there was "no evidence to of impact," no impact that could be measured," and "unknown data." Seven percent of the respondents indicated it was too early to tell if the use of social media would provide details of a potential candidate that would assist in determining teacher retention rates. It was noted that a respondent said, "Relationships are the key to retention." It was also reported that, "Teacher retention is based on salary and evaluation." These responses indicated an agreement with the other reported responses. One response stated that, "if you hire a bad apple you are not going to keep it," from which it could have been inferred that despite the use of social media, teacher retention is a complex matter.

Another theme that emerged was in relationship to the use of social media in recruitment. Seven percent of the HR managers indicated that social media was used in recruitment. It was reported that, "We on occasion post openings on our Facebook page." Additionally, one respondent reported that, "Social media is used to receive high return of applicants."

CONCLUSION

The literature showed initial investigations regarding the effect of social networking sites on hiring decisions within industries. Research about social media or the effect they might have had on HR managers was rapidly evolving (Bondarouk & Olivas-Lujan, 2013). This area had been minimally investigated in the education field. However, this research indicated there was relatively little use of social networking sites by school HR managers in the hiring process. Despite this, it should have been noted that social media had opened various means of communication and was not going away. Although there were many benefits of the use of social media in recruitment, screening and selection when making hiring decisions, there were ethical and legal issues that needed to be considered.

The results indicated that there were no significant differences in the use of social media in Recruitment between HR managers in low retention districts and high retention districts. There were no significant differences in the use of social media in Screening or in selection between HR managers in low retention districts and high retention districts. There were also no significant differences in the perception of the Benefits of Social Media between HR managers in low retention districts and high retention districts. Finally, there were no significant differences in Self-Efficacy between HR managers in low retention districts and high retention districts.

The results indicated that there were no significant differences between the HR managers in high and low retention districts in regards to their use of social media in hiring, selecting, and recruiting district employees, their perception of social media as a benefit in their work, and in their self-efficacy.

Additional research on the two groups' (high retention and low retention) hiring practices needs to be conducted to identify the other factors that contributed to the differences in their retention rates. Punia and Sharma (2008) showed the influence of organizational procurement practices on employee retention intentions based on personal and positional variables of employees. They concluded that the process of identifying candidates to fill open position had a positive relationship with their stay in the organization. From the results, there was a clear linkage of the procurement practices on employee retention intentions.

Baker-Doyle (2010) asserted that the problem of teacher turnover was linked to teacher recruitment, induction, and long-term retention efforts. Alongside the existing knowledge base, social network perceptions research could help provide a comprehensive picture of teacher recruitment and retention policies. Cochran-Smith (2004) argued there was a need to address teacher recruitment as it related to policy initiatives. The relationship between social media tools and teacher retention seemed especially important in the 21st century, when cost-conscious trustees and superintendents needed to find ways to reduce wasteful practices, which contributed to the retention of new teachers.

REFERENCES

Aspiridis, G., Kazantzi, V., & Kyriakou, D. (2013). Social networking websites and their effect in contemporary human resource management – A research approach. *Mediterranean Journal of Social Sciences*, *4*(1), 29–45.

Baker-Doyle, K. (2010). Beyond the labor market paradigm: A social network perspective on teacher recruitment and retention. *education policy analysis archives, 18*, 26.

Bandura, A. (1997). *Self-efficacy: The exercise of control*. USA: W.H. Freeman & Company.

Barber, A. E. (1998). *Recruiting employees*. Thousand Oaks, CA: Sage Publications.

Beard, K. (2009). *Nursing faculty roles in teaching racially and ethnically diverse nursing students in a registered nurse program* [Doctoral Dissertation]. Dowling College.

Bickley, S. L., & Kwok, L. (2011). *Social media as an employee recruitment tool. Sarah L. Bicky. Hospitality Management*. Syracuse University.

Boyd, D. M., & Ellison, N. B. (2008). Social network sites: Definition, history and scholarship. *Journal of Computer-Mediated Communication, 13*(1), 210–230. doi:10.1111/j.1083-6101.2007.00393.x

Brotherton, P. (2012). Social media and referrals are best sources for talent: A new survey shows that companies are investing more and more of their recruitment resources in social media and seeing it pay off. *T + D, 24.*

Cascio, W., & Aguinis, H. (2005). *Applied psychology in human resource management.* New Jersey: Prentice Hall.

Chapman, D. S., Uggerslev, K. L., Carroll, S. A., Piasentin, K. A., & Jones, D. A. (2005). Applicant attraction to organizations and job choice: A meta-analytic review of the correlates of recruiting outcomes. *The Journal of Applied Psychology*, *90*(5), 928–944. doi:10.1037/0021-9010.90.5.928 PMID:16162065

Cochran-Smith, M. (2004). Stayers, leavers, lovers, and dreamers: Insights about teacher retention. *Journal of Teacher Education*, *55*(5), 387–392. doi:10.1177/0022487104270188

Davidson, K. H., Maraist, C., & Bing, M. N. (2011). Friend or foe? The promise and pitfalls of using social networking sites for HR decisions. *Journal of Business and Psychology*, *26*(2), 153–159. doi:10.1007/s10869-011-9215-8

Evans, *T.* (2010). State schools lure more employers: Recruiters like one stop shopping for grads with solid academics, job skills, and record of success. *The Wall Street Journal,* B1- B8.

Finn, D., & Singh, P. (2003). The effects of information technology on recruitment. *Journal of Labor Research* *24*(3), 395-405. Griffin, M. M. & Lake, R. L. (2012). Social networking postings: Views from school principals. *Education Policy Analysis Archives*, *20*, 1–24.

Gatewood, R. D., & Field, H. S. (2001). Human resource selection (5th ed.). Fort Worth, TX: Dyrden Press.

Griffin, M. M., & Lake, R. L. (2012). Social networking postings: Views from school principals. *Education Policy Analysis Archives*, *20*, 1–24. doi:10.14507/epaa.v20n11.2012

Ingersoll, R. (2001). Teacher turnover and teacher shortages: An organizational analysis. *American Educational Research Journal*, *38*(3), 499–534. doi:10.3102/00028312038003499

Ingersoll, R. (2004). Four myths about America's teacher quality problem. In M. Smylie & D. Miretzky (Eds.), *Developing the teacher workforce: The 103rd yearbook of the National Society for the Study of Education* (pp. 1–33). Chicago: University of Chicago Press. doi:10.1111/j.1744-7984.2004.tb00029.x

Jobvite. (2013). Social Recruiting Survey Results. Retrieved from www.jobvite.com

Jones, C., & Behling, S. (2010). Uncharted waters: Using social networks in hiring decisions. *Issues in Information Systems*, *11*(1), 589–595.

Kay, A. (2000). Recruiters embrace the internet. *Information Week*, *778*, 72–80.

Kluemper, D. H., & Rosen, P. A. (2009). Future employment selection methods: Evaluating social networking websites. *Journal of Managerial Psychology*, *24*(6), 567–580. doi:10.1108/02683940910974134

Lipiec, J. (2001).. . *Human Resources Management Perspective at the Turn of the Century Public Personnel Management*, *30*, 137–146.

Lorenz, K. (2009). *Employers are digging up your digital dirt*. Retrieved May 2, 2013 from http:www.theworkbuzz.com/job-surveys/socialnetworks

Luszczynska, A., Scholz, U., & Scwarzer, R. (2005). The general self-efficacy scale: Multicultural validation studies. *The Journal of Psychology*, *139*(5), 439–457. doi:10.3200/JRLP.139.5.439-457 PMID:16285214

NYSED. (2013). The New York State School Report Card retrieved from https://reportcards.nysed.gov/

Pethe, S., Chaudhary, S., & Dhar, U. (1999). *Occupational self-efficacy Scale and Manual*. Agra: National Psychological Corporation.

Pfeiffer, J. (1994). *Competitive advantage through people*. Boston: Harvard Business School Press.

SHRM. (2014). Retrieved from http://www.shrm.org/TemplatesTools/Glossaries/HRTerms/Pages/r.aspx#sthash.4cBgpq2w.dpuf

Smith, P. G., & Wyatt, W. (2010). *Using social networking websites for hiring decisions: Legal and ethical considerations. Best Practices Forum Human Resources* (pp. 1–8). Arlington, TX: NJDHS.

Snell, S., Pedigo, P., & Krawie, G. (1995). Managing impact of information technology on human resource management. In G. Ferris, S. Rosen, & D. Barnum (Eds.), *Handbook of Human Resource Management* (pp. 159–174). Cambridge, Mass: Blackwell.

Tiwari, P., & Saxena, K. (2012). Human resource management practices: A comprehensive review. *Pakistan Business Review*, *13*(4), 667–705.

Van Iddekinge, C., Lanivich, S., Roth, P., & Junco, E. (2013). Social media for selection? Validity and adverse impact potential of a Facebook based assessment. *Journal of Management*, *15*, 1–25.

Waite, B. (2015). School human *resource managers' level of use of social networking websites on the dimensions of self-efficacy, decision making in recruiting, screening and selection of teachers and its impact on teacher retention* [Doctoral Dissertation].

Wilk, S. L., & Cappelli, P. (2003). Understanding the determinants of employer use of selection methods. *Personnel Psychology*, *56*(1), 103–124. doi:10.1111/j.1744-6570.2003.tb00145.x

Woska, W. J. (2007). Legal issues for HR Professionals: Reference checking/ background investigations. *Public Personnel Management*, *36*(1), 79–89. doi:10.1177/009102600703600106

KEY TERMS AND DEFINITIONS

Facebook: Launched in February 2004. It was a social networking website on which users could create personal profiles, share photos and statuses, and communicate with family, friends, classmates, and co-workers. Facebook allowed users to create pages for their businesses that were easily connected with their personal pages. Facebook had seen the biggest gain in overall usage by recruiters seeking potential candidates.

Human Resource Manager: The individual within an organization responsible for hiring new employees. Human resource management practices were defined as organizational activities directed at managing the pool of human resources and ensuring that the resources are employed towards the fulfillment of organizational goals.

LinkedIn: Was created for professional networking. It was launched in May 2003. People used LinkedIn to keep in touch with co-workers, as well as with people in their networking groups. Employers had begun to use this website to hire employees, using a tool called LinkedIn Recruiter.

Recruitment: Those practices and activities carried on by the organization with the primary purpose of attracting, screening, and selecting a qualified person for a job.

Retention: Organizational policies and practices designed to meet the diverse needs of employees created an environment that encouraged employees to remain employed.

Screening: The process in which a prospective employee was investigated to verify qualifications and confirm that the person would be a safe and appropriate match for the workplace.

Selection: The process of collecting and evaluating information about an individual to extend an offer of employment.

Self-Efficacy: Judgments or beliefs about one's capabilities to achieve tasks required to produce outcomes in specific situations or contexts. They affected thought processes and the level and persistency of motivation and emotion. Occupational self-efficacy was a domain-specific measure of self-efficacy. Occupational self-efficacy referred to the belief in one's own ability and competence to perform in an occupation.

Social Media: A connection of Web-based sites that allowed users to share information about them and to create partnerships with other users. Users could connect with other individuals around the globe and maintain a local network group.

Turnover: In the literature on teacher turnover and retention, the general term turnover was used as an umbrella term to describe the departure of teachers from their teaching jobs.

Twitter: Launched in July 2006. Twitter provided a service that allowed users to communicate through short posts known as tweets—posts of up to 140 text characters, which Twitter displayed on the user's profile page and delivered to the user's circle of friends, or by default, allowed anyone access to the user's page.

Compilation of References

21. st Century Partnership. (2008). 21st Century Skills Education and Competitiveness. USA: http://www.p21.org/storage/documents/21st_century_skills_education_and_competitiveness_guide.pdf

Abdalla, S., Thompson, S., & Marks, N. (2008). Estimating Worldwide Satisfaction. *Ecological Economics*, *47*(1), 35–42. retrieved from http://www.uvm.edu/pdodds/files/papers/others/everything/abdallah2007a.pdf doi:10.1016/j.ecolecon.2007.11.009

Abowd, J., & Card, D. (1989). On the Covariance Structure of Earnings and Hours Changes. Econometrica, 57(2), 411-445.

Agosta, L. (2004). Data Mining is Dead-Long Live Predictive Analytics! *Information & Management*, *14*(1), 37.

Aguilar, M. K. (2009, February). SEC Mandates XBRL; Filings to Start by July 2009. *Compliance Week*, *6*(61), 14–15.

Alavi, M., Yoo, Y., & Vogel, D. R. (1997). Using information technology to add value to management education. *Academy of Management Journal*, *40*(6), 1310–1333. doi:10.2307/257035

Allport, G. W. (1954). The historical background of modern social psychology. In G. Lindley (Ed.), *Handbook of social psychology* (Vol. 1). Reading, MA: Addison-Wesley.

Ambrosio, J. (2013). Changing the subject: Neoliberalism and accountability in public education. *Educational Studies*, *49*(4), 316–333. doi:10.1080/00131946.2013.783835

Aron, L., & Loprest, P. (2012). Disability and the education system. *The Future of Children*, *22*(1), 97–122. doi:10.1353/foc.2012.0007 PMID:22550687

Ashmore, R. D., & Del Boca, F. K. (1981). Conceptual approaches to stereotypes and stereotyping. In D. L. Hamilton (Ed.), *Cognitive processes in stereotyping and intergroup behavior* (pp. 1–35). Hillsdale, NJ: Lawrence Erlbaum Associates.

Aspiridis, G., Kazantzi, V., & Kyriakou, D. (2013). Social networking websites and their effect in contemporary human resource management – A research approach. *Mediterranean Journal of Social Sciences*, *4*(1), 29–45.

Astin, A. W. (1997). How good is your institutions retention rate? *Research in Higher Education*, *38*(6), 647–658. doi:10.1023/A:1024903702810

Atenas, J., Havemann, L., & Priego, E. (2015). Open Data as Open Educational Resources: Towards transversal skills and global citizenship. *Open Praxis*, *7*(4), 377–389. doi:10.5944/openpraxis.7.4.233

Augusztinovics, M. (2002). Issues in pension system design. *International Social Security Review*, *55*(1), 21–35. doi:10.1111/1468-246X.00112

Austin, S., Wadlington, E., & Bitner, J. (2001). Effect of beliefs about mathematics on math anxiety and self-concept in elementary teachers. *Education*, *112*(3), 390–396.

Avolio, B. J., Jung, D. I., Murry, W., & Sivasbramaniam, N. (1996). Building highly developed teams: Focusing on shared leadership process, efficacy, trust, and performance.

Ayala, C. C., Shavelson, R. J., Ruiz-Primo, M., Brandon, P. R., Yin, Y., Furtak, E., & Tomita, M. K. et al. (2008). From formal embedded assessments to reflective lessons: The development of formative assessment studies. *Applied Measurement in Education*, *21*(4), 315–334. doi:10.1080/08957340802347787

Baars, H., & Kemper, H.-G. (2008). Management Support with Structured and Unstructured Data—An Integrated Business Intelligence Framework. *Information Systems Management*, *25*(2), 132–148. doi:10.1080/10580530801941058

Bachman, H. J., Coley, R. L., & Chase-Lansdale, P. L. (2009). Is maternal marriage beneficial for low-income adolescents? *Applied Developmental Science*, *13*(4), 153–171. doi:10.1080/10888690903287633 PMID:20485456

Baer, L., & Duin, A. H. (2014). Retain Your Students! The Analytics, Policies and Politics of Reinvention Strategies. *Planning for Higher Education*, *42*(3), 30.

Baker-Doyle, K. (2010). Beyond the labor market paradigm: A social network perspective on teacher recruitment and retention. *education policy analysis archives, 18*, 26.

Baker, M., & Johnston, P. (2010). The Impact of Socioeconomic Status on High Stakes Testing Reexamined. *Journal of Instructional Psychology*, *37*(3).

Baker, M., Sigmon, J., & Nugent, M. (2001). *Truancy reduction: Keeping students in school.* Washington, DC: Office of Juvenile Justice and Delinquency Prevention, U. S. Department of Justice.

Bakula, N. (2010). The Benefits of Formative Assessments for Teaching and Learning. *Science Scope*, *34*(1), 37–43.

Balfanz, R., & Byrnes, V. (2012). The importance of being in school: A report on absenteeism in the nation's public schools. *Education Digest: Essential Readings Condensed for Quick Review*, *78*(2), 4–9.

Bandura, A. (1997). *Self-efficacy: The exercise of control.* USA: W.H. Freeman & Company.

Barber, A. E. (1998). *Recruiting employees.* Thousand Oaks, CA: Sage Publications.

Barlow, A. T., & Reddish, J. M. (2006). Mathematical myths: Teacher candidates' beliefs and the implications for teacher educators. *Teacher Educator, 41*(3), 145–157. doi:10.1080/08878730609555380

Basham, L. M. (2010). Transformational and transactional leaders in higher education. *International Review of Business Research Papers, 6*(6), 141–152.

Beard, K. (2009). *Nursing faculty roles in teaching racially and ethnically diverse nursing students in a registered nurse program* [Doctoral Dissertation]. Dowling College.

Beard, K. S., Hoy, W. K., & Woolfhook-Hoy, A. (2010). Academic optimism of individual teachers: Confirming a new construct. *Teaching and Teacher Education, 26*(5), 1136–1144. doi:10.1016/j.tate.2010.02.003

Becker, G. (1967). *Human capital and the personal distribution of income; an analytical approach.* Ann Arbor: Institute of Public Administration.

Becker, W., & Lewis, D. (1993). *Higher education and economic growth.* London: Kluwer Academic Publishers. doi:10.1007/978-94-015-8167-7

Bellanca, J. (1998, May). Teaching for intelligence: in search of best practices. *Phi Delta kappan, 79*(9).

Benefits of an Advanced Regents Diploma – Guidance Resources. (n. d.). Retrieved May 7, 2016, from http://www.hphsnyc.org/apps/pages/index.jsp?uREC_ID=246434&type=d&pREC_ID=568540

Bertot, J. C., Jaeger, P. T., & Grimes, J. M. (2010). Using ICTs to create a culture of transparency: E-government and social media as openness and anti-corruption tools for society. *Government Information Quarterly, 27*(3), 264–271. doi:10.1016/j.giq.2010.03.001

Best of the best business websites. (2016). *Reference & User Services Quarterly, 56*(2), 130-134. Retrieved from http://jerome.stjohns.edu:81/login?url=http://search.proquest.com.jerome.stjohns.edu:81/docview/1860278455?accountid=14068

Bickley, S. L., & Kwok, L. (2011). *Social media as an employee recruitment tool. Sarah L. Bicky. Hospitality Management.* Syracuse University.

Birdsall, N., & Sabot, R. (Eds.). (1996). *Opportunity foregone: Education in Brazil. Washington, D.C.: Inter-American Development Bank.* Baltimore, Md.: John Hopkins University Press.

Bizarro, P., & Garcia, A. (2010). XBRL—Beyond the basics. *The CPA Journal, 80*(5), 62.

Black, A. T., Seder, R. C., & Kekahio, W. (2014). *Review of research on student nonenrollment and chronic absenteeism: A report for the Pacific Region.* Washington, DC: U.S. Department of Education.

Black, P., & Wiliam, D. (1998). Inside the black box: Raising standards through classroom assessment. *Phi Delta Kappan*, 92(1), 139–148.

Blaug, M. (1985). Where are we now in the economics of education? *Economics of Education Review*, *4*(1), 17–28. doi:10.1016/0272-7757(85)90034-2

Boggs, O. (2011). The rise of childhood poverty in Georgia: Implications for public school planning and pedagogy.

Bok, D. (2010). *The Politics of Happiness: What Government Can Learn from the New Research on Well-Being*. USA: Princeton University Press. doi:10.1515/9781400832194

Boyd, D. M., & Ellison, N. B. (2008). Social network sites: Definition, history and scholarship. *Journal of Computer-Mediated Communication*, *13*(1), 210–230. doi:10.1111/j.1083-6101.2007.00393.x

Brookhart, S. M., & Moss, C. M. (2013, May). Leading by learning. *Phi Delta Kappan*, *94*(8), 13-17.

Brotherton, P. (2012). Social media and referrals are best sources for talent: A new survey shows that companies are investing more and more of their recruitment resources in social media and seeing it pay off. *T + D, 24.*

Bryman, A. (2007). Effective leadership in higher education: A literature review. *Studies in Higher Education*, *32*(6), 693–710. doi:10.1080/03075070701685114

Buhl, H. U. (2013). Interview with Martin Petry on Big Data. *Business & Information Systems Engineering*, *5*(2), 101–102. doi:10.1007/s12599-013-0253-9

Buhl, H. U., Röglinger, M., Moser, F., & Heidemann, J. (2013). Big Data. *Wirtschaftsinformatik*, *55*(2), 63–68. doi:10.1007/s11576-013-0350-x

Burke, M. A., & Sass, T. (2008). *Classroom peer effects and student achievement*. National Center for Analysis of Longitudinal Data in Education Research.

Burns, J. M. (2003). *Transforming leadership: A new pursuit of happiness* (Vol. 213). Grove Press.

Cable, R., & Healy, P. (2013, May). XBRL in the accounting curriculum. *Paper presented at the American Accounting Association Mid-Atlantic Region Annual Meeting*, Parsippany, NJ.

Cai, L., & Zhu, Y. (2015). The Challenges of Data Quality and Data Quality Assessment in the Big Data Era. *Data Science Journal*, *14*(0), 2. doi:10.5334/dsj-2015-002

Cancian, M., & Reed, D. (2009). Family structure, childbearing, and parental employment: Implications for the level and trend in poverty. *Focus (San Francisco, Calif.)*, *26*(2), 21–26.

Capozzoli, E., & Farewell, S. (2010). SEC XBRL filing requirements: An instructional case on tagging financial statement disclosures. *Issues in Accounting Education*, *25*(3), 489–511. doi:10.2308/iace.2010.25.3.489

Carnoy, M., & Rothstein, R. (2013). What Do International Tests Really Show About US Student Performance? Washington, DC: Economic Policy Institute. Retrieved from http://www.epi.org/publication/us-student-performance-testing/

Carnoy, M. (1994). *Economics of education: research and studies*. Oxford: Pergamon.

Carroll, T., Fulton, K., & Doerr, H. (2010). *Team up for 21st century teaching and learning: What research and practice reveal about professional learning*. Washington, DC: National Commission on Teaching and America's Future.

Cascio, W., & Aguinis, H. (2005). *Applied psychology in human resource management*. New Jersey: Prentice Hall.

Chang, H., & Romero, M. (2008). Present, engaged and accounted for: The critical importance of addressing chronic absence in the early grades. *National Center for Children in Poverty*. Retrieved from http://www.nccp.org/publications/pdf/text_837.pdf

Chang, R., Ghoniem, M., Kosara, R., Ribarsky, W., Yang, J., Suma, E., . . . Sudjianto, A. (2007). Wirevis: Visualization of categorical, time-varying data from financial transactions. *Paper presented at the IEEE Symposium on Visual Analytics Science and Technology VAST '07*.

Chang, R. M., Kauffman, R. J., & Kwon, Y. (2014). Understanding the paradigm shift to computational social science in the presence of big data. *Decision Support Systems*, *63*, 67–80. doi:10.1016/j.dss.2013.08.008

Chapman, D. S., Uggerslev, K. L., Carroll, S. A., Piasentin, K. A., & Jones, D. A. (2005). Applicant attraction to organizations and job choice: A meta-analytic review of the correlates of recruiting outcomes. *The Journal of Applied Psychology*, *90*(5), 928–944. doi:10.1037/0021-9010.90.5.928 PMID:16162065

Chaudhuri, S., Dayal, U., & Narasayya, V. (2011). An overview of business intelligence technology. *Communications of the ACM*, *54*(8), 88–98. doi:10.1145/1978542.1978562

Civil Rights Data Collection (CRDC). (n. d.). About the Civil Rights Data Collection. Retrieved from http://ocrdata.ed.gov/downloads/AboutTheCRDC.pdf

Civil Rights Data Collection (CRDC). (n. d.). FAQ/User guide – Overview. Retrieved from http://ocrdata.ed.gov/Overview

Clifford, M., Behrstock-Sherratt, E., & Fetters, J. (2012). *The ripple effect: A synthesis of research on principal influence to inform performance evaluation design*. American Institutes for Research. A quality School Leadership. *Issue Brief*.

Cochran-Smith, M. (2004). Stayers, leavers, lovers, and dreamers: Insights about teacher retention. *Journal of Teacher Education*, *55*(5), 387–392. doi:10.1177/0022487104270188

Cohen, Y. (2015). Structural equation modeling to predict fourth grade student achievement.

Coleman, J. S., Cambell, E., Hobson, C., McPartland, J., Mood, A., Weinfeld, F., & York, R. (1966). *Equality of educational opportunity*. Washington, DC: U.S. Government Printing Office.

Collie, R. J., Shapka, J. D., & Perry, N. E. (2011). Predicting teacher commitment: The impact of school climate and social-emotional learning. *Psychology in the Schools*, *48*(10), 1034–1048. doi:10.1002/pits.20611

Collie, R. J., Shapka, J. D., & Perry, N. E. (2012). School climate and social-emotional learning: Predicting teacher stress, job satisfaction, and teaching efficacy. *Journal of Educational Psychology*, *104*(4), 1189–1204. doi:10.1037/a0029356

Common Core State Standards Initiative. (2015, July 1). Retrieved from http;//www.corestandards.org

Connelly, G. (2014). Where the buck stops. *Principal*, May/June, 56–57.

Corkern, S. M., & Morgan, M. I. (2012). Introduce XBRL to business students. *American Journal of Business Education*, *5*(3), 319–323.

Cronin, J., & Jensen, N. (2104, September). The phantom collapse of student achievement in New York. *Phi Delta Kappan*, *96*(2), 60-66.

Crosnoe, R., & Wildsmith, E. (2011). Nonmarital fertility, family structure, and the early school achievement of young children from different race/ethnic and immigration groups. *Applied Developmental Science*, *15*(3), 156–170. doi:10.1080/10888691.2011.587721 PMID:21894243

Cuff, E. (2014). The effects and importance of technology in the research process. *Journal of Educational Technology Systems*, *94*(3), 75–97. doi:10.2190/ET.43.1.f

Cuillier, D., & Piotrowski, S. J. (2009). Internet information-seeking and its relation to support for access to government records. *Government Information Quarterly*, *26*(3), 441–449. doi:10.1016/j.giq.2009.03.001

Daisi, O. (2011, January 13). The Impact of Human Resource Development on Economic Growth in Nigeria: An Empirical Investigation (1902-2008). doi:10.2139/ssrn.1739492

Daniel, B. (2015). Big Data and analytics in higher education: Opportunities and challenges. *British Journal of Educational Technology*. doi:10.1111/bjet.12230

Daniel, B. K., & Butson, R. (2013). Technology enhanced analytics (TEA) in higher education. *Paper presented at the Proceedings of the International Conference on Educational Technologies*.

Daniel, B., & Butson, R. (2014). Foundations of Big Data and Analytics in Higher Education. Retrieved from http://engineering.nyu.edu/files/ICAS2014-Proceedings-Publication.pdf

DataO. E. C. D. © OECD, https://data.oecd.org

Davenport, T. H., Barth, P., & Bean, R. (2013). How 'big data' is different. *MIT Sloan Management Review*, *54*(1).

Davidson, K. H., Maraist, C., & Bing, M. N. (2011). Friend or foe? The promise and pitfalls of using social networking sites for HR decisions. *Journal of Business and Psychology*, *26*(2), 153–159. doi:10.1007/s10869-011-9215-8

De la Maisonneuve, C. (2015). Reforming the pension system to increase coverage and equity in Colombia (Working Papers No. 1235). OECD Economics Department. Paris: OECD Publishing. doi:10.1787/5js0cqrr97s4-en

De Meulmester, J. C., & Rochet, D. (1995). A causality analysis of the link between higher education and economic development. *Economics of Education Review*, *144*(4), 351-361.

Deal, T., & Peterson, K. D. (1999). *Shaping school culture: The heart of leadership*. San Francisco, CA: Jossey-Bass.

Debreceny, R., & Farewell, S. (2010). XBRL in the Accounting Curriculum. *Issues in Accounting Education*, *25*(3), 379–403. doi:10.2308/iace.2010.25.3.379

Delen, D., & Demirkan, H. (2013). Data, information and analytics as services. *Decision Support Systems*, *55*(1), 359–363. doi:10.1016/j.dss.2012.05.044

Deming, W. E. (1986). *Out of the crisis*. Cambridge, MA: Massachusetts Institute of Technology, Center for Advanced Engineering Study.

DeNavas-Walt, C., & Proctor, B. D. (2014). Income and poverty in the United States - 2013. *U.S. Census –. Current Population Reports. Series P-28, Special Censuses*, (September), 60–249.

Denison, E. F. (1971). Education and the economics of human capital. In R. A. Wykstra (Ed.), Education and Economic Growth. New York Free Press.

DePrince, A., & Morris, P. (2008, April). The Effects of Education on the Natural Rate of Unemployment. *Business Economics (Cleveland, Ohio)*, *43*, 45. doi:10.2145/20080205

Desimone, L. (1999). Linking parent involvement with student achievement: Do race and income matter? *The Journal of Educational Research*, *93*(1), 11–30. doi:10.1080/00220679909597625

Dhar, V., & Sundararajan, A. (2007). Information Technologies in Business: A Blueprint for Education and Research.

Diebold, F. X., Cheng, X., Diebold, S., Foster, D., Halperin, M., Lohr, S., & Pospiech, M. (2012). *A Personal Perspective on the Origin (s) and Development of "Big Data"*.

Diener, E., Emmons, R. A., Larsen, R. J., & Griffin, S. (1985). The Satisfaction with Life Scale. *Journal of Personality Assessment*, *49*(1), 71–75. doi:10.1207/s15327752jpa4901_13 PMID:16367493

Diploma Requirements. (n. d.). Retrieved May 7, 2016, from http://www.p12.nysed.gov/part100/pages/1005.html

Direction, S. (2013). So, are the geeks inheriting the earth?: Big Data, big decisions and best practice for information management. *Strategic Direction*, *29*(9).

Donady, B., & Tobias, S. (1977, November). Math Anxiety. *Teacher, 95*(3), 71-74.

Drago-Severson, E. (2012). New opportunities for principal leadership: Shaping school climate for enhanced teacher development. *Teachers College Record, 114*, 1–44. PMID:24013958

Drigas, A. S., & Leliopoulos, P. (2014). The Use of Big Data in Education. *International Journal of Computer Science Issues, 11*(5), 58.

DuFour, R., DuFour, R., & Eaker, R. (2008). *Revising professional learning communities at work: New insights for improving schools*. Bloomington, IN: Solution Tree Press.

DuFour, R., & Mattos, M. (2013). How do principals really improve schools? *Educational Leadership, 70*(7), 34–40.

Du, H., Vasarhelyi, M. A., & Zheng, X. (2013). XBRL mandate: Thousands of filing Errors and so what? *Journal of Information Systems, 27*(1), 61–78. doi:10.2308/isys-50399

Duncan, G. J., Yeung, W. J., Brooks-Gunn, J., & Smith, J. R. (1998). How much does childhood poverty affect the life chances of children? *American Sociological Review, 63*(3), 406–423. doi:10.2307/2657556

Dupin-Bryant, P. A., & Olsen, D. H. (2014). Business Intelligence, Analytics And Data Visualization: A Heat Map Project Tutorial. *International Journal of Management & Information Systems, 18*(3), 185–200.

Duvall, R. (2001, January) Economic Education: Building on Strength, the Key to the Future

Dworkin, A. G., Haney, C. A., Dworkin, R. J., & Telschov, R. L. (1990). Stress and illness behavior among urban public school teachers. *Educational Administration Quarterly, 26*(1), 60–72. doi:10.1177/0013161X90026001004

Dziuban, C., Moskal, P., Cavanagh, T., & Watts, A. (2012). Analytics that Inform the University: Using Data You Already Have. *Journal of Asynchronous Learning Networks, 16*(3), 21–38.

Eagan, A. (2015). How the Shift in High Stakes Testing Impacts Students of Low Socioeconomic Status in a Suburban Junior High School [Education and Human Development Master's Thesis].

Easterlin, R. (2013, January). Happiness and Economic Growth: The Evidence (IZA Discussion Paper No. 7187). University of Southern California.

Easton, P., & Klees, S. (1990). Education and the economy: Considering alternative perspectives. *Prospects, 20*(4), 413–428. Retrieved from http://poseidon01.ssrn.com/delivery.php?ID=150124106095081120016088118092103022031075 03601204901 810601111101506901504608802408403100402905204012708609009012012 7123 027104126121123102101107082095029121076068104092017115067&EXT=pdf doi:10.1007/BF02195115

Eckerson, W. W. (2006). Deploying dashboards and scorecards. The Data Warehouse Institute, 1-24.

Epstein, J. L., Coates, L., Salinas, K. C., Sanders, M. G., & Simon, B. S. (1997). *School, family and community partnerships*. San Francisco: Corwin Press.

Epstein, J. L., Sanders, M. G., Sheldon, S., Simon, B. S., & Salinas, K. C. (2009). *School, family, and community partnerships: Your handbook for action*. Thousand Oaks, CA: Corwin Press.

Epstein, J., & Rodriguez-Jansorn, N. (2004). School, family, and community partnerships link the plan. *Education Digest*, *69*(6), 19–24.

Evans, J. R. (2012). Business analytics: the next frontier for decision sciences.

Evans, *T*. (2010). State schools lure more employers: Recruiters like one stop shopping for grads with solid academics, job skills, and record of success. *The Wall Street Journal,* B1- B8.

Evans, A. M., & Campos, A. (2013). Open government initiatives: Challenges of citizen participation. *Journal of Policy Analysis and Management*, *32*(1), 172–185. doi:10.1002/pam.21651

Fall, F., & Bloch, D. (2014). Overcoming Vulnerabilities of Pension Systems (Working Papers No. 1133). OECD Economics Department. Paris: OECD Publishing. doi:10.1787/5jz1591prxth-en

Fama, E. F. (1970). Efficient capital markets: A review of theory and empirical work. *The Journal of Finance*, *25*(2), 383–417. doi:10.2307/2325486

Fan, X., & Chen, M. J. (1998). Academic achievement of rural school students: A multi-year comparison with their peers in suburban and urban schools.

Fang, J. (2009). How CPAs can master XBRL. *The CPA Journal*, *79*(5), 70.

Fang, J. (2011). Why is the U.S. XBRL conversion process so slow? *The CPA Journal*, *81*(1), 1.

Fang, J. (2013). The progress of XBRL conversion: Reviewing the rules, consequences, and potential remedies. *The CPA Journal*, *83*(2), 68.

Fedotenkov, I., & Meijdam, L. (2013). Crisis and Pension System Design in the EU: International Spillover Effects Via Factor Mobility and Trade. *De Economist*, *161*(2), 175-197. doi:10.1007/s10645-013-9207-3

Finn, D., & Singh, P. (2003). The effects of information technology on recruitment. *Journal of Labor Research 24*(3), 395-405. Griffin, M. M. & Lake, R. L. (2012). Social networking postings: Views from school principals. *Education Policy Analysis Archives*, *20*, 1–24.

Fitz-Enz, J. (n. d.). The ROI of Human Capital: Measuring the Economic Value of Employee Performance

Forman, K. & Markson, C. (2016, May). The efficacy of teacher evaluations in New York City: A tale of two districts. *New York Academy of Public Education*, *5*.

Forman, K., & Markson, C. (2015). Is "effective" the new "ineffective"? A crisis with the New York State teacher evaluation system. *Journal for Leadership and Instruction*, *14*(2), 5–11.

Franks, E. E. (2014). *State of the art analytics and managers in the defense industry*. CAPELLA UNIVERSITY.

French, E. (2005). The Effects of Health, Wealth, and Wages on Labour Supply and Retirement Behaviour. *The Review of Economic Studies*, *72*(2), 395–427. doi:10.1111/j.1467-937X.2005.00337.x

Frey, B., & Stutzer, A. (2001). *Happiness and Economics: How the Economy and Institutions Affect Human Well-Being*. Princeton University Press.

Fullan, M. (1985). Change process and strategies at the local level. *The Elementary School Journal*, *85*(3), 391–421. doi:10.1086/461411

Fullan, M. (1996). Professional culture and educational change. *School Psychology Review*, *25*(4), 496–500.

Fullan, M. (1998). Leadership for the 21st century: Breaking the bonds of dependency. *Educational Leadership*, *55*, 6–11.

Fullan, M. (2001). *Leading in a Culture of Change*. San Francisco: Jossey-Bass.

Fullan, M. (2011). *Change leader: Learning to do what matters most*. John Wiley & Sons.

Fullan, M., & Scott, G. (2009). *Turnaround leadership for higher education*. John Wiley & Sons.

Futscher, M. R. (2013). Principals' perceptions about the impact of the New York State Annual Professional Performance Review legislation on the instructional practices of New York public schools. *Dissertations Abstracts International Section A, 75*.

Galston, W. A. (2001). Political knowledge, political engagement, and civic education. *Annual Review of Political Science*, *4*(1), 217–234. doi:10.1146/annurev.polisci.4.1.217

Gandomi, A., & Haider, M. (2015). Beyond the hype: Big data concepts, methods, and analytics. *International Journal of Information Management*, *35*(2), 137–144. doi:10.1016/j.ijinfomgt.2014.10.007

Gardner, H. (1983). *Frames of Mind: Theory of multiple intelligences*. New York: Basic Books.

Garmezy, N. (1991). Resiliency and vulnerability to adverse development outcomes associated with poverty. *The American Behavioral Scientist*, *34*(4), 416–430. doi:10.1177/0002764291034004003

Gatewood, R. D., & Field, H. S. (2001). Human resource selection (5th ed.). Fort Worth, TX: Dyrden Press.

Gibson, S., & Dembo, M. H. (1984). Teacher efficacy: A construct validation. *Journal of Educational Psychology*, *76*(4), 569–582. doi:10.1037/0022-0663.76.4.569

Giorno, C., & Adda, J. (2016). Improving the pension system and the welfare of retirees in Israel (Working Papers No. 1288). OECD Economics Department. Paris: OECD Publishing. doi:10.1787/5jm0xf1fsqvf-en

Goddard, R. D., Sweetland, S. R., & Hoy, W. K. (2000). Academic emphasis of urban elementary schools and student achievement in reading and mathematics: A multilevel analysis. *Educational Administration Quarterly*, *36*(5), 683–702. doi:10.1177/00131610021969164

Gordon, M., & Seashore-Louis, K. (2009). Linking parent and community involvement with student achievement: Comparing principal and teacher perceptions of stakeholder influence. *American Journal of Education*, *116*(1), 1–31. doi:10.1086/605098

Gottfredson, G., Gottfredson, D., Payne, A., & Gottfredson, N. (2005). School climate predictors of school disorder: Results from a national study of delinquency prevention. *Journal of Research in Crime and Delinquency*, *42*(4), 412–444. doi:10.1177/0022427804271931

Govan, C. J. (2013, January 1). *Observing the academic performance and student graduation rates of grade 8 students who failed Texas State Assessments*. Retrieved from http://www.proquest.com/en-US/products/dissertations/individuals.shtml)

Gregory, P. (1986). *The myth of market failure, employment and the labor market in Mexico*. Baltimore, London: The Johns Hopkins University Press, Published for the World Bank.

Griffin, M. M., & Lake, R. L. (2012). Social networking postings: Views from school principals. *Education Policy Analysis Archives*, *20*, 1–24. doi:10.14507/epaa.v20n11.2012

Guha, S., & Leonard, J. (2002, January/February). Motivation in elementary mathematics: How students and teachers benefit from computers. *TechTrends*, *46*(1), 40–43. doi:10.1007/BF02772036

Hair, J. F. Jr. (2007). Knowledge creation in marketing: The role of predictive analytics. *European Business Review*, *19*(4), 303–315. doi:10.1108/09555340710760134

Hampden-Thompson, G. (2009). Are two better than one? A comparative study of achievement gaps and family structure. *Compare: A Journal of Comparative and International Education*, *39*(4), 513–529.

Hanushek, E., & Woessmann, L. (2007, February 1). The Role of Education Quality for Economic Growth (Working Paper No. 4122). World Bank Policy Research. Retrieved from http://ssrn.com/abstract=960379

Hanushek, E., & Lindseth, A. (2009). *Schoolhouses, courthouses, and statehouses: Solving the funding-achievement puzzle in America's public schools*. Princeton University Press. doi:10.1515/9781400830251

Hargreaves, C. A., & Ding, L. (2014). Business Analytics as a Framework for an Evolving Multi-Agent System. *Journal on Computing*, *2*(3).

Harris, T., & Morsfield, S. (2012). An evaluation of the current state and future of XBRL and interactive data for investors and analysts (White Paper No. 3). *Columbia University, Center for Excellence in Accounting and Security Analysis*.

Harris, J. G., Craig, E., & Light, D. A. (2011). Talent and analytics: New approaches, higher ROI. *The Journal of Business Strategy*, *32*(6), 4–13. doi:10.1108/02756661111180087

Harrison, L. M. (2011). Transformational leadership, integrity, and power. *New Directions for Student Services*, *2011*(135), 45–52. doi:10.1002/ss.403

Haycock, K. (1998). Good teaching matters... A lot. *Organization of American Historians*, *13*(1), 61–66.

Henry, K. L. (2007). Who's skipping school: Characteristics of truants in 8th and 10th grade. *The Journal of School Health*, *77*(1), 29–35. doi:10.1111/j.1746-1561.2007.00159.x PMID:17212757

Hernandez, D. J. (2011). *Double Jeopardy: How third-grade reading skills and poverty influence high school graduation*. The Anne E. Casey Foundation.

Hill, S. T. (1982). You can't afford, for teachers to be out, so take these steps now to stop absenteeism. *ERIC Document Reproduction Service ED*, *214*, 233.

Hirsh, S. (2005). Professional development and closing the achievement gap. *Theory into Practice*, *44*(1), 38–44. doi:10.1207/s15430421tip4401_6

Hoffelder, K. (2012). *Finance Execs Find XBRL Useless*. Retrieved December 20, 2013 from http://ww2.cfo.com/gaap-ifrs/2012/11/finance-execs-find-xbrl-useless/

Holland, H. (2005). Teaching teachers: Professional development to improve student achievement. Research Points: Essential Information for Educational Policy, 3(1), 1–4. Washington, DC: American Educational Research Association.

Holmstrom, A. (2010). District finds the right equation to improve math instruction. *Journal of Staff Development*, 31(6), 58–62.

Holsapple, C., Lee-Post, A., & Pakath, R. (2014). A unified foundation for business analytics. *Decision Support Systems*, *64*, 130–141. doi:10.1016/j.dss.2014.05.013

Hoover, J. J. (2010). Special Education Eligibility Decision Making in Response to Intervention Models. *Theory into Practice*, *49*(4), 289–296. doi:10.1080/00405841.2010.510752

Hopkins, M. S. (2011). Big Data, analytics and the path from insights to value. *MIT Sloan Management Review*, *52*(2), 21-22. Retrieved from http://0-search.ebscohost.com.library.dowling.edu/login.aspx?direct=true&db=buh&AN=57750727&site=ehost-live

Hosen, R., Solovey-Hosen, D., & Stern, L. (2003, Spring). Education and Capital Development: Capital as Durable Personal, Social, Economic and Political Influences on the Happiness of Individuals. *Education*, *123*(3).

Houchens, G., & Cabrera, J. (2013). Preparing principals for instructional leadership: Integrating the common core standards-research. *Kentucky Journal of Excellence in College Teaching and Learning*, *11*(1), 56-62.

Howard, T., Dresser, S., & Dunklee, D. (2009). *Poverty is not a learning disability*. Thousand Oaks, CA: Corwin Press.

Howe, W. J. (1993). The effects of higher education on unemployment rates. In W. E. Becker & D. R. Lewis (Eds.), *Higher education and economic growth* (pp. 129–145). Netherlands: Kluwer Academic Publishers Group. doi:10.1007/978-94-015-8167-7_6

Hoy, W. (2012). School characteristics that make a difference for the achievement of all students: A 40-year odyssey. *Journal of Educational Administration*, *50*(1), 76-97.

Hoy, W. K., Tarter, J. C., & Hoy, A. W. (2006). Academic optimism of schools: A force for student achievement. *American Educational Research Journal*, *43*(3), 425–446. doi:10.3102/00028312043003425

Hsinchun, C., Chiang, R. H. L., & Storey, V. C. (2012). Business intelligence and analytics: from big data to big impact. *Management Information Systems Quarterly*, *36*(4), 1165–1188. Retrieved from http://0-search.ebscohost.com.library.dowling.edu/login.aspx?direct=true&db=lxh&AN=83466038&site=ehost-live

Hughes, M. F. (1995). Achieving despite adversity: Why are some schools successful in spite of the obstacles they face? A study of the characteristics of effective and less effective elementary schools in West Virginia using qualitative and quantitative methods. Charleston, WV: West Virginia Education Fund. Retrieved from http://eric.ed.gov/PDFS/ED398004.pdf

ILO. (2016). Statistics. Retrieved from http://www.ilo.org/stat/lang--en/index.htm

Imants, J., & Van Zoelen, A. (1995). Teachers' sickness absence in primary schools, school climate and teachers' sense of efficacy. *School Organization*, *15*(1), 77–86.

Ingersoll, R. (2001). Teacher turnover and teacher shortages: An organizational analysis. *American Educational Research Journal*, *38*(3), 499–534. doi:10.3102/00028312038003499

Ingersoll, R. (2004). Four myths about America's teacher quality problem. In M. Smylie & D. Miretzky (Eds.), *Developing the teacher workforce: The 103rd yearbook of the National Society for the Study of Education* (pp. 1–33). Chicago: University of Chicago Press. doi:10.1111/j.1744-7984.2004.tb00029.x

Jacobs, A. (2009). The pathologies of big data. *Communications of the ACM*, *52*(8), 36–44. doi:10.1145/1536616.1536632

Jacobs, J., Gregory, A., Hoppey, D., & Yendol-Hoppey, D. (2009). Data literacy: Understanding teachers data use in a context of accountability and response to intervention. *Action in Teacher Education*, *31*(3), 41–55. doi:10.1080/01626620.2009.10463527

Jacobs, N. (2011). Understanding school choice: Location as a determinant of charter school racial, economic, and linguistic segregation. *Education and Urban Society*.

Jagadish, H. V., Gehrke, J., Labrinidis, A., Papakonstantinou, Y., Patel, J. M., Ramakrishnan, R., & Shahabi, C. (2014). Big Data and Its Technical Challenges. *Communications of the ACM*, *57*(7), 86–94. doi:10.1145/2611567

Jalonen, H., & Lönnqvist, A. (2009). Predictive business – fresh initiative or old wine in a new bottle. *Management Decision*, *47*(10), 1595–1609. doi:10.1108/00251740911004709

Jobvite. (2013). Social Recruiting Survey Results. Retrieved from www.jobvite.com

Johnson, D. R., & Creech, J. C. (1983). Ordinal measures in multiple indicator models: A simulation study of categorization error. *American Sociological Review*, *48*(3), 398–407. doi:10.2307/2095231

Jones, A., & Willis, M. (2003). The challenge of XBRL: Business reporting for the investor. *Balance Sheet*, *11*(3), 29–37. doi:10.1108/09657960310491172

Jones, C., & Behling, S. (2010). Uncharted waters: Using social networks in hiring decisions. *Issues in Information Systems*, *11*(1), 589–595.

Jones, G., Ogawa, N., & Williamson, J. (1993). *Human resources in development along the Asia-Pacific Rim*. New York, Singapore: Oxford University Press.

Jones, M. G., Jones, B. D., Hardin, B., Chapman, L., Yarbrough, T., & Davis, M. (1999). The impact of high-stakes testing on teachers and students in North Carolina. *Phi Delta Kappan*, 199–203.

Jorgenson, H. (1984). The contribution of education to U.S. economic growth. In E. Dean (Ed.), *Education and economic productivity* (pp. 95–163). Cambridge, Massachusetts: Ballinger Publishing Company.

Jorgenson, H., & Fraumeni, M. (1998). *Investment in education and U.S. economic growth*. Netherlands: Kluwer Academic Publishers.

Karen, O. (2016). What is being done with open government data? An exploratory analysis of public uses of New York City open data. *Webology*, *13*(1), 1–12.

Kay, A. (2000). Recruiters embrace the internet. *Information Week*, *778*, 72–80.

Kielman, J., Thomas, J., & May, R. (2009). Foundations and Frontiers in Visual Analytics. *Information Visualization*, *8*(4), 239–246. doi:10.1057/ivs.2009.25

Kılınç, A. Ç. (2013). The relationship between individual teacher academic optimism and school climate. *Journal of Educational Sciences*, *1*(5), 621-634.

King, E., & World Bank. (2011). Education is fundamental to develop and growth. Retrieved from http://blogs.worldbank.org/education/education-is-fundamental-to-development-and-growth

Kiron, D., Ferguson, R. B., & Prentice, P. K. (2013). From value to vision: Reimagining the possible with data analytics. *MIT Sloan Management Review*, *54*(3), 1.

Kiron, D., & Shockley, R. (2011). Creating business value with analytics. *MIT Sloan Management Review*, *53*(1), 57.

Kiron, D., Shockley, R., Kruschwitz, N., Finch, G., & Haydock, M. (2011). Analytics: The widening divide. *MIT Sloan Management Review*, *53*(3), 1–22.

Kiser, L. J. (2007). Protecting children from the dangers of urban poverty. *Clinical Psychology Review*, *27*(2), 211–225. doi:10.1016/j.cpr.2006.07.004 PMID:16979274

Klatt, T., Schlaefke, M., & Moeller, K. (2011). Integrating business analytics into strategic planning for better performance. *The Journal of Business Strategy*, *32*(6), 30–39. doi:10.1108/02756661111180113

Kline, R. B. (2005). *Principles and practices of structural equation modeling* (2nd ed.). New York, NY: The Guilford Press.

Kluemper, D. H., & Rosen, P. A. (2009). Future employment selection methods: Evaluating social networking websites. *Journal of Managerial Psychology*, *24*(6), 567–580. doi:10.1108/02683940910974134

Knapp, M. S., Swinnerton, J. A., Copland, M. A., & Monpas-Huber, J. (2006). *Data-Informed Leadership in Education*. Center for the Study of Teaching and Policy.

Knell, M. (2012). Increasing Life Expectancy and Pay-As-You-Go Pension Systems. *Working Papers (Oesterreichische Nationalbank)*, (179), 1-36.

Knight, J., & Gunatilaka, R. (2012). Subjective Well-being and Social Evaluation in a Poor Country (CSAE Working Paper WPS/2014-09). Centre for the Study of African Economies, University of Oxford.

Koehler, M. J., & Mishra, P. (2009). What is technological pedagogical content knowledge? *Contemporary Issues in Technology & Teacher Education*, 9(1), 60–70.

Kohavi, R., Rothleder, N. J., & Simoudis, E. (2002). Emerging trends in business analytics. *Communications of the ACM*, *45*(8), 45–48. Retrieved from http://0-search.ebscohost.com.library.dowling.edu/login.aspx?direct=true&db=buh&AN=11863428&site=ehost-live doi:10.1145/545151.545177

Kouzes, J. M., & Posner, B. J. (2002). *Leadership challenge* (3rd ed.). San Francisco: Jossey-Bass.

Krishnamurthy, R., & Awazu, Y. (2016). Liberating data for public value: The case of Data.gov. *International Journal of Information Management*, *36*(4), 668–672. doi:10.1016/j.ijinfomgt.2016.03.002

Krueger, A., & Lindahl, M. (2001). Education for Growth: Why and for Whom? *Journal of Economic Literature*, *39*(4), 1101–1136. doi:10.1257/jel.39.4.1101

Kumar, B. S. (2014). Business Analytics: A way forward to Decision Making.

LaMelza, J. (2003). High school resource room teacher attitudes towards the 1997 amendments to the Individuals with Disabilities Education Act and its influence on their instructional practices [Doctoral dissertation].

Lange, C., Range, B., & Welsh, K. (2012). Conditions for Effective Data Use to Improve Schools: Recommendations for School Leaders. *International Journal Of Educational Leadership Preparation*, *7*(3), 1–11.

Lau, L. K. (2003). Institutional factors affecting student retention. *Education-Indianapolis Then Chula Vista*, *124*(1), 126–136.

LaValle, S., Lesser, E., Shockley, R., Hopkins, M. S., & Kruschwitz, N. (2011). Big Data, Analytics and the Path from Insights to Value. *MIT Sloan Management Review, 52*(2), 21-32.

Learn.org. (2016). tertiary education. Retrieved from learn.org

Leech, D., & Fulton, C. (2008). Faculty perceptions of shared decision making and the principal's leadership behaviors in secondary schools in a large urban district. *Education*, *128*(4), 630–644.

Leithwood, K., Aitken, R., & Jantzi, D. (2006). *Making schools smarter: Leading with evidence*. Corwin Press.

Leithwood, K., & Strauss, T. (2009, Spring). Turnaround schools: Leadership lessons. *Education Canada*, 49(2), 26–29.

Leithwood, K., Strauss, T., & Anderson, S. E. (2007). District Contributions to School Leaders' Sense of Efficacy: A Qualitative Analysis. *Journal of School Leadership*, *17*(6), 735–770.

Lessler, K. J. (2010). High-stakes and non-stakes testing states and the transfer of knowledge to students' advanced placement test, advanced placement U.S. history test and SAT exam scores [Doctoral dissertation].

Levey, E. K. (2015, July 1). *Teacher attitudes on personal teaching efficacy and responsive teaching, and principal leadership behaviors in the areas of leader social relationships, leadership/goal setting, and collaboration for learning in low wealth, low and high achieving middles*. Dowling.edu. Retrieved from http;//0-search.proquest.com/library.dowling.edu/docview/1503738159?=10549

Levine, D. K., & Lezotte, L. W. (1990). Unusually Effective Schools: A Review and Analysis of Research and Practice. Madison, Wise: Nat. Centre for Effective Schools Research and Development.

Lipiec, J. (2001).. . *Human Resources Management Perspective at the Turn of the Century Public Personnel Management*, *30*, 137–146.

Lippman, L., Burns, S., & McArthur, E. (1996). *Urban schools: the challenge of location and poverty*. Washington, DC: United States Department of Education.

Lippmann, W. (1922). *Public opinion*. New York: Harcourt Brace.

Li, Q., & Ma, X. (2010). A meta-analysis of the effects of computer technology on school students' mathematics learning. *Educational Psychology Review*, *22*(3), 215–243. doi:10.1007/s10648-010-9125-8

Liu, C. (2013). XBRL: A new global paradigm for financial reporting. *Journal of Global Information Management*, *21*(3), 60–80. doi:10.4018/jgim.2013070104

Lonneville, J. (2014, April). Why some school districts outperform others: A mixed methods study on poverty, student performance on the New York State school assessments, and school district funding across rural, suburban, and urban school districts [Doctoral Dissertation]. Niagara University.

Lorenz, K. (2009). *Employers are digging up your digital dirt.* Retrieved May 2, 2013 from http:www.theworkbuzz.com/job-surveys/socialnetworks

Louis, K., Leithwood, K., Wahlstrom, K., & Anderson, S. (2010). *Learning from leadership: Investigating the links to improved student learning*. New York: Wallace Foundation.

Luan, J. (2002). Data mining and its applications in higher education. *New Directions for Institutional Research, 2002*(113), 17–36. doi:10.1002/ir.35

Luke, A. (2012). After the testing: Taking reading and writing into the world. *Journal of Adolescent & Adult Literacy, 56*(1), 8–13. doi:10.1002/JAAL.00095

Luszczynska, A., Scholz, U., & Scwarzer, R. (2005). The general self-efficacy scale: Multicultural validation studies. *The Journal of Psychology, 139*(5), 439–457. doi:10.3200/JRLP.139.5.439-457 PMID:16285214

Macfadyen, L. P., Dawson, S., Pardo, A., & Gasevic, D. (2014). Embracing big data in complex educational systems: The learning analytics imperative and the policy challenge. *Research & Practice in Assessment, 9*(2), 17–28.

MacIver, M. A., & Groginsky, S. (2011). Working statewide to boost graduation rates. *Phi Delta Kappan, 92*(5), 16–20. doi:10.1177/003172171109200505

Madden, J. V., Lawson, D., & Sweet, D. (1976). *School effectiveness study*. Sacramento, CA: State of California Department of Education.

Malik, A., & Singh, D. (2012). Happiness: A Central Objective of Positive Psychology. *Indian Journal of Positive Psychology, 3*(1).

Malinsky, M., Ross, A., Pannells, T., & McJunkin, M. (2006). Math anxiety in pre-service elementary school teachers. *Education*, 127(2), 274–279.

Mangiante, E. M. S. (2011). Teachers matter: Measures of teacher effectiveness in low-income minority schools. *Educational Assessment, Evaluation and Accountability, 23*(1), 41–63. doi:10.1007/s11092-010-9107-x

Manley, R., & Hawkins, R. J. (2010). *Designing school systems for all students: A toolbox to fix America's schools*. New York: Rowman & Littlefield.

Manyika, J., Chui, M., Brown, B., Bughin, J., Dobbs, R., Roxburgh, C., & Byers, A. H. (2011). Big data: The next frontier for innovation, competition, and productivity.

March, J. G., & Simon, H. A. (1958). Organizations.

Marsh, J. A., & Farrell, C. C. (2015). How leaders can support teachers with data-driven decision making A framework for understanding capacity building. *Educational Management Administration & Leadership*, *43*(2), 269–289. doi:10.1177/1741143214537229

Marzano, R., Toth, M., & Schooling, P. (2012). *Examining the role of teacher evaluation in student achievement: Contemporary research base for the Marzano causal teacher evaluation model* (White paper). Retrieved May 1, 2016 from http://www.marzanocenter.com/files/MC_White_Paper_20120424.pdf

Mayer, S. E. (1997). *What money can't buy*. Cambridge, MA: Harvard University Press.

McBride, S. K. (2009, January 1). The relationship of selected academic and educational factors on student attendance.

McMillan, J. H. (2012). *Educational research: Fundamentals for the consumer* (6th ed.). New York: Longman.

McTighe, J., & Brown, J. L. (2005). Differentiated instruction and educational standards: Is detente possible? *Theory into Practice*, *44*(3), 234–244. doi:10.1207/s15430421tip4403_8

Meier, D., Kohn, A., Darling-Hammond, L., Sizer, T. R., & Wood, G. (2004). Many children left behind (D. Meier, & G. Wood, Eds.). Boston, MA: Beacon Press.

Meyer, L. H. (2012). Freedom, fairness, and justice: What now for severe disabilities?: A response to Turnbull. *Research and Practice for Persons with Severe Disabilities*, *37*(3), 220–223. doi:10.2511/027494812804153480

Militaru, D. N. (2011). The costs of demographic and economic crises – challenges to pension system reform. *Annals Of The University Of Petrosani Economics*, *11*(4), 175–182.

Miller, D. (2013, July-September). Universities and Colleges as Economic Drivers: Measuring Higher Education's Role in Economic Development. *Planning for Higher Education*, *41*(4).

Missett, T. C., Brunner, M. M., Callahan, C. M., Moon, T. R., & Azano, A. P. (2014). Exploring teacher beliefs and use acceleration, ability grouping, and formative assessment. *Journal for the Education of the Gifted*, *37*(3), 245–268. doi:10.1177/0162353214541326

Mitchell, W. C., & United States, President's Research Committee on Social Trends. (1933). Recent Social Trends in the United States: Report of the President's Research Committee on Social Trends (Vol. 1). New York: McGraw-Hill. Retrieved from Questia

Morote, E.-S. (2001). Relationship Among Higher Education, Economic Growth and Employment in Latin American Leading Emerging Markets (Dissertation). University of Pittsburgh.

Mouza, C. (2006). Linking professional development to teacher learning and practice: A multi-case study analysis of urban teachers. *Journal of Educational Computing Research*, *34*(4), 405–440. doi:10.2190/2218-567J-65P8-7J72

Murphy, A. K. (2007). The suburban ghetto: The legacy of Herbert Gans in understanding the experience of poverty in recently impoverished American suburbs. *City & Community*, *6*(1), 21–37. doi:10.1111/j.1540-6040.2007.00196.x

Murtaugh, P. A., Burns, L. D., & Schuster, J. (1999). Predicting the retention of university students. *Research in Higher Education*, *40*(3), 355–371. doi:10.1023/A:1018755201899

Muth, R., Browne-Ferrigno, T., Bellamy, T., Fulmer, C., & Silver, M. (2013). Using Teacher Instructional Leadership as a Predictor of Principal Leadership. *Journal of School Leadership*, *23*(1).

Nandeshwar, A., Menzies, T., & Nelson, A. (2011). Learning patterns of university student retention. *Expert Systems with Applications*, *38*(12), 14984–14996. doi:10.1016/j.eswa.2011.05.048

National Center of Educational Statistics. (n. d.). *What is school district demographics system?* Retrieved from http://nces.ed.gov/surveys/sdds/about.aspx

New York State Department of Education. (2014). Guidance on New York State's annual professional performance review for teachers and principals to Implement education law §3012-c and the commissioner's regulations, 1-166.

New York State Education Department (NYSED). (2016). Race to the top executive summary. Retrieved from https://www2.ed.gov/programs/racetothetop/state-reported-sharing/nyexsumm.pdf

New York State Education Department (NYSED). (n. d.). NYSED Fiscal Analysis & Research Unit. Retrieved from http://www.oms.nysed.gov/faru/Profiles/profiles_cover.html

New York State Education Department Data Site. (n. d.). Retrieved May 13, 2016, from http:// data.nysed.gov/ NYSED/P-12 /Part 100 Regulations/100.5

New York State Education Department. (2002). *Statistics for public school districts*. Retrieved from http://www.p12.nysed.gov/irs/chapter655/2002/ glossary_June_2002.htm

New York State Education Department. (2012). *New York State report cards – Data accuracy*. Retrieved from https://reportcards.nysed.gov/

New York State Education Department. (2013, August). Release of data –August 7 2013, supplemental slides. Proceedings of the New York State Education Department Press Conference. Retrieved from http://www.p12.nysed.gov/irs/pressRelease/20130807/home.html

New York State Education Department. (2014, May). *Reporting data for 2013–14 school year*. Retrieved from http://www.nysldstac.org/wp-content/uploads/ 2014/ 05/SIRS-Manual-v9.14.pdf

New York State Education Department. (2015). *Glossary of Terms - Report Cards Data*. Retrieved from http://data.nysed.gov/glossary.php?report=reportcards

New York State Office of Education Performance Review. (1974). *School-related factors influencing reading achievement: A case study of two inner city schools*. Office of Performance Review. Retrieved from http://www.eric.ed.gov/PDFS/ED089211.pdf

Newmann, F., & Wehlage, G. (1995). *Successful school restructuring: A report to the public and educators by the Center on Organization and Restructuring of Schools*. Madison: University of Wisconsin.

Nichols, S. L., Glass, S. L., & Berliner, G. V. (2006). High-stakes testing and student achievement: Does accountability pressure increase student learning? (S. Dorn, Ed.). Education Policy Analysis Archives, 14 (1), 1-180.

Nichols, J. D. (2003). Prediction Indicators for Students Failing the State of Indiana High School Graduation Exam. *Preventing School Failure*, *47*(3), 112–120. doi:10.1080/10459880309604439

Nichols, S. L., & Valenzuela, A. (2013). Education policy and youth: Effects of policy on practice. *Theory into Practice*, *52*(3), 152–159. doi:10.1080/00405841.2013.804306

Nicolae, E. (2012). Happiness, Economics and Politics. towards a Multi-Disciplinary Approach. *The Journal of Philosophical Economics, 5*(2).

Norton, M. S. (1994). *The personnel administrator in Arizona: A research study*. Tempe, AZ: Arizona State University.

NYSED. (2013). The New York State School Report Card retrieved from https://reportcards.nysed.gov/

Obama, B. (2009a). Transparency and open government. Memorandum for the Heads of Executive Departments and Agencies, Retrieved data from http://www.whitehouse.gov/sites/default/files/microsites/ostp/ostp_public_access_memo_2013.pdf

Obama, B. (2009b). Memorandum for the Heads of Executive Departments and Agencies: Freedom of Information Act (Presidential memorandum). Retrieved from http://www.whitehouse.gov/the_press_office/Transparen

Obidziński, P. (2010). On the need for prevention in the pension system on the example of the demographic reserve fund. In *Folia Oeconomica Stetinensia* (pp. 179-189). doi:10.2478/v10031-010-0012-8

O'Brien, L. M., Meszaros, B., & Pulliam, W. (1985). Effects of teacher use of objectives on student achievement in social studies. In A. Summers (Ed.), *Productivity Assessment in Education.* San Francisco, CA: Jossey-Bass, Inc. doi:10.1080/00933104.1985.10505506

OBrien, R. M. (1983). Reducing grouping distortion in rank category variables. *American Journal of Political Science*, *25*(3), 605–616. doi:10.2307/2110821

OECD DOCUMENTS. (1996). *Employment and growth in the knowledge–based economy*. Paris: OECD.

OECD. (2012). Coverage of Private Pension Systems: Evidence and Policy Options. In *OECD Pensions Outlook 2012*. Paris: OECD Publishing. doi:10.1787/9789264169401-7-en

OECD. (2013). Architecture of national pension systems. In *Pensions at a Glance 2013: OECD and G20 Indicators*. OECD Publishing. doi:10.1787/pension_glance-2013-6-en

OECD. (2014A). Architecture of national pensions systems. In *OECD, IDB and The World Bank, Pensions at a Glance: Latin America and the Caribbean*. Paris: OECD Publishing. doi:10.1787/9789264224964-9-en

OECD. (2014B). Editorial: Demographic change and economic stagnation put pressure on pension systems. In *OECD Pensions Outlook 2014*. Paris: OECD Publishing. doi:10.1787/pens_outlook-2014-2-en

OECD. (2014C). *OECD Reviews of Pension Systems: Ireland*. Paris: OECD Publishing. doi:10.1787/9789264208834-en

OECD. (2014D). Hours worked (indicator). doi:10.1787/47be1c78-en

OECD. (2015A). *Pensions at a Glance 2015: OECD and G20 indicators*. Paris: OECD Publishing. doi:10.1787/pension_glance-2015-en

OECD. (2015B). Pensions statistics (Edition 2015) OECD Pensions Statistics (database). doi:10.1787/f59da966-en

OECD. (2016A). Labour Force Statistics: Summary tables. *OECD Employment and Labour Market Statistics* (database).

OECD. (2016B). Hours Worked: Average annual hours actually worked. *OECD Employment and Labour Market Statistics* (database). doi:10.1787/data-00303-en

OECD. (2016C). *OECD Reviews of Pension Systems: Mexico*. Paris: OECD Publishing. doi:10.1787/9789264245938-en

OECD. (2016D). Hours worked. In *OECD Factbook 2015-2016: Economic, Environmental and Social Statistics*. Paris: OECD Publishing. doi:10.1787/factbook-2015-54-en

Ohtake, F. (2012). Unemployment and Happiness. Japan Labor Review, vol. 9, no. 2, Spring 2012

Oliveras, Y. (2014). *The empirical relationship between administrator ratings of teacher effectiveness and student achievement on the State of Texas assessments of academic readiness*.

O'Neill, B. (2014, January). What's the Economy for, Anyway? Why It's Time to Stop Chasing Growth and Start Pursuing Happiness. *Journal of Financial Counseling and Planning*.

Open Data Charter. (2015). *Principles*. Retrieved from http://opendatacharter.net/principles/

OReilly, K., & Paper, D. (2012). Want Value from Big Data? Close the Gap between the C-Suite and the Server Room. *Journal of Information Technology Case and Application Research*, *14*(4), 3–10. doi:10.1080/15228053.2012.10845709

Osborn, J. (2002). Practical Research, Assessment and Evaluation Retrieved 1/24/15 from http://pareonline.net/getvn.asp?v=8&n=6

Osterman, K. F., & Kottkamp, R. B. (1993). *Reflective Practice for Educators: Improving Schooloing Through Professional Development*. Newbury Park, CA: Corwin Press.

Ovando, M. N., & Cavazos, M. (2004). Principals' Instructional Leadership in Successful Hispanic Majority High Schools. *Scholar-Practitioner Quarterly*, *2*(3), 7–24.

Park, H. J., Roberts, K. D., & Stodden, R. Faculty perspectives on professional development to improve efficacy when teaching students with disabilities. *Journal of Post Secondary Education and Disability, 25*(4), 377-383.

Partnership for 21 Century Skills (2008). 21st Century Skills Education and Competitiveness. http://www.p21.org/storage/documents/21st_century_skills_education_and_competitiveness_guide.pdf 2008

Patterson, J. (2003). *Coming Even Cleaner About Change*. Lanham, MD: Rowman & Littlefield Publishers, Inc.

Pattnaik, J., & Sriram, R. (2010). Father/male involvement in the care and education of children. *Childhood Education*, *86*(6), 354–359. doi:10.1080/00094056.2010.10523169

Pavot, W. G., Diener, E., Colvin, C. R., & Sandvik, E. (1991). Further validation of the Satisfaction with Life Scale: Evidence for the cross-method convergence of well-being measures. *Journal of Personality Assessment*, *57*(1), 149–161. doi:10.1207/s15327752jpa5701_17 PMID:1920028

Pearce, K. L., Lungren, M., & Wince, A. (1998). The effects of curriculum practices on first graders' attitudes, activity preferences, and achievements in mathematics. *Education*, 1998, 82–90.

Pencavel, J. (1993). Higher education, economic growth, and earnings. In W. E. Becker & D. R. Lewis (Eds.), *Higher education and economic growth* (pp. 51–87). Netherlands: Kluwer Academic Publishers Group. doi:10.1007/978-94-015-8167-7_3

Perry, L., & McConney, A. (2010). Does the SES of the school matter? An examination of socioeconomic status and student achievement using PISA 2003. *Teachers College Record, 112*(4), 7–8.

Pethe, S., Chaudhary, S., & Dhar, U. (1999). *Occupational self-efficacy Scale and Manual*. Agra: National Psychological Corporation.

Pfeiffer, J. (1994). *Competitive advantage through people*. Boston: Harvard Business School Press.

Phillips-Wren, G., & Hoskisson, A. (2015). An analytical journey towards big data. *Journal of Decision Systems*, *24*(1), 87–102. doi:10.1080/12460125.2015.994333

Picciano, A. G. (2012). The Evolution of Big Data and Learning Analytics in American Higher Education. *Journal of Asynchronous Learning Networks*, *16*(3), 9–20.

Pierson, A. (2014). *What makes a successful principal?: Incorporating school principal background in state and district policy* [Doctoral dissertation].

Podell, D. M., & Soodak, L. C. (1993). Teacher efficacy and bias in special education referrals. *The Journal of Educational Research*, *86*(4), 247–253. doi:10.1080/00220671.1993.9941836

Podestà, F. (2002). Recent developments in quantitative comparative methodology: The case of pooled time series cross-section analysis. *DSS Papers Soc.*, *3*(2), 5–44.

Polikoff, M. S., Porter, A. C., & Smithson, J. (2011). How well aligned are state assessments of student achievement with state content standards? *American Educational Research Journal*, *48*(4), 965–995. doi:10.3102/0002831211410684

Power, D. J. (2014). Using Big Data for analytics and decision support. *Journal of Decision Systems*, *23*(2), 222–228. doi:10.1080/12460125.2014.888848

Provost, T. (2013). *No-so-happy anniversary, XBRL.* Retrieved December 20, 2013 from http://ww2.cfo.com/gaap-ifrs/2013/01/not-so-happy-anniversary-xbrl

Provost, J., Boscardin, M., & Wells, C. (2010). Perceptions of principal leadership behaviors in Massachusetts in the era of education reform. *Journal of School Leadership*, *20*(5), 532–560.

Prytula, M., Noonan, B., & Hellsten, L. (2013). Toward Instructional Leadership: Principals' Perceptions of Large-Scale Assessment in Schools. *Canadian Journal of Educational Administration and Policy*.

Psacharopolous, G. (1988, Fall). Returns to Education: A further international update and implications. *Journal of Human Resources*, *20*(4), 893-921.

Psacharopoulos, G. (Ed.). (1987). *Economics of education: Research and studies*. New York: Pergamon Press.

Psacharopoulos, G., & Woodhall, M. (1985). *Education for development: An analysis of investment choices*. USA: World Bank, Oxford University Press.

Public Library of Science. (2014). *Data Availability.* Retrieved from http://journals.plos.org/plosone/s/data-availability

Quamruzzaman, A. (2013, February). The Pursuit Of Happiness: An Analysis Of Aggregate Difference In The Distribution of Happiness In The United States. *Mcgill Sociological Review*, *3*.

Raines, T., Dever, B., Kamphaus, R., & Roach, A. (2012). Universal screening for behavioral and emotional risk: A promising method for reducing disproportionate placement in special education. *The Journal of Negro Education*, *81*(3), 283–296. doi:10.7709/jnegroeducation.81.3.0283

Rajesh, K. (2013). Big Data Analytics: Applications and Benefits. *IUP Journal of Information Technology*, *9*(4), 41.

Ravishanker, G. (2011). Doing academic analytics right: Intelligent answers to simple questions. *Research Bulletin (Sun Chiwawitthaya Thang Thale Phuket)*, 2.

Ready, D. D. (2010). Socioeconomic disadvantage, school attendance, and early cognitive development: The differential effects of school exposure. *Sociology of Education, 83*, 271–286. doi:101177/0038040710383520

Ritzen, J. (1977). Education, economic growth, and income distribution. New York: North-Holland Pub. Co.

Rivikin, S. G., Hanushek, E. A., & Kain, J. F. (2005). Teachers, schools, and academic achievement. *Econometerica, 73*(2), 417–458. doi:10.1111/j.1468-0262.2005.00584.x

Rivkin, S. G., Hanushek, J. F., Markman, J. M., & Kain, J. F. (2003). Does peer ability affect student achievement? *Journal of Applied Econometrics, 18*(5), 527–544. doi:10.1002/jae.741

Robinson, V. J. (2010). From instructional leadership to leadership capabilities: Empirical findings and methodological challenges. *Leadership and Policy in Schools, 9*(1), 1–26. doi:10.1080/15700760903026748

Rogers, D. L. (2000). A paradigm shift: Technology integration for higher education in the new millennium. *AACE Journal, 1*(13), 19–33.

Rondinelli, D., & Montgomery, J. (1995). *Great policies: Strategic innovations in Asia and The Pacific Basin. Rotterdam, Netherlands: Erasmus Universiteit Rotterdam, Institute for Economic Research*. Published Westport, Conn: Praeger Publishing.

Rose, M. (2013). The core of the matter. *American Teacher*, May/June, 4-5.

Rossman, G. B., Corbett, H. D., & Firestone, W. A. (1998). Change and effectiveness in schools: A cultural perspective. *Curriculum Inquiry, 21*(1), 127–131.

Rothbart, M., & Taylor, M. (1992). Category labels and social reality: Do we view social categories as natural kinds? In G. R. Semin & K. Fiedler (Eds.), *Language, interaction and social cognition* (pp. 11–36). London: Sage.

Runardotter, M. & Ståhlbröst, A., (2016). CLASH!: The open data policy meets an organizational context. *International Journal of Public Information Systems*, (1), 1.

Ruppar, A. L., Gaffney, J. S., & Dymond, S. K. (2012). Influences on teachers' decisions about literacy for secondary students with severe disabilities. *Exceptional Children, 81*(2), 2 09-226.

Sadler, D. R. (1998). Formative assessment and the design of instructional systems. *Instructional Science*, 18(2), 119–140.

Saha, L., & Faberlind, I. (1994). Education and development. In H. Torsten, & T. Neville (Eds.), The international encyclopedia of education. USA: Pergamon.

Sala-i-Martin, X., Doppelhofer, G., & Miller, R. (2004). Determinants of Long Term Growth: A Bayesian Averaging of Classical Estimates (BACE) Approach. *The American Economic Review, 94*(4), 813–835. doi:10.1257/0002828042002570

Santiago Rivera, D., & Shanks, G. (2015). A Dashboard to Support Management of Business Analytics Capabilities. *Journal of Decision Systems*, *24*(1), 73–86. doi:10.1080/12460125.2015.994335

Sanyal, B. C. (1987). *Higher education and employment*. Great Britain: The Falmer Press, UNESCO.

Scassa, T. (2014). Privacy and open government. *Future Internet*, *6*(2), 397–413. doi:10.3390/fi6020397

Schiller, K. & Muller, C. (2000). External examinations and accountability, educational expectations, and high school graduation. *American Journal of Education*, *108*.

Schubert, J. (2007). Transformation through staff development. *Reclaiming Children and Youth*, *16*(3), 53–55.

Schultz, T. (1988). *Education, investment and returns. In handbook of development economics*. The Netherlands: North Holland.

SEC. (2009). *Interactive Data to Improve Financial Reporting*. Retrieved December 12, 2013 from http://www.sec.gov/rules/final/2009/33-9002.pdf

Senge, P. (1990). *The fifth discipline: the art and practice of a learning organization*. New York: Currency Doubleday.

Senge, P. M. (2014). *The dance of change: The challenges to sustaining momentum in a learning organization*. Crown Business.

Shanks, G., & Bekmamedova, N. (2012). Achieving benefits with business analytics systems: An evolutionary process perspective. *Journal of Decision Systems*, *21*(3), 231–244. doi:10.1080/12460125.2012.729182

Sheridan, B., & Drew, J. (2012, June). The future is now: XBRL emerges as career niche. *Journal of Accountancy*. Retrieved May 23, 2016 from http://www.journalofaccountancy.com/issues/2012/jun/20124962.html

Shin, D., & Johnson, D. (1978). Happiness as the Overall Assesment of the Quality of Life. *Source Social Indicators Research*, *5*(1-4), 475–492. doi:10.1007/BF00352944

SHRM. (2014). Retrieved from http://www.shrm.org/TemplatesTools/Glossaries/HRTerms/Pages/r.aspx#sthash.4cBgpq2w.dpuf

Shultz, P. (1994). Human capital investment in women and men. Occasional Papers (N. 44). San Francisco, California: International Center for Economic Growth.

Shultz, P. (1997). *Latin American education: Comparative perspectives* (C. A. Torres & A. Puiggrós, Eds.). Boulder, Colo.: Westview Press.

Sianesi, B., & Van Reenen, J. (2003). The returns to education: Macroeconomics. *Journal of Economic Surveys*, *17*(2), 157–200. doi:10.1111/1467-6419.00192

Sidanius, J. (1993). The psychology of group conflict and the dynamics of oppression: A social dominance perspective. In S. Iyengar (Ed.), *Explorations in political psychology* (pp. 183–219). Durham, NC: Duke University Press.

Sinai, N., & Martin, M. (June 19, 2013). *Open Data Going Global.* Retrieved from https://www.whitehouse.gov/blog/2013/06/19/open-data-going-global

Smith, P. G., & Wyatt, W. (2010). *Using social networking websites for hiring decisions: Legal and ethical considerations. Best Practices Forum Human Resources* (pp. 1–8). Arlington, TX: NJDHS.

Snell, S., Pedigo, P., & Krawie, G. (1995). Managing impact of information technology on human resource management. In G. Ferris, S. Rosen, & D. Barnum (Eds.), *Handbook of Human Resource Management* (pp. 159–174). Cambridge, Mass: Blackwell.

Soehner, D., & Ryan, T. (2011). The Interdependence of Principal School Leadership and Student Achievement. *Scholar-Practitioner Quarterly*, *5*(3), 274–288.

Sparks, D. (2003). We care, therefore they learn. *National Staff Development Council*, *24*(4), 42–47.

Starnes, B. A. (2011). *Change, Sputnik, and Fast Food. Phi Delta Kappan*, *92*(7), 72–73.

Sterrett, W., & Bond, N. (2012). Beyond tough choices: Prioritizing and preserving education in times of cuts and layoffs. *Kappa Delta Pi Record*, *48*(2), 52–54. doi:10.1080/00228958.2012.680380

Stodolksy, S. S. (1985). Telling Math: Origins of math aversion and anxiety. *Educational Psychologist*, 20(3), 125–133.

Stone, D. A. (2002). *Policy paradox: The art of political decision making*. New York: Norton.

Stronge, J. H., Ward, T. J., Tucker, P. D., & Hindman, J. L. (2012). What is the relationship between teacher quality and student achievement? An exploratory study. *Journal of Personnel Evaluation in Education*, *20*(3-4), 165–184. doi:10.1007/s11092-008-9053-z

Summers, A., & Raivetz, M. (1982). What helps fourth grade students to read? In A. Summers (Ed.), *Productivity Assessment in Education*. San Francisco, CA: Jossey-Bass, Inc.

Summers, A., Wolfe, B., & Columbia Univ, N. (1976). Which school resources help learning? Efficiency and equity in Philadelphia public schools. *IRCD Bulletin*, *11*(3), 1–17.

Taffe, S. W., Laster, B. P., Broach, L., Marinak, B., McDonald Connor, C., & Walker-Dalhouse, D. (2012). Differentiated instruction: Making informed teacher decisions. *The Reading Teacher*, *66*(4), 303–314. doi:10.1002/TRTR.01126

Taylor, E. Z., & Dzuranin, A. C. (2010). Interactive financial reporting: An introduction to eXtensible Business Reporting Language (XBRL). *Issues in Accounting Education*, *25*(1), 71–83. doi:10.2308/iace.2010.25.1.71

Taylor, R. T., & La Cava, G. S. (2011). Urban Principals' Second Order Change Leadership. *Planning and Changing*, *42*(3-4), 224–240.

Teichler, U. (1999). Higher education policy and the world of work: Changing conditions and challenges. *Higher Education Policy*, *12*(4), 285–312. doi:10.1016/S0952-8733(99)00019-7

Teixeira da Silva, J., & Dobránszki, J. (2015). Potential Dangers with Open Access Data Files in the Expanding Open Data Movement. *Publishing Research Quarterly*, *31*(4), 298–305. doi:10.1007/s12109-015-9420-9

The QoG Institute. (2016). The QoG Standard Data Set. Code Book. Retrieved from http://www.qogdata.pol.gu.se/data/qog_std_jan16.pdf (10/4/2016)

The QoG Institute. (2016). The QoG Standard Data Set. http://qog.pol.gu.se/data/datadownloads/qogstandarddata

Thomas, J. J., & Cook, K. A. (2005). Illuminating the Path: The R&D Agenda for Visual Analytics National Visualization and Analytics Center.

Thomas, D., Jeanne, G., David, W., & Alvin, L. (2001). Data to Knowledge to Results, Building an Analytic Capability. *California Management Review*, *43*(2).

Tinto, V. (2006). Research and practice of student retention: What next? *Journal of College Student Retention*, *8*(1), 1–19. doi:10.2190/4YNU-4TMB-22DJ-AN4W

Tinto, V. (2007). *Taking student retention seriously*. Syracuse University.

Tiwari, P., & Saxena, K. (2012). Human resource management practices: A comprehensive review. *Pakistan Business Review*, *13*(4), 667–705.

Tomlinson, C. A. (1999). Mapping a route toward differentiated instruction. *Educational Leadership*, *57*(1), 12–16.

Toutkoushian, R., & Curtis, T. (2005). Effects of socioeconomic factors on public high school outcomes and rankings. *The Journal of Educational Research*, *98*(5), 259–271. doi:10.3200/JOER.98.5.259-271

Tribunella, T., & Tribunella, H. (2010). Using XBRL to analyze financial statements. *The CPA Journal*, *80*(3), 69.

Tschannen-Moran, M., Hoy, A. W., & Hoy, W. K. (1998). Teacher efficacy: Its meaning and measure. *Review of Educational Research*, *68*(2), 202–248. doi:10.3102/00346543068002202

Tucker, B. A., & Russell, R. F. (2004). The influence of the transformational leader. *Journal of Leadership & Organizational Studies*, *10*(4), 103–111. doi:10.1177/107179190401000408

Tucker, P. D., & Stronge, J. H. (2005). *Linking teacher evaluation and student learning*. Alexandria, VA: Association for Supervision and Curriculum Development.

Turnbull, R. H. (2012). "Free at last": Kennedy, King, and the meaning of liberty in the disability movement (M. Agran, Ed.). Research & Practice for Persons with Severe Disabilities, 37(3), 210-216.

U.S. Census Bureau. (2012). Households and families: 2010. 2010 Census Briefs.

United States. (1983). *A nation at risk: The imperative for educational reform*. Author.

University of Gothenburg. Sweden. (2016, 1 1). Quality of Government Institute. Retrieved from http://qog.pol.gu.se/data

Ura, D. K., Alkire, S., & Zangmo, T. (2011). The Gross National Happiness Index of Bhutan: Method and Illustrative Results. Retrieved from OECD presentations: http://www.oecd.org/site/ssfc2011/48920513.pdf

Urick, A., Wilson, A., Paes de Carvalho, C., Oliveira, A. C., Perry, S. M., & Campelo Koslinski, M. (2015). Does school leadership influence opportunity to learn for 15 year olds in US and Brazil? *Paper presented at American Education Research Association annual meeting*, Chicago, IL.

US Bureau of Labor Statistics. (2008, 1 1). US Bureau of Labor Statistics. Retrieved 10 1, 2016 from US Bureau of Labor Statistics: http://www.bls.gov/

van Barneveld, A., Arnold, K. E., & Campbell, J. P. (2012). Analytics in higher education: Establishing a common language. *EDUCAUSE learning initiative, 1*, 1-11.

Van Ewijk, R., & Sleegers, P. (2010). The effect of peer socioeconomic status on student achievement: A meta-analysis. *Educational Research Review*, *5*(2), 134–150. doi:10.1016/j.edurev.2010.02.001

Van Iddekinge, C., Lanivich, S., Roth, P., & Junco, E. (2013). Social media for selection? Validity and adverse impact potential of a Facebook based assessment. *Journal of Management*, *15*, 1–25.

Vescio, V., Ross, D., & Adams, A. (2008). A review of the research on the impact of professional learning communities on teaching practice and student learning. *Teaching and Teacher Education*, *24*(1), 80–91. doi:10.1016/j.tate.2007.01.004

Viaene, S., & Van den Bunder, A. (2011). The secrets to managing business analytics projects. *MIT Sloan Management Review*, *53*(1), 65–69.

Waite, B. (2015). School human *resource managers' level of use of social networking websites on the dimensions of self-efficacy, decision making in recruiting, screening and selection of teachers and its impact on teacher retention* [Doctoral Dissertation].

Waller, M. A., & Fawcett, S. E. (2013). Data science, predictive analytics, and big data: A revolution that will transform supply chain design and management. *Journal of Business Logistics*, *34*(2), 77–84. doi:10.1111/jbl.12010

Waters, J. T., Marzano, R. J., & McNulty, B. (2004). Leadership that sparks learning. *Educational Leadership*, *61*(7), 48.

Watson, H. (2011). Business analytics insight: Hype or here to stay? *Business Intelligence Journal*, *16*(1), 4–8.

Waugh, R. F. (2000). Towards a model of teacher receptivity to planned system-wide educational change in a centrally controlled system. *Journal of Educational Administration*, *38*(4), 350–367. doi:10.1108/09578230010373615

Weaver, K., & Willén, A. (2014). The Swedish pension system after twenty years: Mid-course corrections and lessons. *OECD Journal on Budgeting*, *13*(3), 1–26. doi:10.1787/budget-13-5jxx3sx58x9t

Weisner, T. S., & Garnier, H. (1992). Nonconventional family life-styles and school achievement: A 12-year longitudinal study. *American Educational Research Journal*, *29*(3), 605–632. doi:10.3102/00028312029003605

Welsh, W. (2000). The effects of school climate on school disorder. *The Annals of the American Academy of Political and Social Science*, *567*(1), 88–107. doi:10.1177/000271620056700107

Whitchurch, C. (2004). Administrative managers–A critical link. *Higher Education Quarterly*, *58*(4), 280–298. doi:10.1111/j.1468-2273.2004.00274.x

Wilder, C. R., & Ozgur, C. O. (2015). Business Analytics Curriculum for Undergraduate Majors. *INFORMS Transactions on Education*, *15*(2), 180–187. doi:10.1287/ited.2014.0134

Wilkins, D. (2014). Planning for a future you can't predict. *American School & University*, November, 201–203.

Wilkins, J. L. (2010). Elementary School Teachers Attitudes Toward Different Subjects. *Teacher Educator*, *45*(1), 23–36. doi:10.1080/08878730903386856

Wilk, S. L., & Cappelli, P. (2003). Understanding the determinants of employer use of selection methods. *Personnel Psychology*, *56*(1), 103–124. doi:10.1111/j.1744-6570.2003.tb00145.x

Wilson, D. (2004). The interface of school climate and school connectedness and relationships with aggression and victimization. *The Journal of School Health*, *74*(7), 293–299. doi:10.1111/j.1746-1561.2004.tb08286.x PMID:15493706

Wilson, G. L. (2013, September/October). The math frame reaching common core heights for students who struggle. *Teaching Exceptional Children*, *46*(1), 36–46. doi:10.1177/004005991304600105

Wong, H., & Wong, R. (2010, November). *Developing and retaining effective teachers and principals*. Retrieved May 22, 2016 from http://www.oswego.edu/Documents/project_smart/Summer Institute/Developing and Retaining.pdf

Wong, H., & Wong, R. T. (2004). *The First Days of School*. Mountain View, CA, USA: Harry K. Wong Publications, Inc.

World Economic Forum Global Agenda Council on Employment. (2014, 1 22-25). Matching Skills and Labour Market Needs Building Social Partnerships for Better Skills and Better Jobs. Retrieved from http://www3.weforum.org/docs/GAC/2014/WEF_GAC_Employment_MatchingSkillsLabourMarket_Report_2014.pdf

Woska, W. J. (2007). Legal issues for HR Professionals: Reference checking/background investigations. *Public Personnel Management*, *36*(1), 79–89. doi:10.1177/009102600703600106

Wu, J. H., Hoy, W. K., & Tarter, J. C. (2013). Enabling school structure, collective responsibility, and a culture of academic optimism. *Journal of Educational Administration*, *51*(2), 176–193. doi:10.1108/09578231311304698

XBRL US. (2016). *Who else uses XBRL?* Retrieved May 25, 2016 from https://www.xbrl.org/the-standard/why/who-else-uses-xbrl

Xue, Q. L. (2007). Structural Equational Models. The Johns Hopkins University. Retrieve 1.24.16 from http://ocw.jhsph.edu/courses/structuralmodels/PDFs/Lecture8.pdf

Zhang, K. (2015). Four Changes of Modern Universities from the Perspective of "4V" of Big Data. *Canadian Social Science*, *11*(3).

Zuiderwijk, A., & Janssen, M. (2014). Open data policies, their implementation and impact: A framework for comparison. *Government Information Quarterly*, *31*(1), 17–29. doi:10.1016/j.giq.2013.04.003

About the Contributors

S. Marshall Perry, Ph.D., is an Associate Professor of Education at Saint Mary's College of California. He holds a Ph.D. in Administration and Policy Analysis from the Stanford University School of Education and a B.A. with distinction in Political Science from Yale University. Previously, Dr. Perry taught adult basic education, worked at the New York City Board of Education, consulted with public schools involved in restructuring, and evaluated supplemental education programs. In addition to authoring several articles and chapters, Dr. Perry has presented at conferences of the American Educational Research Association, American Evaluation Association, and World Educational Research Association.

* * *

Jianing (Jade) Fang, CPA, CITP, earned his double-major B.A. in Economics, and Accounting and Information Systems with high honors in 1986 from Queens College, CUNY. He passed the CPA examinations and was certified in 1990. He earned his M.S. in Taxation in 1993 from Washington School of Law and his DPS (Doctor of Professional Studies) in 2006 from Pace University. Dr. Fang has been the Editor-in-Chief for Global Science and Technology Forum's (GSTF) Annual International Conference on Accounting and Finance since 2010. Jade has published three books and numerous research papers in refereed journals.

Kenneth Forman is the off-campus program coordinator and lecturer in the School of Professional Development/Educational Leadership Program at Stony Brook University. He served as an administrator and teacher for the New York City public schools for 27 years and as a school building leader on Long Island for 12 years. He is the author of two educational leadership books: Preparing for Educational Leadership, 2nd Edition, a guide for emerging school and district leaders to successfully complete SBL/SDL New York State licensing examinations and Diving into Data, a resource to help move schools or districts to become highly-effective data-driven organizations.

Craig Markson is an Assistant Dean and Lecturer with the School of Professional Development at Stony Brook University. He is responsible for off-campus graduate programs that meet the professional development needs of aspiring K-12 school leaders. His research interests include the efficacy of online learning in the context of school leadership preparation, State assessments, ISLLC Standards, gender and school leadership, teacher evaluations, and the relationships among poverty and academic achievement.

Claudia McGivney is the Head of Academic Engagement for Stony Brook University Libraries. She holds a Master of Science in Library and Information Science from LIU Post, a Master of Arts in Interdisciplinary Studies from Hofstra University, and is currently working on a Ph.D. in Literacy at Hofstra University. She has published and presented on technology in libraries, reflective practice in first year experience courses, and information literacy. Her research interests include anime and graphic novels in higher education, digital literacies, and reflective practice.

Elsa-Sofia Morote has 20+ years' senior-level experience instructing, motivating and researching at the university-level. She holds two Masters Degrees - a MAP in Public Administration (concentration in Strategic Management) (CIDE, 1991), M.Sc. in Finance (Carnegie Mellon University, 1996) and she is Doctor of Education Ed.D (concentration in Higher Education Administration) (University of Pittsburgh, 2001); and completed a postdoctoral work using quantitative methods analysis at the Massachusetts Institute of Technology (MIT, 2001-2003). Currently, Dr. Morote is the Executive Director of the Long Island Opportunities Center at the State University of New York (SUNY).

Erica Murphy-Jessen, Ed.D. has worked as a special educator for over 15 years in the Huntington Union Free School District. She has earned her Doctorate of Educational Leadership, Administration, and Technology as well as SDL and SBL certifications from Dowling College. Dr. Jessen also holds a MS in Special Education and BA is Psychology and Sociology from SUNY Stony Brook. She is also a NYS certified BCBA. Her research interests are special education and behavior analysis and modification.

Héctor X. Ramírez-Pérez, Ed.D., is the Dean of the School of Economics and Business Administration at Universidad Panamericana, Campus México. He researches on family business, entrepreneurship, and education. He holds a BA in Finance at UP (Mexico), a MBA at Western Illinois University (US), and a Doctoral degree at Dowling College (US). He is professor of strategy and management.

Bridgette Waite Wilson has over 15 years' experience as an elementary school Principal and more recently served as a Director of Human Resources for a school district on Long Island. She has earned a Masters in Educational Technology (LIU) and a Doctorate in Education, Leadership and Technology from Dowling College. She received certification in School Administration and Supervision & School District Administrator from Long Island University, C.W. Post. She also holds a Bachelors in Elementary Education from SUNY College at Old Westbury. Dr. Waite Wilson's research interests are in the areas of human resources, student achievement, curriculum and instruction.

Index

A

Ageing 144-147, 149-150
Annual Professional Performance Review (APPR) 25, 198, 219-220, 226, 229, 236-238, 240-242, 245, 247-248, 250-251, 253-257, 259-267, 269-270, 274
Annual Professional Performance Review (APPR) Teacher Evaluation System 229, 245
Attendance 26, 28, 178, 181-182, 187-188, 190-192, 229, 233, 236-238, 241-242, 245
Attendance Rates 181, 190, 229, 233, 237, 241-242
Average Hours Worked 142, 151-152, 159, 170-171

D

Data Repositories 6, 15, 17
Data.NYSED.gov 25-26, 246, 253-254, 274
Datasets 1, 3-8, 10-14, 16-17, 23-25, 38-39, 42-44, 47, 50, 55, 84, 86, 92
Defined Benefit 174
Defined Contribution 144, 149, 174
Differentiated Professional Development (DPD) 274
Direct and Indirect Effects 85, 87, 112
Disability Classification Rate (DCR) 274

E

Economic Development 119-121, 123-124, 126
Economic Growth 119, 121-127, 133-134
EDGAR 62-65, 67-68, 70, 78-79, 81-82
Education 7, 9, 12-17, 24-25, 27, 32, 38, 41-44, 46-47, 49-50, 53, 63, 85, 90-93, 118-128, 130-134, 140-141, 178-179, 181, 185, 198-205, 207, 210, 219-221, 230, 234, 237, 242, 246, 248, 250-252, 254-255, 257, 259-261, 263-267, 269-270, 274-275, 279-280, 287
Employment 6, 8, 16, 119-121, 123-126, 133-134, 140, 144-146, 148, 150-153, 170, 276-278, 280, 282, 286, 292

F

Facebook 275-277, 279-280, 282, 286-287, 291
Family Academic Resources 85, 112
family structure 179, 188, 192
Financial Analyses 79
Financial Reporting 63-64, 67, 79

G

GDP per Capita 118, 120, 128, 130-134, 140
Gross Domestic Product (GDP) 140, 145

H

Happiness 119, 122-124, 127
High School Graduation Rate 246
Higher Education 38, 42-44, 46-47, 49-50, 53, 118-121, 123-127, 134, 220
High-Stakes accountability (HAS) 274
Hours-Worked 174

HTML 62-64, 67-68, 70, 78-79, 81-82
Human Resource Manager 291

I

IDEA 62-64, 79, 81-82, 126, 155, 202, 270
Instructional Leadership 85, 87-88, 106, 112, 197, 200, 205, 209-214, 216, 218-219, 221
Instructional Practices (IP) 274

L

Labor 6, 11, 66, 120, 122-127, 134, 140, 142, 144-145, 147-153, 155-160, 168, 170-171
Labor Force Size 142, 155-156, 158-159, 168, 171
Life Expectancy 5, 143-144, 146-147, 149
Life Satisfaction 118-121, 128, 130-134, 140
LinkedIn 275-277, 279-280, 282, 292

M

math achievement 26, 31, 94, 97, 100-101, 107, 110, 178, 185, 187-191

O

OECD 15, 86, 93, 124, 141-153, 155-158, 171
Open Data 1-6, 8-9, 11-15, 17, 24

P

path analysis 184-185
Pay-As-You-Go 149, 174
PAYG 144, 149
PISA 84, 86, 92-93
Pool Data Analysis 142, 153
Poverty 24, 90, 123, 126-127, 145, 148-149, 179, 181, 191-192, 210, 229, 232, 235-238, 241-242, 246
Professional Development (PD) 274

R

Recruitment 276-277, 279-280, 282-285, 287-288, 292
Regents Diploma 229, 235-241, 246
Regents Diploma With Advanced Designation 229, 235-241, 246
Registrant 65-66, 70, 81
Retention 38, 42-43, 45-46, 49, 51-52, 55, 146, 275-277, 280-281, 283-285, 287-288, 292
Retirement 144-150, 174
Retirement-Age 174

S

School-Level Opportunities 85, 112
Screening 126, 278, 280, 282-284, 287, 292
SEC 62-66, 68-70, 77-79, 81-82
SEC's XBRL Mandate 82
Selection 1, 67, 171, 185, 210, 213, 276-284, 287, 292
Self-Efficacy 199, 201, 206, 269, 275-277, 280-285, 287, 292
Social Media 5, 10, 43, 250, 275-288, 292
Student Achievement 42, 84-88, 90-93, 97, 106, 112, 178-182, 192, 204, 206, 221, 229-234, 236-237, 241-242, 246, 254, 265
student attendance 188, 190, 229, 233, 237, 242, 245
students with disabilities 27-28, 32, 182, 188, 192, 248-249, 251-255, 257, 259-261, 264, 266-269, 274

T

TALIS 84, 86, 92-93
Teacher Efficacy (TE) 274
Teacher Evaluations 220, 229, 236-237, 241
Tertiary Education 120, 128, 130-134, 140
Transaction Processing 64, 67
Turnover 30, 184, 275, 280-281, 283, 288, 292
Twitter 14, 16, 275-277, 279-280, 282, 286, 292

U

Unemployment 6, 118, 120-121, 124-125, 127-128, 130-132, 134, 140-141, 170

X

XBRL 62-67, 70, 72, 74-79, 81-82
XML 72-75, 82

Y

Years of Schooling 118, 128, 130-131, 134, 140-141

www.ingramcontent.com/pod-product-compliance
Lightning Source LLC
LaVergne TN
LVHW081341300926
849161LV00008B/2041